Jordans
Employment Law
Precedents

Jordans
Employment Law
Precedents

Edward Benson
Partner, Head of Employment Department
Browne Jacobson LLP

Published by
Jordan Publishing Limited
21 St Thomas Street
Bristol BS1 6JS

Whilst the publishers and the authors have taken every care in preparing the material included in this work, any statements made as to the legal or other implications of particular transactions are made in good faith purely for general guidance and cannot be regarded as a substitute for professional advice. Consequently, no liability can be accepted for loss or expense incurred as a result of relying in particular circumstances on statements made in this work.

© Jordan Publishing Ltd 2009

All rights reserved. No part of this publication may be reproduced, stored in a retrieval system, or transmitted in any way or by any means, including photocopying or recording, without the written permission of the copyright holder, application for which should be addressed to the publisher.

Crown Copyright material is reproduced with kind permission of the Controller of Her Majesty's Stationery Office.

British Library Cataloguing-in-Publication Data

A catalogue record for this book is available from the British Library.

ISBN 978 1 84661 103 2

Typeset by Letterpart Ltd, Reigate, Surrey

Printed in Great Britain by CPI Antony Rowe Limited, Chippenham, Wiltshire

PREFACE

Employment law should not be as complicated as it has become. The rules have become so detailed and prescriptive that employers now have to spend time and resources to ensure the rules are followed.

A clear set of procedures, policies, contracts and standard letters should simplify the job of those responsible for managing human resources. Following appropriate policies, all drafted to help employers comply with the law, should minimise the risk of employment tribunal claims and put them in a strong position if claims are made.

The non-contentious section sets out most of the documents employers are likely to require. It includes contracts of employment, statements of terms of employment, specific clauses in contracts, redundancy, disciplinary, grievance, equal opportunities and other procedures. There is also a selection of standard letters for use in redundancy, disciplinary and other situations.

Each precedent is accompanied by an explanation of when and how it should be used; and comments on drafting.

The contentious section contains precedents for standard claims from employees and standard responses from employers involved in employment tribunal proceedings. Again, there are explanatory notes both about the use of the precedents and about the drafting.

I am grateful for all the helpful comments I have received from my colleagues at Browne Jacobson; and the excellent and patient editorial team at Jordans.

The author and Jordan Publishing Ltd would like to thank Nick Randall, Mohinderpal Sethi, Peter Edwards and Ben Lynch, all of Devereux Chambers, for providing a number of precedent documents.

Edward Benson

Partner, Head of Employment Law
Browne Jacobson LLP

CONTENTS

Preface	v
Table of Statutes	xxi
Table of Statutory Instruments	xxiii

A   Recruitment

A1 Application Form	1
Use	1
Precedent	2
Drafting points	4
A2 Offer Letter	5
Use	5
Precedent	5
Drafting points	6

B   Employment/consultancy agreements

B1 Service Agreement	7
Use	7
Precedent	8
Drafting points	21
B2 Statement of Main Terms and Conditions of Employment	27
Use	27
Precedent	27
Drafting points	36
B3 Consultancy Agreement	39
Use	39
Precedent	40
Drafting points	46
B4 Casual Workers	47
Use	47
Precedent	47
Drafting points	49
B5 Sunday Working	50
Use	50
Precedent	50

B6 Betting Shops	51
Use	51
Precedent	51
C Specific clauses	
C1 Use of Software	53
Use	53
Precedent	53
Drafting points	54
C2 Staff Purchases	56
Use	56
Precedent	56
Drafting points	58
C3 Lay-off and Short-Time	59
Use	59
Precedent	59
Drafting points	60
C4 Media Communications	62
Use	62
Precedent	62
D Policies and procedures	
D1 Staff Handbook	63
Use	63
Precedent	67
D2 General Rules of Behaviour	70
Use	70
Precedent	70
D3 IT Rules	72
Use	72
Precedent	72
Drafting points	76
D4 Notification of Employee Information	78
Use	78
Precedent	78
Drafting points	78
D5 Capability Procedure	79
Use	79
Precedent	79
Drafting points	86
D6 Short Capability Procedure	87
Use	87
Precedent	87

D7	**Disciplinary Procedure**	**90**
Use		90
Precedent		93
Drafting points		98
D8	**Dismissal Procedure**	**100**
Use		100
Precedent		101
Drafting points		103
D9	**Redundancy**	**104**
Use		104
Precedent		104
Drafting points		109
D10	**Grievance Procedure**	**112**
Use		112
Precedent		113
Drafting points		115
D11	**Grievance Procedure (Short Version)**	**116**
Use		116
Precedent		116
Drafting points		117
D12	**Harassment Policy and Procedure**	**118**
Use		118
Precedent		118
Drafting points		122
D13	**Whistleblowing**	**123**
Use		123
Precedent		124
Drafting points		126
D14	**Personal Property**	**127**
Use		127
Precedent		127
Drafting points		127
D15	**Accident Reporting**	**128**
Use		128
Precedent		128
Drafting points		128
D16	**Retirement Policy and Procedure**	**129**
Use		129
Precedent		129
Drafting points		132
D17	**Training**	**133**
Use		133
Precedent		133

D18 Appraisals		**134**
Use		134
Precedent		134
D19 Working Time Policy		**135**
Use		135
Precedent		135
D20 Time Off		**137**
Use		137
Precedent		137
Drafting points		138
D21 Company Cars		**139**
Use		139
Precedent		139
D22 Equal Opportunities		**148**
Use		148
Precedent		149
Drafting points		154
D23 Parental Leave		**156**
Use		156
Precedent		156
Drafting points		159
D24 Maternity		**161**
Use		161
Precedent		161
Drafting points		164
D25 Paternity Leave		**165**
Use		165
Precedent		165
Drafting points		167
D26 Adoption Leave		**168**
Use		168
Precedent		168
Drafting points		171
D27 Flexible Working		**172**
Use		172
Precedent		172
Drafting points		177
D28 Smoking		**178**
Use		178
Precedent		178
D29 Sickness		**181**
Use		181
Precedent		181

Drafting points   184

E   Separate agreements

E1   Working Time Regulations   **187**
Use   187
Precedent   187
Drafting points   187

E2   Training Agreement   **189**
Use   189
Precedent   189
Drafting points   191

E3   Compromise Agreement (Executives)   **192**
Use   192
Precedent   193
Drafting points   201

E4   Compromise Agreement (Basic)   **206**
Use   206
Precedent   206
Drafting points   210

E5   Compromise Agreement (Specific Claim)   **214**
Use   214
Precedent   214
Drafting points   215

E6   Relocation   **217**
Use   217
Precedent   217
Drafting points   218

E7   Loans   **219**
Use   219
Precedent   219

F   Standard Forms and Letters

F1   Access to Medical Reports – Information Sheet   **221**
Use   221
Precedent   221

F2   Access to Medical Reports – Letter Seeking Consent   **223**
Use   223
Precedent   223
Drafting points   224

F3   Access to Medical Reports – Letter to Doctor   **225**
Use   225
Precedent   225
Drafting points   226

F4	**Access to Medical Reports – Letter where Access Requested**	**227**
Use		227
Precedent		227
F5	**Capability – Invitation to Formal Meeting**	**228**
Use		228
Precedent		228
Drafting points		228
F6	**Capability – No Further Action**	**230**
Use		230
Precedent		230
F7	**Capability – Warning for Under-performance**	**231**
Use		231
Precedent		231
Drafting points		232
F8	**Capability – Dismissal Letter**	**233**
Use		233
Precedent		233
Drafting points		234
F9	**Capability – Notice of Appeal**	**236**
Use		236
Precedent		236
F10	**Collective Consultation – Redundancy Information Letter**	**237**
Use		237
Precedent		238
Drafting points		239
F11	**Collective Consultation – Requests for Nominations (TUPE)**	**240**
Use		240
Precedent		240
F12	**Collective Consultation – Requests for Nominations (Redundancy)**	**241**
Use		241
Precedent		241
F13	**Collective Consultation – Request for Volunteers**	**242**
Use		242
Precedent		242
Drafting points		243
F14	**Collective Consultation – TUPE Information Letter**	**244**
Use		244
Precedent		244
Drafting points		246
F15	**Disciplinary Procedure – Invitation to Investigation Meeting**	**247**
Use		247
Precedent		247

Drafting points		248
F16 Disciplinary – Suspension Letter		**249**
Use		249
Precedent		249
F17 Disciplinary – Invitation to Formal Meeting		**250**
Use		250
Precedent		250
Drafting points		251
F18 Disciplinary – Warning		**252**
Use		252
Precedent		252
Drafting points		252
F19 Disciplinary – Dismissal Letter		**254**
Use		254
Precedent		254
Drafting points		254
F20 Disciplinary – No Further Action		**256**
Use		256
Precedent		256
F21 Employee Representatives – Candidate Nomination Form		**257**
Use		257
Precedent		257
F22 Employee Representatives – Information Sheet (TUPE)		**258**
Use		258
Precedent		258
F23 Employee Representatives – Information Sheet (Redundancy)		**261**
Use		261
Precedent		261
F24 Employee Representatives – Ballot Form		**264**
Use		264
Precedent		264
F25 Flexible Working – Application		**266**
Use		266
Precedent		266
F26 Flexible Working – Agreement to Request		**268**
Use		268
Precedent		268
F27 Flexible Working – Invitation to Discuss Request		**269**
Use		269
Precedent		269
F28 Flexible Working – Refusal of Request		**270**
Use		270

Precedent	270
F29 Flexible Working – Agreeing Request Subject to Modifications	**272**
Use	272
Precedent	272
F30 Flexible Working – Appeal	**274**
Use	274
Precedent	274
F31 Grievances – Letter to Complainant	**275**
Use	275
Precedent	275
Drafting points	275
F32 Grievances – Instructions to Investigator	**277**
Use	277
Precedent	277
Drafting points	278
F33 Grievances – Invitation to Hearing	**279**
Use	279
Precedent	279
Drafting points	279
F34 Grievances – Notice of Outcome	**281**
Use	281
Precedent	281
Drafting points	282
F35 Harassment – Letter Informing Alleged Harasser	**283**
Use	283
Precedent	283
Drafting points	283
F36 Harassment – Letter to Complainant	**285**
Use	285
Precedent	285
Drafting points	285
F37 Harassment – Invitation to Hearing	**286**
Use	286
Precedent	286
Drafting points	286
F38 Harassment – Instructions to Investigator	**288**
Use	288
Precedent	288
Drafting points	289
F39 Harassment – Notice of Outcome	**290**
Use	290
Precedent	290

Drafting points	291
F40 Redundancy – Invitation to Meeting	**292**
Use	292
Precedent	292
Drafting points	294
F41 Redundancy – Invitation to Second Meeting	**295**
Use	295
Precedent	295
Drafting points	296
F42 Redundancy – Notification of Redundancy	**297**
Use	297
Precedent	297
Drafting points	298
F43 Redundancy – Confirmation of Redundancy after Appeal	**299**
Use	299
Precedent	299
Drafting points	299
F44 Redundancy – Letter Overturning Redundancy	**300**
Use	300
Precedent	300
Drafting points	300
F45 Retirement – Retirement Notification	**302**
Use	302
Precedent	302
F46 Retirement – Request to Continue Working	**303**
Use	303
Precedent	303
F47 Retirement – Invitation to Meeting	**304**
Use	304
Precedent	304
F48 Retirement – Notification of Decision	**305**
Use	305
Precedent	305
Drafting points	306
F49 Retirement – Appeal Letter	**307**
Use	307
Precedent	307
G Contentious Precedents	
G1 Claim for Wrongful Dismissal in High Court	**309**
Use	309
Precedent	310
Drafting points	311

G2 Defence to Claim for Wrongful Dismissal		**312**
Use		312
Precedent		312
Drafting points		313
G3 High Court Claim for Bonus		**314**
Use		314
Precedent		314
G4 Defence to Claim for Discretionary Bonus		**317**
Use		317
Precedent		317
G5 Claim for Unpaid Bonus and Repudiatory Breach		**319**
Use		319
Precedent		320
Drafting points		322
G6 Defence to High Court Claim for a Bonus and Constructive Dismissal		**324**
Use		324
Precedent		325
Drafting points		326
G7 Unfair Dismissal Claim		**328**
Use		328
Precedent		329
Drafting points		332
G8 Response to Unfair Dismissal Claim		**334**
Use		334
Precedent		335
Drafting points		339
G9 Claim for Unfair Dismissal on the Grounds of Union Membership and/or Activities and/or Non-membership etc		**342**
Use		342
Precedent		343
Drafting notes		347
G10 Response to Claim for Unfair Dismissal on the Grounds of Union Membership and/or Activities or Non-membership etc		**348**
Use		348
Precedent		349
Drafting points		350
G11 Claim for Unlawful Deductions from Wages in Employment Tribunal		**351**
Use		351
Precedent		351
Drafting points		352

G12 Response to Claim for Unlawful Deduction from Wages in Employment Tribunal	**354**
Use	354
Precedent	355
Drafting points	356
G13 Employment Tribunal Claim for Unlawful Deduction from Bonus	**357**
Use	357
Precedent	357
Drafting points	358
G14 Response to Employment Tribunal Claim for Unlawful Deduction from Bonus	**359**
Use	359
Precedent	360
Drafting points	361
G15 Employment Tribunal Claim for Unlawful Deductions from Holiday Pay	**362**
Use	362
Precedent	363
Drafting points	364
G16 Response to Employment Tribunal Complaint of Unauthorised Deduction from Holiday Pay	**365**
Use	365
Precedent	365
Drafting points	367
G17 Employment Tribunal Claim for Holiday Pay under Working Time Regulations	**369**
Use	369
Precedent	370
G18 Response to Employment Tribunal Claim for Holiday Pay under Working Time Regulations	**372**
Use	372
Precedent	372
Drafting points	373
G19 Claim for Redundancy Payment	**375**
Use	375
Precedent	376
Drafting points	377
G20 Employment Tribunal Claim for Bonus on Termination of Employment	**378**
Use	378
Precedent	378
Drafting points	379

G21	**Employment Tribunal Claim for Minimum Wage**	**380**
Use		380
Precedent		381
G22	**Response to Employment Tribunal Claim for Minimum Wage**	**383**
Use		383
Precedent		383
Drafting points		384
G23	**Employment Tribunal Complaint of Failure to Inform/Consult over Business Transfer**	**385**
Use		385
Precedent		386
Drafting points		387
G24	**Claim for Failure to Consult Over Collective Redundancies**	**389**
Use		389
Precedent		390
Drafting points		391
G25	**Particulars of Complaint in a Whistle-blowing (Public Interest Disclosure) Claim**	**392**
Use		392
Precedent		392
Drafting points		397
G26	**Response to Equal Pay Claim**	**399**
Use		399
Precedent		399
Drafting points		403
G27	**Employment Tribunal's Directions in Equal Pay for Value Case**	**405**
Use		405
Precedent		405
G28	**Grounds of Resistance to Discrimination Complaint in Employment Tribunal**	**408**
Use		408
Precedent		409
Drafting points		413
G29	**Request for Further Information about Response**	**415**
Use		415
Precedent		416
Drafting points		417
G30	**Response to Request for Further Information**	**418**
Use		418
Precedent		418
Drafting points		419

G31	**Notice of Appeal to the Employment Appeal Tribunal**	**420**
Use		420
Precedent		421
Drafting points		424

Index   **427**

TABLE OF STATUTES

References are to paragraph numbers.

Access to Medical Reports Act 1988	F1.1, F1.2, F2.2
s 4(2)	F3.2
Companies Act 1985	B1.3, E3.2
s 736	B1.2, B3.2, E3.2
Companies Act 2006	
s 188(2)	B1.3
s 188(6)	B1.3
s 189	B1.3
Contracts (Rights of Third Parties) Act 1999	E3.2
Criminal Justice and Public Order Act 1994	D12.2
Data Protection Act 1998	G25.3
s 7	G25.2
Disability Discrimination Act 1995	D5.1, D16.2, D22.2, D29.3, E3.2, E4.2, E5.2
Employment Act 2002	D10.1
s 31	G16.2
Sch 2	G7.2
Sch 4	G15.3
Employment Rights Act 1996	B1.2, D9.3, D13.1, E3.2, E4.2, E5.2, F25.2, G11.1, G15.1, G25.1
Pt III	C3.2
s 1	B2.1, B4.3
s 3	D11.1
s 11	G21.2
s 13	D1.1, G11.2, G13.2, G15.2, G16.2, G20.2, G21.2
s 23	G15.2
s 24(a)	G13.2
s 43B(1)(a)	G25.2
s 43B(1)(b)	G25.2
s 43KA(1)(b)	G25.2
s 47A	G25.2
s 47B	G25.2
s 47C	G25.2
s 50	D20.1
s 94	G7.2
s 95(1)(c)	G25.2
s 98	G7.2, G9.2, G9.3
s 98A	G7.2
s 103A	G25.2
s 163	G19.2

Equal Pay Act 1970	E3.2, E4.2, E5.2, G26.1, G26.3
s 1(2)	G26.2
s 1(3)	G26.2, G27.2
s 2A(2)	G27.2
Health Act 2006	D28.1, D28.2
Income Tax (Earnings and Pensions) Act 2003	E3.2, E3.3
Insolvency Act 1986	B1.2
Mental Health Act 1983	B1.2
National Minimum Wage Act 1998	E4.2, E5.2
s 1	G21.2
Protection from Harassment Act 1997	D12.1, E4.2
s 3	E3.2, E4.2
Public Interest Disclosure Act 1998	B2.2, C4.1, D13.1
Race Relations Act 1976	D22.2, E3.2, E4.2, E5.2
s 32(3)	G28.2
Rehabilitation of Offenders Act 1974	A1.1
Sex Discrimination Act 1975	D22.2, E3.2, E4.2, E5.2
s 41(3)	G28.2
Social Security Contributions and Benefits Act 1992	B2.2
Supreme Court Act 1981	
s 35A	G1.2, G3.2, G5.2
Trade Union and Labour Relations (Consolidation) Act 1992	E3.2, E4.2, E5.2, G9.1
s 152	G9.2
s 156	G9.2
s 160	G9.2
s 161	G9.2
s 161(5)	G9.2
s 188	E3.2, G24.2, G24.3

Trade Union and Labour Relations
   (Consolidation) Act
   1992—*continued*
  s 188(2)(b)   G24.2
  s 189   E3.2

Trade Union and Labour Relations
   (Consolidation) Act
   1992—*continued*
  s 189(2)–(4)   G24.2
  s 195   E2.2

TABLE OF STATUTORY INSTRUMENTS

References are to paragraph numbers.

Civil Procedure Rules 1998,
SI 1998/3132 G1.3, G5.1

Employment Equality (Age)
Regulations 2006,
SI 2003/1031 D22.2, E3.2, E4.2, E5.2
Employment Equality (Religion or Belief) Regulations 2003,
SI 2003/1660 D22.2, E3.2, E4.2, E5.2
reg 22(1) G28.2
Employment Equality (Sexual Orientation) Regulations 2003, SI 2003/1661 D22.2, E3.2, E4.2, E5.2
reg 22(1) G28.2

Maternity and Parental Leave etc Regulations 1999,
SI 1999/3312 D23.1, D23.2, D23.3

Part-Time Workers (Prevention of Less Favourable Treatment) Regulations 2000,
SI 2000/1551 E3.2

Transfer of Undertakings (Protection of Employment) Regulations 2006,
SI 2006/246 B2.3, E3.3, E4.3
reg 13(3)(a) G23.2
reg 3(1)(a) G23.2
reg 13 E3.2, G23.2, G23.3
regs 13–16 G23.1
reg 13(2) G23.2
reg 13(6) G23.2
reg 14 E3.2
reg 15(1) G23.2
reg 15(8) G23.2

Working Time Regulations 1998,
SI 1998/1833 B1.3, B2.3, B3.1, B4.1, D19.1, D19.2, E1.2, E1.3, E3.2, E4.2, F21.1, G15.1, G17.1, G18.1
reg 15 B1.2, B2.2
reg 16(1) G17.2, G18.2
reg 30 G17.2

A

RECRUITMENT

A1 APPLICATION FORM

A1.1 USE

The job application form should ask for sufficient information to enable you to shortlist those who you think would be able to carry out the job. It assumes that anyone applying will have seen or had access to a job description, unless the advertisement itself gives sufficient information about the job to enable potential job applicants to decide whether or not they are suitable for the job.

The form also asks to see documents proving an employee's entitlement to work in the United Kingdom. All job applicants should be asked this at some stage – either at the job application stage or as a condition before finally agreeing to employ the individual, irrespective of race or nationality – otherwise you are at risk of a race discrimination complaint if, for example, you only ask to see documents for those with addresses abroad or with foreign sounding names.

For the same reason, when asking for qualifications, do not limit them to UK qualifications unless there is some legal requirement for a UK qualification (for example in the case of solicitors or accountants).

When asking about criminal convictions, you are not allowed to ask about 'spent' convictions except where a particular job is exempted from the Rehabilitation of Offenders Act 1974 (see Division A of *Jordans Employment Law Service*). For jobs involving working with children or vulnerable adults, you should ask for a Criminal Records Bureau check (see Division A of *Jordans Employment Law Service*).

If the information given on this form turns out, after employment has started, to be incorrect, you may have valid grounds for terminating that person's employment, if the correct information might have caused you to decide not to offer employment.

A1.2   **Precedent**

Application form

Job application form

> Name:
>
> Address:
>
> Contact telephone number:
>
> Position applied for:
>
> Please state here your employment history in the last five years:
>
> If the job involves driving, do you have a valid driving licence?
>
> Do you have any criminal convictions? (You do not need to disclose spent convictions)
>
> Please state why you consider yourself suitable for the above position, including details of all relevant experience:
>
> State whether you have any of the following qualifications or any other qualifications showing a similar level of knowledge or expertise: [list]
>
> If asked to attend an interview, do you have any medical condition we should be aware of to facilitate the interview process?
>
> Do you have any medical condition which might affect your ability to carry out the duties of this position as specified in the job description? If so, what adjustments may be necessary to your working conditions to enable you to carry out those duties?
>
> Please give the names and addresses of two people we can approach to ask for references. These should include someone from your current or last employment.
>
> Is there any other information you would like us to take into account when short-listing for interview?
>
> **Warranty**
>
> I hereby warrant that all the information given on this form is true and complete to the best of my knowledge and belief. I also accept that the information contained in this application form will become part of my contract of employment if I am offered a position with the company and that I would be liable to summary dismissal if, at any time, it transpires that any of the information given herein was either false or materially incomplete.

Signed

Please include with your application form a document or documents showing you are entitled to work in the United Kingdom. These can include:

– A birth certificate or full adoption certificate issued in the United Kingdom coupled with an official document on which your National Insurance number is stated, such as a P45, P60, pay slip or a document issued by HMRC, or the Employment Service. a passport showing that you are a British or EU citizen or which has a stamp on it showing that you have a right of abode in the United Kingdom or have a right to stay indefinitely in the United Kingdom;

– a certificate of registration or naturalisation in the United Kingdom coupled with an official document on which your National Insurance number is stated, such as a P45, P60, pay slip or a document issued by HMRC, or the Employment Service. a document showing you are a national of the European Economic Area of Switzerland (either a passport or a National identity Card);

– a work permit or a letter from the Immigration authorities saying that you have a right to work in the United Kingdom coupled with a passport or other travel document confirming you have a right to work in the United Kingdom.

A full list of the types of document which are acceptable for these purposes can be obtained from the Home Office Border and Immigration Agency website.

Monitoring

You do not have to complete the next section but the information will be used for the purposes of monitoring only and will not be seen by those involved in short-listing or determining whether to offer you a position:

Sex:

Race:

Date of birth:

Do you have any disability? If so please specify.

Religion:

Sexual orientation:

A1.3 DRAFTING POINTS

Qualifications: Consider what qualifications you require a person to have in order to carry out the job. For some jobs, there are statutory requirements for particular qualifications. Generally, however, you should indicate on the form that an equivalent qualification in another country will suffice. You should always consider whether it is really necessary to require that a person has a particular qualification. If it is not necessary, you may be excluding categories of individuals unnecessarily. If an excluded category is likely to be predominantly of one sex or racial group, you could be indirectly discriminating.

CRB checks: If the job involves working with children or vulnerable adults, include a request to produce the appropriate CRB document.

Monitoring: Only include the monitoring section if you intend to carry out monitoring of applications for the purposes of ensuring that your selection process does not indirectly discriminate on grounds of race, sex, age etc.

A2 OFFER LETTER

A2.1 USE

The offer letter constitutes an offer of employment. If accepted, the employer and employee will be regarded as having entered a binding contract of employment. The offer letter should either set out the terms of employment intended to apply, or should attach a draft contract of employment, so that acceptance of the letter constitutes acceptance of the terms of employment.

We suggest that the offer letter should actually enclose the draft contract. If it does not do so, then any terms in the contract eventually provided by the employer which do not appear or are not referred to in the offer letter may not be binding because the employee will never have accepted the contract.

Continuing to work under a written contract, without ever formally accepting or signing the contract, generally amounts to acceptance by conduct. That is not so, however, where the employee expressly objects to one or more of the written terms of the contract. Arguments such as this often arise where an employer seeks to enforce post-termination restrictions in the contract.

A2.2 Precedent

Offer letter

   Dear,

   [Position]

   I am delighted to be able to offer you the above position. I enclose a [service contract] [statement of terms and conditions of employment] [together with the Company Handbook. The Handbook sets out information about the company and various policies and procedures but, unless otherwise indicated, it is not part of the terms of employment.]

   If you are happy with these terms and wish to accept this offer, please sign the enclosed terms and return them to me.

   If you accept this offer, your start date will be [. . .] or such other date as may be agreed.

   If you have any queries about this job or the terms on which it is offered, please contact me.

[Add something welcoming.]

Yours sincerely

A2.3 DRAFTING POINTS

You can either set out the main terms of employment within the offer letter or (as this precedent envisages) enclose with the offer letter a draft contract. The advantage of enclosing the draft contract with the letter is that there cannot then be any discrepancy between the terms of the offer letter and the terms of the contract. You can also be sure that the employee has agreed to all the terms of the contract.

If you have not already requested documents proving the right to work in the United Kingdom, you should ask to see those documents at this stage (see 'Drafting Points' for the precedent application form). So long as you have seen those documents and retained a copy and have taken reasonable steps to check the documents are genuine, you will have a defence to any proceedings for illegally employing someone who has no right to work in the United Kingdom. You should ensure that all job applicants are asked for these documents. If you only ask those who you think might be foreign nationals, you may discriminate unlawfully on grounds of race.

B

EMPLOYMENT/CONSULTANCY AGREEMENTS

B1 SERVICE AGREEMENT

B1.1 USE

For there to be a binding contract of employment, the terms must have been offered and accepted.

Generally, the employer offers the terms of employment by sending a copy of the agreement and the employee accepts by signing it.

Even if the employee has not signed the contract, simply continuing to work without protest under the terms offered is generally sufficient evidence to constitute acceptance.

It is a requirement of the legislation that all employees are given either a contract of employment or a statement of the main terms of employment within two months of starting.

It is advisable to get the employee to sign the contract right from the start, or even before they start, to ensure that all the terms are agreed.

This contract is suitable for senior employees or directors. For junior employees, a statement of the main terms of employment should be sufficient.

The Service Contract is drafted as if the employer were a Limited Company. Other organisations should adapt the precedent accordingly – for example, a local authority might substitute the word 'Company' by 'Authority'.

For fuller details, see Division B of *Jordans Employment Law Service*.

B1.2 Precedent

Service agreement

>**Date:**
>
>**Parties:**
>
>(1) [LIMITED] registered number [number], whose registered office is at [address] (the "Company")
>
>(2) [   ] whose address is [address] (the "Executive")
>
>**THE PARTIES AGREE** as follows:

1 Interpretation

In this Agreement the following words and expressions have the following meanings:

Expression	Meaning
"Board"	the board of directors of the Company for the time being;
"Group Company"	the Company, any subsidiary (as defined by section 736 of the Companies Act 1985) of the Company, any holding company (as so defined) of the Company and any subsidiary of such holding company, in each case for the time being.

2 Appointment

> 2.1 The Company appoints the Executive and the Executive will serve the Company as [title] [for a fixed period of [ ] years] which appointment may be terminated as provided in clause 14. [The Company may appoint any other person or persons to act jointly with the Executive in his appointment.]
>
> 2.2 The Executive warrants that by entering into this Agreement he will not be in breach of any implied or express terms of any contract with, or of any obligation to, any third party binding upon him.

3 Duties

> 3.1 While his appointment continues the Executive will:

3.1.1 perform the duties of [title as in clause 2] [and be responsible for – *if it is desirable to be more specific*];

3.1.2 (without further remuneration) perform whatever other duties in relation to the business of any Group Company the Board may from time to time assign to him and obey lawful and reasonable directions of the Board;

3.1.3 devote substantially the whole of his time and attention to his duties (during office hours and whatever additional hours may be required to fulfil such duties);

3.1.4 use reasonable endeavours to promote the welfare, interests and reputation of each of the Group Companies, and do nothing which could damage the welfare, interests and reputation of any of the Group Companies;

3.1.5 keep the Employer (or a person designated by the Employer) promptly and fully informed (in writing if requested) of his conduct in the performance of his duties, and of any matters which may come to his notice and which may affect the welfare, interests and reputation of any of the Group Companies including the activities or planned activities of any other person, company or organisation (including the Executive) which may compete with the Company or any Group Company or whose activities may otherwise affect the business of the Company or any Group Company.

3.2 Notwithstanding clause 3.1 or any other term of this Agreement, the Company may [at any time]/[during all or part of any period of notice whether given by the Company or by the Executive] require the Executive to perform such duties as it may [reasonably] require under this clause 3 or no duties provided that at all times the Executive shall continue to observe all obligations not to use or divulge confidential information, not to act against the interests of the Company or any Group Company and not to do any work for or assist in any way any competitor of the Company or any Group Company and the Company may exclude the Executive from any Group Company's premises without giving any reason for doing so but his salary and other benefits will not cease to be payable simply because the Company exercises its powers under this clause 3.2 unless and until his appointment is terminated.

3.3 Unless the Company gives prior written approval (which approval shall not release the Executive from any other duties owed to the Company unless such approval expressly provides), the Executive will not during this appointment be involved in any actual or prospective business (including a profession). The Executive will disclose to the Company such details of any such business as the Company may from time to time require.

3.4 In clause 3.3 "involvement" includes direct or indirect involvement and applies even if the Executive receives no remuneration for his involvement; being an employee of (at whatever level of responsibility) or a consultant to a business; and having any financial or other interest in a business even if this does not involve active participation in the business; but does not include the holding of shares or securities of a company which are quoted or dealt in on any recognised investment exchange so long as the holding is held by way of bona fide investment only.

3.5 The Executive will disclose to the Company any actual or prospective business in which his spouse or dependant children are involved [which may prejudice or otherwise affect the interests of the Company].

3.6 The Company shall have the right to remove the Executive as a member of the Board of the Company and/or any Group Company by notice served on the Executive and from such date the Executive shall cease to be entitled to receive notice of or attend or vote at board meetings.

4 Location

4.1 The Executive's place of work will be at the Company's address set out at the beginning of this Agreement (or) [name the place] [or at any other place [within the United Kingdom] where he can best perform his duties [or where the Board [reasonably] directs him to work]].

5 Confidential information

5.1 For the purposes of this Agreement, "Confidential Information" means trade secrets or confidential information belonging or relating to any Group Company and including, without limitation, information or secrets relating to business or manufacturing methods and processes, inventions, research and development activities, designs, drawings, sources and supplies of materials used, the identity of customers and potential customers, personal contacts with or within customers and potential customers, prices, margins, special arrangements with customers of and suppliers to any Group Company, pricing strategy, marketing strategy and development strategy, product and future product details, computer systems and computer software.

5.2 Both during the appointment and after it ceases, the Executive will not (unless expressly authorised by the Board or unless the Executive needs to do so in order to perform his duties) disclose to any person any Confidential Information which may come to his knowledge and will not use or attempt to use any Confidential Information for his own benefit or for the benefit of anyone else.

5.3 Following termination of his appointment, the obligations of the Executive under clause 5.2 above will not apply to any information which is or becomes generally known to the public on a non-confidential basis through no act or default on the part of the Executive. Nothing in this clause 5 will prevent the Executive from using his personal skills in any business in which he may lawfully be engaged after the termination of his appointment.

5.4 All notes, memoranda, records and other writings including those recorded on electromagnetic media made by the Executive in the course of his duties or relating to the business of any Group Company and any copies of them (in whatever form) and any documents or other records prepared from the notes, memoranda, records and other writings or information contained in them will be and remain the property of the relevant Group Company and will be handed over by the Executive to the Company on demand.

6 Remuneration

6.1 The Executive's salary is £[amount] per annum payable by equal monthly instalments in arrears on the last business day of each calendar month. The salary accrues on a daily basis.

6.2 The Executive's salary will be reviewed by the Board in [month] of each year and may as a result be increased if that is what the Board, which has complete discretion in the matter, decides.

6.3 [The Executive shall be entitled to a bonus calculated and payable in accordance with Schedule 1.]

OR

[The Executive has no contractual or other right to or expectation of a bonus. The Company may from time to time award a bonus and any bonus awarded shall be entirely in the discretion of the Board. In determining whether to pay a bonus and the amount of the bonus, the Board may take into account such factors as it considers appropriate in all the circumstances.]

OR

[In order to reward and/or encourage loyalty and/or performance; and/or to provide an incentive and /or to motivate employees generally or any particular group of employees or any individual employee, the Company may from time to time award a bonus and any bonus awarded shall be entirely in the discretion of the Board. In determining whether to pay a bonus and the amount of the bonus, the Board may take into account such factors as it considers appropriate in all the circumstances.]

7 Holidays

7.1 The Executive will be entitled (in addition to all English public holidays) to [number] working days paid holiday in each complete [calendar] [financial] year [(a year for these purposes commencing on [start date of holiday year])] to be taken at the times the Board approves. The rules laid down in Regulation 15 of the Working Time Regulations 1998 (SI 1998/1833) concerning approval of holiday shall not apply.

7.2 The Executive may not (without the consent of the Board) carry unused holiday entitlement forward to a subsequent holiday year.

7.3 Upon termination of his appointment, the Executive will be entitled to pay in lieu of unused holiday entitlement equal to the payment the Executive would have received for any accrued but untaken holidays. If more holiday than the accrued entitlement has been taken, the Executive will be required to repay any sums received for holiday taken in excess of that entitlement: any sums so due may be deducted from the Executive's salary.

7.4 For the purpose of calculating any pay due to or owed by the Executive under clause 7.3 one day's pay will be [1/260th] of annual salary.

8 Sickness or injury

8.1 If the Executive is absent from work because of sickness or injury, he will inform the Company as soon as possible and must keep the Company regularly informed of the situation and must provide such information about the reason for the absence and its likely duration as the

Company may reasonably require. If the absence from work is for eight or more consecutive days the Executive will provide a medical practitioner's statement on the [eighth] day and then regularly thereafter for the whole of the remainder of the absence.

8.2 If the Executive complies with clause 8.1, the Executive will continue to receive during any period of incapacity due to sickness or injury:

8.2.1 for the first [number] days of absence in any period of [365] days, his full salary; and

8.2.2 after that, whatever salary the Company decides for such period and in such amount as the Company may in its absolute discretion decide so long as it is not less than any statutory pay to which the Executive is entitled,

[provided that if the Executive qualifies for benefits under any Permanent Health Insurance scheme set up by the Company then the Executive shall receive no further benefits under this Agreement other than those provided under the Permanent Health Insurance scheme.] For statutory sick pay purposes, the qualifying days will be the Executive's normal working days.

8.3 If the Executive is awarded or receives damages or compensation for any illness or injury caused by a third party, then any payments made by the Company to the Executive for any period of absence caused by the illness or injury will be treated as a loan repayable on demand.

9 Expenses

Subject to any rules laid down by the Board from time to time, the Company will reimburse the Executive all reasonable travelling and other out of pocket expenses properly incurred by him in the performance of his duties. All claims for expenses must be supported by relevant invoices or receipts.

10 Car

The Company will (subject to any rules laid down by the Board from time to time and in accordance with the Company's car policy from time to time) provide a [suitable] car chosen by the Board) for the use of the Executive during his appointment and will pay all reasonable running costs of the car including the cost of fuel (excluding/including [delete] fuel for private use), licence, insurance and maintenance.

11 Pension

[The Executive may join the Company's pension scheme, subject always to the rules of such scheme from time to time. Information about the scheme has already been supplied to the Executive].

[The Company will make a contribution of [ ]% of the Executive's basic salary to a personal pension plan of his choice, subject to the Executive making a contribution of [ ]% of his basic salary to such plan.]

12 Insurance benefits

[The Executive shall be entitled to be a member of the Company's private medical insurance scheme for the benefit of the Executive, [his spouse and dependant children,] offering such benefits as may be determined by the Company from time to time.]

[The Company will take out and pay the premiums in respect of a policy of insurance on [the life of] the Executive providing for the payment of [a sum equal to [ ] times] the Executive's basic salary to [the Executive or named beneficiaries (as the case may be)] [on the death [or critical illness]] of the Executive and on such other terms as the Board determines.]

The benefits under this clause 12 shall apply provided and from such time as the Executive is accepted under the relevant policies by the relevant insurer and satisfies any conditions of such policies (including a medical examination if appropriate).

13 Inventions and creative works

13.1   The Executive agrees that any inventions, ideas, discoveries, developments or improvements made or conceived by him (whether individually or with others and whether inside or outside working hours) during the course of his duties will promptly be disclosed in full to the Company and will belong exclusively to the Company.

13.2   The Executive agrees that any trade or service marks, logos, designs, drawings or other works created or devised by the Executive (whether individually or with others and whether inside or outside working hours) during the period of his appointment and which:

13.2.1   affect, or relate to the business of, any Group Company; or

13.2.2   are capable of being used or adapted for use in the business of any Group Company; or

13.2.3 involve the use of any equipment, supplies, facilities, Intellectual Property or time of any Group Company,

will promptly be disclosed to the Company and will belong, together with all Intellectual Property subsisting or which may in the future subsist in any of these works, exclusively to the Company.

14   Termination

14.1   The Executive's appointment may be terminated as follows:

14.1.1   by one party giving to the other [number] months' notice in writing [so long as the notice does not expire before [the [number] anniversary of this Agreement] (or) [date]];

14.1.2   by the Company without notice or payment in lieu of notice if the Executive:

(a)   commits a serious breach or persistent material breaches of this Agreement;

(b)   is guilty of any act of dishonesty or serious misconduct or any conduct which, in the reasonable opinion of the Board, damages the interests of the Company or any Group Company or tends to bring himself or any Group Company into disrepute;

(c)   is convicted of any criminal offence [(excluding an offence [other than one of drink driving] under road traffic legislation in the United Kingdom or elsewhere for which he is not sentenced to any term of imprisonment whether immediate or suspended [or for which his licence is not suspended]]);

(d)   commits an act of bankruptcy or compounds with his creditors;

(e)   is disqualified from holding office in another company because of wrongful trading under the Insolvency Act 1986 or any statutory modification or re-enactment of that Act;

(f)   becomes of unsound mind or a patient

under the Mental Health Act 1983 or any statutory modification or re-enactment of that Act; or

(g) [is, in the reasonable opinion of the Board, incompetent in the performance of his duties.]

14.1.3 [where a notice has been given under clause 14.1.1 by the Company or the Executive,] by the Company with immediate effect by giving to the Executive the salary [and specify any other benefits the employee may receive] he would have received during the unexpired period of such notice.

14.2 The Executive's appointment will terminate automatically on the Executive reaching his [number]th birthday; or if the Executive ceases to be a director of the Company [and any other Group Company] for any reason [other than by an act of the Company]; or if the Executive becomes prohibited by law from being a director for any period.

14.3 On the termination of this Agreement for any reason the Executive will promptly:

14.3.1 resign without claim for compensation from all offices held by him in any Group Company (but without prejudice to any claim that may arise or have arisen by reason of the termination of the Executive's employment);

14.3.2 deliver up to the Company at the place of work set out in clause 4 all the items specified in clause 5.4 and all equipment, stocks, samples and other property (including any car and its keys) belonging to any Group Company which may be in his possession or under his control; and notify the Company of any computer password and any other information necessary to enable access to be obtained to data held on any computer or similar device used by the Executive in the course of his employment.

15 Protection of company's interests during his appointment

The Executive will not during the course of his appointment:

15.1 make any contact whether formal or informal, written or oral, with any customers or clients of the Company or any other Group Company with whom the Executive has had dealings, for any purpose other than for the legitimate business interests of the Company or another Group Company. Without limiting the scope of the previous sentence it will be a breach of this clause 15.1 if any unauthorised contact arises out of an intention to set up a competing business or to seek employment with a competitor of the Company or any other Group Company. This clause will not prevent the Executive from seeking employment with a competitor, but clause 16.2.1 will still apply;

15.2 either for himself or for any third party try to entice away from or discourage from being employed by the Company or any other Group Company any person whom the Executive knows to be an employee or prospective employee of the Company or any other Group Company nor will the Executive employ or offer employment to such a person on his own or any third party's account.

16 Protection of company's interests after appointment has terminated

16.1 In this clause 16, the following definitions are used:

"Competing Products" and "Competing Services" mean any products or services competitive with products or services supplied by the Company or any other Group Company where the Executive had any involvement in the supply, manufacture, design, marketing, development or selling of those products or services during the [six] months preceding the termination of the Executive's appointment.

"Customer" means any person or company who has been supplied with or offered any products or services by the Company or any other Group Company during the six months preceding the termination of the Executive's appointment or has been in a negotiation with a Group Company for the supply of products or services during that period of six months and with whom the Executive personally dealt in connection with this supply, offer or negotiation during those six months;

"Prohibited Area" means [state an area which is clearly defined]. The Prohibited Area is intended to represent the area in respect of which Group Companies sell or attempt to sell their products and services and in respect of which the Executive has sufficient dealings to gain confidential or sensitive information which would give him a competitive advantage if he were to leave the employment of the Company or where the Executive has sufficient contact with or knowledge of customers to give him a competitive advantage in the same circumstances. If the Group Companies cease to sell or attempt to sell in any area or start to sell or attempt to sell in a new area or if the Executive's duties change in a relevant respect or if geographical boundaries change in a way that affects the meaning of this term, the Company reserves the right to amend the area defined as the "Prohibited Area".

16.2 [Subject to clause 16.7] after termination of the Executive's appointment, the Executive will not, without the prior written consent of the Board, directly or indirectly, either alone or jointly with or on behalf of any other person and whether on his own account or in any other capacity whatever:

16.2.1 for a period of [six] months commencing with the date of termination, carry on or be engaged or employed or interested in any business which is carried on in the Prohibited Area and which competes with any business of any Group Company in which the Executive had any involvement during the period of [number] months preceding the date of termination [but it will not be a breach of this clause 16.2.1 for the Executive to be engaged or employed or interested in this way if he is only required to perform and he only does perform duties which relate solely to a business or part of a business which does not compete with any business of any Group Company];

16.2.2 for a period of [six] months commencing with the date of termination canvass, solicit, interfere with or approach any Customer for the purposes of the supply of Competing Services or Competing Products;

16.2.3 for a period of [six] months commencing with the date of termination accept any order or custom from a Customer in respect of the supply of Competing Services or Competing Products;

16.2.4 for a period of [six] months commencing with the date of termination canvass or solicit for employment any person who was at the date of termination and continued to be until canvassed or solicited a director or employee of any Group Company in a managerial, sales, marketing or product development position;

16.2.5 for a period of [six] months commencing with the date of termination employ any person who was at the date of termination a director or employee of any Group Company in a managerial sales, marketing, product-development position;

16.2.6 [for a period of [six] months commencing with the date of termination solicit or interfere with any person, firm or company who was a supplier of goods or services to any Group Company in the six months preceding the date of termination and with whom the Executive was concerned or had personal contact during those six months if the solicitation or interference would cause the supplier to cease supplying or materially reduce its supply of products or services to any Group Company;]

16.2.7 induce or assist any other person to do any of those things set out in clauses 16.2.1 to 16.2.6 if this would cause a breach of that person's contract of employment with the Company or any other Group Company.

16.3 Each of the covenants in clause 16.2 will constitute a separate and independent covenant and will be construed as such and if any one or more of such undertakings or any part of an undertaking is held to be against the public interest or unlawful or in any way as an unreasonable restraint of trade, the remaining undertaking or undertakings or the remaining part of such undertaking or undertakings shall continue in full force and effect and shall bind the Executive.

16.4 The Executive acknowledges that he has taken independent legal advice in relation to the terms of the undertakings given in clause 16.2 and that each such undertaking is reasonable and for the proper protection of the business of the Company and each relevant Group Company and further acknowledges that damages may not be an adequate remedy to the Company (or the relevant Group Company) for breach of those undertakings.

16.5 If the Executive contravenes any of the sub clauses in clause 16.2 (taking account of any extension of the periods they refer to because this sub-clause has already operated) the periods of [six] months which they refer to will be extended to last for [six] months after the date the contravention ceased.

16.6 After the date of termination of his appointment the Executive will not represent himself or permit himself to be held out as being in any way connected with or interested in the business of any Group Company (except if and for so long as he remains a director or an employee of that Group Company) or use any name which is identical or similar to or likely to be confused with the name of any Group Company or of any business which it carries on or any product or service which it produces or provides or which might suggest a connection between the Executive with that company or any of its products or services.

16.7 The periods of [six months] in clause 16.2 shall be reduced by any period of notice to terminate this Agreement where the Company pursuant to clause 3.2 requires the Executive to perform only some or none of his duties.

16.8 The covenants shall continue to apply after termination of the Agreement and, in the event the Company and the Executive enter into a compromise agreement, the restrictions shall continue to apply unless specifically released by the Company.

16.9 The Executive agrees to draw to the attention of any future or prospective employer who employs or agrees to employ the Executive during the currency of any restriction imposed by this clause 16 to the existence and contents of this clause 16.

17 Third party rights

It is intended that the provisions of this Agreement should be enforceable by any Group Company or any successor in title to the business of the Company (or the Group Company concerned).

18 Right to hold personal data

As part of the Executive's conditions of service, the Executive gives the Company permission to collect, retain and process information about the Executive, such as sex and ethnic origin. This information will be used by the Company to monitor the Company's compliance with the law and best practice in terms of equal opportunity and non-discrimination. Should the Executive's personal circumstances change, the Executive must notify the Company immediately.

19 Particulars

The following particulars are given for the purposes of the Employment Rights Act 1996 but do not create any contractual rights:

19.1 the Executive's employment under this Agreement began on [date], [and his period of continuous employment with the Company began on [date]].

19.2 if the Executive has any grievance relating to his employment he may apply to the Board to seek redress by submitting details of the grievance in writing. The Executive will be invited to a meeting to discuss the grievance and after the meeting the Executive will be informed of the outcome and the right of appeal in the event that he is dissatisfied with any decision.

19.3 there are no specific disciplinary rules affecting the Executive. Should disciplinary action be necessary, the Executive will be notified in writing, invited to attend a meeting with the Board or an appropriate Board member or members, the outcome of which will be communicated to the Executive in writing and the Executive will have the right of appeal against any decision taken by notifying the Board in writing and setting out the reasons for the Executive's dissatisfaction with any disciplinary action.

IN WITNESS of these matters the parties have executed this Agreement [as a Deed] on the date stated at its beginning.

SIGNED by [   ]   )

for and on behalf of   )

[   ] LIMITED   )

SIGNED by [   ]   )

B1.3 DRAFTING POINTS

Definitions section: In the case of limited companies, it is advisable to include a definition of "Group" even if, at the time of drafting, the company is not part of a group of companies. The situation may change in the future.

Clause 2: This precedent has been drafted as if for employment with a limited company. It can be adapted for use by other organisations such as local authorities by substituting the word "Employer" for "Company" and removing references to "Group Companies".

Where the employee may be required to work for non-UK companies, there may be tax advantages in having separate agreements for those companies. Specialist tax advice on this should be taken.

Clause 2.1: Having the right to appoint someone else to act jointly with the employee gives you greater flexibility when dealing with poor performers or those who take a lot of time off for health reasons.

Clause 2.2: This clause should protect you against the possibility of becoming embroiled in litigation with a former employer of the employee. If you employ someone in breach of that person's contract with a former employer, then you could be sued by that former employer for inducing a breach of contract. To succeed, the former employer would have to establish that you knew or ought to have known about the restrictive covenants. That may not be difficult in the case of senior employees, because senior employees are likely to have some sort of restrictions in their contracts.

Clause 3.1.3: This defines the employee's hours of work. If those hours could average more than 48 hours a week, then consider asking the employee to 'opt-out' of the requirement in the Working Time Regulations 1998 (SI 1998/1833). This can be done by a separate agreement (see precedent at [E1.2]). It is advisable to have the opt-out in a separate agreement rather than the Service Agreement itself because employees have a right to opt back in to the 48-hour maximum average working week. If they do so, then the Service Agreement will no longer accurately state the terms of employment unless the opt-out is kept separate.

Clause 3.1.5: This clause makes it extremely difficult for any employee to leave and set up in competition without you knowing about it. If they do and do not tell you, then they are in breach of this clause. This gives you more remedies than a breach of a restrictive covenant because the courts are more willing to enforce contractual terms which apply during employment. A court might be prepared to order what is sometimes known as a 'springboard injunction' – that is, an injunction preventing a former employee of taking any advantage from a breach of contract occurring during employment.

Clause 3.2: This is sometimes known as a 'garden leave' clause, entitling the employer during any notice period (whether given by the employer or the employee) to require the employee only to perform limited duties or no duties at all (other than the duties not to act against the interests of the employer). The clause could be drafted wider to entitle the employer to exclude the employee at any time – whether or not during the notice period.

Clause 3.5: This clause supplements clause 3.1.5. It prevents any employee seeking to set up a competing business via members of his family.

Clause 5.1: Confidential information should be defined to include any information not generally known to the public which could be used by a competitor to damage the company's interests. Without a comprehensive definition, the courts may imply a fairly limited definition of confidential information (*Faccenda Chicken Limited v Fowler* [1986] IRLR 69).

Clause 6.3. Even where a benefit is stated to be discretionary, the courts may imply a limit on the extent to which a discretion may be exercised, particularly if the purpose of the bonus is stated either within the contract or elsewhere. Any award or non-award of a bonus for a reason which does not appear to fall within the stated purpose of the clause may be attacked as a breach of contract. There are two approaches that could be taken when drafting clauses intended to give employers a wide discretion. The first is to state that the employer may exercise the discretion for any reason – thereby attempting to preclude any implied term that the reasons have to be limited to achieve some particular purpose (as in the first option in the precedent). The second is to state the purpose but to state it as widely as possible (as in the third option).

You should decide whether you want bonuses to be taken into account in determining pension entitlement. If it is not already clear from the rules of the pensions scheme that bonuses are not to be included, then you should make it clear in this Agreement.

Clause 7: The Working Time Regulations 1998 (SI 1998/1833) entitle employees to a minimum of 28 days' holiday a year (including bank and public holidays) for holiday years beginning on or after 1 April 2009 (between 24 and 28 days for holiday years beginning before that date). The regulations prohibit payments in lieu of holiday entitlement under the regulations, except on termination of employment. See Division C7 of *Jordans Employment Law Service*.

Clause 8: Apart from regulations on statutory sick pay, there is no legislation governing sick pay entitlement. Most employers pay full pay for a period. Sometimes employers specify strict periods during which full pay is paid; and sometimes those periods are entirely discretionary. The same comments apply to discretionary sickness payments as apply to discretionary bonuses. Those employers who operate Permanent Health Insurance schemes often intend that payments under those schemes should take over from any entitlement (express or implied) to payment under the contract. Although this is probably implicit in most contracts, particularly where sick pay is stated to be discretionary, it is better to spell this out expressly.

Clause 8.3: This enables employers to recover salary and other payments made to employees injured by third parties from the third party's insurer.

Clause 11: You should check that the rules and eligibility conditions of any pension scheme satisfy the requirements to exempt from stakeholder schemes. If they do not, then a stakeholder scheme will have to be introduced.

Clause 14.1.1: Shareholder's approval is now required for service contracts of two years or more (s 188(2) of the Companies Act 2006), unless the company is not registered in the United Kingdom or is a wholly owned subsidiary of another company (s 188(6) of the Companies Act 2006). Any term in a contract providing for longer notice than two years, or for a fixed term of more than two years, is void and there will be implied a term that the employment can be terminated on reasonable notice (s 189 of the Companies Act 2006). These sections only apply to contracts made on or after 1 October 2007. For contracts made earlier than that, the provisions of the Companies Act 1985 apply. The Combined Code on Corporate Governance 2006 recommends a one-year maximum for the notice period, to avoid rewarding poor performance on termination of employment.

Clause 14.1.2(g): Employers may wish to omit this ground for termination of employment. It gives the employer considerable scope for dismissal but some may consider it gives too much scope.

Clause 14.1.3: This entitles the employer to terminate with immediate effect but with payment of the salary (and such other payments as the employer may specify) for the period of the notice. Without this clause, employers who give a payment in lieu of notice may technically breach the contract of employment by not giving actual notice. That could put any restrictive covenants (ie any obligations on the employee restricting their activities after termination of employment) in jeopardy. The disadvantage of such a clause for employees is that they make the payment fully taxable, whereas without such a clause, the payment would amount to an advance payment of damages for breach of contract, attracting the tax exemption for the first £30,000. The current approach of HMRC, however, is that any payment in lieu of notice, if such payments are habitually made, is regarded as an emolument of employment and so taxable unless the amount is clearly calculated so as to compensate for financial loss – taking account of other earnings, mitigation and deductions of tax from pay.

Clause 16: The enforceability or otherwise of restrictive covenants applying after termination of employment is a large subject, dealt with in Division D1, Section 2 of *Jordans Employment Law Service*. Broadly, such covenants will only be enforced if they are strictly necessary and no wider than necessary to protect some legitimate business interest of the employer. The legitimate interests may include customer and trade connections, confidential information and the stability of the workforce.

Generally, this means that non-compete clauses (ie clauses preventing a former employee from working for a competitor) will only be enforceable if they are limited in time and area. Non-compete clauses lasting six months are generally enforceable. Clauses lasting 12 months are borderline. Clauses for more than 12 months will probably not be unless there is some particular reason why the longer period is necessary to protect the employer.

Non-solicitation and non-dealing clauses (ie clauses preventing a former employee from soliciting or dealing with clients or customers) are only enforceable if they only apply to those clients and customers with whom the former employee dealt personally. Such clauses may also restrict the employee from soliciting or dealing with prospective customers – ie potential customers with whom the former employee was negotiating for business. Again, the clause should be limited in duration. Restrictions lasting for more than 12 months are generally only enforceable if contact with clients and customers is only occasional, so that a 12-month restriction would not prevent significant customer contact.

Non-poaching clauses (ie clauses prohibiting former employees from enticing employees of the former employer to leave and join a competitor) are only enforceable if they prohibit poaching of senior employees or employees with significant contact with the customer base, such as sales staff. They should also be restricted to those employees who were employed at or shortly before termination of the former employee's employment.

Clause 16.5: This clause may be useful if the restrictions only last for a short period – say three or six months. The advantage of restrictions only lasting for a short period is that they are more likely to be enforced by the courts. The disadvantage is that it often takes time first to discover that an employee is or may be breaching a restrictive covenant; and then a further period to gather sufficient evidence to apply to the courts for an injunction; and then a further period to apply to the court for an interim injunction to enforce the clause. This automatic extension of the periods of restrictive covenants means that the period runs from the date the breach ceases rather than from termination of employment. This clause has yet to be tested in the courts and there is no certainty that a court would enforce it. However, it may be useful at least as a deterrent and should improve the former employer's negotiating position.

Clause 16.9: The former employer may wish to enforce the clause not only against the former employee but also against any future employer. Most employers will abide by restrictive covenants, rather than risk getting involved in litigation with a competitor. Requiring former employees to draw any restrictions to any future employer's attention may often deter the future employer from allowing or encouraging the former employee to breach the covenants; or if they knowingly allow the employee to breach a restrictive covenant, will render that future employer liable to the former employer for inducing a breach of contract.

B2 STATEMENT OF MAIN TERMS AND CONDITIONS OF EMPLOYMENT

B2.1 USE

Unlike the Service Agreement, this precedent is intended to be a straightforward, easy to understand explanation of an employee's main terms of employment. It includes all the terms which are required by s 1 of the Employment Rights Act 1996 (see Division B2 of *Jordans Employment Law Service*).

Either a contract of employment (see the Service Agreement set out above) or a statement of main terms of employment must be provided to the employee within two months of starting employment. To ensure that the employee has agreed to all these terms, it is advisable to send this statement or a contract with the offer letter.

Most of the main terms must be included within a single document. Certain terms may be included by reference to other documents. This includes terms relating to sick pay, pensions and notice pay. The statement must also contain a note about disciplinary and grievance procedures and can refer to other documents for those procedures. Typically, disciplinary and grievance procedures may be contained in a Company Handbook.

Any changes to terms of employment must be notified within one month of the change. You can either notify by stating which term has changed or you can provide a completely new statement. Pay rises, for example, should be notified in writing.

There are certain terms which are not actually required by s 1 of the Employment Rights Act 1996 but which you may wish to include. In retail employment, for example, you may wish to include a term about staff purchases. For sales staff, you may wish to include some restrictive covenants. There are separate additional clauses set out later in this section which can be incorporated or you can borrow clauses from the Service Contract (for example, restrictive covenants or terms about intellectual property and copyright).

B2.2 Precedent

Statement of main terms and conditions of employment

 Employer:

 Employee:

 1. Date employment began: [ ]

[Your employment with [ ] counts towards your period of continuous employment and accordingly your period of continuous employment began on [ ].]

[No other employment counts towards your period of continuous employment.]

2. **Job title:** [ ]

3. **Duties:**

   Your duties shall be as indicated by your job title. In addition:

   (1) You may be required to carry out any other duties within your capacity which the Employer may reasonably require

   (2) You shall obey all reasonable rules and instructions given to you by the Employer.

   (3) You shall, during working hours, devote the whole of your time and attention exclusively to the interests of the business and throughout the period of your employment shall take all reasonable steps to preserve and protect the property, goodwill and reputation of the Employer and shall do nothing to damage the Employer.

   (4) During the period of your employment, you shall not, except with prior written consent of a director of the Employer, work for, be employed by or have any interest in any other business.

4. **Location:**

   [You will be employed [initially] at][Your employment will be based at][ ][but you may be required to work [at any other premises occupied by the Employer [or any customer or client of the Employer] within [ ] elsewhere [within [the United Kingdom][for temporary periods] as directed by the Employer].

5. **Confidentiality:**

   (1) Both during the period of your employment and thereafter, you shall not disclose to any person or make use of for your own benefit or for the benefit of any other person, any trade secret or confidential information of the Employer unless you have obtained the written consent of a director of the Employer or such use or disclosure is required for the proper performance of your duties.

   (2) For these purposes, confidential information means any information which would, if disclosed to a competitor,

damage the interests of the Employer, and accordingly shall include but shall not be limited to designs, prices, mark-ups, special arrangements with suppliers, special arrangements with and requirements of particular customers, pricing strategy, sales and marketing strategy, research and development activities and plans for new products.

6. **Hours of work:**

[Your normal hours of work shall be [ ] hours per week, [from [ ] am to [ ] pm] [Monday to Friday] and such further hours as may be necessary to fulfil your duties.] [Overtime may be required from time to time [by agreement between you and your manager] [and reasonable notice will be given to you of any requirement to work overtime].

7. **Remuneration:**

(1) You will be paid £[ ] per [year][month][week][hour], payable [weekly][monthly] in arrears by credit transfer or any other arrangement acceptable to the Employer.

(2) Overtime will be paid at [time and a half] [or double time if the overtime hours are worked between the hours of [midnight and 7 am] or on Saturdays or Sundays]][for hours worked in excess of [ ] in any week [one day's holiday or certified sickness counting for these purposes as [ ] hours' work].

(3) [The Employer may also, in the complete discretion of the Employer, pay a bonus [of an amount to be determined by the Employer] [in accordance with any bonus scheme which may be issued by the Employer [at the start of each year] [from time to time] [but the Employer reserves the right in any year not to operate any such scheme [either generally or in respect of any category of employee]] and any bonus scheme introduced may be altered or withdrawn at any time and for any reason entirely at the discretion of the Employer. That discretion shall not be limited by any express or implied term of the contract].

(4) [You will also be paid commission [calculated in accordance with any commission scheme which may be issued by the Employer [each year][from time to time] [or set out method of calculation of bonus].

8. **Holidays:**

(1) The holiday year commences on [ ]. In each holiday year you will be entitled to [ ] days' paid holiday [reduced pro rata in respect of part-time employees] [in addition to

public holidays] [which includes any entitlement to public holidays]. Prior approval must be obtained from the Employer before any holiday. Approval will only be given if the proposed holiday will not unduly interfere with the smooth running of the business. The rules about gaining approval for holidays set out in Regulation 15 of the Working Time Regulations 1998 (SI 1998/1833) shall not apply and the only rules that shall apply shall be those set out in this paragraph.

(2)   [You may not carry unused holiday entitlement forward to a subsequent holiday year.][You may carry forward up to [ ] day's holiday from one holiday year to the next [provided that holiday is taken before [ ]].

(3)   On termination of your employment, you will be entitled to a payment in lieu of all holiday accrued but not taken during the part of the holiday year prior to the termination of your employment. The amount of the payment shall be the holiday pay that would have been paid in respect of such holiday unless your employment was terminated by reason of gross misconduct or you terminated your employment without giving the notice required under clause 12, in which case the amount of the payment shall be £1 unless sub-clause 4) applies.

(4)   If, when you leave your employment, you have taken in excess of your holiday entitlement, any excess holiday payments made must be repaid to the Employer. Any sums so owing may be deducted from your salary.

(5)   For the purposes of calculating holiday pay, one day's pay shall be [1/260th of annual basic salary] [[ ] hours' pay].

9.   **[Public holidays:**

You will be entitled to all statutory and public holidays and to be paid for such days. If you are required to work on a public holiday, you will be entitled to an additional day's holiday at some other time.]

10.   **Pensions:**

[There is no Company pension scheme [but the Employer will pay [ ]% of your annual salary into a personal pension scheme arranged by you.]]

[You will be entitled to join the Company's pension scheme subject to your satisfying the eligibility conditions. Details of the scheme are available from [ ]].

11. Sickness or injury:

(1) If you are absent from work by reason of sickness or injury, you must notify [a colleague] [your supervisor or manager] as soon as possible on the first day of your absence and keep the Employer regularly informed of the situation and the likely duration of the absence until you return. You must also provide any further information which the Employer may request in relation to any absence.

(2) [You should comply with any rules laid down in the Company Handbook and/or in any sickness procedure.]

(3) If the absence continues for less than eight days (including weekends) you must complete a self-certification form when you return. If the absence lasts for eight days or more, you must obtain medical certificates to cover the whole period of your absence.

(4) [Provided you comply with the above requirements [and the requirements of the sickness policy and procedure], you will be paid [full pay for the first [ ] days of absence due to sickness or injury in any 12 month period and thereafter] statutory sick pay (if entitled to it) in accordance with the Social Security Contributions and Benefits Act 1992. For the purposes of statutory sick pay, qualifying days are [Monday to Friday].]

or

[The Company may in its absolute discretion pay full pay for a limited period.]

(5) [The Employer has the right to require you to attend for a medical examination by any doctor nominated by the Employer and you will co-operate with any such requirement. You will also consent to your medical practitioner supplying a medical report.]

(6) If you are awarded damages in respect of any illness or injury caused by a third party, then any payments over and above statutory sick pay made by the Employer to you in respect of any period of absence caused by such illness or injury shall be treated as a loan repayable on demand.

12. Termination of employment:

Your employment may be terminated by the Employer by notice in writing of [ ] [weeks] [months] [subject to a minimum of] [one week for each completed year of employment subject to a maximum of twelve weeks [and a minimum of one week]. You may terminate your employment by [ ] [one week's] notice.

13. Grievance and disciplinary procedures:

(1) If possible, grievances and matters of a disciplinary nature will be dealt with informally but the following procedures are available if an informal procedure is not considered appropriate or has not resolved the problem. Even the formal procedure will be approached and operated flexibly as the main objective will be to resolve the problem.

(2) If you have a grievance relating to your employment, you should raise it first with your line manager either orally or in writing. If the matter is not settled you should raise it with [fill in next person up eg a director]. If it is not appropriate to raise the matter with either of these (eg if the complaint is against one or both of them) then you should raise it with another director or manager and this procedure will be treated as adapted as appropriate.

(3) All grievances will be treated as strictly confidential and will not be disclosed to others in the company unless you wish it.

(4) Disciplinary rules are set out [below] [in the Company Handbook, [a copy of which has been provided to you] [a copy of which is available from [ ]].

(5) Disciplinary action may be taken in the event that an Employee's conduct or performance is not regarded as acceptable. In serious cases, Employees may be dismissed for a first offence, but normally a first instance of misconduct or poor performance should result in a warning. Before any disciplinary action is taken, an Employee shall be notified in writing of the complaints against him or her and shall then be invited to attend a disciplinary hearing with a colleague or official of a trade union as representative if they so wish and to make any points they may wish the Employer to take into account before deciding whether to take disciplinary action. In appropriate cases, the Employee may be suspended on full pay while the matter is being investigated.

(6) Unless otherwise stated in the warning, warnings will be disregarded after twelve months' satisfactory conduct or performance, provided no further warnings have been issued during that period. If further warnings are given during the currency of an earlier warning, that earlier warning shall continue in force until all warnings have expired.

(7) The following will be regarded as gross misconduct which could lead to dismissal:

   (i) theft, fraud and deliberate falsification of records;

   (ii) physical violence;

   (iii) serious bullying or harassment;

   (iv) deliberate damage to property;

   (v) serious insubordination;

   (vi) misuse of an organisation's property or name;

   (vii) bringing the employer into serious disrepute;

   (viii) deliberate rudeness;

   (ix) serious incapability whilst on duty brought on by alcohol or illegal drugs;

   (x) serious negligence which causes or might cause unacceptable loss, damage or injury;

   (xi) serious infringement of health and safety rules;

   (xii) serious breach of confidence (subject to the Public Interest Disclosure Act 1998).

   This list is not intended to be exhaustive.

   An Employee may appeal against any disciplinary action by giving notice in writing within 7 days to [fill in appropriate person eg managing director] who will consider the appeal at an appeal hearing, at which the Employee may be represented by a colleague or official of a trade union.

14. **Protection of employer's interests:**

   (1) You shall not, without the prior written consent of a director, directly or indirectly, either alone or jointly with or on behalf of any other person:

      (a) for a period of 12 months commencing with the date of termination, carry on or be engaged or employed or interested in any undertaking which is carried on within the United Kingdom which competes with [that part of] the business of the

Employer [in which you worked at the date of termination [or at any time during the period of six months prior to the date of termination] [provided it shall not be a breach of this clause 14(1)(a) if you are employed in a part of such undertaking [or in a capacity] which does not compete with the [part of the] business of the Employer [in which you were employed at the date of termination of employment [or at any time during the period of six months prior to the date of termination]]]];

(b)   for a period of 12 months commencing with the date of termination canvass, solicit, interfere with or approach any customer for the purposes of the supply of products or services competitive with products or services supplied by the Employer;

(c)   for a period of 12 months commencing with the date of termination accept any order or custom from a customer in respect of products or services competitive with products or services supplied by the Employer;

(d)   for a period of 12 months commencing with the date of termination, canvass or solicit for employment or employ any person who was at the date of termination of this Agreement and continued to be until so canvassed, solicited or employed a director, designer or sales representative employed by the Employer;

(e)   for a period of 12 months commencing with the date of termination, solicit, interfere with or approach any person firm or company or entity who was a supplier of goods or services to the Employer in the 6 months preceding the date of termination and with whom you had personal contact during the those 6 months where the result of such solicitation, interference or approach is or would be the interference with or disruption of supplies to the Employer.

(2)   For the purpose of sub-clause (1) above, a "customer" shall mean any person or company who, to your knowledge, was supplied with or offered any products or services by the Employer or with whom the Employer was negotiating during the period of six months preceding the date of termination and with whom you personally dealt in connection with such supply, offer or negotiation during those 6 months.

B2 Statement of Main Terms and Conditions of Employment 35

    (3)   If you contravene one or more of the sub-clauses within sub-clause (1) (taking account of any of the extension of the periods referred to therein by reason of this sub-clause), the period of 12 months therein referred to shall be extended to last until 12 months after the date the contravention ceased.

    (4)   After the termination of this Agreement, you shall not represent yourself or permit yourself to be held as being in any way connected with or interested in the business of the Employer (except if and for so long as you remain a director or employee of the Employer) or use any name which is identical or similar to or likely to be confused with the name of the Employer or any product or service produced or provided by the Employer or which might suggest a connection with the Employer or any of its products or services.

    (5)   Immediately on termination of your employment, you shall return to the Employer all property belonging to the Employer, including all documents and any copies thereof in whatever form those copies may be made, whether on paper, tape, computer disc or otherwise. If you hold any information on any equipment which you own, you shall forthwith copy that information onto an appropriate medium, supply that copy and any other copies in your possession to the Employer and then delete such information from all equipment in your possession.

15.   **Right to hold personal data:**

As part of your conditions of employment, you give the Employer permission to collect, retain and process information about you, such as age, sex, ethnic origin and health records. This information will be used by the Employer for a number of purposes, including but not limited to monitoring the Employer's compliance with the law and best practice in terms of equal opportunity and non-discrimination. Should your personal circumstances change, you must notify the Employer immediately.

16.   **Collective and workforce agreements:**

Your employment is subject to the terms of the following collective and workforce agreements:

[list]

17.   **Company Handbook:**

The Company Handbook sets out various policies and procedures and certain information about the company. Except where the Handbook indicates otherwise, the contents of the Handbook are not intended to be contractual. The Handbook (including any contractual terms included within it) may be updated and/or amended from time to time.

18. **Terms of employment:**

These terms supersede all previous terms of employment, agreements, arrangements and understandings, whether formal or informal.

Signed on behalf of the Employer   **Signed by the Employee**

....

Dated:

B2.3 DRAFTING POINTS

Clause 1: For the rules on continuous employment, see Division B2 of *Jordans Employment Law Service*. Generally, the period of continuous employment starts when the employment starts. Breaks in employment generally break continuous employment but there are a few exceptions, for example where the break is due to sickness or where it has been agreed that employment is to be regarded as continuous despite the break.

The general rule is that continuous employment should always be with the same employer, but again there are a few exceptions. Transfers of employment within the same group of companies, or where the make-up of a partnership changes, do not break continuous employment; and a change of employer when a business is transferred in circumstances where the Transfer of Undertakings (Protection of Employment) Regulations 2006 (SI 2006/246) apply again does not break continuity of employment.

Clauses 2 and 3: It is a statutory requirement to state either the job title or a brief description of the duties. In this precedent various other duties have been added in clause 3. These clauses, although not mandatory requirements of the legislation, are useful to ensure that you have a remedy if the employee acts against the interests of the employer.

Clause 5: There is no statutory requirement to include a term about confidentiality and such a term is probably implied into the contract of employment anyway (see Drafting Points on clause 5 of the Service Agreement). However, it is still useful to include this clause to clarify what information you regard as confidential and to remind employees of their duties to maintain confidentiality. Also, if you want the obligation not to use or disclose confidential information to continue after termination of employment, you will have to state this.

Clause 7(3): However much you try to clarify that a bonus scheme is discretionary and that it can be altered or withdrawn at any time, the courts generally imply a term of the contract that the discretion should not be exercised arbitrarily or capriciously. This term as drafted attempts to give the employer maximum discretion but employers should always be prepared to justify how they have exercised their discretion. It is a good idea to record brief reasons why the discretion has been exercised in a particular way, in case the employee seeks to challenge the bonus by relying on an implied term or on the basis that it is discriminatory.

Employers should be careful about any statements they may make about the purpose of the bonus. For example, if the employer states in a document (for example, a Company Handbook or a letter explaining the bonus) that it is to reward hard work, then a refusal of a bonus because the employee has handed in notice of resignation may be challenged on the basis of an implied term that only the employee's previous hard work should be taken into account. If you do want to describe the purpose of the bonus, you should do so in the widest possible terms, to avoid inadvertently fettering your discretion.

Clause 8(1): The Working Time Regulations 1998 (SI 1998/1833) require a minimum of 5.6 weeks' holiday a year (including public holidays), for holiday years commencing on or after 1 April 2009.

If you employ part-time workers, then in order to ensure part-time workers benefit in the same way, pro rata, as full-time employees from public holidays, include the eight public holidays in the annual entitlement.

Clause 8(3): The Working Time Regulations 1998 (SI 1998/1833) require employers to pay any accrued holiday pay on termination of employment. That is so even where the employee has been summarily dismissed. However, the regulations appear to allow employers to make their own rules about how payment for accrued holiday pay is calculated. This precedent therefore provides that, in cases of gross misconduct, the accrued holiday pay is calculated as £1. This has not yet been tested in employment tribunals.

Clause 8(4): Without this clause, employers will have no right to recover excess holiday pay where an employee leaves their employment having taken more holiday than has accrued as at the date of termination of employment.

Clause 9: This clause should be omitted if public holidays are included within clause 8.

Clause 10: Payments into personal pension schemes will not exempt employers from the requirement to provide stakeholder schemes unless there are fewer than 5 employees.

You should check that the rules and eligibility conditions of the pension scheme satisfy the requirements to exempt from stakeholder schemes. If they do not, then a stakeholder scheme will have to be introduced.

Clause 11: If you want sick pay to be discretionary, you should state this in this clause. See the comments about the exercise of discretion in relation to bonuses in the comment on clause 7(3) above. If sick pay is to increase with length of service, this should also be stated here. There is a risk, where benefits improve with length of service, of an age discrimination claim, since younger employees cannot clock up the same length of service as older employees (see Division E4 of *Jordans Employment Law Service*).

If there are separate rules in the Company Handbook or in a separate sickness policy or procedure, then you can refer to them here and make payment of sick pay (over and above statutory sick pay) conditional on complying with those rules. In that case, you should include the paragraph (2) in square brackets and the first square bracketed section in clause 11(4).

Clause 13: You can either set out a basic disciplinary procedure within this statement (as here) or you can refer to another document such as a Company Handbook for the disciplinary, grievance and appeal procedures. If you do not have a Company Handbook or separate disciplinary procedure, then you should use this clause. The rules about gross misconduct are based on ACAS' recommendations in its Code of Practice on Disciplinary Procedures.

Clause 14: See the comments on restrictive covenants in the Drafting Points for Service Agreement (clause 16). Restrictive covenants such as these are only likely to be appropriate for senior employees, sales staff or those who have regular dealings with customers or clients.

Clause 17: By including this clause within the statement of terms and conditions of employment, you draw employee's attention to the Company Handbook (so that they cannot later claim that they were unaware of its provisions) without making the Handbook itself a contractual document. There are certain clauses within the Handbook which you may wish to be contractual – for example, rules about parental leave (see notes to the precedent Parental Leave Policy) or about making deductions from wages. This can be achieved by indicating within the Handbook if any provision is intended to be contractual.

B3   CONSULTANCY AGREEMENT

B3.1   USE

This agreement is designed to ensure that the consultant is not treated as an employee. This may be appropriate, for example, where the consultant is required to provide particular services as and when required but it is left to the consultant to decide how, when and where to provide the services.

This may suit both parties, particularly where the extent to which the 'employer' will need the services and the extent to which the consultant will be able and willing to provide them is uncertain. There will be no risk of an unfair dismissal claim if it turns out that the services are not required to the extent originally envisaged. The consultant may, however, be treated as an employee for the purposes of discrimination legislation, where the definition of 'employee' is far wider than for unfair dismissal legislation (see Division E of *Jordans Employment Law Service*); and the consultant may also be a 'worker' for the purposes of the Working Time Regulations 1998 (SI 1998/1833) (see Division C3 of *Jordans Employment Law Service*) and the minimum wage legislation (see Division C1 of *Jordans Employment Law Service*).

The consultant is likely to be treated as self-employed for tax purposes. Broadly the same tests are applied for determining whether a person is an 'employee' for the purposes of employment legislation as for tax legislation.

Key determining factors for determining employment status are:

– The degree of control exercised by the 'employer' over the worker – the greater the degree of control, the more likely it is that a court of tribunal or HMRC will conclude that the 'consultant' is an employee;

– whether the worker receives a regular salary or wages (suggesting employment);

– whether the worker can determine his or her own hours of work, method of working and place of working (suggesting self-employment);

– whether the 'employer' is under any obligation to provide work (suggesting employment);

– whether the worker is obliged to accept any work offered (suggesting employment);

- whether the worker is integrated into the 'employer's' business (suggesting employment);

- whether the worker has to provide his or her own stationery, tools, equipment, office etc (suggesting self-employment);

- whether the worker is entitled to delegate some duties to his or her own employees or sub-contractors (suggesting self-employment);

- whether payment is against invoices (suggesting self-employment).

The use of this form of contract and the title 'consultant' does not guarantee that HMRC or an employment tribunal will accept without further enquiry that the individual is not employed. What matters is how the contract is operated in practice.

B3.2 **Precedent**

Consultancy agreement

DATED 20[ ]

AN AGREEMENT made the day of 200

BETWEEN

(1) [ ] LIMITED whose registered office is at [ ] (the "Company")

(2) [ ] of [ ] (the "Consultant")

IT IS AGREED as follows:

1. Definitions

The following terms shall have the meanings set out below:

["Group Company": the Company, any subsidiary (as defined by Section 736 of the Companies Act 1985) of the Company, any holding company (as so defined) of the Company and any subsidiary of such holding company, in each case for the time being;]

"Services": the services to be provided by the Consultant hereunder and detailed in clause 2.

2. Consultancy services

2.1 The Company engages the Consultant to provide the Services to the Company [and all Group Companies] and the Consultant agrees to provide such services upon the terms and conditions set out in this Agreement.

2.2 The Consultant is engaged to provide the following services: [*set out details of the consultancy services to be provided*]

3. Consultancy fee

3.1 The Company shall pay the Consultant a fee of £[ ] per [hour] [week] [month] [year] (such fee to be [inclusive] [exclusive] of VAT if applicable) payable [in 12 equal monthly instalments] [monthly] [in arrears] [on the last working day of each calendar month] [within [14] days of the Consultant delivering to the Company his [VAT] invoice]. [For any part day, the fee will be reduced on a pro rata basis]. A normal day shall be between [ ] and [ ] but the fee shall not be increased if longer hours are worked on a particular day.

3.2 The Consultancy Fee shall be payable upon delivery by the Consultant to the Company of a valid [VAT] invoice.

4 Duration

This Agreement shall commence on [ ] and shall continue (subject to clause 7) [for a fixed period of [ ] terminating on the [ ]] [until terminated by either party giving to the other not less than [30] [60] [90] days' notice] [not to expire before [ ]].

5 Consultant's services

5.1 The Consultant is retained on a [non-exclusive] "when-needed" basis to provide the Services to the Company [and all Group Companies] for up to [ ] hours during each week of this Agreement at such times and at such locations as may reasonably be required by the Company.

5.2 The Consultant shall:

5.1.1 faithfully and diligently perform his duties;

5.1.2 provide his services with reasonable care and skill and to the best of his ability;

5.1.3 use his best endeavours to promote the interests of the Company [and the Group Companies]; and

5.1.4 comply with all statutes and regulations together

with any bye-laws and regulations of local and other authorities applicable to the Services.

5.3 [The Consultant shall give priority to the provision of the Services over all other business activities undertaken by the Consultant.] [The Consultant shall provide his services exclusively to the Company and shall not undertake any other business during this Agreement.]

5.4 The Consultant shall be responsible for providing, without reimbursement from the Company, all tools and equipment and any stationery or other items necessary for the proper performance of the Services.

6 Expenses

6.1 The Company shall reimburse the Consultant for out of pocket expenses reasonably incurred by him in the proper provision of the Services in accordance with the Company's scale of allowable expenses.

6.2 The Consultant shall on request by the Company provide such vouchers or other evidence of actual payment of such expenses as the Company may [reasonably] require.

7 Termination

7.1 The Company may by notice in writing with immediate effect terminate this Agreement if the Consultant shall:

7.1.1 commit a [material] breach of any of the terms of this Agreement [which, in the case of a breach capable of remedy, shall not have been remedied by the Consultant within 21 days of receipt by the Consultant of a notice from the Company specifying the breach and requiring its remedy];

7.1.2 be grossly incompetent, guilty of gross misconduct and/or any serious or persistent breach of this Agreement or serious or persistent negligence in the provision of the Services;

7.1.3 fail or refuse after written warning to provide the Services reasonably and properly required of him under this Agreement;

7.1.4 have a receiver appointed over any of his assets or have a petition issued for his bankruptcy or propose any composition with his creditors;

7.1.5 through injury and/or illness become unable to

perform the Services for a consecutive period of [6] weeks [or an aggregate of 40 days] in any period of [12] calendar months;

7.1.6 be convicted of a criminal offence other than a minor motoring offence.

7.2 Termination of this Agreement for whatever reason shall not affect the accrued rights of the parties arising in any way out of this Agreement as at the date of termination.

8 Confidential information

8.1 For the purposes of this Agreement "Confidential Information" means trade secrets or confidential information belonging or relating to any Group Company and including (without limitation) information or secrets relating to business or manufacturing methods and processes, inventions, research and development activities, designs, drawings, sources and supplies of materials used, the identity of customers and potential customers and agents, personal contacts with or within customers and potential customers or with agents, prices, margins, special arrangements with customers of and suppliers to any Group Company, pricing strategy and marketing strategy, product and future product details.

8.2 Both during the continuation of this Agreement and thereafter, the Consultant shall not (unless authorised to do so by the Company or by a court of competent jurisdiction or unless required to do so by law or any competent authority or in order to perform his duties hereunder or unless such confidential information is generally available to the public (through no default on the part of the Consultant)) disclose to any person any Confidential Information which may come to his knowledge and shall not use or attempt to use any such Confidential Information for his own benefit or for the benefit of any person.

8.3 Following termination of this Agreement, the obligations of the Consultant under clauses 8.1 and 8.2 above shall not apply to any information which is or becomes generally available to the public on a non-confidential basis through no act or default on the part of the Consultant.

8.4 Nothing contained in this clause 8 shall be construed so as to prevent the Consultant from using his personal skills in any business in which he may lawfully be engaged in after the termination of this Agreement.

8.5 All notes, memoranda, records and other writings

(whether recorded on paper, computer memory or discs or otherwise) made by the Consultant in the course of his duties or relating to the business of any Group Company and any copies thereof on any documents or other records prepared from such notes, memoranda, records and other writings or information contained therein shall be and remain the property of the relevant Group Company and shall be handed over by the Consultant to the Company from time to time and on demand.

9 [*Note: Restrictive Covenants after cessation may sometimes be irrelevant – use wording from the Precedent Service Agreement but this may increase the risk of the contract being deemed a contract of services.*]

10 Rights and consultant's works

10.1 The Consultant acknowledges that the product and/or results of all work carried out by him for the Company under this Agreement shall belong exclusively to the Company. Accordingly, the Consultant shall execute all such documents and do all such acts as the Company shall from time to time require in order to give effect to its rights pursuant to this clause.

[*Note: More extensive provisions are contained in clause 13 of the Precedent Service Agreement.*]

11 Status and tax liabilities

The parties declare that it is their intention that the Consultant shall have the status of a self-employed person and shall not be entitled to any pension, bonus or other fringe benefits from the Company and it is agreed that the Consultant shall be responsible for all income tax liabilities and National Insurance or similar contributions in respect of his fees and the Consultant agrees to indemnify the Company against all demands for any income tax, penalties, interest in respect of the Consultant's services hereunder and against its reasonably and properly incurred costs of dealing with such demands.

12 Notice

Any notice required to be given under this Agreement shall be in writing and shall be deemed to be sufficiently served on the Company if left at or sent by first class post to the registered office of the Company for the time being and shall be sufficiently served on the Consultant if left at or sent by first class post to his last known place of residence. Proof of posting of any such notice shall be sufficient without proof of delivery and any such notice posted as aforesaid shall be deemed to have been served on the 2nd day (excluding Sundays and public holidays) following that on which it was posted.

13 [Indemnity

The Consultant shall be liable for and shall indemnify the Company for all losses, costs, damages and expenses arising from any injury or sickness, disease or death of any person or loss of or damage to any property arising out of this Agreement caused by the negligence or deliberate act of the Consultant [or any person employed by the Consultant or to whom the Consultant delegates any responsibility under this Agreement] except where such injury, sickness, disease, death, loss or damage is caused or contributed to by the negligence of the Company.]

14 Entire agreement

The Agreement comprises the entire agreement between the Parties to the exclusion of all other terms and conditions, prior or collateral agreements, negotiations, notices of intention and representations. The Parties agree that they have not been induced to enter into the contract on the basis of any representation or warranty save that this clause shall not limit liability for fraudulent misrepresentations. The Parties shall not be bound by or be liable for any statement, representation, promise, inducement or understanding of any kind or nature not set forth in the contract and no amendment to the contract shall be binding on either Party unless in writing and signed by each Party.

15 Non assignment

[This Agreement is personal to the Consultant and] the Consultant shall not assign or sub-contract the benefit or burden of this Agreement without the prior written consent of the Company [but the Consultant shall be entitled to employ his own staff to assist in the provision of the Services].

16 Jurisdiction

This Agreement shall be governed and construed in all respects and in accordance with English law and the parties submit to the exclusive jurisdiction of the courts of England and Wales.

SIGNED by

[   ]

for [   ] Limited

SIGNED by [   ]

B3.3 DRAFTING POINTS

Definitions: Generally you should include a definition of group companies. Even if there are no other companies in the group at the time the contract is drawn up, there may be in the future.

Clause 2: Duties should be set out in general terms, describing broadly the sort of work the employee may be asked to undertake. The more specific the duties are, the greater the risk that the consultant will be regarded as an employee.

Clause 3: Anything that looks more like a salary than a fee – for example regular payments each month, will make it more likely that the consultant will be regarded as an employee.

Clause 5.3: Actually prohibiting the consultant from working for anyone else would tend to indicate employment rather than self-employment. You can, however, ask the consultant to give priority to working for you over all other business activities of the consultant. You can also require the consultant not to work for a direct competitor or to disclose to you all his or her other business activities. The more stringent the requirements, however, the greater the risk of the consultant being regarded as an employee.

Clause 8.1: Include within the definition of 'confidential information' any information which is not generally known to the public and which, if disclosed to or used by a competitor, could put you are a competitive disadvantage. The precedent here includes types of information generally included in the definition, but you should consider whether it covers all information you would like to be treated as confidential.

Clause 13: This clause should be included to ensure that no earlier contracts govern the relationship. This is particularly important, for example, where a former employee's employment is terminated but his or her services are retained under a consultancy agreement.

Clause 14: This prevents the Consultant claiming bonuses, commission or other payments not referred to in the Agreement.

Clause 15: Only include the second section in square brackets if the Consultant has a right to delegate any responsibilities under this Agreement. The right of the Consultant to sub-contract, or delegate the work to his or her own staff is a strong indicator of self-employment.

B4 CASUAL WORKERS

B4.1 USE

This precedent is meant to cover cases where individuals have an arrangement with a company or other organisation whereby they can be called on if and when required; and if they are required, they get paid for that assignment. A new form should be completed for each assignment. The intention is to avoid an 'over-arching' or 'umbrella' contract, by providing for a series of mini employment contracts each of short duration. There is then no contract during the periods between assignments, because an assignment can only be made by agreement.

This could similarly be used for casual workers who only work evenings or weekends as and when required, so that each assignment would only last for a few hours. This form could then effectively be used as a written notification of the times an individual is meant to start and finish. It may be too cumbersome in that situation to complete this form for each assignment in which case the alternative first paragraph may be used.

This should avoid the individual acquiring sufficient continuous employment to qualify for certain employment rights such as the right not to be unfairly dismissed and the right to a redundancy payment when the assignment ends. If assignments are going to be so regular or of such duration that employment protection rights are going to be acquired anyway, then this arrangement will not be suitable.

The individual will probably be an employee during each assignment and so qualify for statutory sick pay, holiday pay and other rights under the Working Time Regulations 1998 (SI 1998/1833), the national minimum wage and the right not to be discriminated against on grounds of sex, race, etc.

B4.2　　　　　　　　　Precedent

Casual workers' terms of engagement

　　DETAILS OF TEMPORARY ASSIGNMENT

　　　　[ ] Limited of　　　　　　　　　　("the Company")

　　[You will work from [date] to [date] at [location]. Starting time shall be [start time] and finishing time shall be [finishing time].]

　　　　or

　　[This document sets out the terms of engagement that will apply if and when you agree to work for the Company. Actual times and dates of working will be agreed with you from time to time.]

TERMS

Job Title: [ ]

[**Duration:** This engagement shall start on the start date indicated above and terminate on the finishing date indicated above.]

or

[**Duration:** Each engagement will finish at the time and on the date agreed.]

Continuous Employment: No other employment counts towards continuous employment.

Pay: £[ ] per hour worked paid weekly in arrears.

Absence and Illness: You must notify the Company as soon as possible if you cannot attend work on a date on which you have agreed to work.

Company Sick Pay and Pensions: None of these are applicable to your employment but provided you have done some work under this engagement, or under another engagement ending within eight weeks before this engagement starts, you will qualify for statutory sick pay subject to the rules of the statutory sick pay scheme.

Holiday Pay: One thirteenth of the pay rate quoted above represents holiday pay. It will be withheld until the earlier of the pay date in respect of any holiday taken or the termination of this engagement. Your holiday pay will be shown separately on your pay slip.

Rules and Regulations: [Add here any rules and regulations you wish to apply during the engagement.]

Notice of Termination of this Engagement: Normally an engagement will terminate at the time and on the date we have agreed that it will end. However, there may be circumstances in which your engagement will have to be terminated earlier – for example, if the work anticipated ceases or does not arise or if your conduct or performance is not acceptable. In the latter case, the disciplinary procedure will apply.

Disciplinary Action: Disciplinary action may be taken against you in the event that your conduct or performance is not regarded as acceptable. Before disciplinary action is taken, you will be notified in writing of the complaints against you and invited to attend a disciplinary hearing with a colleague or union official as representative if you wish. You may appeal against any disciplinary action by giving written notice within 7 days to the Company.

Grievance Procedure: If you have a grievance relating to your employment you should raise it with [ ] or if this is not appropriate you should raise it with [ ]. A meeting will then be held. If you are not happy with the outcome you may appeal within 5 working days to [ ].

Date ....

Signed by the Employer

....

B4.3 DRAFTING POINTS

This precedent sets out the bare minimum terms necessary to comply with s 1 of the Employment Rights Act 1996. You may wish to add other clauses from the precedent statement of terms and conditions of employment for employees or one or more of the precedent individual clauses.

Where engagements are for single days or of very short duration, so that new terms of engagement are not issued for each engagement, use the alternative 'Duration' clause.

B5 SUNDAY WORKING

B5.1 USE

Employers who wish their employees to work in a shop on Sundays must give their employees a statutory notice about their rights to opt-out of Sunday working. This does not apply to workers who are employed to work only on Sundays. This precedent may be used.

B5.2 Precedent

Statutory rights in relation to Sunday shop work

> You have become employed as a shop worker and are or can be required under your contract of employment to do the Sunday work your contract provides for.
>
> However, if you wish, you can give a notice, as described in the next paragraph, to your employer and you will then have the right not to work in or about a shop on any Sunday on which the shop is open once three months have passed from the date on which you gave the notice.
>
> Your notice must:
>
> – be in writing;
>
> – be signed and dated by you;
>
> – say that you object to Sunday working.
>
> For three months after you give the notice, your employer can still require you to do all the Sunday work your contract provides for. After the three-month period has ended, you have the right to complain to an employment tribunal if, because of your refusal to work on Sundays on which the shop is open, your employer:
>
> – dismisses you; or
>
> – does something else detrimental to you, for example, failing to promote you.
>
> Once you have the rights described, you can surrender them only by giving your employer a further notice, signed and dated by you, saying that you wish to work on Sundays or that you do not object to Sunday working and then agreeing with your employer to work on Sundays or on a particular Sunday.

B6 BETTING SHOPS

B6.1 USE

Employers who wish their workers to work in a betting shop on Sundays must give their employees a statutory notice about their rights to opt-out of Sunday betting work. This does not apply to workers who are employed to work only on Sundays. This precedent may be used.

B6.2　　　　　　　　　　Precedent

Statutory rights in relation to Sunday betting shop work

You have become employed under a contract of employment under which you are or can be required to do Sunday betting work, that is to say, work:

– at a track on a Sunday on which your employer is taking bets at the track; or

– in a licensed betting office on a Sunday on which it is open for business.

However, if you wish, you can give a notice, as described in the next paragraph, to your employer and you will then have the right not to do Sunday betting work once three months have passed from the date on which you gave the notice.

Your notice must:

– be in writing;

– be signed and dated by you;

– say that you object to doing Sunday betting work.

For three months after you give the notice, your employer can still require you to do all the Sunday betting work your contract provides for. After the three-month period has ended, you have the right to complain to an employment tribunal if, because of your refusal to do Sunday betting work, your employer:

– dismisses you; or

– does something else detrimental to you, for example, failing to promote you.

Once you have the rights described, you can surrender them only by giving your employer a further notice, signed and dated by you, saying that you wish to do Sunday betting work or that you do not object to doing Sunday betting work and then agreeing with your employer to do such work on Sundays or on a particular Sunday.

C

SPECIFIC CLAUSES

C1 USE OF SOFTWARE

C1.1 USE

Employers who allow their employees access to computers, for example to prepare documents, letters, invoices etc or for sending emails or accessing the internet, will need rules regulating use of computers. Because employers are likely to update and supplement their software from time to time, those rules are more appropriately included in a Company Handbook than in a contract or statement of main terms and conditions of employment. Nevertheless, it is useful to include a provision in the contract or statement of main terms and conditions of employment a requirement on employees to comply with rules set out in the Handbook or elsewhere. This would enable the employer to enforce the rules by injunction or seek compensation for any loss arising from an employee's breach of the rules.

This clause, therefore, should be used in conjunction with a section in the Company Handbook.

Employers are unlikely to want to sue their employees to enforce terms such as these, but they may wish to if the employee has left employment.

C1.2 Precedent

Use of software

1. The Employee must not attempt, alone or with others, to gain access to data or programs without authority to do so.

2. In accessing or using any computer software, the Employee shall observe any rules laid down by the Company in the Handbook or otherwise.

3. The Employee shall not load into any computer via disk, typing, electronic data, transfer or any other means any program unless authorised to do so and, if so authorised, shall do so only in accordance with rules laid down by the Company in the Handbook or otherwise.

4. The Employee must not use any modem link to access any other computer or bulletin board or information service except with specific written prior authority from the Employee's Line Manager and, if so authorised, shall do so only in accordance with rules laid down by the Company in the Handbook or otherwise.

5. The Employee shall comply with any Licence Agreements entered into by the Company and in particular must not copy computer software or any related documentation, including user guides and user manuals. Any employees learning of unauthorised copying of computer software or related documentation must notify their line manager immediately.

6. The Employee shall comply with copyright law in the United Kingdom and in any other country in which the Company may operate. Breach of copyright, including illegal copying or use of software shall be regarded as gross misconduct.

7. The consequence of any breach of these rules or any rules set out in the Company Handbook or otherwise could be so serious for the Company that any breach will be regarded as gross misconduct which could lead to summary dismissal.

8. Because of the pace of change in technology and in management systems, the Company has the right to amend or add to this clause from time to time or to introduce new or amended rules concerning the use of software, protection against computer viruses, protection of copyright or otherwise.

C1.3 DRAFTING POINTS

Before deciding whether to include a clause about use of the computer, you should consider:

— which if any of your employees have access to the computer;

— whether you are prepared to allow some use of your computer network for private purposes;

— which programs will employees have access to;

— what sort of actions would you want to prevent.

Once these points have been considered, you can decide which of the above terms should be included in the Service Agreement or statement of main terms and conditions of employment; and then decide what to include in the Company Handbook.

Inappropriate use of computers can lead to legal action against the employer – for example, offensive emails, particularly ones with a sexual or racist content, may lead to complaints of sexual or racial harassment; illegal copying of programs or user guides may lead to breach of copyright claims. The rules should be very clear that any such action will be treated very seriously. This should be stated both in the contract or statement of main terms and conditions of employment and in the Company Handbook.

Clause 8 allows you to amend the clause from time to time. Although this precedent is drafted in fairly general terms, it is impossible to predict with certainty what changes in software technology there may be in the future and a general and wide-ranging right to amend the clause is therefore essential.

C2 STAFF PURCHASES

C2.1 USE

This clause is useful in those employments where employees may be permitted to purchase goods from the employer. Employees may be entitled to a staff discount, in which case you may wish to ensure that that privilege is not abused. For example, you would not want your employees to buy goods cheaply with the intention of selling them on to their friends.

Allowing employees to purchase goods may also make prevention of theft by employees more difficult. In shops, for example, an employee caught with goods from the shop which they have not paid for may use as an excuse the fact that they were planning to pay for the goods later. It will then be difficult if not impossible to prove an intention to steal. The solution is to lay down clear rules about the procedure to be followed by employees if they wish to purchase goods, with a clear statement, ensuring everyone is aware of it, that a failure to follow the rules will be regarded as gross misconduct which could render the employee liable to summary dismissal. With a clause like that, employers will only need to prove a breach of the rules – not an intention to steal.

To lessen the likelihood of theft, some employers restrict the times at which employees may be permitted to purchase goods from the employer.

Finally, you may wish to allow employees to buy goods and have the cost deducted from their wages. You are only allowed to do this if the employee has agreed in writing (see Division C1 of *Jordans Employment Law Service*).

C2.2 Precedent

Staff purchase clause

> [The Employee may only purchase goods from the Employer at those times notified to him or her from time to time by the Manager or Area Manager, as appropriate.]

Procedure

> The procedure for purchasing goods from the Employer is as follows:
>
> (a) goods intended to be purchased must be taken immediately to the [Manager/check-out] for purchase;
>
> (b) the Employee must then inform the [Manager/check-out operator] than the Employee intends to purchase the goods [using the staff discount] [under this Staff purchase clause];

(c) the [check-out operator/manager] will then give the Employee [a receipt/written authorisation to purchase] recording the fact that he or she [has purchased/intends to purchase] the goods under these staff purchase arrangements;

(d) the receipt must be kept with the goods until the Employee leaves the premises;

(e) prior to purchase, the goods must remain visible at all times and under no circumstances may goods be put inside any property belonging to the Employee (including pockets or handbags or any vehicle) or left unattended.

[Staff discount

Employees are entitled to a staff discount of [X%] for purchases made for themselves or for their immediate family (ie parents, children, spouse and siblings). Under no circumstances may the staff discount be used to purchase goods for friends or for resale.

[Staff may only purchase goods up to an aggregate value (after applying the staff discount) of £[ ] on any one [day/week/month].]

[Deductions from wages

The Employer shall be entitled to deduct from the wages of the Employee any sums owing in respect of any purchase of goods by the Employee which have not already been paid for.]

Defective goods

If the Employee wishes to purchase defective or damaged goods, the full price [subject to the usual staff discount] must be paid unless the Employee has the written agreement of [a Manager].

Breach of any of these rules shall constitute gross misconduct which will generally lead to summary dismissal. Furthermore, the Employee agrees that the Employer shall be entitled to deduct from the Employee's wages an amount equal to the full retail price of goods in question (without discount) and the employers are hereby authorised to make such a deduction in these circumstances.

Right to Search

The Employer reserves the right to search the Employee and any of the Employee's belongings (including any vehicle belonging to or used by the Employee) at any time while on or leaving the Employer's premises. During such a search, the Employee is entitled to be accompanied by a colleague, who must be an employee of the Employers.

C2.3 DRAFTING POINTS

These clauses should be adapted to suit the particular circumstances. For example, in retail employment, it may be useful to restrict the times at which staff may purchase goods to periods outside opening hours or during periods when the shop is unlikely to be particularly busy. You may wish to limit the overall amount spent in any particular period, particularly where you provide for a staff discount.

In manufacturing employment, you may need to devise a more rigorous procedure for staff purchases, requiring a written record signed by an appropriate manager that the purchase has been authorised prior to purchase; and some means of recording the purchase, so that if an employee is caught removing goods from the premises or hiding goods in handbags or pockets without good explanation, you can be sure whether or not the purchase is legitimate. You would need to ensure that managers understand the need to insist that all staff purchases are authorised in advance in writing and that they must never merely give verbal consent to a staff purchase. If it becomes well-known that a particular manager gives verbal consent to staff purchases, then you will not have the proof you may need if you suspect an employee of stealing.

It is important to provide within these terms a right to make appropriate deductions from wages or salary. Without written authorisation, you may be treated as having made an unauthorised deduction from wages. The employee would be entitled to recover the amount of the deduction in an employment tribunal and you would lose the right to recover that amount from the employee (see Division C1 of *Jordans Employment Law Service*).

C3 LAY-OFF AND SHORT-TIME

C3.1 USE

Lay-off and short-time clauses are used particularly in industries in which workload regularly fluctuates. Without such a clause, lay-offs and short-time working without the consent of the employees may amount to a breach of contract by the employer. By laying off employees or putting them on short-time working, redundancies can be avoided. During the initial period of any period of lay-off or short-time working, employees are entitled as a minimum to 'guarantee pay' from their employers; and thereafter, employees may be entitled to state benefits.

Broadly, lay-off means the employee is not required to carry out any work during a particular week and as a result is not entitled to any payment (other than statutory guarantee pay). If workers are entitled to payment (apart from guarantee pay) even when not required to work, then they are not treated as 'laid off' during periods when no work is provided.

Short-time working occurs when the work required of employees or a group of employees reduces so that their remuneration drops to half a week's pay or less.

If the period of lay-off continues for more than four consecutive weeks, or for six weeks not more than three of which are consecutive in any period of 13 weeks, then employees are entitled to resign and to claim a redundancy payment. The rules are explained in Division D4 of *Jordans Employment Law Service*.

Employers are only entitled to impose a lay-off or short-time working if there is a clause in the contract to that effect. Although such a clause can be implied, in practice it is much better to have an express term, to avoid arguments about whether there is such a right and, if so, how it may be exercised. Laying off or putting on short-time working without such a clause (express or implied) is a breach of contract entitling employees to sue for any lost wages or to resign and claim constructive dismissal.

Many lay-off and short-time clauses are contained in collective agreements and require consultation with a recognised trade union.

C3.2 Precedent

Lay-off and short-time working

Lay-off and short-time

1. If there is a cessation or shortage of work or a reduction in the Company's requirements for employees to carry out work

generally or any particular kind of work, whether such cessation, shortage or reduction is temporary or permanent and whatever the reason for such cessation, shortage or reduction, the Company shall have the right either:

(a) to lay-off without remuneration (except any remuneration required to be paid under Part III of the Employment Rights Act 1996) all or some employees for all or part (by using a rota or otherwise) of the period of the cessation or shortage of work however long that period may be; or

(b) to place on short-time working all or some employees for all or part (by using a rota or otherwise) of the period of the cessation or shortage of work (however long that period may be) and may reduce compensation according to the number of hours actually worked.

2. For the purposes of this clause, an employee shall be treated as laid off during any week throughout which he or she is required by the Company not to work and not to attend for work and accordingly is not entitled to any remuneration (other than as required by Part III of the Employment Rights Act 1996 or any statutory re-enactment of modification thereof).

3. For the purposes of this clause, an employee shall be treated as placed on short-time working for any week during which he or she is required by the Company to work such reduced hours that the employee's remuneration is less than half that employee's normal week's pay.

4. [Before any period of lay-off or short-time working, the Company shall inform [trade union]/[employee representatives] of the reasons for the proposal to lay-off or place on short-time working and the expected duration; and the Company shall consult [trade union]/[employee representatives] about ways of avoiding or lessening the impact of such lay-off or short-time working.]

C3.3 DRAFTING POINTS

In industries in which workload regularly fluctuates, lay-off and short-time are often attractive alternatives to redundancy. During any period of lay-off, employees are entitled to claim state social security benefits; and there is a statutory limit on how long employees can be laid off for before they become entitled to redundancy payments.

To ensure that employees understand the rules about lay-off and short-time working, many employers include within the Company Handbook a section explaining the impact lay-off and short-time working have on employment rights. This will include an explanation of the right to guarantee payments during the initial period of any lay-off; and the right to a redundancy payment after four consecutive weeks of lay-off or six weeks in any period of 13 weeks of which not more than three are consecutive.

Lay-off and short-time clauses that are contained in or derive from collective agreements often require consultation before lay-off or short-time working are imposed.

C4 MEDIA COMMUNICATIONS

C4.1 USE

This clause may be inserted into a Service Agreement or statement of main terms and conditions of employment. The advantage of including it within the contractual documents rather than in a Company Handbook is that it makes a breach of this term a breach of contract. That may give employers a wider range of remedies, including for example an injunction or claim for damages, than if this is included within a Handbook.

Employers should bear in mind the provisions of the Public Interest Disclosure Act 1998, under which employees are protected from disciplinary action or dismissal for making a 'protected disclosure' – ie a disclosure about any wrongdoing the employee believes another employee or the employer has committed. In most cases, to be protected, the disclosure must be to someone within the employing organisation but there are a few limited circumstances where a disclosure to the press may be protected – see Division C6 of *Jordans Employment Law Service*.

C4.2 Precedent

Media communications

Media communications

> Employees must not make contact with or communicate with any member of the press or media or anyone so connected, in relation to the Company or its business or any Group Company unless they obtain the prior written permission of [their line manager/a director]. Employees are not permitted to publish any letter, articles or otherwise purport to represent the Company or any Group Company unless they have obtained the prior permission from [their line manager/a director].

D

POLICIES AND PROCEDURES

D1 STAFF HANDBOOK

D1.1 USE

Staff handbooks set out information about the employer and often include a variety of policies and procedures. They may also include sample forms for employees to invoke a particular procedure. They are generally not regarded as contractual documents, so that the provisions in the handbook cannot be enforced and a failure by either party to follow them will not constitute a breach of contract. Nevertheless, rules contained in the handbook are generally expected to be followed. For example, if the handbook contains a disciplinary procedure, a failure by the employer to follow the procedure may render a dismissal unfair.

There may be certain provisions in the handbook which an employer will want to be contractually binding. Such terms may include:

- rules permitting deductions from wages or receipt by the employer of a payment from the employee. This is because, under s 13 of the Employment Rights Act 1996, a deduction may not be made from wages unless there is a written term of the contract permitting such a deduction. There is a similar provision in relation to payments from the employee. For fuller details, see Division C1 of *Jordans Employment Law Service*;

- rules about sick pay. For example, the employer may wish to provide that a failure to follow the correct notification procedure will result in loss of sick pay. A failure to follow the rules laid down in the statutory sick pay regulations can result in a loss of statutory sick pay – see Division C7 of *Jordans Employment Law Service*;

- provisions for claiming expenses.

There is nothing wrong with including such terms in the handbook so long as you remember to incorporate them somehow into the contract of employment or statement of main terms of employment.

This can be achieved by either duplicating the terms in the contract or statement of main terms, or stating in the contract of statement a provision that, for example:

– any sums owing by the employee to the employer under any provision in the handbook may be deducted from wages or a payment received by the employer;

– sick pay will only be payable if the rules laid down in the handbook are followed.

To avoid any possible argument that a change in the handbook amounts to a variation of the terms of employment (which would require the employee's consent), it is useful to include a clear statement, probably at the start of the handbook, that the handbook may be updated from time to time.

Rules setting out standards of behaviour, dress codes and how to deal with particular situations may be set out in the handbook. Such rules may include:

– General behaviour

– Computer software

– Dress code

– Media communications

– Personal property

Employers should consider introducing policies on the following matters and including them within the handbook:

– Access to personal information policy

– Accident/incident reporting

– Aids policy

– Alcohol and drug abuse policy

– Appraisal policy

– Bereavement policy

– Changes in personal circumstances

- Competence policy
- Computer software
- Court attendance
- Disciplinary procedure
- E-mail and internet policy
- Equal opportunities and discrimination policy
- Flexible working
- Grievance procedure
- Harassment and bullying
- Health and safety policy
- HM forces and similar bodies
- Maternity rights policy
- Media communications
- Paternity leave policy
- Personal property
- Public service
- Retirement
- Right to hold personal data
- Training and development policy
- Parental and family leave policy
- Smoking policy
- Suggestion scheme
- Work-related health policy
- Working-time regulations

Examples of all these policies appear in this section.

The handbook may also contain a summary of the benefits available to employees. Often these will be contractual. Even if they are not, a failure to provide a benefit stated in the handbook may be regarded as a breach of contract because it may damage the relationship of mutual trust and confidence (see Division B2 of *Jordans Employment Law Service*). Benefits that may be provided for in the handbook may include:

– Bonus scheme

– Private medical insurance

– Staff group pension plan

The handbook may also include a statement of the various means by which the employer communicates with its employees. If there is a 'Works Council' or staff forum, or an 'Information and Consultation' procedure (for which see Division G of *Jordans Employment Law Service*), a brief description could be included. A typical section on communication may refer to the following matters:

– Purpose

– AGM

– Corporate intranet

– Information and consultation procedure

Finally, the handbook may set out forms for the employee to use in certain circumstances. Typically, these may include:

– Appraisal forms

– Family and parental leave request form

– Flexible working request

– Holiday booking form

– Overtime claim form

– Request to work beyond retirement age

– Sickness self-certification form

Again, precedents for all these matters appear in this section.

D1.2　　　　　　　　　Precedent
Staff handbook

CONTENTS

Welcome to [　] Limited

Foreword

Company rules

Employment policies

Employee benefits

Communication and consultation

Forms

Welcome to [　] Limited

[Describe [　] Limited's philosophy and culture. Describe the Company and its business. For example:

[　] Limited is a major manufacturer and distributor of [　]. It operates worldwide and is part of a major international group.

We treat our employees as our major asset. We want all employees to find [　] an enjoyable and rewarding place to work. We are confident that our philosophy, outlook and culture provides the right environment for everyone to fulfil their full potential. We pride ourselves on our ability to develop the skills of our employees as well as making work enjoyable.

Good communication between staff at all levels is part of the key to our success. We encourage employees to raise any matters that may concern them, whether it is some relationship at work that they are finding difficult, or whether it is concern about the ethics of what any other member of staff is doing, or whether you have simply thought of a better way of doing things, we want our employees to feel free to discuss whatever it is that concerns them with their line manager or any other manager or a director. We aim for continual improvement in everything we do, and the best source of ideas for improvement is you, our employees. No employee should ever feel that they will be criticised or ostracised for raising a matter which is of concern to them.

I wish you all a very pleasant and fulfilling time working with us here at [　] Limited.]

Signed: [Managing Director]

Foreword

Please read this handbook carefully. If you have any queries do not hesitate to refer them to [your supervisor or to the Human Resources department]

The Company reserves the right to amend this handbook as and when appropriate.

Your Statement of Terms and Conditions of Employment sets out the legal basis of your employment – that is your legal obligations to the Company and the Company's legal obligations to you. It is important that you read and understand your terms and conditions. If you have any queries about them, please refer to [your supervisor or to the Human Resources Department].

It is a term of your employment that you comply with the rules laid down in this Handbook. The business can only succeed for everyone's benefit if everyone from top management downwards works as a disciplined team and this is only possible if everyone works by the same rules. You should find these rules are as much a benefit to you as they are to the Company. They should help you to understand what is expected of you and what you can expect of the Company.

This handbook also lays down procedures to be followed in certain situations. Again, these should be as much for your benefit as for the Company. They should enable you to understand how to handle particular situations and the process the Company intends to follow when those situations arise.

Certain situations require a degree of formality. This ensures fairness and consistency of treatment. This is another reason why we have rules and procedures. There are also forms set out at the end of the handbook which you should use if and when appropriate.

We do not want these procedures to operate inflexibly. They are there to help but if you and/or the Company decide that some other procedure would be better, for whatever reason, then the rules should be adapted as appropriate. Departure from the rules, however, should be the exception rather than the rule so we encourage you to follow the rules unless you think there are very good reasons not to. You can always discuss the application of the rules with the Human Resources Department if for any reason you feel that they are not working for you. If appropriate, you and the Human Resources Department can then agree to amend the rules either generally or to suit your particular situation.

Company rules

[Set out general rules of behaviour]

Company policies and procedures

[Set out procedures]

Communication and consultation

[Set out means of communication between employer and employee]

Forms

[Set out standard forms]

D2 GENERAL RULES OF BEHAVIOUR

D2.1 USE

General rules of behaviour should set out the basic rules that you expect your employees to observe. They should help your employees to know what is expected of them, but they may also be useful when applying the disciplinary procedure. They should be stated as widely as possible, so that employees can have no legitimate complaint if they are disciplined for breach of the rules. This is particularly important in the case of gross misconduct. Generally employers are entitled to dismiss summarily, without prior warnings, for gross misconduct. However, an employer may not be able to do this if employees are given no clear explanation of what constitutes gross misconduct.

This precedent should be adapted to suit the particular circumstances of the employer. For example, employees who regularly deal with the public, such as till assistants in shops, or nurses in hospitals, can be expected to comply with rules about dealing with the public such as politeness, patience, helpfulness etc, whereas this may not be so important for, for example, technicians who do not deal directly with the public.

D2.2 Precedent

General standards of behaviour

Employees are expected to conduct themselves in a manner compatible with the aims and culture of the Company. This means that:

– they should obey all reasonable instructions issued to them by their line manager or by any other appropriate manager;

– they should report any matters that are of concern to them about the conduct of other employees or of members of the public;

– they should behave with courtesy and consideration for and show respect to fellow employees and members of the public with whom they come into contact;

– they should be aware of the Company's policies and comply with them. If an Employee has any difficulty in complying with a particular policy, they should raise the matter with their line manager or with a member of the Human Resources Department;

– they should comply with any rules, for example about use of Company equipment and health and safety rules, which may be issued from time to time;

– they should attend for work punctually;

- they should comply with all rules about notifying sickness absence or absences for any other reason;

- they should not do anything which exposes either themselves or others to any avoidable health and safety risk;

- they should observe all rules about confidential information and not discuss work matters outside the workplace, particularly where that information could reach a competitor;

- they should not take on work outside of this employment without express permission from an appropriate manager;

- they should take proper care of Company property, including any Company car.

Any failure in any of the above respects could result in the disciplinary procedure being invoked.

Gross Misconduct

Certain issues are regarded by the company as so serious as to warrant summary dismissal without notice. Matters which justify summary dismissal include, but are not limited to:

(i) theft, fraud and deliberate falsification of records;

(ii) physical violence;

(iii) serious bullying or harassment;

(iv) deliberate damage to property;

(v) serious insubordination;

(vi) misuse of an organisation's property or name;

(vii) bringing the employer into serious disrepute;

(viii) deliberate rudeness;

(ix) serious incapability whilst on duty brought on by alcohol or illegal drugs;

(x) serious negligence which causes or might cause unacceptable loss, damage or injury;

(xi) serious infringement of health and safety rules;

(xii) serious breach of confidence (subject to the Public Interest (Disclosure) Act 1998).

D3 IT RULES

D3.1 USE

As noted in the comments on the clause on use of software, there should generally be a clause in the Service Agreement or statement of main terms of employment, dealing with use of computers, as well as a policy set out in the Company Handbook. The fact that this policy is set out in the Handbook rather than the contract or statement of main terms and conditions of employment means that it can be changed from time to time without the employer having to negotiate; but the rules nevertheless have contractual force (at least so far as the employer is concerned) so long as there is an express requirement in the Service Agreement or statement of main terms and conditions of employment making compliance with the rules a requirement under the contract.

D3.2 Precedent

IT rules

Introduction

The use of the Company's computer system, including the e-mail system and the internet, is encouraged, as its appropriate use helps communication and improves efficiency. Its inappropriate use, however, causes problems ranging from minor distractions to legal claims against the Company. This policy sets out the Company's IT rules and policies. Failure to comply may lead to disciplinary action including, in serious cases, dismissal.

Use of computers

Computers are provided for business use only. They are not to be used for computer games, private correspondence or for any other personal matter [except in cases of emergency or with specific permission from your line manager].

The system has been set up for business use and must not be adapted to suit personal preferences/tastes. For example, the Company does not permit personalised screensavers.

Copyright

The Company uses computer software distributed by a variety of outside companies who write or distribute computer software. The Company does not own this software or its related documentation but is allowed to use the computer software under various Licence Agreements with software developers. Unless the Company is authorised by the software developers, it does not have the right to copy licensed computer software in any way.

As an employee of the Company, you must comply with Licence Agreements entered into by the Company and ensure that you and anyone you supervise does nothing to put the Company in danger of legal action for breach of a Licence Agreement. This means, in effect, that you must not copy computer software or any related documentation which include user guides and user manuals.

Any employees learning of unauthorised copying of computer software or related documentation must notify their line manager immediately.

According to UK copyright law, illegal copying of software is an infringement of copyright in the software and can be subject to civil damages, with no financial limit, and criminal penalties (including fines and imprisonment). The Company does not condone the illegal copying of computer software. Making, acquiring or using unauthorised copies of computer software will be regarded as misconduct or in serious cases or cases which have serious consequences for the Company, gross misconduct.

Passwords

If you are issued with a password, you must not write this down. If you forget your password, you must seek assistance.

Use of e-mail and internet

The e-mail system and the internet are available for communication on matters directly concerned with the business of the Company. Personal use of e-mail and the internet on the Company's system is not permitted [except in cases of emergency or with specific permission from your line manager].

Employees using the e-mail system should give particular attention to the following points.

1. The standard of presentation. The style and content of an e-mail message must be consistent with the standards that this Company expects from written communications, ie courteous, polite and helpful.

2. The extent of circulation. E-mail messages should only be sent to those employees for whom they are particularly relevant.

3. The appropriateness of e-mail. E-mail should not be used as a substitute for face-to-face communication.

4. Abusive e-mails can be a source of stress and can damage work relationships. Hasty messages, sent without proper consideration, can cause unnecessary misunderstandings.

5. The visibility of e-mail. If the message is confidential, the user must ensure that the necessary steps are taken to protect confidentiality. The company will be liable for any defamatory material of unauthorised disclosure of confidential information

circulated either within the Company or to external users of the system. To lessen the risk of unauthorised disclosure, all e-mails to external users should contain the message given at paragraph 7 below.

6. E-mail contracts. Offers or contracts transmitted via e-mail are as legally binding on the company as those sent on paper. Care must therefore be taken not to create a binding contract by anything sent by e-mail. For this reason, all e-mails to external sources should include the statement set out in paragraph 7 below.

7. All e-mails to external users should contain the following:

> "The e-mail and any attachments contains information from .... which may be privileged or confidential. The information is intended to be for the exclusive use of the person named.
>
> If you are not that person, we apologise. You have received this by mistake. Please return this e-mail to us and delete any copies you may have. You should be aware that any disclosure, copying, distribution or use of this e-mail or its contents which has not been authorised by us is prohibited and could lead to legal action. Thank you for your co-operation.
>
> Nothing in this e-mail is intended to constitute a binding offer or contract and there is no intention on the part of the sender, whether on his own behalf or on behalf of any other person, by this e-mail to enter legal relations with your or any other person."

Any failure to follow these guidelines satisfactorily can result in disciplinary action being taken against you which may result in your summary dismissal.

Unauthorised Use

Any use of the e-mail system or internet which is not related to the business is contrary to the Company's rules and could lead to disciplinary action. The following are regarded as particularly serious and are likely to be regarded as gross misconduct:

- any message that could constitute bullying or harassment. What matters is how it affects the recipient, so thoughtlessness or "just a bit of fun" is no defence;

- excessive or unnecessary personal use, eg social invitations, jokes, cartoons or chain letters;

- on-line gambling;

- accessing pornography;

- downloading or distributing copyright information and/or any software available to the user;

- posting confidential and/or personal information about other employees, the Company or its clients or suppliers;

- circulation of unsolicited e-mail;

- responding to chain e-mails;

- issuing warnings about viruses (see below).

Implementation of the Policy

The Company has appointed **[insert name of individual]** to be responsible for the management of the system. This person will be available for advice on all aspects of the policy.

All incoming and outgoing e-mail and internet access is logged. These logs are subject to regular review, carried out by **[the IT department]**. Hard copies of e-mail messages may be used as evidence in disciplinary proceedings.

Access to all the Company's systems (including e-mail and internet) is controlled through a system of user identifications and passwords. All users are issued with a unique individual password which must be changed at regular intervals and is confidential to the user. Disclosing a password to any other employee is likely to result in disciplinary action, including summary dismissal. Should a circumstance arise where it is necessary for an employee to access a system using another employee's credentials, then authorisation must be sought from your manager who will instruct **[the IT department]** to grant such access.

Users must ensure that critical information is not stored solely within the e-mail system. Hard copies must be kept or stored separately on the system. If necessary, documents must be password protected.

Users are required to be familiar with the requirements of the data protection legislation and to ensure that they operate in accordance with the requirements of the Act.

Employees who believe they have cause for complaint as a result of e-mail communications should raise the matter initially with [their line manager] and/or [the system manager]. If necessary, the complaint can then be raised through the grievance procedure.

Viruses

Computer viruses can cause serious damage to our computer system and in some cases could be catastrophic. It is vitally important that you comply with all instructions from [our IT department] to prevent viruses entering or damaging our system.

You must not open attachments to e-mails without checking with [our IT department] first unless you know the source of the e-mail and you know it is reliable. If in doubt, check with our IT department.

Any discs used from a source other than the Company must be checked for viruses first by our IT department.

If you receive a warning about a virus DO NOT E-MAIL the warning to everyone in the Company – that will clog up the system, which is precisely what the virus itself aims to do. Most virus warnings are hoaxes unless they come from an authoritative source. If you receive a virus warning, contact [our IT department] who will check on the authenticity of the warning and whether any action need be taken.

Breach of these rules

The consequence of any breach of these rules could be so serious for the Company that any breach will be regarded as gross misconduct which could lead to summary dismissal.

Amendments

Because of the pace of change in technology and in management systems, it may be necessary to amend or add to this clause from time to time. The Employer reserves the right to introduce new rules for the protection of its software and data and to protect against misuse or unauthorised disclosure of confidential information and breach of copyright.

D3.3 DRAFTING POINTS

You should consider the extent to which you are prepared to allow your employees to use the computer system for their own private purposes. That would include the use of computer games, access to the internet for example to book holidays or theatre tickets etc. Completely unrestricted use for private purposes is probably dangerous and will invite abuse by employees. A sensible compromise is to allow limited use for emergencies or with permission from a line manager. Employees who regularly work late may need greater access to e-mails for private purposes than others, both because they may have less opportunity to access the internet or send e-mails at home because of their late working and because they may need to rearrange private appointments by e-mail because of late working.

Accessing the internet for inappropriate purposes may be a 'grey area' so far as imposing disciplinary sanctions is concerned, particularly if the inappropriate use occurs outside working hours. It is therefore a good idea to specify that inappropriate use will be regarded as gross misconduct and then to describe what you would regard as inappropriate use.

You should consider what steps you wish to take to protect information kept on your computer system; and then explain in the rules on computer use that any attempt at undermining those rules will be regarded as misconduct or gross misconduct. At the moment, suitable protection includes the use of passwords and abuse can be prevented by requiring that employees do not disclose their passwords to anyone else. That will be sufficient in most cases, but you should consider whether there are any further safeguards you wish to impose and what action you might take if those safeguards are breached.

D4 NOTIFICATION OF EMPLOYEE INFORMATION

D4.1 USE

Employers should keep up-to-date information about their employees. The best way to keep records up-to-date is to have a rule requiring employees to notify of any changes.

D4.2 Precedent

Notification of employee information

> In order that our records can be kept up-to-date, it is important that the Human Resources department are notified of any changes in personal circumstances during the course of your employment. Changes to be notified include, but may not be limited to:
>
> - Home address and telephone number
>
> - Bank address, sort code and account number
>
> - [Change in marital status]
>
> - Change of name
>
> - Birth of a child
>
> - Next of kin – name, address and relationship
>
> - [Driving licence details/changes]

D4.3 DRAFTING POINTS

Any further information you wish to keep about your employees should be included here.

D5 CAPABILITY PROCEDURE

D5.1　USE

Although not strictly necessary as a matter of law, it is recommended that the disciplinary procedure should be adapted in cases of under-performance or lack of ability to do the job. This is because there may be factors outside the control of the employee that are causing the under-performance. These factors should be explored and dealt with. If they are not, any dismissal may be unfair.

Employees should also be given a reasonable opportunity to improve before any dismissal for under-performance. Only in the most extreme cases would it be regarded as fair to dismiss for under-performance without any prior warnings. Warnings in relation to under-performance should give a clear indication of what the problem is, what improvement is sought and the time-scale within which improvement is to be achieved.

A failure in any of these respects could render any dismissal unfair. Furthermore, if the reason for the under-performance is related to health, there is a risk of a claim under the Disability Discrimination Act 1995.

Unfair dismissal is dealt with in Division D3 of *Jordans Employment Law Service* and Disability Discrimination is dealt with in Division E3.

D5.2　Precedent

Capability policy and procedure

Capability policy and procedure

1. **Policy statement**

    1.1　The Company recognises that its employees are its most important asset. If employees are performing the duties of their post at a sub-standard level, then the service which is offered to our clients and customers may be affected. There will also be significant "hidden costs" associated with additional cover and management time which will have a detrimental effect on others attending work.

    The aim of this Capability Procedure is to enable any employee experiencing difficulty in achieving the required standards of performance to work closely with their line manager to find ways of improving performance and of eliminating possible causes for the performance. All those involved in this procedure, including the line manager and the employee, should appreciate that poor performance can be caused by a number of different factors, including:

- temporary personal difficulties experienced by the employee, which may be affecting concentration (in which case, temporary redeployment may be considered or a temporary adjustment to duties);

- personality clashes with colleagues or a manager, in which case, a permanent or temporary adjustment could be made to the location of the employee's workplace or reporting lines;

- health problems, in which case a referral to occupational health should be considered. Note that apparent non-health related matters may become a health matter due to stress related to poor performance;

- lack of understanding of the standards expected or of the requirements of the job, in which case appropriate discussions should take place, coupled with any training or mentoring which may be considered appropriate;

- lack of appropriate training;

- lack of the skills necessary for the job.

The intention of this procedure is to identify the causes of poor performance and to develop an appropriate plan to deal with those causes. The emphasis during any such period will be on support for the employee and co-operation between the parties in planning for improvements and evaluating the outcomes.

1.2. The Company is committed to dealing with any actual or perceived under-performance in a fair and reasonable way. Generally this will involve an agreed process which:

- takes account of any particular characteristics, circumstances and experience of the employee;

- offers support and appropriate training within a framework of regular performance reviews.

1.3 At all stages within this procedure, the employee will be entitled to be accompanied by a representative of a trade union or work colleague.

1.4 Where in the reasonable view of the manager, an employee has been negligent or has deliberately failed to work or conduct him or herself to an acceptable standard, then such issues should be addressed as a matter of misconduct. under the Disciplinary Procedure.

2   Standards of performance

2.1   Poor performance may be identified by the line manager, the employee concerned, or a colleague. It may also be brought to light by formal complaint or client feedback.

2.2   Line managers and supervisors should ensure that all employees are aware of the performance and standards of work expected of them and the range of duties to be undertaken. Where possible these standards of performance should be agreed with the employee at appraisals or other meetings.

2.3   Standards of performance should be applied consistently to employees occupying the same job and/or performing the same duties. These duties and standards should be drawn from the job description, person specification, directorate/departmental business plans and the performance review and development process.

3   Principles

The following are key principles that underpin the procedure. Further advice and information is available from the Human Resources Department. Managers should:

3.1   Consider each individual employee's circumstances and bear in mind that poor performance may be linked to factors outside of the working environment or personal factors within it;

3.2   Identify the causes of poor performance and explore ways in which those causes can be dealt with;

3.3   Attempt to retain an employee in their current post and give them the opportunity to improve. Temporary redeployment should only be considered in serious cases of poor performance where there is a risk in maintaining the employee in the post. The purpose of temporary redeployment is to help to explore whether there might be other positions within the Company which might be more suited to the employee's abilities and/or to give the employee time to improve and/or provide a temporary respite for the employee if the reasons for poor performance are factors such as personal problems which are likely only to be temporary;

3.4   Consider retraining or further training and redeployment within the monitoring and support process;

3.5 Operate regular review periods. These can vary in length due to the different complexity of jobs and the normal learning periods associated with them;

3.6 Record and keep details of all formal discussions/interviews with the employee, as well as evidence relating to monitoring work targets;

3.7 Ensure that standards of performance are realistic and where possible measurable.

While every effort will be made to help an employee improve their performance and retain them in post, the Company cannot guarantee to maintain employment if satisfactory performance is not achieved following the exhaustion of this Procedure.

4. Informal procedure

Where employees are experiencing difficulties with performance, the problem should be addressed when it first becomes apparent, either through the performance review process or in a non-formal supportive way, through dialogue between the manager and employee. The first step should be informal discussions. These should concentrate on:

- Identifying the problem and discussing any supporting information;

- The standards of job performance required;

- The shortcomings in reaching these standards;

- Exploring possible reasons for poor performance;

- Devising a plan to deal with those reasons;

- Reaching agreement on how and when acceptable performance might be achieved and by what means;

- The environment in which the employee is working and whether this may have an adverse impact upon performance such as staffing levels, availability of equipment, personality clashes etc.

With support, performance may reach or return to expected standards, but if this is not the case, normally within three months, a more formal approach will be required and the formal procedure should be followed.

5 Formal procedure

When it becomes apparent that an informal approach to improving performance has failed or is likely to fail, the employee will be advised of, and receive written confirmation that a formal procedure will be adopted involving a formal interview.

Stage 1 – Formal meeting and review

(a) Managers should prepare for this meeting by informing the employee in writing of its purpose and issues to be discussed at the meeting, the employee's right to be accompanied and adequate notice to allow them to prepare (at least two working days).

(b) Managers should have a clear picture of the ways an employee is under-performing or under-achieving, with records and evidence to support this.

The purpose of the meeting is to:

(a) Identify clearly and fairly the ways in which an employee is under-performing/under-achieving. This should be evident from documents such as job descriptions, person specifications, the line managers file notes, evidence of complaints or pieces of work;

(b) Ensure that the employee is aware of the concerns about his/her performance, the standards required and where actual performance has fallen short of the standards. Possible causes should be identified and discussed and an agreed programme of support and monitoring should be implemented. The employee should have the opportunity to challenge and/or put forward any facts or evidence for consideration;

(c) Consider means to improve performance which may include the following:

- Counselling/welfare assistance from within or outside of the organisation depending on the nature of the problem;

- An appropriate referral to Occupational Health and acting upon the advice contained within any subsequent report;

- Extra support and supervision from the line manager;

- Retraining or further training either on or off the job;

- Setting and reviewing work targets that must be achievable, clear, specific, measurable and agreed between the parties;

- A temporary or permanent change of hours/duties/workplace subject to the agreement of all parties and where feasible;

- A temporary placement in another department where unacceptable performance has been attributed to factors specific to where an employee works pending further investigation. All parties must agree any such temporary placement;

- Arranging for a colleague to act as a role model and mentor on areas of shortfall. The mentor should not be employed within the same team as the subject as the close proximity of the mentor may create unacceptable stresses on all parties.

The manager and the employee should seek to agree a monitoring review period to ensure the employee is clear about timescales and when their performance will next be discussed. Even if performance has improved, agreed support and monitoring meetings should take place. If it is apparent that the employee's difficulties are due to an inability to adjust to significant change in either the nature of the tasks to be undertaken, or the equipment used, it may be appropriate to agree redeployment to a different position.

The key points of this meeting and any action agreed should be confirmed in writing to the employee along with the potential consequences of failure to achieve a significant and sustained improvement within the agreed time period. Whilst the emphasis in this correspondence should be on the problem and the agreed course of action put in place to rectify it, it should be clear to the employee that ultimately their employment may be at risk. They should also be informed that records will be kept during the monitoring period, and any other relevant information retained.

This review period should not normally be less than one month nor more than three months (also interim reviews should be utilised) but the period will depend on the nature of the problem and its causes. Where possible, this review period should be agreed but if agreement cannot be reached, it is ultimately up to the manager to determine.

Where the required standard has not been achieved but significant improvement has been made by the end of the review period the manager may agree to a further review of up to three months to enable performance to meet the required standard.

Stage 2 – Consequences of a failure to improve

Where it is clear that the employee, despite the support measures introduced, is not able to improve to the required standards, then the following forms of action (not necessarily consecutively) should be considered by the appropriate Director at Stage Two of the Procedure.

The employee should, where possible and practicable, be offered redeployment to an alternative post. Any such redeployment may be made on the following basis:

(a)   A trial basis of not less than four weeks;

(b)   Subject to agreed monitoring and review periods;

(c)   A clear indication of the consequences of a failure to perform to the required standards.

Should the employee refuse such an offer, or where such a position is not available, or where there is a continuing failure to perform at the required standards in the new post, then dismissal may be considered, in accordance with the process outlined below.

Stage 3 – Termination of employment

The employee should be informed in writing of the concerns about their performance and be invited to attend a formal meeting at which the employee will be given the opportunity to state their case. The written invitation should remind the employee of his or her right to be accompanied by a trade union representative or work colleague. The invitation to the meeting should make it clear that a possible outcome of the meeting could be his or her dismissal.

The formal hearing will be chaired by an appropriate Director and the format/process will be the same as used for disciplinary hearings.

Where a decision is reached to dismiss it will be on the grounds of capability and following a formal hearing. The required notice will be given under the employment contract.

Stage 4 – Appeal against dismissal

A right of appeal exists against dismissal on the grounds of capability in accordance with the procedure for hearing appeals under the disciplinary procedure. The employee will be informed of this right and how to exercise it in the letter of dismissal. The decision of the Appeal Panel will be final.

The employee has the right to be represented/accompanied by a trade union representative, or a work colleague.

6 Monitoring and review

The application of this policy will be monitored by the Head of Human resources as and when required.

D5.3 DRAFTING POINTS

This may be regarded as cumbersome particularly for small employers. Employers should consider what resources are available to it and adapt this procedure to what is practicable. The key points that should be present in any capability procedure are:

– a requirement to explore the reasons for poor performance. If the reason is that expectations are unrealistic, or there are health issues or domestic problems or the employee is simply unaware of the standards expected, an employment tribunal will expect the employer to be aware of the reason and to have taken appropriate action;

– an indication that only in the most extreme cases should dismissal be considered without any prior warnings;

– warnings should set out a clear timetable for improvement, detailing precisely the improvement sought;

– there should be a right of appeal.

Small employers who do not have the resources to implement a procedure such as this one may rely on the shorter version of the capability procedure or the disciplinary procedure to deal with under-performance but should bear the above points in mind when implementing the procedure.

D6 SHORT CAPABILITY PROCEDURE

D6.1 USE

This procedure, rather than the lengthier one set out above, may be used for smaller employers who do not have the resources to deal with under-performance in the way set out in the lengthier procedure. The same general points and the drafting points apply equally to this procedure.

D6.2　　　　　　　　Precedent

Capability procedure

> At all times the Employer endeavours to ensure that employees achieve and maintain a high standard of performance in their work. It will ensure the standards are established, performance is monitored and employees are given appropriate training and support to meet these standards.

Procedure

> 1. Where the line manager first establishes that an Employee's performance is below the standard required, an informal discussion will be held with the Employee to try to establish the reason. Should this discussion result in a decision that the established standards are not reasonably attainable, the standards will be reviewed.
>
> 2. If it becomes apparent that the under-performance constitutes misconduct, the disciplinary procedure will be invoked.
>
> 3. If it is decided that the under-performance emanates from a change in the organisation's standards, those standards will be explained to the Employee and consideration will be given to assist the Employee achieve the standards required.
>
> 4. Should the Employee show no (or insufficient) improvement over an agreed review period, the Employee will be invited to a formal interview. The invitation will be in writing and will set out the respects in which it is considered that performance is below the standard required. The invitation will remind the Employee of his or her right to be accompanied by a representative of a trade union or a work colleague.
>
>   The aims of this interview will be to:
>
>   (a)　identify the cause(s) of the under-performance and to determine what if any assistance (eg training, retraining, support, etc.) can be given;

(b) explain clearly the shortfall between the Employee's performance and the required standard;

(c) obtain the Employee's commitment to reaching that standard;

(d) set a reasonable period for the Employee to reach the standard and agree on a monitoring system during that period;

(e) tell the Employee what will happen if that standard is not met (which could be dismissal, so long as the Employee has been given all reasonable opportunity to improve, both during the informal and the formal stages of this procedure).

The outcome of this interview will be recorded in writing and a copy will be given to the employee. This written record will state:

(a) the respects in which the Employee is not meeting the required standards;

(b) the improvement sought;

(c) the time-scale within which improvement is to be achieved;

(d) the consequences of not achieving that improvement within the timescale.

5. At the end of the review period a further formal interview will be held (at which the Employee may be accompanied by a colleague or representative of a trade union), at which time:

(a) if the required improvement has been made, the Employee will be told of this and encouraged to maintain the improvement;

(b) if some improvement has been made, but the required standard has not yet been met, the review period may be extended;

(c) if there has been no discernible or insufficient improvement, it will be explained to the Employee that he or she has failed to meet the standard required. Consideration will be given to whether there are alternative vacancies which the Employee would be competent to fill. If there are, the Employee will be given the option of accepting such a vacancy or being dismissed;

- (d) if such vacancies are available, the Employee will be given full details of such vacancies before being required to make a decision;

- (e) in the absence of suitable alternative vacancies, the Employee will be invited to give his/her views. In the absence of exceptional circumstances, however, the Employee may be dismissed.

6. Employees may appeal against their dismissal following the Disciplinary Appeals Procedures.

D7 DISCIPLINARY PROCEDURE

D7.1 USE

Regulations concerning statutory dismissal and disciplinary procedures came into force on 1 October 2004. They were intended to encourage disputes to be resolved in the workplace rather than in employment tribunals. These procedures proved to be fraught with difficulty, being over-technical and prescriptive. As a result, they are to be repealed for disciplinary procedures starting on or after 5 April 2009. However, while they remain in place, it is important that the basic principles underlying the statutory procedures are reflected in the Company disciplinary procedure. Even after their repeal, the procedures represent the minimum that employment tribunals generally expect of employers when operating disciplinary procedures.

The Standard Dismissal and Disciplinary Procedure should always be followed whenever you are contemplating a dismissal on <u>any</u> ground including conduct; competence; ill health; redundancy; non-renewal of fixed-term contract and retirement, subject to limited exceptions.

The standard procedure will also have to be followed if you are contemplating taking 'relevant disciplinary action', ie action short of dismissal as a result of the employee's conduct or capability ('capability' here probably includes ill health):

including	but not
• demotion;	• warnings (oral or written); or
• suspension without pay;	• suspension on full pay
• (possibly) non-payment of or reduction in discretionary bonus; and	
• (possibly) non-payment of discretionary sick pay	

Demotion and suspension without pay may only be used as disciplinary sanctions if the contract of employment so provides (which is rare) or if the employee agrees (which is even rarer).

A modified dismissal procedure can be used for gross misconduct which warrants dismissal without investigation, where the evidence against the employee is unarguable and overwhelming. We anticipate tribunals will be reluctant ever to accept that the modified procedure is appropriate.

Employees who qualify for unfair dismissal rights (generally those with one year's service or more) will, in almost all cases where the employer has not followed the statutory procedure, receive a minimum of four weeks' pay by way of compensation (this provision is to be repealed for disciplinary proceedings starting on or after 6 April 2009). The Employment Tribunal will in most cases increase or decrease any award by between 10% and 50% depending on whether the employer or employee is responsible for the failure to follow the procedure. This increase will apply not only to unfair dismissal compensation but also to any other award made as part of the employees' claim eg discrimination. Again, this provision is to be repealed.

If the dismissal is unfair but the statutory procedure has been complied with, then there is no adjustment to compensation.

Exemptions when neither statutory disciplinary procedure needs to be followed include:

- collective dismissals (20 or more redundancies);

- the employer's business suddenly ceases to function because of an event unforeseen by the employer;

- continued employment would contravene a legal duty or restriction.

The following requirements apply to the statutory dismissal and disciplinary procedures:

- each step must be taken without unreasonable delay;

- the timing and location of any meetings has to be reasonable;

- the meetings must be conducted in such a way as to allow both parties to explain their cases;

- a manager senior to the original decision-maker who chaired the disciplinary or grievance meeting should, where reasonably practicable, hear the appeal;

- the employee has the right to be accompanied to the step two meeting and/or step three appeal by a colleague or trade union representative; and

- the employee must take all reasonable steps to attend meetings.

If the employee does not turn up for a meeting without good reason, then the employee will be in breach of the procedure. The employer is then released from all further obligations under the statutory procedure. If there is a good reason, however, employers should re-arrange the meeting. The employer need only re-arrange the meeting once. If the meeting falls through a second time for unforeseeable reasons then neither party will be under any further obligation under the statutory procedures. Both parties will be treated as having complied with the relevant statutory procedures.

Although these requirements will no longer automatically make dismissals unfair for disciplinary procedures starting on or after 6 April 2009, the principles should generally still be followed. Unless there are exceptional circumstances, failure to follow the above is likely to make a dismissal unfair on general unfair dismissal principles.

For a full explanation of the statutory dismissal and statutory disciplinary procedures, see Division C6 of *Jordans Employment Law Service*.

Complying with the statutory dismissal and disciplinary procedures is necessary to ensure that any dismissal is fair, but employers must also have a sufficient reason for dismissal and have carried out a reasonable investigation. The disciplinary procedure is designed to ensure this happens. For full details of unfair dismissal law in the context of disciplinary dismissals, see Division D3 of *Jordans Employment Law Service*. The following is a brief summary.

The employer must:

- have a genuine belief in the employee's guilt;

- based on reasonable grounds;

- following as much investigation into the case as was reasonable in all the circumstances.

Conclusive proof of misconduct is not necessary – only a genuine and reasonable belief following a reasonable investigation.

Once the investigation is complete, employers should:

- notify the employee in writing of the allegations he or she has to answer;

- give the employee details of the evidence against him or her. This may be done by providing copies of statements from witnesses or (if these witnesses wish to remain anonymous) a reasonable summary of what the witnesses say;

- invite the employee to a disciplinary hearing. The invitation should be in writing and the employee should be informed in writing of the right to be accompanied or (if the disciplinary procedure so provides) represented. Representation may be appropriate if, for example, English is not the employee's first language. Failure to allow an employee to be accompanied at a disciplinary hearing by a union official or work colleague will result in a penalty of up to two weeks' pay;

- the disciplinary hearing should be conducted by someone who has had no (or if that is not practicable, as little as possible) connection with the matters complained of – bearing in mind that someone independent will need to be reserved for an appeal;

- the employee should be given reasonable notice of the disciplinary hearing – normally at least 48 hours;

- take notes of the disciplinary hearing;

- at the disciplinary hearing listen to any points the employee wants to make;

- do not make a decision immediately. Give yourself at least half an hour to consider the points the employee makes – otherwise it looks as if you pre-judged the matter;

- inform the employee as soon as possible once the decision has been reached;

- if the decision is to impose a disciplinary sanction, remind the employee of his or her right to appeal;

- if the employee appeals, arrange an appeal hearing, to be heard by someone with no (or if that is not practicable, as little as possible) connection with the matters complained of.

The following precedent is designed to ensure all the above happens. You should ensure that those involved with the disciplinary process are fully aware of the requirements of the policy.

D7.2　　　　　　　　　Precedent

Disciplinary procedure

Introduction

> The disciplinary procedure is there to help resolve problems created by a person's conduct or performance. The aim is improvement rather than punishment. Wherever possible, we try to resolve problems with a person's conduct or performance by informal discussion, but this disciplinary procedure may be used where the informal approach is unsuccessful.

This procedure may be used in cases of under-performance, in conjunction with capability procedure.

Investigation

It will normally be necessary to carry out an investigation into allegations of misconduct or under-performance. This will generally include interviewing witnesses and potential witnesses, including (in many cases) the person against whom the complaints are made. Witness statements or notes of interview will generally be prepared. Occasionally, witnesses may wish to remain anonymous. In that case, the wishes of those interviewed will be respected. Either the statement or interview notes will be 'redacted' to remove any information from which the identity of the interviewee could be determined or a summary of that person's evidence will be prepared – again ensuring that no information is contained in the summary from which the interviewee's identity could be determined. Any such statement, interview notes or summary should include a statement that the interviewee wishes to remain anonymous.

Interviewees will generally be asked to sign their statement or interview notes to ensure they agree the contents. The signature will be removed from any statement or notes given to the employee against whom the allegations are made.

Suspension

During the period of the investigation and/or pending any disciplinary hearing, the Company may suspend the employee against whom the allegations are made on full pay. This may be appropriate, for example, where relationships have broken down, or where there could be risks to individuals or property or responsibilities to others, or to allow any investigation to go on unhindered. Suspension should only be considered in the most serious cases – generally where the allegations are of gross misconduct or involve bullying or intimidation. The period of suspension should be kept to a minimum – generally no longer than one month.

Notification

If the investigation suggests there is a case to answer, the employer will send the employee:

- a summary of the allegations;

- a copy of any statements by witnesses or notes of interviews with them or such information as the company considers appropriate in the circumstances;

- copies of any relevant documents – for example, in the case of time-keeping offences, records of attendance, arrival times and departure times;

- notification of the time, date and place for any disciplinary hearing;

- notification of the right to be accompanied.

Re-arranging time of disciplinary hearing

The Company will always attempt to find a date and time for the disciplinary hearing which is convenient for all parties. If the date for the hearing turns out to be inconvenient either for the employee concerned or the person the employee wishes to accompany them, then the employee should notify the person who arranged the meeting immediately and a new hearing will be arranged.

IT IS IMPORTANT THAT EMPLOYEES ATTEND THE DISCIPLINARY HEARING. IF AN EMPLOYEE FAILS TO ATTEND A DISCIPLINARY HEARING WITHOUT REASONABLE EXCUSE THE DISCIPLINARY HEARING MAY PROCEED IN THAT EMPLOYEE'S ABSENCE.

Occasionally, unforeseen circumstances may arise which prevents the employee attending. If this happens, the employee should notify the person who arranged the hearing at the earliest opportunity so that a mutually convenient date can be arranged. If this happens more than once, the point may be reached where the hearing will have to go ahead in the Employee's absence. If this point is reached, alternatives to attendance at the hearing may be offered – for example, the Employee may be invited to put his or her points in writing, or attendance could be via a representative who will be permitted telephone contact with the Employee.

Disciplinary hearing

At the disciplinary hearing, the Employee will have the right to be accompanied by a colleague or official of a trade union. The purpose of the hearing is to give the Employee the opportunity to present his or her side of the story and any points he or she would like the disciplinary panel to take into account.

[The Employee may wish to call witnesses to back up his or her version of events, or may wish to provide documents to the hearing. The employee should notify the person who arranged the meeting so that arrangements can be made for the witnesses to attend and sufficient copies of the documents are made for the person conducting the hearing and for the person presenting the management case.

Generally, the procedure at the hearing will be as follows:

– a representative of management or the person who carried out the investigation will present the management case, unless this is unnecessary because the statements and documents prepared by the investigator are sufficient;

– any witnesses the management side wishes to call should then be called. This will not be necessary in all cases and in some cases (for example, where the information comes from a customer) this may not be practicable;

- if the management side does call witnesses, the employee or person accompanying the employee may question those witnesses;

- the person conducting the disciplinary hearing may then question the witness;

- the employee will then be invited to present his or her case;

- the person presenting the management case may then question the employee;

- the person conducting the disciplinary hearing may then question the employee;

- if the employee wishes to call witnesses, those witnesses should then be called to answer questions from the Employee or person accompanying the Employee;

- the person presenting the management case may then question those witnesses;

- the person conducting the disciplinary hearing may then question those witnesses;

- the person presenting the management case may then address the hearing to argue the management viewpoint;

- the employee may then address the hearing to present his or her viewpoint;

- the person conducting the disciplinary hearing will then adjourn to consider what decision to make. That person may need more than a day to consider all the evidence and arguments before coming to a conclusion.]

Notes of the disciplinary hearing should be taken.

Outcome

The Employee will be notified of the outcome as soon as possible. The outcome may be:

(a) in cases of under-performance, the Employee may be offered, wherever practicable, assistance through training or coaching or otherwise, and given a reasonable period to reach the required standard [for details, see the Capability Procedure);

(b) an oral warning for the purpose of improving future conduct or performance. In the case of warnings for poor performance, clear targets and time-scales will be set;

(c) a written warning for under-performance or misconduct. In the case of warnings for under-performance, clear targets and time-scales will be set;

(d) a final written warning for under-performance or misconduct following earlier warnings or for under-performance or misconduct which is regarded as serious enough to justify a final written warning. In the case of warnings for under-performance, clear targets and time-scales will be set.

Warnings generally remain on your record for 12 months unless otherwise stated.

(a) dismissal for under-performance or misconduct following a final written warning or for under-performance or misconduct which is regarded as serious enough to justify dismissal;

(b) summary dismissal without notice in the case of gross misconduct (see below).

The letter notifying the employee of the outcome should:

– state the outcome;

– generally enclose notes of the disciplinary hearing or, if there is likely to be any delay in preparing the notes, those notes should be sent as soon as practicable;

– inform the employee of his or her right to appeal.

Gross misconduct

The following will be regarded as gross misconduct which could lead to dismissal:

(a) theft, fraud and deliberate falsification of records;

(b) physical violence;

(c) serious bullying or harassment;

(d) deliberate damage to property;

(e) serious insubordination;

(f) misuse of an organisation's property or name;

(g) bringing the employer into serious disrepute;

(h) deliberate rudeness;

(i)　　serious incapability whilst on duty brought on by alcohol or illegal drugs;

(j)　　serious negligence which causes or might cause unacceptable loss, damage or injury;

(k)　　serious infringement of health and safety rules;

(l)　　serious breach of confidence (subject to the Public Interest (Disclosure) Act 1998).

This list is not intended to be exhaustive.

Appeals

If you disagree with a disciplinary decision you may appeal by writing to [ ] or, if [ ] was involved in the original disciplinary decision, the [ ], within [ ] days of the decision.

You have the right to be accompanied by a colleague or official of a trade union at any disciplinary or appeal hearing.

At the appeal hearing, witnesses will not generally be called as it will usually be sufficient to rely on the documents and statements produced to the disciplinary hearing and any notes of the disciplinary hearing.

D7.3　DRAFTING POINTS

Investigation: Whatever the size and administrative resources available to the employer, employers are always expected to carry out a reasonable investigation before disciplining for misconduct. If the disciplinary process leads to dismissal, a failure to carry out a reasonable investigation may render the dismissal under. If the disciplinary process leads to a formal warning, then a failure to follow a fair procedure could possibly provide grounds for an unfair constructive dismissal, or an unfair dismissal in the future if further misconduct occurs which, because of the warning, leads to dismissal.

Notification: It is a requirement of the statutory dismissal and statutory disciplinary procedure that the employee should be informed in writing of the allegations he or she has to face, together with sufficient information to show the basis of the allegation. That will generally include all the evidence, including witness statements or interview notes or a summary. The notification should also remind the employee of his or her right to be accompanied. This is likely to remain true, under general principles of unfair dismissal law, after the repeal of the statutory dismissal procedure.

The legislation requires employers to permit the employee to be accompanied by a trade union representative or a work colleague. Some disciplinary procedures go further and allow representation by a friend or even a legal representative. This may be acceptable in larger organisations, but employment tribunals generally accept that employers are entitled to insist that only those with a connection with the workplace and knowledge of the employer's procedures should be allowed to represent or accompany employees. Friends, family or professional advisors (for example legal or health advisors) may have too much of a personal interest in the outcome to be objective or helpful in internal disciplinary proceedings, so tribunals generally accept that it is permissible to exclude them.

The legislation permits the companion to ask questions and to make points on behalf of the employee but not to answer questions on behalf of the employee. There is therefore little difference in practice between permitting a person to be accompanied and permitting him or her to be represented.

Re-arranging the time of the hearing: The legislation for disciplinary procedures starting on or before 6 April 2009 requires the employee to take reasonable steps to attend the disciplinary procedure. If the employee fails to attend, therefore, without reasonable excuse, the employee is in breach of the statutory procedure and the employer is released from further obligations under the statutory procedure. However, in order to demonstrate that the employer has acted reasonably, it is generally advisable to allow at least one re-arrangement of the meeting.

If the employee fails to attend for unforeseen reasons, then the employer must re-arrange the meeting – this is a requirement of the rules on statutory dismissal and disciplinary procedures.

Disciplinary hearing: This procedure sets out a fairly formal process for the disciplinary hearing. This may not be appropriate for smaller employers without substantial resources or expertise at presenting disciplinary cases. The section in square brackets, therefore, can be omitted in the case of smaller employers.

Gross misconduct: ACAS recommends that categories of misconduct which will be regarded as gross misconduct justifying summary dismissal should be set out either in the company's rules or in the disciplinary procedure itself. Failure to do so may render a dismissal for gross misconduct, even one which would otherwise be justified, unfair.

D8 DISMISSAL PROCEDURE

D8.1 USE

Dismissal may be the outcome of the disciplinary procedure but there are other circumstances that could lead to dismissal. These include:

- absence due to ill health over such a long period, or likely to continue for such a long period, that we have to appoint a replacement;

- regular intermittent absence which is so disruptive to the business that we cannot reasonably be expected to continue to employ that employee;

- redundancy;

- other substantial reasons which make it impossible to continue to employ a person, for example reorganisations which do not amount to redundancy, irreconcilable clash of personalities etc;

- non-renewal of a fixed-term contract.

For dismissals where the procedure has been started before 6 April 2009, the statutory dismissal procedure applies just as much to these types of dismissal as for disciplinary dismissals. This means the same basic steps have to be followed, ie:

– the employee must be invited to a hearing and must be informed in writing of the reasons why the employer is contemplating dismissal;

– the employee must be informed of the basis on which the employer is contemplating dismissal;

– a hearing must then be held at which the employee is entitled to be accompanied by a work colleague or representative of a trade union;

– after the hearing, the employee must be informed of the outcome and reminded of the right of appeal;

– if the employee wishes to appeal, an appeal hearing must be held at which the employee again has the right to be accompanied.

A failure to follow the statutory dismissal procedure renders the dismissal automatically unfair and compensation can be increased by between 10% and 50%.

For details of the statutory dismissal procedure, see Division D3 of *Jordans Employment Law Service*.

Where the dismissal procedure starts on or after 6 April 2009, these rules will no longer apply but under ordinary unfair dismissal principles, a failure to follow the above procedure or something like it is likely to make the dismissal unfair.

The disciplinary procedure will generally be used in the case of dismissals for disciplinary reasons. The following procedure may be used for dismissals for other reasons. Employers are not required to have a dismissal procedure, but it is a good idea to have one, so that managers responsible for dismissals are aware of the procedure they should follow and so that employees know what the procedure will be. It also means that employers have a procedure to follow which is not called a 'disciplinary procedure' to use in cases of dismissal for non-disciplinary reasons. It never looks good for an employer, when considering a dismissal for ill health for example, to talk about a 'disciplinary hearing'.

D8.2 Precedent

Dismissal procedure

> This procedure will be used when the Employer is contemplating dismissal for reasons other than misconduct or under-performance. In the case of misconduct or under-performance, the disciplinary procedure should be used.

Investigation/fact-gathering

> It is important for the Employer to have as much information as possible about the reasons behind any proposal to dismiss, first so as to decide whether the situation really does deserve consideration of dismissal and secondly to decide whether the situation can be better resolved in ways that do not involve dismissal. To do this, it will often be necessary to carry out an investigation or fact-gathering exercise. This may include interviewing witnesses and potential witnesses, including the person whom it is proposed to dismiss. For example:
>
> - in the case of proposed dismissal because of a lengthy absence for ill health, this may involve obtaining a medical report from the Employee's General Practitioner (GP) or consultant; conferring with the GP or consultant, discussion with the Employee's colleagues to find out how they are coping during the absence and how long they expect to be able cope with the absence without having to appoint a replacement.
>
> - in the case of reorganisations or redundancy, the Employer will obtain enough information to enable it to explain the proposal and the reasons to any individuals potentially affected. In some cases, the investigation may be minimal – for example, where an important client or customer is lost or a type of work ceases, but

even in those cases, the Employer should investigate whether there is any way in which redundancies or dismissals can be avoided or minimised. In some cases, the Employer may have to select who out of a number of people to select for redundancy, in which case the investigation/fact-gathering exercise will include obtaining all information relevant to the matters the employer proposes to take into account in making the selection.

- in the case of apparently irreconcilable personality clashes, the Employer will investigate whether it is possible for the two (or more) parties to be reconciled, or whether it is possible for both/all individuals to be retained in different locations. That may not be possible if there are personality clashes between one individual and a number of other individuals.

Except where misconduct is alleged, it will not normally be appropriate to suspend.

Notification

If the investigation/fact-gathering suggests there may be a case for dismissal, the Employer will write to the Employee setting out:

- a summary of the relevant facts;

- a copy of any statements by witnesses or notes of conversations with them or such other information and documents as the employer considers appropriate in the circumstances. Where a selection for redundancy has to be made, this information will include details of any assessment carried out of the employee, together with overall scores of other employees omitting the names of those other employees;

- notification of the time, date and place for a hearing to discuss the situation;

- notification of the Employee's right to be accompanied by a work colleague or representative of a trade union.

Re-arranging time of hearing

The Employer should attempt to find a time for the hearing which is convenient for all parties. If the date for the hearing turns out to be inconvenient for the Employee or the person the person accompanying the Employee, then the Employee should notify the person who arranged the hearing immediately and a further hearing will be arranged.

It is important for the Employee to attend the hearing. If an Employee fails to attend the hearing without reasonable excuse the hearing may proceed in that Employee's absence.

If the Employee or person accompanying the Employee is unable for unforeseen reasons (such as illness) to attend the hearing, then the Employer will rearrange the hearing once. If the same thing happens as second time, then the hearing may continue in the Employee's absence.

Further investigations/fact-gathering and further meetings

Further matters to be investigated may arise out of the first hearing. Sufficient hearings should be held to enable the Employer to discuss with the Employee thoroughly all facts relevant to the decisions to be made. Once the employer has reached this stage, a decision will be made. The employee will be informed in writing as soon as possible after the decision has been made.

Appeals

If the decision is to dismiss, the employee may appeal by writing to [ ], within [ ] days of receiving written notification of the decision.

Right to be accompanied

The employee has the right to be accompanied by a colleague or official of a trade union at all hearings throughout this procedure, including the appeal procedure.

D8.3   DRAFTING POINTS

Investigation/fact-gathering: There is no need strictly for the employer to set out the examples of the types of investigation that may need to be carried out in particular cases (as this precedent does), but it is helpful to do so, if only to remind managers of the sort of investigation they should carry out and the information that should be provided to the employee.

D9 REDUNDANCY

D9.1 USE

There is no statutory requirement to have a redundancy procedure, but it may help:

- to remind managers of the procedure they should follow in the event that redundancies are necessary;

- to clarify the process for employees;

- to set out any rules about redundancy payments and selection criteria, to try to avoid disputes.

Where 20 or more redundancies are proposed, the employer must consult with employee representatives or representatives of a recognised trade union. If there is no recognised trade union and employee representatives have not been appointed, the employer will have to arrange for the election of employee representatives – see the appropriate forms in the Standard Forms and Letters section.

D9.2 Precedent

Redundancy procedure

Introduction

Redundancy means any dismissal attributable wholly or mainly to the fact that:

- the employer has ceased, or intends to cease to carry on the business for the purposes of which the employee was employed by him; or

- has ceased, or intends to cease to carry on that business in the place where the employee was so employed; or

- the requirements of that business for:

    - employees to carry out work of a particular kind; or

    - for employees to carry out work of a particular kind in the place where the employee was so employed,

have ceased or diminished or are expected to cease or diminish.

Redundancy will thus cover the following situations:

- closure of part of the business;

- ceasing to carry on a particular type of work;

- loss of a particular client or customer, resulting in a reduced workload;

- any reorganisation whereby the same amount of work can be carried out but by fewer employees;

- a need to reduce the number of employees in order to prevent further losses.

Where any of these circumstances apply the following procedure will be followed.

Investigation/fact-gathering

It is important to have as much information as possible about the reasons behind any proposal to dismiss on the grounds of redundancy, first so as to decide whether the situation really does deserve consideration of dismissal and secondly to decide whether the situation can be better resolved in ways that do not involve dismissal. To do this, it will often be necessary to carry out an investigation or fact-gathering exercise.

In the case of reorganisations or redundancy, it is important for us to obtain enough information to enable us to explain the proposal and the reasons to any individuals potentially affected. In some cases, the investigation may be minimal – for example, where an important client is lost or a type of work ceases, but even in those cases, we will investigate whether there is any way in which redundancies or dismissals can be avoided or minimised. In some cases, we may have to select who out of a number of people to select for redundancy, in which case the investigation/fact-gathering exercise will include obtaining all information relevant to the matters we propose to take into account in making the selection.

If the investigation/fact-gathering suggests there may be a case for making redundancies, the employer will first determine how many redundancies are likely to be required. The procedure that applies after that will depend on whether there are likely to be:

- less than 20 redundancies;

- between 20 and 99 inclusive) redundancies; or

- 100 or more redundancies.

Consultation

Legislation requires employers to consult with trade union or employee representatives when proposing 20 or more redundancies in a three-month period and stipulates that there must be at least 30 days between the start of consultation and the date of the first redundancy or redundancies and at least 90 days where there are more than 100 proposed redundancies.

[Although not required to by the legislation, we intend to consult employee representatives or trade union representatives over all redundancies.]

Once we have enough information, we will formulate proposals about the following:

- the numbers and descriptions of employees whom it is proposed to make redundant;

- the proposed method of selecting those who are to be made redundant;

- the proposed method of carrying out the redundancies;

- how redundancy payments are to be calculated. The legislation determines the minimum redundancy payments that must be made but we may consider enhancing those payments, depending on the circumstances.

Where collective consultation is required or decided on

If we are required to or we decide to, we will then give the employee representatives and/or trade union representatives the following information in writing:

- the reasons for the proposals;

- the numbers and descriptions of employees whom it is proposed to make redundant;

- the total number of employees of that description;

- the proposed method of selecting those who are to be made redundant;

- the proposed method of carrying out the redundancies;

- proposals for calculating redundancy payments.

In consultation with the employee representatives and/or trade union representatives, we will then try to agree on all of the above points. If it becomes apparent that agreement cannot be reached on any particular point or points, then ultimately it is up to us to decide, taking account of any representations made by the representatives. However, every effort should be made on both sides to reach agreement.

Once agreement has been reached, we will then move on to selecting and consulting individuals about the redundancies.

Selection for redundancy

We will then apply the selection criteria which have either been agreed with the employee representatives or trade union representatives or been decided on by us. Generally, selection criteria will include some or all of the following:

- disciplinary records;

- absenteeism records;

- performance, as recorded in appraisal records or other documents or, if there are no such records, the opinion of at least two managers acting independently of each other;

- length of service.

Other factors may be used if considered appropriate.

Length of service may be used where all other factors are equal.

Notifying those proposed to be made redundant

Those it is proposed to make redundant will then be notified of the following:

- a summary of the reasons for the redundancies;

- an explanation of the selection criteria;

- an explanation of why, applying those criteria, it is proposed to make that employee redundant. Where selection is on the basis of a score under different headings, the employee will be notified of his or her particular score and of the total scores (without names being attributed) of others from whom the selection was made;

- details of all vacancies;

- notification of the time, date and place for a meeting to discuss the situation;

- notification of the employee's right to be accompanied by a work colleague or trade union representative.

Meeting

We will always attempt to find a time for the meeting which is convenient for all parties. If the date for the meeting turns out to be inconvenient for either party or for the person accompanying the employee, then the employee should notify the person who arranged the meeting immediately and a further meeting will be arranged.

It is important that employees attend the meeting. If an employee fails to attend such a meeting without reasonable excuse the meeting may proceed in that employee's absence.

Further matters to be investigated may arise out of the first meeting. Sufficient meetings should be held to enable us to discuss thoroughly all facts relevant to the decisions we will have to make including any alternative employment options that may be available. Once we have reached this stage, a decision will be made.

You will be informed in writing as soon as possible after the decision has been made. This notification will state:

– the date the employee's employment will end;

– details of any redundancy payment to which the employee may be entitled;

– the employee's right to appeal.

[During the notice period

During the notice period, every assistance will be given to help employees to find other employment. They will be permitted a reasonable amount of time off and the Human Resources Department will arrange interviews with all those under notice of redundancy to discuss their particular situation. Assistance will be provided or arranged to help people prepare CVs and prepare for interviews and also to suggest ways in which to look for other employment.]

Notification of vacancies

Vacancies will be notified via [notice board/ intranet/ regular updates]. Any employee who is interested in or would like to find out more about any particular vacancy should contact [the Human Resources Department].

Appeals

If the decision is to dismiss, and you disagree with that decision, you may appeal by writing to [ ] or, if [ ] was involved in the original decision, [ ], within [ ] days of the decision.

If the decision to make you redundant is overturned, then you may return to work on a mutually agreed date. All arrears of wages/salary will be paid and your employment will be treated as continuous. If you return to work, however, you will be required to repay any redundancy payment and/or payment in lieu of notice and such sums may be deducted from your remuneration (including the arrears of pay).

[Redundancy payments

[We will enhance the statutory redundancy payment as follows:

- the redundancy payment will be calculated in the same way as the statutory redundancy payment but without applying the weekly cap on wages;

- the payment so calculated will then be multiplied by [ ].]

[Whether or not we decide to enhance redundancy payments is entirely within our discretion. We may take into account when exercising that discretion whatever factors we may consider appropriate. This may (but will not necessarily) include the cost of such enhancement, the number of people made redundant at around the same time, whether further redundancies may be necessary but not past practice. Each redundancy situation will be reviewed independently of any previous redundancy situations.]]

Right to be accompanied

You have the right to be accompanied by a colleague or official of a trade union at all meetings throughout this procedure, including the appeal procedure.

D9.3 DRAFTING POINTS

Introduction: The definition of redundancy quoted here is the definition used in the Employment Rights Act 1996, which deals with unfair dismissal and redundancy. The definition used in the rules on consulting with employee representatives is considerably wider and covers all dismissals for reasons not related to the individual concerned, so it could cover dismissals to achieve a change in terms of employment. The narrower definition is used in this precedent but employers should bear in mind that there may be a need to consult employee representatives or trade union representatives in certain other situations as well.

Consultation: Consultation with employee representatives or trade union representatives is required if 20 or more redundancies are proposed within a three-month period; and minimum periods between the start of consultation and the date of the first redundancy (ie the first date on which redundancy notice expires). Some employers, particularly those who recognise trade unions, will consult with those trade unions anyway. Those employers with a Works Council or similar body will also consult over possible redundancies irrespective of the number of redundancies proposed. This precedent should be adapted to incorporate references to any recognised trade union and to any Works Council.

Consultation should be 'with a view to reaching agreement'. So long as the employer has tried to reach agreement, it will have complied with the legislation. If agreement cannot be reached, employers are not expected to continue trying to reach agreement indefinitely. Generally, once it becomes clear that agreement is not going to be reached, then consultation is probably complete. The employer should nevertheless take account of any points the representatives have made when deciding what to do.

Selection for redundancy: Some employers have a settled procedure for selecting for redundancy. This may be inevitable if that procedure has been agreed and there is no prospect of agreeing changes to it. However, different redundancy situations can require different approaches. For example, if a number of redundancies are required from a group of people all doing roughly similar jobs, then 'last in first out' may be appropriate. But if redundancies are needed across the board, for example, because the business is losing money and it is necessary to find a number of redundancies which are not necessarily in one particular area, it may be a lot more complicated to devise suitable criteria. Employment tribunals accept that employers must be allowed to ensure that the retained workforce, after redundancies, has all the requisite skills and the appropriate balance of skills. This precedent is drafted on the basis that there is no set procedure for selection but that selection criteria will be the subject of consultation with the appropriate representatives.

Whatever selection criteria are adopted, they should be as objective as possible. Last in first out is generally safe (although it has been unsuccessfully challenged on the ground of age discrimination) as it is completely objective. Some subjective criteria are sometimes inevitable. For example, employers may not have any way of objectively measuring performance. If that is the case, subjectivity should be kept to a minimum by getting at least two managers acting independently of each other to assess performance.

Notification and meeting: It is a requirement of the statutory dismissal procedure that employees should be informed in writing of the reasons for any proposal to dismiss and should be invited to a meeting to discuss the proposal. They must be given sufficient information in advance of the meeting in order to prepare any points they may wish to be taken into account. We recommend that this information should include information about any assessment made of the particular employee and well as overall assessments or scores of other employees. Cases on this point are not entirely consistent but if the above is followed it is highly unlikely that a tribunal will conclude that insufficient information was provided to the employee. This precedent therefore represents the minimum necessary to comply with the statutory dismissal procedure. Failure to follow these steps is likely to render the redundancy unfair. Note that the statutory dismissal procedure only applies to dismissals taking effect before 6 April 2009 or for which the dismissal procedure has started before that date. For dismissals after that date, the same process should generally be followed under ordinary unfair dismissal principles.

Notification of vacancies: Employees should be notified of any suitable vacancies. To avoid any possible arguments about whether a vacancy is suitable and whether the employee should have been notified about it, we recommend that the employer notifies all vacancies to all employees under notice of redundancy. This can be done easily by circulating vacancy lists or by posting vacancies on the notice board or intranet.

Enhancing redundancy payments: Many employers enhance the statutory redundancy payment. There are various ways in which this can be done. The regulations on age discrimination recognised that most redundancy pay schemes (including the statutory one) to some extent discriminate on grounds of age. Rather than scrapping the redundancy pay scheme and starting again, an exemption was included within the regulations that exempts redundancy payments from age discrimination so long as the only departures from the statutory formula are the removal of the cap on a week's pay and multiplying the overall result by a factor. Many enhanced redundancy pay schemes do not quite work like this. The age discrimination legislation therefore limits the enhanced redundancy payments that are permissible. The formula set out here reflects most enhanced redundancy schemes. Another permissible option is to add a lump some which is the same for everyone to all redundancy payments. That could not possibly be discriminatory because all employees would be treated equally.

Alternatively, some employers may wish to treated enhancements to redundancy payments as completely discretionary, in which case the second alternative should be used.

D10 GRIEVANCE PROCEDURE

D10.1 USE

Employers are required, either in the contract or in the statement of main terms and conditions of employment, to explain to employees what they should do if they have a grievance. This can be done by reference to another document, such as the handbook or a separate policy.

Various minimum requirements are laid down by the Employment Act 2002. These minimum requirements are to be repealed in respect of grievances arising on or after 6 April 2009 or where the action on which the grievance is based starts before that date and continues after it, so long as the employee presents a claim to the tribunal on or before 4 July 2009 (or 4 October 2009 in equal pay and redundancy cases). However, the requirements still represent good practice and following them should protect against employment tribunal claims. These requirements are:

- that any complaint in writing must be treated as a grievance;

- when a grievance has been submitted to the employer, then the employee may be required to explain the basis on which the grievance is made. Once that has been done, the employer must arrange a meeting with the employee;

- the employee has a right to be accompanied at any grievance meeting;

- the employee must take all reasonable steps to attend the meeting;

- if the employee or the person accompanying him or her is unable to attend the meeting for unforeseen reasons, then the meeting must be re-arranged. If this happens a second time, then the statutory grievance procedure is treated as having been complied with;

- after the grievance hearing, the employer must notify the employee in writing of the outcome;

- the employer must also inform the employee of his or her right to appeal;

- if the employee appeals, the employer must arrange a meeting to hear the appeal.

Employees have to raise a grievance before they can rely on the subject matter of the grievance in a claim to an employment tribunal, and they must wait 28 days before they submit any claim to the tribunal. If a grievance has been submitted, then the normal time limits for bringing a claim are extended by three months.

For full details, see Division C6 of *Jordans Employment Law Service*.

D10.2 **Precedent**

Grievance procedure

Informal stage

> In most cases, any problems you are having with your employment are best resolved by informal discussions with the people involved. We encourage you, therefore, to discuss any concerns you may have with your line manager or with the Human Resources Department.
>
> If the matter is successfully resolved at this stage, then that fact will be noted in your file and you will be asked to sign the file note to confirm this. If it is not resolved, the formal procedure will be explained to you, in particular, the requirement to put your grievance in writing.

Formal stage

> If you have a grievance about your employment and either:
>
> - you have tried unsuccessfully to resolve the matter by discussion; or
>
> - you do not think the problem can be resolved by discussion,
>
> you should raise the matter in writing with [ ]. You should set out in writing the basis of your complaint and suggestions about how you think the problem could be resolved.
>
> NOTE that this procedure should NOT be used to challenge dismissals (for which you should use the right of appeal under the dismissal procedure). The grievance procedure can be used to challenge disciplinary warnings or suspensions (although in most cases the appropriate means of challenging a disciplinary warning or suspension will be through an appeal) but any such grievance may be dealt with at any hearing under the disciplinary procedure.

Meeting

> [ ] will then set up a meeting to discuss your grievance.
>
> You should make every effort to attend the meeting. Failure to attend without a reasonable explanation may result in the meeting going ahead in your absence.

Re-arranging time of meeting

> We will always attempt to find a date and time for the meeting which is convenient for all parties. If the date for the meeting turns out to be inconvenient then you should notify the person who arranged the meeting immediately and a further meeting will be arranged.

Notification of outcome

> [ ] will notify you as soon as possible of the outcome.

Appeals

> If you disagree with that decision, you may appeal by writing to [ ] or, if [ ] was involved in the original decision, [ ], within [ ] days of the decision.

Right to be accompanied

> You have a right to be accompanied by a colleague or official of a trade union at all meetings under this procedure, including the appeal meeting.

Grievances after termination of employment

> Normally, we will continue to deal with your grievance even if your employment terminates. In some cases, however, this will not be possible, for example:
>
> - where you have obtained other employment and do not have time to pursue your grievance;
>
> - where you have relocated and do not wish to return to meetings with us to pursue your grievance.
>
> If you do not wish us to continue to deal with your grievance after your employment has terminated, you should let us know either orally or in writing and you should give a brief explanation.
>
> Alternatively, you may want us still to consider your grievance but without holding a meeting with you. If that is the case, again, please let us know (either orally or in writing) and we may agree to deal with your grievance in writing without a meeting.

Employment tribunals

> For grievances about matters arising or starting before 6 April 2009, in most cases you will not be able to bring a claim in an employment tribunal for matters other than dismissal (eg discrimination, equal pay, unlawful deductions from wages, unlawful detriment, working time) unless you have first tried to resolve the matter within the workplace through the grievance procedure. This should be borne in mind if you are considering bringing a complaint in a tribunal. This rule does not apply to grievances in respect of matters occurring on or after 6 April 2009.

D10.3 DRAFTING POINTS

Formal/informal stage: Many grievance procedures provide for an informal stage. Care needs to be taken when trying to resolve grievances informally because of the statutory grievance procedure (applicable to grievances in respect of matters starting before 6 April 2009). If a formal grievance is treated as having been raised, then the statutory grievance procedure must be followed. Therefore, employers who try to resolve a grievance informally without a hearing could fall foul of the rules on statutory grievance procedures. There are two ways of dealing with this. The first is to treat the informal meeting as the grievance hearing, but then a right of appeal must be offered. The second is to get the employee's agreement, if the matter is successfully resolved informally, to withdraw the formal grievance.

The first method is not satisfactory, since offering a right of appeal makes the process more formal, defeating the object of the informal stage.

This precedent seeks to ensure there is no confusion between the informal stage and the formal stage, by requiring the manager or Human Resources Department to record the fact that the grievance has been resolved and asking the employee to sign that record, so that the employee can be treated as having withdrawn the grievance; and making it clear to the employee that if they wish to pursue the grievance further, they must put the complaint in writing.

If an employer thinks their managers may not always do this, it may be safest to omit reference to the informal stage within the grievance procedure. The only benefit of the informal procedure is that it may be possible to resolve the grievance without recourse to any formal procedure.

D11 GRIEVANCE PROCEDURE (SHORT VERSION)

D11.1 USE

All employers should have a grievance procedure. It is a requirement of the legislation (s 3 of the Employment Rights Act 1996) that the statement of terms and conditions of employment or the contract of employment contains a note of how employees should raise grievances. This precedent grievance procedure represents the bare minimum that employers should have. Larger organisations, or those with a full-time Human Resources Department, may wish to have a lengthier, more sophisticated procedure.

The statutory grievance procedures also generally apply (with a few exceptions). Note that the statutory grievance procedure is to be repealed for grievances arising or starting on or after 6 April 2009.

For full details of the rules on statutory grievance procedures, see Division C6 of *Jordans Employment Law Service*.

D11.2 Precedent

Grievance procedure

> An employee raising a grievance should in the first instance discuss it with his or her immediate line manager.
>
> If the grievance is not resolved within two days the employee should submit the grievance in writing to the line manager and the line manager will arrange a formal grievance hearing at which the grievance will be discussed formally between the line manager and the employee and/or his or her chosen representative (who must be a colleague or trade union representative). This hearing will be held as soon as reasonably practicable.
>
> If the grievance is against the employee's line manager, or if for any other reason the employee considers it inappropriate to raise the grievance with that line manager, the grievance should be raised with any other manager. This may be appropriate, for example, if the grievance involves a complaint of racial or sexual harassment against the line manager.
>
> If the matter remains unresolved after the formal hearing, it may then be referred by way of appeal to a director of the Company, who will then discuss the grievance with the employee and/or with his or her chosen representative, who must be a work colleague or representative of a trade union.

Employees may be assured that any grievances brought will be treated as confidential. At all stages of the grievance procedure, an employee may be accompanied or represented by a colleague or representative of a trade union.

The prime objective for all parties is to achieve a solution as quickly as possible.

D11.3 DRAFTING POINTS

Employers with a full-time Human Resources Department will probably want to include within the grievance procedure some reference to the Human Resources Department. For example, they may wish formal grievances to be raised with the Head of Human Resource, so that the Human Resources Department can decide how the grievance should be dealt with. A representative of the Human Resources Department may wish to be present at any grievance hearing.

D12 HARASSMENT POLICY AND PROCEDURE

D12.1 USE

Having a harassment procedure should first ensure that any problems are brought to your attention at an early stage; and secondly provides a way in which complaints of harassment may be dealt with. There is no statutory requirement for such a policy, but having a policy on harassment should lessen the likelihood of harassment causing you a serious problem and should also enable you to better defend any complaints to an employment tribunal based on harassment.

Harassment on grounds of age, creed, disability (past or present), nationality, race, racial origins, religion, religious belief, gender, gender re-assignment or sexual orientation, trade union membership or non-membership, part-time or fixed-term status is likely to be unlawful and complaints may be brought in an employment tribunal.

Serious forms of harassment, whether or not on any of the above grounds, may constitute a criminal offence under the Protection from Harassment Act 1997.

For more details on when harassment could be unlawful under the discrimination legislation, see Division E of *Jordans Employment Law Service*.

For written complaints of harassment occurring or starting before 6 April 2009, the statutory grievance procedure will apply (see notes to the precedent grievance procedure). This precedent should ensure compliance with that procedure. While this is strictly unnecessary for complaints about matter occurring on or after 6 April 2009, it is still good practice to comply with those requirements.

D12.2　　　　　　　　　　Precedent

Harassment policy and procedure

>The Employer is committed to providing a working environment that ensures all employees are treated with dignity and respect, free from harassment and bullying.

Definition of harassment

>Harassment is any unwanted conduct which has the purpose or effect of violating the dignity or creating an intimidating, hostile, degrading, humiliating or offensive environment for an employee. Harassment is unwanted, unwelcome and unreciprocated behaviour.

Such behaviour will constitute unlawful harassment if it is on grounds of age, creed, disability (past or present), nationality, race, racial origins, religion, religious belief, gender, gender re-assignment or sexual orientation, trade union membership or non-membership, part-time or fixed-term status and is unwanted by the recipient. This behaviour is unacceptable and, if it occurs, measures will be taken to stop it, including disciplinary action if necessary. Sexual harassment also includes unwanted conduct of a sexual nature (whether or not that conduct is on grounds of sex) which has the purpose or effect set out in the previous paragraph.

Harassment is to a degree, a subjective question and can take many forms: verbal, non-verbal, physical and bullying ranging from physical attack to more subtle conduct which makes the recipient uneasy. It can be persistent or an isolated incident. All employees must be aware of the sensitivities of others. It is no excuse that behaviour is tolerated by other employees. If one employee is offended or feels bullied by a particular type of behaviour, then that behaviour constitutes harassment even if others are not offended.

We treat any form of harassment as serious misconduct.

Managers must ensure that any alleged harassment is investigated and action taken to prevent recurrence.

The Criminal Justice and Public Order Act 1994 created a criminal offence of 'causing intentional harassment, alarm or distress'. A person will be guilty if they use 'threatening, abusive or insulting words or behaviour'.

Harassment is unlawful in many cases and individual employees may be legally held liable for their actions. In some cases their behaviour may also amount to a criminal offence.

Harassment includes:

Sexual Harassment

- Unwelcome sexual remarks, such as jokes, teasing and verbal abuse

- The display of pin-ups, pornographic pictures or sexually suggestive subject matter

- Unwelcome remarks about a person's appearance or marital status

- Unwelcome physical contact or demands for sexual favours

- Unwelcome physical contact

- Offensive or sexually explicit language

- Offensive or suggestive gestures

Racial Harassment

- Racially derogatory remarks or racial jokes
- Display of racially offensive material

Harassment on grounds of sexual orientation

- Unwelcome remarks about a person's sexuality or marital status
- Unwelcome remarks, such as jokes, teasing and verbal abuse

Harassment on grounds of gender re-assignment

- Jokes about a person's gender re-assignment
- Adverse comments, whether to their face or behind their backs

Harassment of people with disabilities

- Harassment, undignified treatment, ridicule or exclusion of people because of their disability

Religious Harassment

- Unwelcome remarks, such as jokes, teasing and verbal abuse
- Display of religiously offensive material
- Pressure to take part in religious activities

Harassment on grounds of age

- Unpleasant comments about a person's age
- Comments suggesting that people of a certain age are less able than others

Bullying in the workplace

- Includes insulting behaviour, threats or physical assault, the intention of belittling someone through the misuse of power or position which leaves them feeling hurt or upset
- Bullying can take various forms, physical, verbal or attitude

These are not complete lists of all the types of conduct which could constitute harassment

Dealing with complaints of Harassment – informal action and advice

All allegations of harassment will be dealt with seriously, promptly and in confidence. Employees who believe they have been harassed are encouraged to use this procedure. They should not fear victimisation. Retaliation against an employee who brings a complaint of harassment is a serious disciplinary offence which may constitute gross misconduct and could result in dismissal.

[The Human Resources Department] will provide confidential advice to anyone who believes they have been harassed about the best way to deal with the situation. Any employee who is not sure whether the behaviour from others that they are experiencing amounts to harassment should discuss the situation with [the Human Resources Department].

In some cases it may be possible to rectify matters informally. Sometimes individuals are not aware that their behaviour is unwelcome and an informal discussion may be all that is required to ensure a greater understanding and the ceasing of the behaviour. The individual should initially undertake this discussion, although they may enlist the support of their manager or a member of personnel.

Where an informal resolution is not possible then the employee should make a formal complaint as defined under the Employer's grievance procedure. Any complaint made out of malice will be a disciplinary issue.

Formal action

The allegation of harassment will then be investigated. Consideration will be given to the separation whilst at work of the complainant and the alleged harasser, taking into account the views of the complainant. In serious cases the alleged harasser may be suspended in order for the complaint to be investigated.

You will be interviewed by [a member of the Human Resources department] to establish full details of the conduct you are complaining about. [You may bring a work colleague or representative of a trade union with you to this meeting if you choose]. They will then carry out an independent, impartial and objective investigation as quickly as possible. This will normally involve interviewing the alleged harasser and anyone else who may have witnessed the conduct complained of. The alleged harasser will have the right to be accompanied by a work colleague or representative of a trade union. Those carrying out the investigation will so far as is practicable not be connected with the conduct complained of. An investigation will be carried out sensitively in a way that respects the rights of both you and the alleged harasser.

When the investigation is completed, you will be informed whether or not your allegation is considered to be well founded.

If a case of harassment is considered proven then action taken will follow the Disciplinary procedure. The level of action taken will depend upon the seriousness of the harassment.

If the allegation is found to be not well founded, consideration may be given to whether it is necessary to transfer or reschedule the work of both or either party, if it is considered that it would not be appropriate for either of you to continue to work in close proximity to each other.

D12.3　DRAFTING POINTS

Examples of harassment: The examples given here should be reviewed and amended to suit the particular workplace.

Informal and formal stages: The employer should review the procedure set out here to check that it is practicable. If the employer simply does not have the resources to carry out the investigations envisaged in these stages, then the procedure should be simplified. For example, in a small workplace, it may be impossible or impracticable to separate the complainant and the alleged harasser, in which case it would be pointless and possibly damaging to include the sections dealing with separation.

D13 WHISTLEBLOWING

D13.1 USE

The Public Interest Disclosure Act 1998 inserts into the Employment Rights Act 1996 protection for employees and workers who make a 'protected disclosure'. It is now unlawful to victimise a worker for making a protected disclosure; it is automatically unfair to dismiss an employee for making a protected disclosure (irrespective of length of service and compensation is unlimited); and any agreement is void in so far as it precludes the worker from making such a disclosure.

The aim of the Act is to protect workers who raise genuine concerns about malpractice at work, including breach of a legal obligation (eg negligence, breach of contract, breach of administrative law); miscarriage of justice, danger to health and safety or to the environment and any attempts to cover up any of these.

There are various levels of protection, depending on the circumstances. Disclosure to the employer is the most common form of disclosure. Workers who make such a disclosure to their employers are protected provided they have an honest and reasonable suspicion that malpractice has taken place and they act in good faith.

Disclosure to a regulatory body may also be protected, but here the conditions for protection are more stringent. There must be a good reason why the employee has not raised the matter internally and the employee must honestly and reasonably believe that the allegations are true. The Act lists the appropriate regulatory bodies. These include the Health and Safety Executive and the Financial Services Authority.

For more details, see Division C6 of *Jordans Employment Law Service.*

We recommend that whistleblowing procedures should be kept separate from the normal grievance procedure, given the difference in the nature of the complaints covered and the way that they should be handled. Grievance procedures are suitable for complaints relating specifically to action taken by the employer in relation to an individual employee, while the whistleblowing procedure is used for complaints that affect the organisation as a whole.

There is no legal requirement for employers to adopt a whistleblowing policy, but there are good reasons for having one and following it. First, employers are less likely to be exposed to claims, since they will be able to demonstrate that they have taken measures to address the concerns of employees.

Secondly, the policy may help management identify and rectify malpractice – for example, the majority of frauds are detected because workers who are not involved in the fraud report their suspicions to their employers.

Thirdly, there are a few very limited circumstances where disclosure to the press is protected, one of the conditions being that it was reasonable to make the disclosure. The existence of an appropriate whistleblowing policy makes it less likely that any court or tribunal would conclude that disclosure to the press is reasonable.

D13.2 **Precedent**

Whistleblowing

> All organisations face the risk of things going wrong or of unknowingly harbouring malpractice. We believe we have a duty to identify such situations and take the appropriate measures to remedy the situation. By encouraging a culture of openness within our organisation we believe that we can help prevent malpractice – prevention is better than cure. That is the aim of this policy.
>
> We want to encourage you to raise issues which concern you at work. You may be worried that by reporting such issues you will be opening yourself up to victimisation or detriment, or risking your job security; that is quite understandable. However, all our staff now enjoy statutory protection if concerns are raised in the right way. This policy is designed to give you that opportunity and protection. Provided you are acting in good faith, it does not matter if you are mistaken. There is no question of you having to prove anything.
>
> If there is anything which you think we should know about, please use the procedure outlined in this policy. By knowing about malpractice at an early stage, we stand a good chance of taking the necessary steps to safeguard the interests of all staff and protect our organisation.
>
> In short, please, don't hesitate to 'blow the whistle' on malpractice.
>
> [*Note: This policy is not our normal Grievance Procedure. If you have a complaint about your own personal circumstances then you should use our normal Grievance Procedure. If you have concerns about malpractice within the organisation then you should use the procedure outlined in this policy.*]

Our guarantee

> The management is committed to this policy. If you use this policy to raise a concern, we give you our assurance that you will not suffer any form of retribution, victimisation or detriment. We will treat your concern seriously and act according to this policy. We will not ask you to prove anything. If you ask us to treat the matter in confidence we will respect your request and only make disclosures with your consent. We will give

you feedback on any investigation and be sensitive to any concerns you may have as a result of any steps taken under this procedure.

How to raise your concern internally

1. TELL YOUR IMMEDIATE SUPERIOR [LINE MANAGER]

    If you are concerned about any form of malpractice you should normally first raise the issue with your [line manager]. There is no special procedure for doing this – you can tell him or her about the problem or put it in writing if you prefer.

2. IF YOU FEEL UNABLE TO TELL YOUR IMMEDIATE SUPERIOR [LINE MANAGER]

    If you feel you cannot tell your [line manager], for whatever reason, please raise the issue with [the Head of Human Resources/ a Director].

    Name: [*insert name(s)*]

    Contact Details: [*insert details, including telephone number*]

3. IF YOU STILL HAVE CONCERNS[1]

    If you have raised your concerns and you are still concerned, or the matter is so serious that you feel you cannot discuss it with either of the two persons named above, you should raise the matter with [the Chief Executive/ the Managing Director].

    Name: [*insert name*]

    Contact Details: [*insert details, including telephone number*]

How we will respond

After you have raised your concern we will decide how to respond in a responsible and appropriate manner under this policy. Usually this will involve making internal enquiries first, but it may be necessary to carry out an investigation at a later stage which may be formal or informal depending on the nature of the concern raised.

As far as possible, we will keep you informed of the decisions we take and the outcome of any enquiries and investigations we carry out. However, we will not be able to inform you of any matters which would infringe our duty of confidentiality to others.

---

[1] Whistleblowers working for a public body subject to ministerial appointment (eg the NHS and many 'quangos') may raise their concerns with the sponsoring Department. In such cases, the policy should include relevant contact details.

Raising your concern externally (exceptional cases)

> The main purpose of this policy is to give you the opportunity and protection you need to raise your concerns internally. We expect that in almost all cases raising concerns internally will be the most appropriate action for you to take.
>
> However, if for whatever reason, you feel you cannot raise your concerns internally and you honestly and reasonably believe the information and any allegations are true, you should consider raising the matter with [the appropriate regulator].
>
> Name of appropriate regulator: [*eg Health & Safety Executive or Financial Services Authority*]
>
> Contact Details: [*insert details, including telephone number*]

Caution

> *If you have good reasons for not using the internal or regulatory disclosure procedures described above, you may consider making wider disclosure by reporting the matter to the police or to the media, for example. However, whistleblowers who make wider disclosures of this type will only be protected from victimisation and suffering detriment in certain circumstances. We recommend that you take legal advice before following this course of action since we believe it will be in your own interests to do so.*

D13.3 DRAFTING POINTS

For workers working for a public body subject to ministerial appointment (eg the NHS and many quangos), the policy should state that workers may raise their concerns with the sponsoring Department. In such cases, the policy should include relevant contact details.

D14 PERSONAL PROPERTY

D14.1 USE

This paragraph may be useful where employees may have to leave personal property unattended – for example, where they may be required to change into uniform or safety clothing. Generally, where this applies, employers may be expected to provide some sort of protection for employees' property.

It could be used in any employment, however, where the employer believes employees' property may be vulnerable to theft.

A notice such as this, included in a handbook or put up on notice boards, should protect employers from being sued in respect of theft of personal items, as well as providing a reminder to employees to look after their property sensibly.

D14.2 Precedent

Personal property

Personal property

> The Company understands that Employees may [sometimes wish/have] to bring items of personal property onto Company premises. We try to provide a place of work that will be safe from theft and damage but ultimately, it is the Employee's responsibility to look after their property. [Lockers are provided where clothing and valuable items such as jewellery may be stored. These should be locked at all times when appropriate. Any loss of the locker key should be reported immediately to [the Human Resources Department].] Employees are advised not to leave personal property unattended at any time [other than inside lockers]. Employees should be careful, therefore, about leaving jackets or handbags or other property unattended. The Company cannot accept responsibility for personal property which is lost, stolen or damaged on the Company's premises.

D14.3 DRAFTING POINTS

You may wish to include specific rules for the protection of personal property. Providing lockers where employees may be required to change while at work is a sensible precaution, but there may be other steps employers could take, such as providing lockable desks of filing cabinets.

The disciplinary procedure should provide that theft of anyone's property would amount to gross misconduct.

D15 ACCIDENT REPORTING

D15.1 USE

This may either be included in the contract of employment, or in the handbook, or in a separate policy. It may be part of a health and safety policy.

D15.2 Precedent

Accident reporting

Accidents

> If you suffer an accident at work, you must ensure that the circumstances of the accident are entered in the Accident Book which is kept in [the Human Resources department] and that your line manager is informed as soon as possible.

> If you witness or are involved in an incident which might have caused injury, you must inform your line manager.

> [If you see a situation, for example damaged machinery or equipment, which you think could represent a danger or health hazard, you should report it to your line manager.]

D15.3 DRAFTING POINTS

The final paragraph should be included wherever potentially dangerous machinery is used.

D16 RETIREMENT POLICY AND PROCEDURE

D16.1 USE

Since the new rules on retirement came into force in October 2006, employers may wish to have a retirement policy and procedure. This ensures that all employees are aware of their rights on retirement, in particular the right to request continued working beyond retirement age, and that they exercise those rights correctly.

This precedent sets out the correct procedure to follow in cases of retirement. So long as it is followed, there should be no risk of an age discrimination or unfair dismissal claim. If it is not followed, the defence to such claims will not apply and you will have to be able to demonstrate that the retirement was justified.

D16.2 Precedent

Retirement policy and procedure

Introduction

This policy and procedure explains the Company's approach to retirement and the process it applies. The Company's aim is, so far as possible, to help you plan your retirement by giving plenty of notice of when we are expecting you to retire; and to ensure you understand what options are available to you.

Retirement age

The Company's normal age for retirement is [65].

You can retire earlier if you wish to do so by liaising with your [Manager/Supervisor] and submitting appropriate notice in accordance with the terms and conditions of your employment. The amount of your pension may be affected, however, and we recommend you take advice from a qualified financial advisor before doing so. If you do want to retire early, it would help us if you could discuss this with [your Manager/Supervisor] to make sure you are aware of all options open to you and to assist us with succession planning.

Time lines

Between 12 and 6 months before proposed retirement date	Between 6 and 3 months before proposed retirement date	Within a reasonable period of receiving the request	Within a reasonable period after that:
The Company will give you written notification of the date it proposes you will retire and of your right to ask to continue working beyond retirement age.	If you wish to continue working beyond the retirement date, submit request.	The Company will: • agree the request; or • hold a meeting with you to discuss the request; or • if not practicable to hold a meeting within a reasonable period consider the request.	The Company will notify you of its decision and of your right of appeal.

What will happen?

Between six and twelve months before you reach retirement age, we will write to you advising you of the date we anticipate you will retire. This will normally be the end of the month in which your [65th] birthday falls.

If you wish to retire on that date, you do not need to take any further action and your employment will come to an end on that date.

If you wish to continue to work beyond your retirement date, you should make a formal written request (you can use the attached form). This should be sent between six and three months before the proposed retirement date. Your request should be sent to [your Line Manager/Supervisor/the Human Resources Department].

Procedure for continued working request

On receipt of your request to continue working beyond your retirement age, we will notify you if your proposal is accepted. If so, we will write to you setting out any revision to your terms of employment. If we do not immediately agree to your proposal] you will be invited to a meeting where your request to continue working will be fully considered, and you will be advised of the decision within two weeks of the meeting. Sample invitation letters and notification letters appear at the end of this handbook.

IF YOUR REQUEST IS ACCEPTED

If it is agreed that you can continue to work beyond your proposed retirement date, this will be confirmed to you in writing, along with any changes to your terms and conditions of employment. [The Company's offer of continued employment will generally be on the basis of a fixed-term contract for a specified period.] If you are not happy with the terms proposed, you have a right of appeal (see sample appeal letter attached).

IF YOUR REQUEST IS DECLINED

If your request to continue working is declined, this will be confirmed to you in writing with details of your proposed retirement date, your right to appeal and the appeal procedure. Your employment will continue until the proposed retirement date or, if later, the day after you are notified of the decision.

If you wish to appeal then you must do so within two weeks of receiving the decision, clearly stating in writing your reasons for appealing. You should send the appeal to [your Line Manager/the Human resources Department] who will make the appropriate arrangements for the appeal hearing.

Where possible, the appeal hearing will be held within two weeks of receiving your grounds of appeal. Where this is not reasonably practicable, then a meeting will be arranged as soon as possible, no later than four weeks after receiving the letter. If you are unable to attend the initial meeting or your appeal meeting within two months of the original date of the request to continue working, a decision will be made based upon the information available. The outcome will be confirmed to you in writing and this decision will be final.

ACCOMPANIMENT

We recognise that retirement is a significant life event, and will endeavour to ensure that you are supported during this time. When you are invited to your meeting to discuss your options, or any subsequent hearings or meetings, you may be accompanied by a work colleague.

Considering your request to continue working

The Company will give careful consideration to all requests to continue working beyond retirement age. When considering the request the Company will consider whether any of the following circumstances apply to you. In general the Company will not agree to a request if, in the Company's view, none of the circumstances set out below apply:

- Your continued employment would be particularly beneficial or necessary for the completion of a specified task or project;

- Your continued employment would enable you to pass on your skills/experience and/or provide training to other employees;

- There is a shortage within the Company of employees with your skills/experience;

- You are carrying out a key role within the Company and the Company has not been able to find a suitable replacement;

- [add any other circumstances in which you may agree working beyond retirement, ensuring they do not discriminate on unlawful grounds such as disability. For example, refusing continued working for health reasons could amount to a breach of the Disability Discrimination Act 1995 unless justified].

In most cases where the Company agrees to continued working beyond retirement age, it will do so on the basis of a fixed term. That fixed term may be extended if the same circumstances apply at the end of the period.

D16.3 DRAFTING POINTS

Retirement age: Any retirement age below 65 could amount to unlawful age discrimination unless it is justified. For details, see Division E4 of *Jordans Employment Law Service*.

Time lines: The time-scales set out here are those set out in legislation. Retirement at the normal retirement age cannot normally amount to an unfair dismissal, provided the correct procedure is followed. In particular, notice of retirement must be given between 12 and six months before the proposed retirement date; and employees must be informed of their right to request to work beyond their retirement date. The request must be in writing and must be submitted between six and three months before the proposed retirement date. If the request is agreed, there is no need to hold a meeting to discuss it. If it is not agreed, however, a meeting must be held.

Procedure: Employers may wish to provide that continued working is for a fixed term only. Alternatively, the employer may specify a new retirement date. As that new retirement date approaches, the same procedure will apply unless the new retirement date is within six months of the old and this is stated within the employer's notification of its decision.

Considering the request for continued working: If the employer follows the correct procedure, there should be no danger of age discrimination nor of unfair dismissal. If the procedure is not followed, however, there may be such a risk. It may still be possible to justify compulsory retirement. It should be easier to justify retirement and to ensure that the policy is applied in a consistent way if the policy sets out the circumstances in which requests for continued working may be granted. If this is not done, there is a danger of discrimination claims on grounds, for example, of disability. By applying a consistent non-discriminatory policy on granting and refusing requests, employers should be able to justify refusals of requests for continued working.

D17 TRAINING

D17.1 USE

There is no need for employers to have a policy specifically dealing with training, but if you want to use a training agreement whereby employees have to repay course fees if they leave within a specified period, it helps to warn employees of this in advance, to avoid possible disputes.

D17.2 Precedent

Training policy

> We are committed to providing and paying for training and development for employees where we believe this will improve individual and company performance and/or help employees acquire additional skills and knowledge that will enable them to achieve their personal career aspirations. We regard this as a benefit both to employees and to ourselves – you gain valuable skills and knowledge and we gain the benefits of improved performance.
>
> To make sure we get some benefit from any training provided, we may ask employees to sign a training agreement, whereby you agree to remain in this employment for a minimum period and if you leave during that minimum period, you will repay all or part of the training fees.
>
> Annually, all employees will have an appraisal discussion with their line manager. Areas for training and development may be discussed and identified at these discussions. Employees who consider they would benefit from training in any particular area should raise the matter at these appraisal discussions.

D18 APPRAISALS

D18.1 USE

There is no need for employers to have a policy on appraisals other than to inform employees of the process.

D18.2 Precedent

Appraisals

Appraisals provide an opportunity for employees to discuss with their line managers their own performance, aspirations, objectives, ambitions and any matters which they consider may be holding them back. Generally, formal appraisals take place once a year but they should reflect discussions that have taken place throughout the year. It is important for employees to know and understand what is expected of them and what they would need to achieve promotion. It is equally important for line managers to understand the aspirations and concerns of those who report to them.

The formal appraisal process should not be seen in isolation from general discussions that should take place about performance. The purpose of a formal appraisal is to ensure that the employee's concerns and aspirations are recorded, and the line manager's views of the employee's performance are also recorded, so that any objectives, aspirations, ambitions, problems or concerns can be highlighted and appropriate action taken.

Appraisals take place in [the winter/spring/ summer/autumn] each year and your contribution to this process is extremely important.

Prior to the formal appraisal meeting, you are expected to complete the employee section of the appraisal form which should then be forwarded to the person appraising you.

At the formal appraisal meeting, both parties' views are exchanged and discussed based on objectives set in the previous year. There should be no surprises and discussions should be open, frank and confidential to both parties. Agreement should be reached on the forthcoming year's objectives and any training needs identified.

The meeting will normally involve a recap on achievements against previously set objectives, to identify areas of strength and weakness, to identify any training needs and as an opportunity for employees to communicate not only the problems they may have encountered during the previous year, but also the areas which have given employees development opportunities and job satisfaction. This is also an opportunity for the employee to review his or her aspirations and ambitions, including any new ambitions not previously discussed or recorded.

D19 WORKING TIME POLICY

D19.1 USE

The only reason you might want to have a working time policy is to inform employees and managers about the requirements of the Working Time Regulations 1998 (SI 1998/1833). This briefly summarises the regulations.

D19.2 Precedent

Working time policy

Working time policy

It is the Company's policy to comply with the spirit as well as the letter of the Working Time Regulations 1998 (SI 1998/1833) to ensure a safe working environment and safe conditions for all staff. The following is intended only as a summary of the Working Time Regulations 1998. The regulations may be updated, amended or replaced from time to time. If there is any discrepancy between this summary and the regulations, then the regulations will prevail.

Scope

This policy applies to all staff within the Company.

In brief, the Regulations stipulate the following:

- *Hours* – A maximum working week of 48 hours averaged over a rolling 17-week period, unless a voluntary Opt-Out Agreement has been signed.

- *Paid Annual Leave* – A minimum of four weeks holiday per annum in addition to statutory holidays.

- *Daily Rest Period* – Employees are entitled to a rest period of 11 consecutive hours between each working day (12 hours in any 24-hour period for adolescent workers).

- *Weekly Rest Period* – Employees are entitled to a rest period of not less than 24 hours in each seven-day period. This may be averaged over a two-week period, ie two days' rest over a fortnight.

- *In-work rest breaks* – Employees are entitled to an uninterrupted break of 20 minutes when the daily working time is more than six hours (30 minutes for adolescent workers when the daily working time is more than 4.5 hours).

- *Records* – Where employees have agreed to work in excess of the 48-hour weekly working limit, their employer is required to keep records of their names. For staff who have not signed an Opt-Out Agreement, there is a requirement to keep records as far as is reasonably practicable. These records must be kept for a minimum period of two years.

- *Employee Rights* – Employees should not suffer detriment for exercising their rights under the Regulations.

Procedures

New starters

Where it is considered appropriate you will receive an Opt-Out Agreement together with explanatory notes on the Regulations. This is a voluntary arrangement and can be terminated, if agreed to by you, by giving three months' notice. No criticism or detrimental treatment will result if you decide not to sign the Opt-Out Agreement; and once you have signed it, you can terminate that agreement on three months' notice.

Time monitoring

It is considered that compliance with the Regulations can be achieved through the use of existing systems.

Where staff have not signed an Opt-Out Agreement, it is their responsibility to ensure that they do not exceed the hours stipulated in the Regulations. If you are concerned about the Regulations or experience any problems regarding working hours, breaks, etc. you should raise it with your line manager in the first instance. If you feel you are being forced to work longer hours than is permitted by the regulations, and if discussing the matter informally with your line manager has not resolved the problem, then you can discuss the matter with the Human Resources Department; or if that fails, then you should raise a formal grievance in writing.

Holidays

It is the responsibility of managers to ensure that staff take their full holiday entitlement within the holiday year. The Regulations do not allow employers to buy out untaken holiday entitlement, except on termination of employment, and staff should be encouraged to take their full holiday entitlement.

Assistance

Should you require any clarification on the provisions of this Policy and Procedures, please contact the Human Resources Department.

D20　TIME OFF

D20.1　USE

Employees are entitled to reasonable time off for public duties. These are defined in s 50 of the Employment Rights Act 1996. Normally this will be unpaid but some employers may want to encourage participation in such bodies, in which case all or part of the time off may be paid. The policy reminds employees and managers of the right to time off and enables the employer to clarify whether or not they are prepared to pay for such time off.

D20.2　　　　　　　　Precedent

Time off for public service, jury service or in the armed services

Employees participating in local government (eg local authorities, health authorities, police and fire authorities) and those elected to local councils or other authorities may be granted reasonable leave of absence to attend meetings. What is reasonable will depend on:

- your position;

- the amount of time off for similar purposes that you have already taken;

- you current workload;

- [add any other factors you would want to include which it would be reasonable to include – for example, the availability of other staff to cover.]

[We do not pay for time off for these purposes and such time off will be unpaid unless it is taken as holiday.]

[Where you receive payment from the relevant authority for such duties you will not be paid by us, unless the payment you receive would be less than normal pay or normal earnings, in which case the Company will make up the difference. No payments will be made for time off for local authority candidates to attend meetings or other activities for the purposes of seeking election.]

If you are called up for jury service or have to attend Court as a witness you [will] /[will not] receive pay whilst away from work. Instead, you are entitled to attendance expenses from the Court. The Court will supply you with a claim form which the Company will complete on your behalf. You then return the completed form to the Court for reimbursement at the end of the attendance period.

If you who wish to participate in service in the Reserve or Auxiliary Forces you will be allowed a maximum of [one] week's leave without pay. Any further weeks must be taken from holiday entitlement

D20.3　DRAFTING POINTS

There is no requirement for employers to pay for such time off but employees do have a statutory right to reasonable unpaid time off for these purposes. This precedent should therefore be adapted to indicate whether you are prepared to pay for such time off. In certain employments where the employer may want to encourage membership of public bodies, the employer may want to pay for time off.

D21 COMPANY CARS

D21.1 USE

This policy is intended to cover all possible situations in which cars may be used on company business. It deals with health and safety issues, environmental issues, types of car permitted, rules on smoking, drugs and alcohol, tax, insurance, looking after the car and accidents.

D21.2 Precedent

Company car policy

> We take seriously our responsibilities to the environment and to the communities in which we operate. One of the major environmental impacts we make is through our car fleet.
>
> Employees will be aware that the taxation of Company cars has changed, significantly reducing for some the attractiveness of the company car as a benefit. The taxation of private fuel given as a benefit has increased dramatically.
>
> Employees issued with a Company Fuel Card must only use this for fuel and oil for the company vehicle. Using the card for any other vehicle will be regarded as gross misconduct.

Health and safety

> We recognise our responsibility for the health and safety of employees and members of the public resulting from necessary driving on Company business. So this Policy applies to all employees who are required to drive as part of their job and includes:
>
> – all drivers of company registered vehicles
>
> – those driving privately registered cars on company business
>
> – personnel who drive hire vehicles on company business
>
> Our intention is to make both the professional and personal lives of employees safer. The objective of the Car Policy is to achieve this by reducing the number of driving incidents in which employees are involved. Reducing these incidents also reduces potential injury to employees and members of the public.
>
> It is the responsibility of all employees to inform their line manager of any health/fitness reasons, which may affect their safety whilst driving on Company business. It is the responsibility of the line manager to assess these risks and to take appropriate measures. All employees' behaviour whilst driving is a reflection on the Company's corporate image. Drivers

are expected to be courteous and abide by the Highway Code and road traffic laws in place (including speed restrictions).

Smoking in vehicles

It is a requirement that an enclosed vehicle must be smoke free if it is:

(a) used by members of the public or a section of the public; or

(b) used in the course of paid or voluntary work by more than one person (even is those persons use the vehicle at different times, or only intermittently).

Any person who has management or control over that smoke-free vehicle shall be under a duty to ensure that at least one no smoking sign is displayed in a prominent position in each compartment of the vehicle in which people can be carried.

Notwithstanding this, there is an exemption to the above requirements, where a vehicle is used primarily for the private purposes of a person who owns it or has a right to use it, which is not restricted to a particular journey.

In summary therefore:

- Where a vehicle is used primarily for private purposes, it is not required to be smoke free or contain a no smoking sign;

- Where a vehicle is used primarily for work purposes and only used by one person, it is not required to be smoke free or contain a no smoking sign;

- Where a vehicle is used primarily for work purposes and by more than one person (whether or not those persons use the vehicle at different times or intermittently), then it must be smoke-free and it must carry the relevant no smoking signs.

Driving under the influence of drugs/alcohol

Certain prescription and 'over the counter' drugs can cause side effects such as drowsiness. Normally, there would be a written warning on the bottle or in the instructions. Employees are expected to take notice of any such warnings. Employees should seek further advice from their GP/Pharmacist and if appropriate, discuss any adverse effect with their line manager.

Employees whose work involves driving should not consume alcoholic drinks during working hours. All employees likely to drive should be aware that heavy drinking during the evening before work can affect their ability to drive safely the following day and may leave them over the legal drink drive limit. Any employee who has their licence suspended must immediately inform their Manager, who in turn should inform the Human Resources Department.

Provision of company cars

Company cars are provided to employees based on the following criteria:

Essential business need:

If a car is necessary to perform the employee's duties, and these cannot be performed economically by using a private car, a company car may be provided. It generally requires driving more than [ ] miles on business each year to qualify. The necessity to provide a car under such provision should be reviewed each year, and the car will be withdrawn if the business reason for its provision ceases to apply.

Additional benefit for Managers:

A car will be provided, if necessary, to remain competitive in the employment market. This benefit will normally apply to Managers. In this instance, we may also offer a cash alternative, which can be more beneficial to the employee for tax reasons if the vehicle is not used solely for business mileage. Please see 'Car Allowance' below. If you are authorised to use the vehicle for private use then this is limited to social and domestic purposes only. The vehicle may never be used for any outside business activity, or for racing, pace making, speed testing or rally activities.

All cars used for business purposes must be kept in a good, clean and roadworthy condition both inside and out. Failure to do so could result in disciplinary action.

Cars will normally be saloon or estate cars with four / five doors and be appropriate for business use; including customer visits and transportation. All company cars should be available for business use during normal hours.

Cars must be chosen and driven with substantial use in mind. Those with excessive running costs or reputation for poor resale value should be avoided. The normal replacement period is [ ] years.

APPROVAL PROCEDURE

It is the responsibility of each individual to seek approval for his or her Company vehicle, which should be sought from the [ ].

CAR LEASING LEVELS

Leasing limits are agreed with the employee on commencement of employment and reviewed on a regular basis.

Once the car has been leased, cars should not be altered or additional optional equipment added under any circumstances

Car allowance

If we agree to a cash alternative, the car allowance is equivalent to [ ]% of the monthly lease cost of the vehicle.

The car allowance does not count towards pensionable pay and does not count as salary for purposes of merit awards, bonuses etc. It remains the responsibility of the employee to inform Her Majesty's Revenue and Customs of any Company vehicle issued to them.

Business mileage

The employee may claim for business mileage in their private vehicle in accordance with the section 'Employee Owned Vehicles' below.

When we are paying a car allowance to an individual, in lieu of a Company car, the following become the absolute responsibility of the employee:

– lease or purchase of the private vehicle;

– appropriate insurance cover;

– maintenance, repair, MOT, road refund license, etc;

– contact with HMRC on tax allowances available for business use of a private vehicle.

Allowance for fuel

Drivers provided with a company car or cash allowance may reclaim fuel costs, in accordance with rates approved from time to time, via the standard expense reclaim procedure.

[Drivers provided with company cars for business **and** personal use will be issued with a Fuel card by the company. The Fuel card can be used to purchase only fuel and oil for the Company vehicle.]

Please note that the use of a car, or car and fuel for private purposes, is a taxable benefit and is liable for Income Tax and Employers' National Insurance Contributions.

Tax implications

Details of how cars are taxed may be obtained from HMRC's website – www.hmrc.gov.uk.

(A) EMPLOYEE-OWNED VEHICLE

If you use your own car for business use (this does not include travel to and from work) you are entitled to reclaim the appropriate business mileage rate from the Company. These rates are set by the Company, and compensated on a per mileage basis for fuel, wear and tear, insurance, depreciation, etc.

The Company determines the fuel reimbursement rate from time to time taking account of various factors, including petrol prices. The rates may be found [*identify where the rates may be found*]. Where a journey commences from home, the employee must deduct the usual mileage incurred when travelling to their place of work.

Those with cash allowances must make claims for petrol as a Company car user.

(B) ADDITIONAL INFORMATION

It remains the responsibility of each employee to keep records of Company mileage for HMRC, if required.

Selection of company cars available

In keeping with the Company's commitment to sustainable development, the range of cars available for selection by staff under a traditional Company car scheme will be restricted to those representing "best-in-class" environmental performance in each cost bracket. Cost will be assessed on the whole-life cost of the vehicle, while environmental performance will be assessed primarily on the following criteria:

- carbon monoxide and dioxide, sulphur dioxide and other emissions;

- fuel economy;

- the environmental policies of the manufacturer;

- any other relevant data available.

The permitted choice can be found [ ].

Insurance

We are responsible for the insurance of any Company car provided to employees either as a benefit or business need car. Employees taking up their entitlement to a Company car must hold a full driving licence, a copy of which must be provided to [the Human Resources Department]. [This is restricted to partner/spouse and any such individual must be over the age of 21 and produce a full driving licence.]

Details of any subsequent endorsements, prosecutions pending or disqualification must be notified to [the Human Resources Department] forthwith.

Driving licence checks will be undertaken on an annual basis by [the Human Resources Department.]

No mobile phone should be used in a Company car unless the correct hands-free equipment has been installed. All calls should be kept to an absolute minimum whilst driving.

Maintenance

We will bear the proper cost of all expenses incurred by employees in the maintenance of Company cars with the exception of cleaning costs.

Poor maintenance can reduce fuel efficiency by up to 30%, with significant implications for both running costs and the car's environmental impact. Employees must ensure that any car provided to them is regularly inspected and that any fault is attended to promptly. **UNDER NO CIRCUMSTANCES SHOULD ANY CAR BE DRIVEN IN AN UNSAFE, ILLEGAL OR UNROADWORTHY CONDITION.**

The employee is also responsible for ensuring that:

– Servicing takes place in accordance with manufacturers recommendations and the service agent stamps the service record;

– The vehicle is maintained in a clean and roadworthy condition, including tyres, lighting, bodywork, etc;

– The vehicle has the correct type of fuel, top-up fluids (oil, coolant and windscreen washer fluid) and correct tyre pressure;

– Cars are refuelled using only standard unleaded or diesel fuel – no premium fuels are to be used;

– A valid road fund licence is displayed and current MOT where relevant is in effect.

Fines and penalties

The employee is responsible for any fines or penalties incurred whilst the employee or any other driver authorised by them is in charge of the vehicle, whether the fine is imposed on the employee or on the Company. Employees will therefore be required to reimburse the Company for any payment the Company may make in respect of any fine. The Company may deduct such amounts from any salary or other sums owing to the employee.

The Company will reimburse normal parking charges (but not penalties) incurred whilst the vehicle is being used for business purposes. In no circumstances will the Company reimburse parking fines or penalties regardless of how they were incurred.

Personal safety guidance for drivers

Road rage

Road rage is an increasingly prominent feature of driving on Britain's roads today. Drivers should be alert for potentially dangerous situations and avoid them. When unavoidably encountering such a situation employees are advised to:

- not take your eyes off the road;

- avoid eye contact with an aggressive driver;

- stay calm – do not react or respond in any way to provocation;

- if annoyed by the driving or behaviour of another driver do not communicate in any way with that other driver, whether by gestures, mouthing words or otherwise;

- keep away from drivers behaving erratically.

Accidents

All accidents, whether or not the employee's fault, must be reported to the Company together with the condition of your vehicle as soon as practicable and in any event before the end of the next working day. You should complete an accident report form and then forward it to the Company within 24 hours. All the information required on the form must be completed. The following particulars should appear in the form:

- the name and address of the third party and the name and address of his/her insurers;

- the names and addresses of all passengers in both the Company vehicle and the third party's vehicle;

- names and addresses of all witnesses. It will be of considerable assistance if statements can be obtained from witnesses at the time of the accident;

- particulars of the police attending ie name, number and division; and

- a detailed sketch must be provided showing the relative position of the vehicle before and after the accident, together with details of the roads in the vicinity. Eg whether they are major or minor roads and as many relevant measurements as possible.

At no time must any statement be made which may be taken as an admission of guilt (eg sorry!). Only exchange the particulars above and nothing more. Please note also that no statements should be made to the police without written permission from the Company. This is particularly important in cases involving death or injury and leading to an inquest or inquiry as the driver will have to be legally represented and the Company would not wish to prejudice your position in any way.

If the vehicle is leased you must contact the appropriate leasing company to obtain permission to hire a similar replacement vehicle.

The Company reserves the right to deduct any insurance policy excess from any sums including salary due to you.

Security issues

Consider keeping your car doors locked and windows wound up in slow-moving traffic.

- always lock the doors when you leave the vehicle
- fill up with fuel regularly to avoid running out
- pull over to read maps and papers or to use a mobile phone
- beware of other drivers signalling faults about your vehicle; do not immediately stop, drive on slowly until it is safe to stop and check
- do not keep car and house keys together
- never leave the car unattended with the keys in the ignition

Breakdown guidance

Your vehicle should be serviced and maintained as per the driver's instructions in the manufacturers handbook. In the event of breakdown, you should refer to either the driver's handbook or Lease Company driver pack.

Employment termination

On the termination of employment, any Company vehicle should be returned to the Company in a clean and roadworthy condition on the last day of work, or such other date agreed in writing in advance with the Company.

Responsibility

Individual Managers are responsible for the implementation of this Policy within their own area. Any queries on the application or interpretation of this Policy must be discussed with [the Human Resources department] prior to any action being taken.

[The Human Resources department] has the responsibility for ensuring the maintenance, regular review and updating of this Policy.

This Policy will be open to review after a period of 12 months or, at an earlier stage if we have reason to question its effectiveness, spirit or fairness.

D22　EQUAL OPPORTUNITIES

D22.1　USE

The various Codes of Practice issued by the Disability Rights Commission, the Equal Opportunities Commission and the Commission for Racial Equality (now replaced by the Commission for Equality and Human Rights) recommend employers to have an Equal Opportunities Policy and to involve employees in the drafting and operation of the policy. This precedent should therefore be used as a draft for discussion with employees rather than something that is imposed by the employer.

Having such a policy should help employers ensure that discrimination does not occur in the first place. It should also help employers when defending tribunal complaints of discrimination. In order to be effective, however, it is important to communicate the policy to employers. This can be done:

– at induction, when employees are introduced to the workplace and their jobs;

– in the handbook;

– on notice boards;

– thorough training.

Employers must also ensure that the policy is followed. Having a policy and not following it is sometimes worse than not having a policy at all: any complaint of discrimination in an employment tribunal will be considerably strengthened if the employer has not followed its own procedure.

Most public authorities have a legal duty to promote equal opportunities both in employment and more generally. They are also responsible for any failures to promote equal opportunities of their contractors. For this reason, when putting work out to tender by private companies, public authorities need to take steps to satisfy themselves that the tenderers are able to comply with those duties; and there is generally a term in any contracting out document requiring compliance with those duties. Public authorities may, therefore, wish to expand this policy considerably. Private companies hoping to pick up work from public authorities are likely to find themselves excluded it they do not have a comprehensive equal opportunities policy.

D22.2 Precedent

Equal opportunities policy

General statement

[Employer] is committed to providing equal opportunities in employment. This means that all job applicants and employees will receive equal treatment regardless of race, colour, ethnic or national origin, sex, marital status, religion, belief, age, sexual orientation or disability. All job offers and promotions will be based on merit and suitability of the individual for the job in question.

Staff at all levels have a responsibility to see that this policy is observed.

Legislation

It is unlawful to discriminate against individuals either directly or indirectly in respect of their race, sex, marital status, sexual orientation, religion, belief, age or disability. The relevant legislation is a follows:

– the Race Relations Act 1976

– the Sex Discrimination Act 1975

– the Disability Discrimination Act 1995

– the Employment Equality (Religion or Belief) Regulations 2003 (SI 2003/1660)

– the Employment Equality (Sexual Orientation) Regulations 2003 (SI 2003/1661)

– Employment Equality (Age) Regulations 2006 (SI 2003/1031)

Codes of Practice relating to race, sex and disability discrimination have been produced by the Commission for Racial Equality, the Equal Opportunities Commission, the Government and the Law Society and have been used as the basis for this policy. There is also a Code of Good Practice on the Employment of Disabled Persons published by the Department of Employment (Training) which is reflected in this policy. The Company is fully committed to implementing these codes or any future codes which replace or amend those codes.

Although deliberate acts of discrimination will generally be regarded as a disciplinary matter, the Company encourages its employees to question their own actions and those of others to help to promote equality of opportunity and the absence of discrimination; and no adverse action, disciplinary or otherwise, will be taken against individuals who draw practices which may be discriminatory to the attention of the Company – even if those individuals were in part responsible for the discrimination.

Understanding some of the terms within the legislation

This is intended to be a summary of the relevant legislation. We have tried to keep this fairly short and straightforward. However, unlawful discrimination can generate complex problems and may not always be recognised as unlawful – particularly by those responsible for the discrimination. Therefore if you are not sure about a particular situation or practice which you think may be discriminatory, we recommend you consult [the Human Resources Department] rather than relying on this. Summary. If there are any discrepancies between the relevant legislation and this summary, the legislation will prevail.

Direct discrimination: Direct discrimination means less favourable treatment on one of the prohibited grounds. For example, it could include not putting somebody forward for training or promotion because of their race, sex etc.

Indirect discrimination: This means the application of a provision, criterion or practice which adversely affects members of the protected group (eg one sex, or those of a particular ethnic or national origin or those of a particular religion or belief etc).

The provision, criterion or practice in question is not indirect discrimination if it is a proportionate means of achieving a legitimate aim. For example:

- excluding part-time workers from certain benefits probably amounts to indirect sex discrimination since generally more women than men seek to work part-time;

- refusing a request from a female employee to change her hours from full-time to part-time may amount to a provision criterion or practice which adversely affects women. However, if the Company can demonstrate that there were sound reasons for the refusal amounting to a proportionate means of achieving a legitimate aim, then there will be no indirect discrimination. For example, it may be that the Company justifiably believes that the job cannot be done on a part-time basis;

- a blanket ban on beards in a food production or packaging factory may not be a proportionate means of meeting health and safety requirements if face masks could satisfactorily overcome health and safety risks and so could amount to indirect discrimination on grounds of race and/or religion;

- language requirements could amount to race discrimination unless an ability to speak a particular language or a high level of competence in English or any other language is an essential ingredient for a job (eg language teachers, interpreters).

Disability discrimination: Disability for the purposes of the discrimination legislation means any mental or physical impairment which has a substantial and long-term adverse effect on his or her ability to carry out day-to-day activities. An impairment is long-term if it has lasted for at least 12 months or can reasonably be expected to last for at least 12 months or is likely to last for the rest of the life of the person affected. Day-to-day activities mean the following:

- mobility (so people who use a wheelchair, or who cannot walk more than a short distance, or for any reason are unable to use public transport would be covered);

- manual dexterity (so conditions such as arthritis are likely to be covered);

- physical co-ordination;

- continence;

- ability to lift, carry or otherwise move everyday objects. Difficulty in moving large heavy objects would not count as a disability since lifting or carrying them would not be regarded as a day-to-day activity;

- memory or ability to concentrate, learn or understand;

- perception of risk of physical danger.

Less favourable treatment because of a person's disability amounts to direct discrimination which is likely to be unlawful. For example, a manager who is prejudiced against those with a mental impairment and as a result treats them less favourably than others directly discriminates on grounds of disability. This sort of discrimination cannot be justified.

Less favourable treatment for a reason related to disability (rather than the disability itself) does not amount to discrimination if it can be justified as a proportionate means of achieving a legitimate aim. For example, training for a position that requires physical strength may justifiably be refused for an employee who, because of a disability, does not have the requisite strength. The reason the training was refused was not the disability itself, but a reason related to the disability – ie physical strength.

Where any feature of the Company's premises or any arrangements the Company makes in relation to an employees working conditions places an employee at a disadvantage because of a disability that that person has, the Company is under an obligation to make such adjustments to the premises or working conditions as are reasonable to mitigate or eliminate that disadvantage.

For example, if it is practicable to do so, ramps will be provided for wheelchair users to ensure they have access to all areas of the premises they may wish to visit. Aids may be available for those who are visually impaired or have hearing difficulties. If you have a disability which you consider is putting you at a disadvantage in comparison with other employees, please discuss this with the Human resources Department who will then find out what aids are available or what adjustments could be made to the premises or working conditions to reduce the impact of or eliminate the disadvantage.

Victimisation: This means treating a person in an unfavourable way because they have complained, given information or brought legal proceedings about discrimination.

Harassment: Harassment on any of the prohibited grounds is also unlawful. Harassment for these purposes means unwanted conduct which has the purpose of violating a person's dignity or creating an intimidating, hostile, degrading, humiliating or offensive environment for that person. Sexual harassment also includes conduct of a sexual nature which has that effect, whether or not that was the purpose.

Equal opportunities training

Appropriate training will be provided to all employees about equal opportunities and the implementation of this policy. This policy will be explained to all employees at induction.

Recruitment, training and promotion

Recruitment and promotion are based on merit and suitability for the position in question, without regard to race, colour, ethnic or national origin, sex, marital status, religion, sexual orientation, age or disability.

To avoid indirect discrimination, all vacancies will generally be advertised internally and/or externally unless there is an obvious internal candidate or there is an urgent need for a temporary appointment pending a more rigorous selection process. We will not rely on 'word of mouth recruitment'.

Wherever possible, more than one person will be involved in short listing candidates, to reduce the chance of bias. Any marking or assessment system used will be determined beforehand and will be applied consistently. Each person involved in the process will assess candidates separately before meeting to agree a final mark or assessment for each candidate.

Short listing will then be on the basis of information provided in any job application forms, covering letters, CVs and, in the case of internal applicants, appraisal or assessment documents and disciplinary records.

Any tests used in the selection process [will be professionally validated and] will correspond to the levels of skill and the abilities required for the job.

Staff involved in interviews will receive equal opportunities training.

References will only be taken after selection for recruitment or promotion has been made, to avoid any risk of the selection process being influenced by the subjective views of third parties.

Monitoring and review

This policy will be monitored periodically by [the Human Resources Department] to review its effectiveness. Any changes required will be made when and where reasonably practicable. To facilitate monitoring, all job applicants will be asked to state their ethnic origin, religion, sexual orientation and whether or not they have a disability. No applicant is obliged to answer, but such answers as are given may be used for monitoring purposes only.

Recruitment, promotion, transfer and training records will be periodically examined to ensure that the Company's practices in relation to those matters are not prejudicing one sex, racial group etc. If it is so found, such steps as are reasonably practicable shall be taken to remedy the situation.

Similarly, instances of the use and outcomes of the disciplinary and grievance procedures will be monitored, in particular to see if members of a particular race, sex etc are using or being subjected to the policy more than others or if there is any evidence that the outcome is being influenced by such matters. If there does appear to be such an influence, the Company will take steps to try to understand what is causing that influence and how to remedy the situation.

Disciplinary procedure

Allegations of deliberate acts of discrimination or harassment on grounds of race, colour, ethnic or national origin, sex, marital status, religion or belief, sexual orientation, age or disability by employees of the company will be taken seriously and where appropriate will result in the application of the disciplinary procedure. If such discrimination is found to have occurred, appropriate disciplinary action will be taken. The policy applies to all who are employed in the Company.

What to do if you consider you are the victim of discrimination or harassment

The grievance procedure is available but in the first instance, it may be preferable to seek advice from [the Human Resources Department]. Sometimes an informal discussion with the person responsible may resolve the matter. If it does not, you should put your concerns in writing to [the Human Resources Department] who will investigate the complaint and attempt to reach a resolution of the matter.

The Company will treat seriously and take prompt action on any employee grievance concerning unlawful, unfair or unreasonable discrimination, victimisation or harassment on any prohibited ground. It will not be assumed that a person who complains on these grounds is being over-sensitive. If any employee considers he or she has a grievance as a result of discrimination or harassment on any prohibited ground, he or she should discuss the matter with [ ]. [ ] will then carry out such investigation or arrange for such investigation to be carried out as he or she considers appropriate, bearing in mind the need to keep such complaints confidential. If any individual employee is accused of discriminatory behaviour or harassment on any prohibited ground, that employee may be suspended on full pay during the investigation. Full details of the complaint must be given to such employee, who must be given an opportunity to answer the complaint under the normal disciplinary procedure. Following such investigation, the Company may:

- if the complaint is against an employee, try to resolve the situation amicably, bearing in mind that the complainant and employee may have to continue working together; and/or

- if satisfied that an employee is guilty of a deliberate act of discrimination, take appropriate disciplinary action; and/or

- if the situation cannot be resolved amicably, and it is not thought that disciplinary action is appropriate, transfer either the complainant or those against whom the complainant complains to another area of the Company. The complainant will not normally be transferred unless he or she agrees or it is concluded that the allegation of discrimination was made for some improper motive.

D22.3 DRAFTING POINTS

General statement: A general statement, even if vague and aspirational, nevertheless creates a positive image with job applicants, employees, public bodies and employment tribunals. As with the policy as a whole, however, a general statement will have little impact or benefit if it is not backed up by what happens in practice.

Legislation: It is helpful for employees to have a rudimentary understanding of the legislation. Without this some employees may not appreciate the seriousness of any breach of the equal opportunities legislation. Employers will, however, need to ensure that employees are not so over-concerned about discrimination that they do not disclose or, worse still, try to cover up acts of discrimination by themselves or others. The disciplinary procedure should, therefore, only generally be used for deliberate acts of discrimination. Ensuring that employees understand the basic terms of the legislation, therefore, should help employers distinguish inadvertent from deliberate discrimination.

For this reason, in this section of the policy, employers may wish to include examples of discrimination which they think are particularly likely to arise in the particular workplace.

The examples of indirect discrimination should be adapted to reflect the sorts of situations that could arise in the particular workplace.

Recruitment: Some of the requirements set out in this section may need to be relaxed or omitted for some employers. For example, only substantial employers are likely to have the time and resources to have any selection tests professionally validated; some smaller employers may not have the resources to allocate two managers to short-list in the way described here.

Word of mouth recruitment can be effective in some types of employment. Word of mouth recruitment is widely used, as are 'headhunters' who often use personal recommendation or information coming to them about individuals via word of mouth for the initial contact. Although the discouragement of word of mouth recruitment is included within all the statutory codes of practice, many employers still use 'word of mouth' methods at some stage in recruitment. Many employers encourage the use of word of mouth methods by offering bonuses to employees who introduce suitable candidates to the employer who are eventually appointed. Employers who do this often save thousands of pounds a year on fees for recruitment consultants. Employers who do so, or who use headhunters who do so, should either omit all reference to word of mouth recruitment within the policy, or state that word of mouth recruitment may be acceptable for senior positions or where a particularly suitable candidate has been identified.

Monitoring and review: Employers should only promise here what they are able to deliver. Monitoring to the extent set out in this policy would only be practicable for employers with a fully resourced Human Resources Department. Other employers should consider what monitoring, if any, is practicable.

Disciplinary procedure: Disciplinary action should generally only be taken in respect of deliberate acts of discrimination. However, even inadvertent acts of discrimination can damage morale and leave the employer open to costly discrimination complaints. Where discrimination is identified, even if inadvertent, the steps taken to remedy the situation should include training for employees or bringing to their attention by any other means the particular risk of discrimination, so that if such discrimination occurs thereafter, the employer can be more certain that it was deliberate.

Employers may, therefore, consider including within this section of the policy, examples of discrimination that any employer would regard as deliberate. This may include applying practices which have been identified in the section on indirect discrimination as discriminatory.

What to do if you consider you are the victim of discrimination or harassment: Some employers may have a separate harassment procedure. If they do, that procedure should be referred to in this section.

D23 PARENTAL LEAVE

D23.1 USE

This precedent sets out the main statutory provisions concerning parental leave. The governing regulations are the Maternity and Parental Leave etc Regulations 1999 (SI 1999/3312). Those regulations also set out in a schedule certain provisions which will apply unless an alternative procedure has been included within the contracts of employment of employees and within a collective or workforce agreement (see Division D2 of *Jordans Employment Law Service*). Those alternative provisions will therefore apply even if you include this precedent in a Handbook and even if this procedure is incorporated into the contracts of employment, unless the procedure has been agreed in a collective or workforce agreement.

A policy such as this one is therefore useful to inform employees of the rules on parental leave; and secondly to reflect any collective or workforce agreement reached in respect of parental leave.

D23.2   Precedent

Parental leave policy and entitlements

This Policy outlines the contents and scope of parental leave entitlements for employees. [It aims to summarise the provisions of the Maternity and Parental Leave etc Regulations 1999 (SI 1999/3312) or any amendments to or replacements of those regulations. Therefore if there are any discrepancies between the relevant regulations and this policy, the regulations will prevail.]

[The contents of this policy form part of your contractual terms of employment.]

Who may take parental leave?

Employees with one year's continuous employment may be eligible to take up to 13 weeks' unpaid parental leave in respect of each individual child provided that the employee:

- has parental responsibility for a child born on or after 15th December 1999;

- has adopted a child under the age of 18 on or after 15th December 1999, or

- has been registered as the child's father provided that the child was born or adopted on or after 15th December 1999.

Parental responsibility

The following are treated as having parental responsibility for a child:

- the child's natural mother and father if they were married to each other at the time of birth;

- the natural mother if the mother and father were not married to each other at the time of birth;

- the father if the court has made an order on the father's application that the father has parental responsibility;

- the father if he has been granted parental responsibility by a "parental responsibility agreement" (ie an agreement in prescribed form filed and sealed with the principal registry;

- the father if a court has made a residence order in favour of the father;

- any person who is appointed guardian of a child;

- any person in whose favour a residence order has been made, for so long as the order remains in force;

- a person who obtains a care order or an emergency protection order (but this is unlikely to be relevant, as such orders are usually obtained by organisations such as local authorities).

A person who is registered as a child's father may not have "parental responsibility" but still qualifies for the right to unpaid parental leave.

If you have already taken some parental leave with another or a previous employer, you should notify [ ] of how much parental leave you have already taken.

When parental leave can be taken

An employee is entitled to take parental leave until the child's 6th birthday, or where the child has been adopted, within the first five years of adoption but no later than the child's 18th birthday.

Parents of children with disabilities, who are entitled to disability living allowance, are permitted to take parental leave until the child's 18th birthday.

How to take parental leave

If you wish to take parental leave, you must inform [ ] of the dates that you want to take as parental leave at least 21 days before the date on which the parental leave is to begin.

Parental leave can only be taken in minimum blocks of one week. If you choose to take less than one week of parental leave, you will nevertheless be treated as taking one full week of parental leave. However, if you are a parent of a disabled child (who is eligible for disability living allowance), you do not have to take leave in minimum blocks of one week, and are entitled to take leave in minimum blocks of one day.

For those who work regular hours each week, (eg 9.00 – 5.00 five days a week), one week's leave is simply leave during the times when that employee is required to work.

For those whose working hours vary from week to week, one week's leave is equal to the total time the employee is normally required, under the contract of employment, to work over a year divided by 52.

Employees are only permitted to take a maximum of four weeks' parental leave in respect of each individual child in any one-year period.

Expecting parents

If you are expecting to be a father of a child, and wish to take parental leave beginning on the date that the child is born, you must notify your employer of the expected week of childbirth and the duration of the period of leave requested at least 21 days before the beginning of the expected week of childbirth.

If you expect to adopt a child, and wish to take parental leave beginning on the date that a child is placed with you for adoption, you must notify your employer of the week in which the placement is expected as well as the duration of the leave requested at least 21 days before the beginning of that week, or where this is not reasonably practicable, as soon as is reasonably practicable.

Alternatively, you may wish to take paternity leave. This is limited to two weeks and must be taken within eight weeks of birth or adoption but paternity leave is paid. Or you can take both parental leave and paternity leave. For details of your rights to paternity leave and pay, see the Company's Paternity Leave Policy.

Proof of entitlement

You may not take any parental leave unless you have provided sufficient evidence indicating:

- your responsibility or expected responsibility for the child in respect of which you wish to take parental leave;

- the child's date of birth, or if the child has been adopted, the date on which the child was placed for adoption; and

- details of the child's entitlement to disability living allowance where appropriate.

Exceptions

Although we will always try to accommodate your request to take parental leave, where your absence would cause undue disruption to the business, your requested leave may be postponed after consultation with you for up to 6 months from the date the parental leave would have started under the original request. Factors which might contribute towards a decision to postpone the parental leave could include a peak business period or a peak absence period, the level of the employee's skill and responsibility or the difficulty in finding a short-term replacement or covering the absence by other means.

Where your request for leave is postponed, you will be notified in writing no later than 7 days after we have received your request for leave. The notice will state the reason for the postponement and will specify dates during which the employer will permit you to take parental leave.

Leave will not be postponed in cases where an expectant parent wishes to take leave beginning on the expected week of childbirth or placement for adoption provided that the above requirements have been complied with.

Rights and duties during parental leave

The only rights of an employee which continue during parental leave are:

- terms entitling the employee to give notice of termination of employment;

- terms about compensation in the event of redundancy; and

- rights under the disciplinary or grievance procedure.

There is no right to remuneration during parental leave.

The only duties which continue are the duty of good faith and any duties not to disclose confidential information or to participate in any other business.

Our right to terminate employment by giving notice and any terms regulating the acceptance of gifts or other benefits also continue during parental leave.

Please do not hesitate to contact [ ] if you have any questions regarding your entitlement to parental leave.

D23.3 DRAFTING POINTS

Contractual or non-contractual? The policy will have to be contractual if it is intended to supplant the rules set out in the schedule to the 1999 Regulations. This policy can only do so if it is incorporated into a contract of employment (the purpose of the second section in square brackets at the start of the policy) and if it has been agreed in a collective or workforce agreement. You should try to make the policy contractually enforceable if there are any additional rules you want to impose about taking parental leave – for example you may wish to prohibit parental leave at certain times of year or at times when annual leave is not permitted.

If the policy is not intended to be contractual, then this policy does no more than explain the relevant statutory provisions. In that case it is better to say that the policy is in fact just a summary of the statutory provisions so that, if there are any discrepancies between this policy and the regulations, or if subsequent cases interpret the regulations differently from this policy, the regulations will prevail. This is the purpose of the first section in square brackets at the start of the policy.

Therefore, if you want to include rules about parental leave that do not appear in the regulations (summarised in this policy) you should:

– agree those rules in a collective or workforce agreement; and

– include the second section in square brackets but not the first section in square brackets.

If you do not want to include any other rules, then you should:

– include the first section in square brackets but not the second.

D24 MATERNITY

D24.1 USE

This precedent summarises the statutory rules on maternity leave and pay. Employers may provide employees with greater rights than those granted by statute but may not reduce those rights.

D24.2 Precedent

Maternity rules and policy

The following is a summary of the statutory rights to maternity leave and maternity pay. Legislation is updated from time to time so if there is any discrepancy between the legislation (including regulations) and this summary, the legislation will prevail (except where indicated otherwise in these rules).

Time off for ante-natal care

All women expecting the birth of a child are entitled to paid time off to keep an appointment for ante-natal care regardless of whether or not they qualify for maternity leave.

After the first appointment, this right will depend upon you producing, on request, a certificate stating that you are pregnant and the relevant appointment card.

Where it is possible to do so, you should arrange appointment times at the start or the end of the working day in order to minimise disruption to work.

Statutory maternity leave

Any woman expecting the birth of a child, irrespective of the length of service and the hours normally worked, is entitled to take a period of 26 weeks Ordinary Maternity Leave and 26 weeks Additional Maternity Leave, making a total on one year's leave.

Additional Maternity Leave will commence on the day after the last day of Ordinary Maternity Leave.

BENEFITS

During Ordinary and Additional Maternity Leave, contractual benefits, except for remuneration, will be maintained.

Employees have the right not to be victimised at work or suffer detrimental treatment on the grounds of pregnancy, childbirth or maternity.

Date Maternity Leave Starts

You may choose to begin your maternity Leave at any time during the 11 weeks before the expected week of childbirth (EWC).

The statutory maternity leave period is automatically triggered if you are absent from work for a pregnancy-related reason during the 4 weeks before the EWC.

If the child is born before the EWC, the maternity leave will start on the day following the date of childbirth.

Notification

1. You must notify the company of the week you expect your leave to start not later than 15 weeks before the EWC, or as soon as is reasonably practicable if you are unable to give notice then. In order to exercise your right to return after maternity leave you must notify the company of:

   - the fact that you are pregnant;

   - your EWC (or the actual date of birth if this has already occurred);

   - the date you wish the leave to start.

The Company may request to see a medical certificate from your doctor, or midwife confirming your EWC.

Return to work

Ordinary Maternity Leave

At the end of your Ordinary Maternity Leave, you have the right to return to the position you held before leaving, on terms and conditions not less favourable than those which would have applied had you not been absent.

In the unlikely event we have to make your position redundant, we will offer you, if available, a suitable alternative position.

Additional Maternity Leave

Following Additional Maternity Leave you will be entitled to return to the same position you held before leaving, unless this is not reasonably practicable, in which case you will be offered an alternative suitable and appropriate position.

Two or more consecutive leave periods

If you return following two consecutive periods of maternity leave, in respect of two separate births, you will have the right to return to a position which is not less favourable in respect of seniority and all other rights, than the position which you held before leaving.

You may not return to work before the end of the two weeks following the date of childbirth. [4 weeks for factory workers].

You must give at least eight weeks' notice if you wish to return to work before the end of the additional maternity leave period. If the eight weeks' notice is not given the Company may postpone your return date, to ensure that eight weeks' notice is provided. If you return to work before the postponed date, the Company does not have to pay you.

The period of maternity leave (ordinary or additional) may not be extended in any circumstances but other periods of leave (eg sickness, holidays or parental leave) may be added to the end.

You may not return to work before the end of the two weeks following the EWC.

Statutory maternity pay

You are eligible for Statutory Maternity Pay if you have been continuously employed by the company for 26 weeks by the end of the 15th week before the EWC and you are still employed by the company at the beginning of the 11th week before EWC.

To qualify you must have average earnings at or above the lower earnings limit for the payment of National Insurance contributions.

Statutory Maternity Pay is paid for a maximum of 39 weeks.

The first six weeks of Statutory Maternity Pay is payable at a higher rate which is equivalent to 90% of your average weekly earnings. The remaining 33 weeks are paid at whichever value is the lowest of the following: £117.18 a week (this is the rate for the year to 31 March 2009 but this amount is increased each year), or 90% of your weekly wage. [However, the Company will pay 90% of your normal earnings for a period of [ ] weeks, after which you will revert to statutory maternity pay. This right is over and above the right conferred by legislation.]

Statutory Maternity Pay generally begins at the same time as Ordinary Maternity Leave commences and is subject to deductions for tax and National Insurance contributions.

Keep in touch days

You can agree to work for the Company or agree to attend training, for up to 10 days during the maternity leave period. These can be 10 consecutive or individual days. You are encouraged to keep in touch with the Company during maternity leave. This has been found to make return to work a lot easier. Any day during maternity leave when an employee either works under her contract of employment, or attends for training to keep in touch, are known as "Keep in Touch Days".

You will be paid your basic salary for any keep in touch days, but this will be off-set against your SMP for that day. Part of any day worked will be paid on a pro-rata basis.

Keep in touch days can be worked without bringing the period of maternity leave to an end and without any loss to SMP payments.

To apply to use a keep in touch day you should contact your manager in the first instance in order to discuss and arrange work activity, seek authorisation and in some instances to review the current risk assessment. General social visits by you will not be recognised by the Company's keep in touch days.

The Company does not have to offer these days and nor will you be obliged to agree to accept work offered. Any keep in touch days worked do not extend the period of maternity leave. No more than 10 days are allowed to be worked without loss to SMP.

Reasonable contact between you and the Company is encouraged throughout maternity leave and either party is entitled to make contact from time to time without affecting the right to SMP.

D24.3 DRAFTING POINTS

If you grant greater rights than those set out in the legislation, those rights should be included in this policy. For example, many employers pay full pay of 90% of earnings for longer than the statutory six weeks. If you do grant greater rights, then you should indicate where appropriate that these rights are over and above those granted by legislation. For example, if you pay 90% of earnings for the first six months of maternity leave, you should include the sentence within square brackets in the 'maternity pay' section.

The same is true of any other rights you may wish to grant which are over and above those granted by legislation.

D25 PATERNITY LEAVE

D25.1 USE

This precedent summarises the statutory rules on paternity leave and pay. Employers may provide employees with greater rights than those granted by statute but may not reduce those rights.

D25.2 Precedent

Paternity leave policy

The following is a summary of the legislation and is not intended to confer any rights over and above those conferred by legislation. If there is any conflict between these rules and the legislation, the legislation will prevail.

Fathers are entitled to take two weeks' paid leave, at the rate of Statutory Maternity Pay ("SMP"), as long as they meet certain criteria.

Eligibility

To be entitled to paternity leave you must:

- Have 26 weeks' service at the end of the 15th week before the Expected Week of Confinement ("EWC"), or (in adoption cases) by the week when an approved adoption agency matches you, or your partner with a child; and

- Have an enduring family relationship with the child and with the mother, or other adoptive parent or be the biological father of the child, or be married to, or be the partner of the child's mother, and;

- Have or expect to have, responsibility for the upbringing of the child.

Leave entitlement

You may choose to take either one week's leave, or two consecutive weeks' leave. The leave may only be taken during the period that begins with the date the child is born, or placed for adoption, and 56 days after that date.

If you have chosen to begin your period of leave on the date of birth and you are at work that day your period of leave begins on the day after that date.

Notification

You are required to give notice of the intention to take paternity leave in or before the 15th week before the EWC; or 28 days before the placement of an adoptive child, or as soon as is reasonably practical.

The notice of intention to take paternity leave must specify:

- The EWC or date of placement;

- The length of the period of leave that you have chosen to take (ie either one or two weeks);

- The date you wish your leave to commence.

If you have notified your wish to take leave from the date of the birth you may do so whenever that occurs. If you wish to vary the request you must provide notice 28 days before the EWC or date of placement, or as soon as is reasonably practicable.

If you have provided a fixed start date for leave you must give 28 days' notice if you wish to change the date or notify us as soon as reasonably practicable.

If you have chosen to specify that your leave should commence a set number of days after the child's birth, to change this date you must give 28 days' notice from the specified number of days after the first day of the EWC, or as soon as is reasonably practicable.

Paternity pay

- In order to qualify for SPP you must have average weekly earnings at or above the lower earnings limit for National Insurance.

- Statutory Paternity Pay (SPP) is the lower Statutory Maternity Pay rate, currently £117.18 (this is the rate for the year to 31 March 2009 but this amount is increased each year). [However, the Company will pay your full normal earnings for a paternity leave period. This right is over and above the right conferred by legislation.]

Return to work

An employee who returns to work after a period of paternity leave is normally entitled to return to the position in which he or she was employed before his or her absence. However if:

- The paternity leave is combined with Additional Maternity leave, Additional Adoption leave or Parental Leave of more than four weeks duration and;

- It is not reasonably practicable to permit the employee to return to his/her old job,

the employee is entitled to return to another job, which is both suitable and appropriate with seniority, pension rights and similar rights regarding terms and conditions, which are not less favourable than those before.

We may request that you provide a signed declaration, stating the purpose of your absence and why you are entitled to such an absence.

You have the right not to suffer detrimental treatment because you took or sought to take Paternity Leave.

D25.3   DRAFTING POINTS

If you grant greater rights than those set out in the legislation, those rights should be included in this policy. For example, many employers pay full pay during paternity leave. If you do grant greater rights, then you should indicate where appropriate that these rights are over and above those granted by legislation. For example, if you pay full pay for the period of the paternity leave, you should include the sentence within square brackets in the 'paternity pay' section.

The same is true of any other rights you may wish to grant which are over and above those granted by legislation.

D26 ADOPTION LEAVE

D26.1　USE

This precedent summarises the statutory rules on adoption leave and pay. Employers may provide employees with greater rights than those granted by statute but may not reduce those rights.

D26.2　　　　　　　　Precedent

Adoption leave policy

The following is intended to be a summary of the legislation on adoption leave and is not intended to confer any rights over and above those conferred by legislation [except where indicated]. If there is any conflict between these rules and the legislation, the legislation will prevail.

Entitlement

Adoptive parents who have at least 26 weeks' continuous employment are now entitled to Adoption Leave. This right only applies in relation to children whose match is notified to the prospective adopter on or after 6 April 2003, or children placed for adoption on or after that date. (Adoption leave and pay is not available in circumstances where a child is not newly matched for adoption, for example when a step-parent is adopting a partner's child).

The adoption leave lasts for 52 weeks, consisting of 26 weeks' ordinary adoption leave ('OAL') and a further 26 weeks additional adoption leave ('AAL') for the person adopting the child (the "adopter").

Only one person may take adoption leave in respect of a child at any one time; so where a couple proposes to adopt a child jointly, one may take adoption leave but the other may only take paternity leave.

Eligibility

Employees with 26 weeks continuous employment by the week in which the approved adoption agency matches the adoptive parent with the child will qualify for OAL and AAL. The adoptive parent must also have notified the agency that he or she agrees that the child should be placed with him or her and the date of the placement. The placement of more than one child still has the same leave entitlement.

The Company may ask the adoptive parent to provide evidence in the form of documents issued by the adoption agency specifying details of the child, the placement and the adoption agency.

D26   Adoption Leave

Date of commencement

You can choose to begin OAL on the date on which the child is placed for adoption or a predetermined date which is no more than 14 days before the child is expected to be placed with you and no later than the expected date of placement.

Notification

You must notify the company of your intention to take OAL no more than seven days after the date on which you are notified of having been matched with the child for the purposes of adoptions or as soon as is reasonably practicable.

The notice must specify:

- The date on which the child is expected to be placed with you for adoption; and

- The date on which you have chosen that your period of leave should begin.

The above notice of intention to take OAL, should be given in writing to your line manager.

If you wish to vary the OAL as notified to the company, you must give 28 days' notice before the date on which the child was expected to be placed with you for adoption, or as soon as is reasonably practicable or where you have chosen to begin the period of leave on a predetermined date 28 days before the predetermined date specified in the notice

Within 28 days of receiving a notice of intention to take adoption leave the company will write to you stating your expected date of return.

Notification of return

If you intend to return to work earlier than the end of your AAL you must give the Company at least 28 days' notice of the date on which you intend to return. If you fail to do so the Company may postpone your return until the requirement for 28 days' notice is fulfilled. If you return before the 28 days' notice is complete the company is not required to pay contractual remuneration for any work done before the end of the 28 days.

On return from a period of OAL you are normally entitled to return to the position you were employed in before the absence. However, if:

- the OAL is combined with additional maternity leave, additional adoption leave or parental leave of more than 4 weeks; and

- it is not reasonably practicable to permit you to return to your old job, then you will be allowed to return to another job which is both suitable for you and appropriate for you to do in the circumstances.

Keep in touch days

You can agree to work for the Company or agree to attend training, for up to 10 days during the adoption leave period. These can be 10 consecutive or individual days. You are encouraged to keep in touch with the Company during adoption leave. This has been found to make return to work a lot easier. Any day during adoption leave when an employee either works under her contract of employment, or attends for training to keep in touch, are known as "Keep in Touch Days".

You will be paid your basic salary for any keep in touch days, but this will be off-set against your SAP for that day. Part of any day worked will be paid on a pro-rata basis.

Keep in touch days can be worked without bringing the period of adoption leave to an end and without any loss to SAP payments.

To apply to use a keep in touch day you should contact your manager in the first instance in order to discuss and arrange work activity, seek authorisation and in some instances to review the current risk assessment. General social visits by you will not be recognised by the Company's keep in touch days.

The Company does not have to offer these days and nor will you be obliged to agree to accept work offered. Any keep in touch days worked do not extend the period of adoption leave. No more than 10 days are allowed to be worked without loss to SAP.

Reasonable contact between you and the Company is encouraged throughout adoption leave and either party is entitled to make contact from time to time without affecting the right to SAP.

Statutory Adoption Pay (SAP)

Statutory Adoption Pay (SAP) will be paid for the first 39 weeks only. The weekly rate of SAP is the smaller of £117.18 (this is the rate for the year to 31 March 2009 but this amount is increased each year), or 90% of your normal weekly earnings. [However, the Company will pay 90% of your normal earnings for a period of [ ] weeks, after which you will revert to statutory adoption pay. This right is over and above the right conferred by legislation.] Adopters who have average weekly earnings below the Lower Earnings Limit for National Insurance Contributions will not qualify for SAP.

You have the right not to suffer detrimental treatment because you took or sought to take Adoption Leave.

D26.3 DRAFTING POINTS

If you grant greater rights than those set out in the legislation, those rights should be included in this policy. For example, many employers pay full pay of 90% of earnings for longer than the statutory six weeks. If you do grant greater rights, then you should indicate where appropriate that these rights are over and above those granted by legislation. For example, if you pay 90% of earnings for the first six months of adoption leave, you should include the sentence within square brackets in the 'maternity pay' section.

D27 FLEXIBLE WORKING

D27.1 USE

Employers are now required to consider applications for flexible working from any employee to enable that employee to care for children up to the age of six, disabled children up to the age of 18 or certain categories of dependent adults. For details, see Division C4 of *Jordans Employment Law Service*.

This precedent explains the statutory rules so that managers and employees know of these rights and the correct procedure to follow. Employers may provide greater rights than those granted by the legislation.

D27.2 Precedent

Flexible working policy

> Employees with at least six months' continuous employment have the right to request a change in their terms and conditions of employment to enable them to work on a more flexible basis in order to care for a child or for a dependent adult. The Company recognises that at various stages in employees' working lives, personal and family commitments may conflict with their ability to fulfil all their work responsibilities. Where these conflicts are not easily resolved, flexible working may provide the solution.
>
> The following procedure sets out who is entitled to this right and how to apply for it. It summarises the relevant legislation. Legislation is amended from time to time so if there is any discrepancy between the provisions of the relevant legislation and this summary, the relevant legislation shall prevail [except where otherwise indicated].
>
> [You are encouraged to use the Forms included at the end of this Handbook. Copies are available from [the Human Resources Department]]

To qualify for this right an employee must

> (In relation to applications to care for a child under the age of 6):
>
> a. have been continuously employed for a period of not less than six months;
>
> b. be either:
>
> > i. the mother, father, adopter, guardian, special guardian or foster parent of the child; or
> >
> > ii. married to or the partner or civil partner of anyone listed in paragraph i; and

c. have, or expect to have, responsibility for the upbringing of the child;

d. make the application before the 6th birthday of the child in question or 18th birthday if the child is disabled.

(in relation to applications to care for a dependent adult):

a. have been continuously employed for a period of not less than six months; and

b. be:

　　i. married to the dependant adult or be the dependant adult's civil partner or partner; or

　　ii. a close relative (ie parent, child, spouse, sibling, aunt, uncle or grandparent, including step, in-law and adoptive relationships); or

　　iii. living at the same address as the dependant adult.

All eligible employees wishing to make an application should do so in accordance with this policy.

What can be requested?

An eligible employee can apply to the Company for a change to be made to one or all of the following:

a. the hours he or she is required to work;

b. the times he or she is required to work;

c. where, as between home and a place of business of the employer, he or she is required to work.

The purpose of the application must be to enable the eligible employee to care for the child or dependant adult.

The Application

The employee's application for flexible working must:

a. be in writing;

b. be made to [the Human Resources Department];

c. state whether a previous application has been made by the employee and if so when;

d. specify the change applied for and the date on which it is proposed the change should become effective;

e. explain what effect if any the employee thinks making the change requested would have on the Company and how, in his opinion any such effect might be dealt with;

f. explain how the employee meets in relation to the child or dependant adult concerned the conditions as set out under the eligibility criteria of this policy;

g. be dated.

Once an application has been made and considered, the employee may not make a further application for 12 months from the date the previous application was made.

Receipt of an application

Within 28 days of the receipt of this application (or longer if agreed or if the relevant manager is not available during that time) the Company will either agree the application or arrange a meeting with the applicant to discuss the application. The employee is entitled to be accompanied by a colleague. This colleague will be entitled to address the meeting and to confer with the employee during the meeting. The time and place of this meeting will be convenient to all attending parties.

Notification of a decision

Within 14 days of the date of the meeting (or longer if agreed) the Company will inform the employee of its decision.

This notification must:

a. be in writing;

b. (if the decision is to agree to the application) specify the contract variation agreed to and state the date on which this variation is to take effect, the length of any trial period, (if there is to be a trial period) the fact that the agreement to vary the terms will not be finalised until the end of the trial period and the date (if any) on which it is agreed that the contract variation will end;

c. (if the decision is to refuse the application):

– state the grounds for refusal;

– explain why those grounds apply to this case; and

– set out the appeal procedure including the name of the person who will consider any appeal This person should be different from the person who dealt with the initial decision e g next level up or Head of Human Resources;

d. be dated.

E-mail will suffice for the purposes of this notification.

Duration of variation

The agreed variation will last until a further agreement is made to vary the contract or for the period (if any) it has been agreed that the contract variation will last. At the end of this period the employee will return to the terms and conditions of employment that existed before the variation unless otherwise agreed.

If the employee continues to satisfy the eligibility criteria then they may make a fresh application for the variation to continue. This new application can be made during the lifetime of the current variation. Due to the time-scale involved an employee would be advised to make such an application at least two months prior to the period coming to an end. Any new application will be considered in line with this policy. There is no guarantee that such a request will be granted.

Trial periods

The arrangement may be subject to a trial period of up to three months. If either party concludes during that trial period that the arrangement is not working, it may submit to the other party proposals for amending or terminating the arrangement setting out reasons why that party believes the arrangement is not working. A meeting will be held within 28 days of submitting the proposal to discuss it or longer if agreed or if the relevant manager is not available. Employer and employee will discuss the proposed changes and the reasons for them with a view to reaching agreement. If no agreement is reached, the arrangement may be terminated by the either party and the employee will revert to the working pattern in place before the last variation.

If the employer decides to return to the previous working pattern, it must notify the employee in writing giving reasons, which must fall within one of the permitted grounds for refusing applications. The employee may appeal within 14 days of receiving notification. An appeal hearing will be held within 14 days after that. At all meetings, the employee has a right to be accompanied.

Grounds for refusal

The application will only be refused if one or more of the following grounds apply:

a. the burden of additional costs;

b. there is a detrimental effect on the ability to meet customer demands;

c. inability to reorganise work of existing staff;

d. inability to recruit additional staff;

e. detrimental impact on quality;

f. detrimental effect on performance;

g. insufficiency of work during the periods the employee proposes to work; or

h. planned structural changes.

Appeal

Employees who are dissatisfied with the Company's decision may appeal. To exercise this right the employee must submit a notice, which must:

a. be in writing;

b. be made to the person named in the employee's written notification of decision;

c. set out the grounds of appeal; and

d. be dated.

Upon receipt of this notice of appeal the Company will arrange a meeting to discuss the appeal within 14 days of this notice. The employee is entitled to be accompanied by a colleague. This colleague will be entitled to address the meeting and to confer with the employee during the meeting. The time and place of this meeting will be convenient to all attending parties.

The Company must then notify the employee of the decision of the appeal within 14 days of the date of the meeting. This notice will:

a. be in writing;

b. state whether or not the Company upholds the appeal;

c. (where the appeal is allowed) the contract variation agreed to and the date upon which it is to take effect, the length of any trial period, (if there is to be a trial period) the fact that the agreement to vary the terms will not be finalised until the end of the trial period and the date (if any) on which it is agreed that the contract variation will end; or

d. where the appeal is dismissed the grounds for this decision and a sufficient explanation of why these grounds apply;

e. be dated.

D27.3 DRAFTING POINTS

Employers may wish to grant rights over and above those granted by the legislation. For example, the legislation does not currently permit flexible working requests in respect of children aged between 6 and 18 who are not disabled. If so, the conditions for qualifying for the right should be amended so that the age of '6' is substituted by a higher age. There should then be a sentence as follows:

> 'This right is more generous than that permitted by legislation, which only permits applications for flexible working to care for able-bodied children up to the age of 6.'

Without this sentence, there will be a discrepancy between this policy and the legislation so that, according to the opening paragraph, the policy will be overridden by the legislation.

D28 SMOKING

D28.1 USE

The Health Act 2006 requires employers to ensure that smoking does not take place within buildings and within vehicles. Furthermore, permitting smoking could cause non-smokers to have to breath smoke which could damage their health. The employer could then be held responsible for that health damage.

For these reasons, employers may wish to introduce a 'smoke-free policy'. If there has been no such policy previously, employers may be expected to provide assistance to those employees who smoke and may find it hard to adapt. If employers fail to provide assistance, then any dismissals as a result of enforcing the policy could be unfair. The sort of assistance that might be provided could include:

– giving plenty of notice of the introduction of the policy;

– directing employees to appropriate sources of help;

– providing areas where and times when smoking is permitted. Under the Health Act 2006, these areas may not be inside buildings – a 'building' is defined in the legislation and includes most structures.

Policies such as this are more likely to be observed if they are negotiated with employees or their representatives; or at least if they follow a period of consultation with the workforce. The policy could not then be challenged on the ground that it is being imposed by management without regard to the wishes of the workforce.

D28.2 Precedent
Smoke-free policy

Introduction

> Second-hand exposure to tobacco smoke is now believed to be a risk factor for lung cancer, heart disease and other illnesses in non-smokers. Smoking is also a fire hazard.
>
> This policy has been developed [following consultation with employee representatives,] to protect all employees, customers and visitors from exposure to second-hand smoke, to help us to comply with the Health Act 2006 effective 1 July 2007 in England and to avoid fire risks.
>
> This Policy will come into force on [*date*].
>
> Failure to comply with this policy may lead to disciplinary action up to and including dismissal.

Restrictions

Smoking will not be permitted at any time in any area of the Company's premises either inside or outside [except in areas specifically designated as smoking areas].

Vehicles

Smoking will **not** be permitted in Company vehicles at any time.

Smoking will **not** be permitted in an employee's own vehicle whilst being used for business purposes where passengers are carried.

Smoking will **not** be permitted in an employee's own vehicle or by visitors and contractors in their vehicles whilst in work car parks.

Communication of the Policy

The contents of this policy will be communicated as follows:

– at induction sessions for new employees;

– using 'no smoking signs' inside the premises and within vehicles used on Company business. [The Company Car policy explains the rules about smoking in cars and the signs within cars that are required];

– visitors badges/passes for contractors and other visitors will set out a summary of this policy.

Help for those who smoke

It is recognised that the Smoke-Free policy could be challenging for those who smoke.

Any employee who smokes and requires support to comply with the policy or wishes to stop smoking is encouraged to seek guidance and assistance. They should speak to [the Human Resources Department] for any information regarding support available.

Other sources of support include Smokeline 0800 848484, www.can-stopsmoking.com, the Public Health Department, your local NHS PCT or your local GP surgery.

Enforcement

Although the Company will be sympathetic towards those who will have to adapt in order to comply with this policy, it believes it has provided appropriate assistance to any employee who needs it. Therefore, unless there are special reasons, anyone failing to observe the Smoke-Free policy may be subject to disciplinary action up to and including dismissal. Failure to observe the policy will be seen as a serious breach and treated as Gross Misconduct which could lead to Summary Dismissal.

The company will endeavour to support employees through the transitional period through education and counselling.

Further information

Please contact [the Human Resources Department] which has overall responsibility for the implementation of this policy should you have any further queries in relation to this policy.

D29 SICKNESS

D29.1 USE

This precedent sets out rules to apply for informing employees about when the employer may contemplate terminating employment on grounds of long-term or persistent absenteeism and on the payment of sick pay.

Clarifying the rules on when you might consider terminating employment will help in defending unfair dismissal claims on grounds of ill health; and disability discrimination claims arising from termination of employment or the issue of warnings for long-term and persistent absence.

It will also help when seeking to justify non-payment of sick pay.

These rules could be set out in a Handbook or in a separate policy. Entitlement to sick pay is generally a contractual right, so the rules on sickness absence reporting and on sick pay should be referred to in the contract or statement of main terms of employment. It is permissible to refer in the contract or statement of terms to a separate document such as a Company Handbook or policy – see for example the precedent contract of employment and precedent statement of terms of employment.

D29.2 Precedent

Long-term or persistent absences for illness or injury

> The Company will be sympathetic to health problems experienced by employees. However, this has to be balanced against the needs of the business and any difficulty the Company experiences with high levels of absenteeism.
>
> The Company expects you to co-operate by providing as much information as possible to enable it to cope with your absence and make arrangements to cope with your absence. In particular, you should:
>
> – remain in regular contact with your line manager to provide any information requested which may help others to carry out any duties that you are unable to carry out;
>
> – provide as much information as you can about the nature and likely duration of your illness;
>
> – inform your line manager if you consider there are any duties you could still carry out while off sick or whether any temporary changes could be made to your duties, hours of work or working conditions which you think might enable you to return to work earlier than if those changes were not made.

[Sick pay

[The Company pays full sick pay for a limited period set out in your [contract of employment/ statement of main terms and conditions of employment], but that is conditional on your complying with the requirements of this policy. If you do not comply, full sick pay may be refused but you will still be entitled to statutory sick pay. If for any reason you are unable to comply with these requirements, for example because the nature of your illness makes it difficult or impossible for you to comply, you should do whatever you reasonably can do towards compliance – for example, asking others such as a relative, friend, neighbour, colleague or trade union representative to provide information to the Company.]

or

[The Company may in its absolute discretion pay full sick pay for a limited period. Unless there are exceptional circumstances, this will not be for longer than [ ] weeks. The matters which the Company will take into account when exercising this discretion are the length of the absence, any other absences within the previous 12 months, the reasons for the absence and the extent to which you have complied with these rules.]

Long-term absences

Generally, we try to cope with absences by asking other employees to share some of the responsibility for the absent employee's work. This is not a satisfactory solution if the absence continues for more than about 14 days. We may then have to use agency staff or engage another employee on a temporary basis.

Depending on the nature of the work and the current workload, this solution may be satisfactory for a period of up to about 3 months, but it is unsatisfactory in the long run because agency and temporary staff may not have the experience of full-time staff, it may not be possible to guarantee that the same agency or temporary staff will be available throughout the whole period of absence and sometimes it is easier to obtain high quality workers by offering permanent rather that temporary work.

For this reason, after 3 months continuous absence (or earlier in the case of key positions), the Company may have to consider engaging a permanent replacement which could result in our having to terminate your employment. We will only do so, however, after taking the following steps:

1. Asking you for your permission to approach your GP and thereafter approaching your GP for a report.

2. If the report does not provide sufficient information for us to judge how long you are likely to be off work, or whether it would be possible for you to return to work on light duties, or if you disagree with your GP's report, we may ask you to attend an examination with an independent medical practitioner. The Company will pay for this examination.

3. Once we have the doctor's report and/or the independent medical practitioner's report (if any), we will invite you to attend a meeting to discuss the situation generally and to explore the possible options to cope with your continued absence. The medical reports should indicate whether there are any steps we could take to cope with your absence or to enable you to return to work perhaps on reduced duties or reduced hours. At the end of the meeting, the Company will decide what action to take. This action may be:

   a. to take no action at present but to review the situation again after a further specified period;

   b. to allow you to return on light duties on a trial basis;

   c. terminate your employment, but if this happens, it will normally be on the basis that if you re-applied for employment when fit, your application would be viewed favourably;

   d. any other action which the Company considers appropriate.

4. If you disagree with the decision that the Company decides to take, you will have a right of appeal to the Managing Director or, if the Managing Director was involved in the first decision, to another director.

At all stages of this procedure, you will have the right to be accompanied by a work colleague or representative of a trade union.

Persistent Absences

Persistent short-term absence can sometimes be indicative of an underlying health problem, particularly if all the absences appear to be for similar reasons. The Company may, therefore, ask you to consent to our approaching your GP for a medical report or may ask you to attend an independent medical practitioner or both. In either case, you will be expected to co-operate [and it is a requirement of your contract of employment that you do so].

There may come a point where your absences are so disruptive to the business that we would have to consider employing you on different duties or terminating your employment. If that is the case, the procedure adopted will be similar to that for long-term absences.

For persistent absences for different reasons where there does not appear to be underlying medical cause, the Company may apply the [disciplinary/dismissal] procedure if the level of absences reaches a point where the Company cannot reasonably be expected to put up with further absences.

[To give a rough idea of levels of absence which would not be regarded as acceptable, the Company shall have regard to the following table, but this is a guideline only. The Company will generally take a more lenient approach if all or most absences are due to a specific illness or condition. Illnesses related to pregnancy will generally not be taken into account.

No. of periods of absence in 12 months→	1	2	3	4	5	6	7	8+
No. of days of absence in 12 months ↓								
10							1	1
15						1	1	F
20					1	F	F	D
25				1	1	F	D	D
30				1	F	D	D	D
35				1	F	D	D	D
40				1	D	D	D	D
45			1	F	D	D	D	D
50			1	F	D	D	D	D
60			1	F	D	D	D	D
70			1	D	D	D	D	D
80			F	D	D	D	D	D
90			F	D	D	D	D	D
100			F	D	D	D	D	D
100 +		1	D	D	D	D	D	D

1 = 1st warning

F = Final warning

D = Dismissal

D29.3 DRAFTING POINTS

Sick Pay: The rules for payment of sick pay should generally be contained in the Service Contract or statement of main terms and conditions of employment. Those rules may refer to the Handbook or sickness policy and require that the terms of the sickness policy are complied with as a condition of paying full pay for a period. You should ensure that the rules in the contract are consistent with those set out in this policy.

If sick pay is discretionary, this should be stated both in the Service Contract and in the statement of main terms and conditions of employment.

Long-term absences: If a long-term absence is due to disability, then employers are required under the Disability Discrimination Act 1995 to make such reasonable adjustments are necessary to accommodate that disability. It is all the more important in such cases to ensure that a detailed medical report is obtained and that this is discussed with the employee to see if anything can be done to enable the employee to return to work. There may come a point, however, even in cases of disability, where the employer cannot be expected to put up with the absence any longer. At that point, it may be reasonable to consider terminating the employment but the statutory dismissal procedure must be followed. When that point is reached will depend on the type of job and the type of employer. You should consider whether the time limits set out in this section are realistic. Smaller employers may find it more difficult to cope with the absence of key individuals and the time limits in such cases may therefore be shorter. In larger organisations where there are more employees who could cover for the employee, employment tribunals may expect employers to be able to cope with long-term absences for a longer period.

Persistent short-term absences: It has been held that employers may apply the disciplinary procedure in the case of persistent short-term absences where each absence is for a different reason, provided there is no under-lying health reason behind the absences. In applying the disciplinary procedure, however, employers should still be seen to be acting sympathetically and should still explore with the employee anything that can be done to improve the employee's attendance.

Applying the disciplinary procedure in such cases may be regarded as heavy-handed and unsympathetic. Larger employers may be expected to apply a more sympathetic procedure. Some employers have a dismissal procedure which is separate from the disciplinary procedure, to deal with dismissals that are necessary through no fault of the employee – such as redundancy or ill health. If that is the case, then the reference here should be to that dismissal procedure rather than the disciplinary procedure.

If employers wish to apply a disciplinary or dismissal procedure, then the table for warnings leading eventually to dismissal as set out here would probably be regarded as fair but employers should ensure that it is followed. If an employee has clocked up sufficient absences to justify a warning then that warning should be given – otherwise it would probably not be fair to dismiss for further absences even if there are sufficient absences to justify dismissal.

Smaller employers may find the rigidity of process set out in the table to rigid and may wish to leave it entirely to the manager's discretion. The test should then simply be whether the manager can reasonably be expected to put up with that level of absence and the section in square brackets including the table should be omitted.

E

SEPARATE AGREEMENTS

E1 WORKING TIME REGULATIONS

E1.1 USE

Without this opt-out, workers must not work more than 48 hours in a week on average. The average is normally taken over a rolling period of 17 weeks. For more details, see Division C3 of *Jordans Employment Law Service*.

Because of the right of the worker to opt back into the 48-hour maximum working week, and because employers are not permitted to put any pressure on employees to opt-out, it is not normally appropriate to include an opt-out provision within the Service Contract or statement of main terms and conditions of employment.

E1.2   Precedent

Opt-out clauses

Agreement to exclude 48-hour average working week

1. I agree that the maximum weekly working time of an average of 48 hours for each seven-day period laid down in the Working Time Regulations 1998 (SI 1998/1833) shall not apply to my employment.

2. This agreement may be terminated by me by giving three months' notice in writing.

Signed by the Worker ....

E1.3 DRAFTING POINTS

Workers are always entitled to end the opt-out agreement by giving notice. If no notice is specified in the agreement, then the agreement can be ended on seven days' notice. The agreement can provide for a longer period of notice but that period cannot be longer than three months.

Clause to be included in statement of terms of employment or separate letter amending terms of employment which worker signs to indicate acceptance

"Exclusion of Maximum Working Week"

You agree that the limit of 48 hours average working time in each seven-day period laid down in the Working Time Regulations 1998 (SI 1998/1833) shall not apply to your employment. This exclusion may be terminated by you by giving three months written notice to the company stating that you wish to terminate the exclusion.

I agree to the above terms:

.... (Signature)

E2 TRAINING AGREEMENT

E2.1 USE

Employers may pay considerable amounts of money to train their employees. This benefits the employee, making him or her more marketable and improving promotion prospects, and benefits the employer who can then expect higher level of performance from the employee. The benefit for the employer, however, may be lost or considerably reduced if the employee leaves. Some employers, therefore, ask employees to sign an agreement such as this one, whereby all or part of the training fees have to be reimbursed by the employee if the employee leaves within a specified period.

Such agreements are arguably in restraint of trade, since they prevent the employee from working for whoever they wish to work for. They are only therefore enforceable to the extent that they are necessary and no wider than necessary to protect some legitimate interest of the employer. In this case, the legitimate interest is the benefit they expect to gain from their investment in the employee's training. Because the employer will receive greater benefit the longer an employee continues to work for the employer, it is advisable to reduce the amount of the pay-back to diminish down to nothing over a period. The period suggested here is two years or 104 weeks.

E2.2 Precedent

Training agreement

To enable the Employee to participate in and attend:

.... ['The Training Course'] [provide sufficient details to identify the course]

.... of .... ['The Employer'] and

.... ['The Employee']

agree as follows:-

1. The Employer shall arrange for the Employee to attend the Training Course and shall pay all fees in respect of the Training Course.

2. The Employer shall allow the Employee such time off as is necessary for the Employee to attend the Training Course and shall pay the Employee his/her normal rate of remuneration during that time off.

3. The Employer and the Employee recognise that the Training Course is an investment by the Employer in the skills of the Employee and that the terms of this agreement are necessary and reasonable to provide reasonable protection for the Employer of that investment.

4. If, on or before [the second anniversary] of the last day upon which the Employee was absent from work by reason of attendance on the Training Course:

   a. the Employee resigns from his employment with the Employer; or

   b. the Employee is dismissed for a reason other than redundancy (as defined by Section 195 of the Trade Union and Labour Relations (Consolidation) Act 1992 as amended),

   the Employee shall pay to the Employer the amount calculated in accordance with clause 4.

4. The amount payable by the Employee to the Employer under clause 3 shall be:

$$£ \frac{([104] - M) \times F}{[104]}$$

WHERE

F = the Cost the Training Course calculated in accordance with clause 5.

M = the number of complete weeks (ie Sunday to Saturday) which fall within the period starting on the last day upon which the Employee was absent from work by reason of attendance on the Training Course and ending on the date upon which the dismissal or resignation referred to above takes effect.

5. The Costs of the Training shall include:

   a. Course fees, examination fees and the cost of course materials;

   b. [salary, pension contributions, and employers' National Insurance contributions paid by the Employer during the periods in which training is provided];

   c. any expenses paid (eg travelling expenses) to enable the Employee to attend the course;

d. (where training is provided internally) any payments made to the trainer, whether by way of salary, fees or otherwise, divided proportionately amongst all those attending the training.

6. The Costs of the Training will be notified to the Employee before the Training Course starts, or where those costs are not known (because for example, the likely expenses are not known), the Employer shall notify the Employee of the Cost of the Training in so far as it is able to.

7. The Employee hereby consents to the Employer receiving any payment which may be required under this Agreement and also consents to any sums owing under this Agreement being deducted from his/her wages or from any other sums which would otherwise be due from the Employer to the Employee.

Signed ....   Signed ....

(The Employee)   (The Employer)

Dated the day of 20[   ]

E2.3 DRAFTING POINTS

Two years or 104 weeks is probably the longest period a court would consider appropriate for the pay-back provisions to apply. Any longer than this would be difficult to justify. For junior employees, even that period may be considered to be too long and a shorter period should be substituted in clause 3 and a corresponding number of weeks should be included in clause 4.

It is unusual for such agreements to require repayment of salary received during the period of the training course but so long as the Employee is notified of those costs and agrees to repay them if required, there is no reason why those costs should not be recoverable.

Because the employee's written consent is needed before the employer can receive any payment from the employee or before any deduction is made from wages/salary, a specific provision (in this precedent, clause 5) must be included permitting receipt of the payment and the deduction.

E3 COMPROMISE AGREEMENT (EXECUTIVES)

E3.1 USE

Any agreement to exclude or limit the operation of the employment legislation is generally void and of no effect. For details see Division H1 of *Jordans Employment Law Service*. This means that an agreement to settle a claim in an employment tribunal is void unless one of the exceptions apply.

The two main exceptions are:

- settlements negotiated through ACAS (known as form COT3, which for some reason is the title appearing on the form); and

- compromise agreements in the form of this precedent.

In order to settle an employment tribunal complaint, therefore, the only safe way to do so is either through ACAS or through a compromise agreement. Agreements negotiated through ACAS are drawn up by ACAS. They are normally extremely simple, setting out the claims that have been settled, the amount of the payment and they may include a clause requiring the terms of settlement to be kept confidential and a clause clarifying that the settlement is made without admission of liability. The scope for including further more complex terms is limited because there is no direct contact between the parties or their representatives. Although in theory there is no reason why a lengthy complex agreement cannot be negotiated in this way, in practice where this happens the parties decide to opt for a compromise agreement.

ACAS is only required to conciliate in certain situations. The former rules on fixed conciliation periods are shortly to be repealed and in the meantime ACAS has indicated that it will exercise its discretion in favour of conciliating even after the fixed conciliation periods have expired.

Another situation where a compromise agreement may be used is to facilitate an agreed termination of employment with a leaving package.

This precedent includes detailed provisions which may only be appropriate for senior executives and directors. These include detailed terms about confidentiality and restrictive covenants. For other employees, use the precedent compromise agreement for non-executives.

E3.2 Precedent

Compromise agreement

THIS AGREEMENT is made on the   of   200[ ]

BETWEEN:

1   [   ], a company incorporated in England and Wales and having its registered office at .... (the "Company"); and

2   [   ] of [address] .... (the "Executive")

1   DEFINITIONS

"Contract of Employment"   the agreement between the Company and the Executive dated [date] including any variation;

"Employment"   the Executive's employment with the Company and all other employments with any of the Group Companies;

"Group Company"   the Company, any subsidiary (as defined by section 736 of the Companies Act 1985) of the Company, any holding company (as so defined) of the Company and any subsidiary of such holding company, in each case for the time being;

"Termination Date"   [   ]

2   TERMINATION OF EMPLOYMENT

[The parties agree that] the Employment and the Contract of Employment (except for those terms stated either in the Contract of Employment or in this Agreement to continue beyond the termination of the Contract of Employment) [shall terminate] [terminated] with effect from the Termination Date [and the Company shall pay and/or provide the Executive with any salary, holiday pay and other benefits (if any) accrued up to the Termination Date subject to appropriate deductions for tax and national insurance contributions] [and the Executive agrees that he has received all salary and other benefits [including accrued holiday pay] due to him in respect of the period up to and including the Termination Date].

3   COMPENSATION /BENEFITS

3.1   In consideration of the Executive's obligations set out in clause 5 hereof, the Company agrees, as compensation for [loss of office and] termination of employment, within [ ] days after the date of signature by both parties of this Agreement or (if later) within 7 days after the conditions in clause 6 are fulfilled, to pay to the Executive a sum of £[ ] less such deductions (including without limitation tax and national insurance contributions) as the Company may be required to make and to pay such amounts as may be deducted to the relevant authorities. [The said payment of £[ ] shall be paid in [ ] equal instalments on [ ], [ ], [ ]].

3.2   [The parties consider that the payments and benefits under this clause [and clause 4] shall not be subject to tax [for the first £30,000] but] the Executive agrees that he is responsible for and will keep the Company indemnified in respect of the payment of all income tax pursuant to the Income Tax (Earnings and Pensions) Act 2003 (in the United Kingdom or elsewhere) and all employees' national insurance and social security contributions in respect of any benefits received by him during the course of or in connection with his employment (including the payments made under clause 3 hereof and any other benefits under this Agreement to the extent that tax and national insurance contributions have not already been deducted by the Company on behalf of the Executive from such sums) together with any reasonable costs and expenses, penalties and interest which the Company may incur in respect of such payments.

4   [MOTOR CAR] [AND] [INSURANCE]

4.1   [The Company hereby agrees to continue to allow the Executive to retain possession of the motor car [provided under clause [ ] of the Contract of Employment] [registration number [ ]] for private use only until [ ] on which date the Executive undertakes to hand over the motor car to the Company without compensation in a clean undamaged and roadworthy condition. The terms of clause [ ] of the Contract of Employment shall apply during the Executive's period of possession of the motor car as if repeated herein mutatis mutandis [save that the Company shall not be liable for running costs incurred in private motoring from [ ]]].

OR

4.1   [The Company will transfer ownership of the motor car

[provided under clause [ ] of the Contract of Employment] [registration number [ ]] with effect from [date] on which date it will deliver to the Executive the keys and all relevant documents in its possession (including the registration document) and from which date the Executive shall be responsible for insuring taxing and maintaining the motor car and for paying therefor and for payment of all running costs. The motor car has been valued by [ ] at £[ ].]

4.2 [The Executive shall purchase the motor car [provided under clause [ ] of the Contract of Employment] [registration number [ ]] on [the Termination Date] [ ] for the sum of £[ ] and from that date the Executive shall be responsible for insuring taxing and maintaining the motor car and for paying therefor and for payment of all running costs.]

4.3 The Company will continue to provide and pay for private medical insurance for the benefit of the Executive [and [his][her]] spouse [and family] on the same terms as such insurance was provided under the Contract of Employment until [ ] or (if earlier) until the Executive obtains further employment providing similar cover.

5 EXECUTIVE'S OBLIGATIONS

In consideration of the payment set out in clause 3 the Executive:

5.1 accepts such payment in full and final settlement of and [he][she] agrees [he] [she] will not bring pursue or continue to pursue and (if a complaint has already been presented) agrees that [he][she] will forthwith withdraw any of the following complaints which have been or which may be brought before an employment tribunal, the high court, county court or other court of law in England and Wales:

5.1.1 any complaint of unfair dismissal, wrongful dismissal or breach of contract;

5.1.2 any complaint of unlawful deductions from wages;

5.1.3 any claim for a redundancy payment, whether under statute, contract or otherwise;

5.1.4 any claim for notice pay, payment in lieu of notice, holiday pay or payment in lieu of holiday pay;

5.1.5 any other claim or complaint under the

Employment Rights Act 1996 in relation to his employment with the Company and/or the termination thereof;

5.1.6 any complaint that [he] [she] has been unlawfully discriminated against under the Sex Discrimination Act 1975, the Race Relations Act 1976, the Employment Equality (Sexual Orientation) Regulations 2003, the Employment Equality (Religion or Belief) Regulations 2003, the Employment Equality (Age) Regulations 2006 or the Disability Discrimination Act 1995;

5.1.7 any claim for equal pay under the Equal Pay Act 1970;

5.1.8 any claim under the Working Time Regulations 1998;

5.1.9 any claim under Section 3 of the Protection from Harassment Act 1997;

5.1.10 any claim alleging a contravention of the Part-Time Workers (Prevention of Less Favourable Treatment) Regulations 2000;

5.1.11 [any other claim raised by the Executive in [his][her] complaint to the Employment Tribunal number [ ]];

5.2 warrants that clause 5.1 above sets out a complete list of all claims and complaints under the legislation (including regulations) therein referred to of which the Executive is aware at the date hereof which the Executive may have against any Group Company and that all the claims and complaints there listed have been raised with the Company or its solicitors or are hereby treated as having been so raised;

5.3 accepts such payment in full and final settlement of all and any other claims or other rights of action whatsoever and howsoever arising (whether under the law of England and Wales or any other law) which he has now or may have in the future against any Group Company or against any officer or employee of any Group Company arising out of or in connection with his employment with the Company and/or its termination or otherwise or any directorships of any Group Company, their termination or otherwise and accordingly the Executive hereby waives any such claims or rights of action including without limitation any claim for arrears of salary, accrued holiday pay, sick pay, maternity pay, bonuses, commission or contractual redundancy payment or other benefit under [his][her] Contract of Employment or otherwise arising in respect of [his][her] employment (including any claim in respect of share options) and any claim for wrongful dismissal, pay in lieu of notice or breach of contract by any Group Company [but not including any claim for compensation for personal injury [arising from matters in respect of which the Claimant is not aware at the date of this Agreement] [arising from matters unrelated to the subject matter of employment tribunal claim number [ ]] or in respect of accrued pension rights];

5.4 [acknowledges that prior to [the transfer of his employment to the Company, regulations 13 and 14 of the Transfer of Undertakings (Protection of Employment) Regulations 2006 (SI 2006/246) were complied with] [and prior to] [the termination of his employment sections 188 and 189 of the Trade Union and Labour Relations (Consolidation) Act 1992 were complied with];]

5.5 acknowledges that before signing this Agreement [he][she] received advice from .... of .... a relevant independent advisor ('the advisor') as to the terms and effect of this Agreement and, in particular, its effect on the Executive's ability to pursue [his][her] rights before an employment tribunal and shall procure that the advisor supplies to the Employer a certificate in the form attached at Schedule 1 hereto.

6 CONDITIONS

The payments referred to in clause 3 and the provision of the motor car in terms of clause 4 above are subject to the following:

6.1 The Executive delivering to the Company signed letters of resignation from all directorships and all other employments and offices which the Executive holds in any Group Company in the form of Attachment 1;

6.2 The Executive returning to the Company all keys, mobile phones, faxes, computers, books, correspondence and documents (including copies) belonging to or leased by any Group Company which the Executive has in [his][her] possession or which is under the Executive's control [(other than the motor car referred to in clause 4 above)];

6.3 The Executive deleting from any computer or other equipment not belonging to or leased by any Group Company in his possession or under his control any Confidential Information (as defined in the Contract of Employment) and any software which is licensed to any Group Company.

6.4 The Executive delivering to the Company a duly executed Stock Transfer Form transferring the [ ] Shares in the capital of the Company held by [him][her].

7 [EXECUTIVE'S WARRANTIES

7.1 The Executive warrants that [he/she] is not aware of any matter which is not known to the Company which if known would entitle the Company to terminate the Executive's employment without notice and without compensation;

7.2 The Executive warrants that [he][she] has not been offered and has not accepted employment with any other employer as at the date of this Agreement [save as disclosed in writing to the Company]];

7.3 The Executive warrants that [he/she] has complied with clauses [confidentiality and restrictive covenants] of the Contract of Employment from the Termination date to the date of this Agreement;

7.4 In the event that the Company discovers any matter which was known to the Executive at the date of this Agreement but was not known to the Company which would have entitled the Company to dismiss the Executive without notice, the Executive shall repay to the Company on receipt of a written demand from the Company setting out the said matter or matters the payment referred to in clause 3 hereof. If the Company discovers that the Executive was offered or accepted employment before the date of this Agreement and that such offer or acceptance was not disclosed to the Company as required by clause 7.1 hereof, the Executive shall repay to the Company all sums earned, in respect of such employment during the period of [ ] months commencing with the Termination Date.

8 CONFIDENTIALITY

The Executive agrees to keep the terms of this Agreement confidential and shall not disclose them to any person save [his][her] immediate family and [his][her] professional advisers and [he][she] agrees to instruct any person to whom [he][she] discloses these terms that they must be kept confidential.

9 STATEMENTS

The Executive will not make, publish or issue or cause to be made, published or issued any disparaging or derogatory statements concerning any Group Company, or any employee or officer of any Group Company. [The Company shall procure that its directors shall not make any disparaging or derogatory statements about the Executive.]

10 COMPANY ANNOUNCEMENT

The Company shall make the announcement set out in Schedule 3 to this Agreement to its staff.

11 REFERENCE

The Company shall provide the Executive with a reference in the form of Schedule 4 to this Agreement and shall not in response to any question from a prospective employer make any statement inconsistent with such reference.

12 CONDITIONS REGULATING COMPROMISE AGREEMENTS

The conditions regulating compromise agreements under the Employment Rights Act 1996, the Trade Union and Labour Relations (Consolidation) Act 1992, the Working Time Regulations 1998, the Sex Discrimination Act 1975 the Race Relations Act 1976, the Employment Equality (Sexual Orientation) Regulations 2003, the Employment Equality (Religion or Belief) Regulations 2003, the Employment Equality (Age) Regulations 2006 and the Disability Discrimination Act 1995 are satisfied in relation to this Agreement.

13 CONTINUATION OF OBLIGATIONS

The Executive shall continue to be bound by his obligation towards the Company to keep confidential and not to use for his own benefit or for the benefit of any other person any trade secret or confidential information [specify terms in Service Contract which the Company wants to continue]. [In addition] in consideration of the payment of £[ ] the Executive agrees as follows [set out here any further restrictions you wish to impose on the Executive].

14 THIRD PARTY RIGHTS

The parties intend that each Group Company should be able to enforce in its own right the terms of this Agreement which expressly or impliedly confer a benefit on that company subject to and in accordance with the provisions of the Contracts (Rights of Third Parties) Act 1999.

15 LEGAL FEES

The Company agrees to pay directly to the relevant independent advisor a contribution towards the Executive's legal fees for advice on the terms of and effect of this Agreement [and in respect of the termination of [his][her] employment] up to a maximum of £[ ].

16 GENERAL

16.1 This Agreement is governed by and interpreted in accordance with the laws of England.

16.2 This Agreement may be executed in two counterparts each of which will be deemed an original, but all of the counterparts will together constitute one and the same instrument.

Signed ....

Dated ....

For and on behalf of the Company

Signed ....   Dated ....

By the Executive

Schedule 1

To be completed on the Advisor's headed notepaper

INDEPENDENT ADVISER

I confirm that I am a relevant independent adviser for the purposes of the legislation referred to in clause 12 of the Compromise Agreement between [*Employer*] and [*Executive*] ('the Executive') and that I have advised the Executive on that Compromise Agreement and its effect on the Executive's right to bring a claim in an Employment Tribunal. I confirm that at the time the advice was given, there was in force a policy of insurance or there was an indemnity provided for members of a professional body covering any claim that might be brought by the Executive in respect of such advice.

Name .... Signature

                                        Date ....

Schedule 2

[Address to any company of which Executive is a director]

Dear Sirs

I hereby resign without claim for compensation as a director of [ ].

Yours faithfully

Schedule 3

Announcement to staff

It is with regret we have to announce that [ ] [has decided to resign from the Company] [is leaving the Company by mutual agreement] [will be leaving the Company by reason of redundancy] to pursue other interests. We would like to record our thanks to [ ] for [his/her] major contribution to the Company over the years and I am sure you will all join me in wishing [him/her] every success in the future.

Schedule 4

Reference

E3.3 DRAFTING POINTS

Clause 2: Only include these words if this agreement itself it to terminate the employment. The advantage is largely cosmetic in that the parties may prefer to announce the termination as by mutual consent rather than dismissal or resignation. The disadvantage is that it may tempt the Executive to prevaricate to keep the employment (and hence his salary) going as long as possible – that will be so particularly if the Termination Date is defined as the date of the Agreement.

Clause 3.1: Only include reference to office-holder if the individual receives separate remuneration for holding that office.

If the payment is made after the P45 has been issued, the employer needs only to deduct tax at basic rate. Tax exemption for the first £30,000 generally applies to termination payments unless the Contract of Employment contains a clause expressly providing for payment in lieu of notice.

If pension payments are being made, check the scheme rules, particularly as to whether payment should be made during employment.

Clause 3.2: Only include these words if the payment exceeds £30,000. Delete the entire first bracketed section of the payment will be fully taxable. The general rules is that termination payments are tax free for the first £30,000 unless they fall within any other provision of the tax legislation requiring it to be taxed. Payments in lieu of notice which are habitually made or which are provided for in the contract of employment are regarded as emoluments of employment and so fully taxable. For the rules on when termination payments may be taxable, see *Jordans Employment Service* at H2[63].

Clause 5.1: Following a 2005 case care needs to be taken to ensure that all potential claims have been specifically identified and set out in the clause. This list includes just about every possible claim that could be brought. Claims that are obviously irrelevant could safely be deleted. Some employers and their advisors still leave in every claim. Otherwise, if the employer only includes claims they think the employee could bring, the employer could be putting ideas into the employee's head. Certain claims cannot be settled by compromise agreement – for example complaints of failure to inform and consult under the Transfer of Undertakings (Protection of Employment) Regulations 2006 (SI 2006/246) and complaints of failure to consult in respect of collective redundancies. If you want to settle such claims, you could use this agreement but recognise that it will not be enforceable or you could let the claim be brought and then ask the tribunal to record the agreement as a tribunal order.

Clause 5.3: Until recently, it has been normal practice to exclude personal injury claims and pension rights. Now that personal injury claims arising from the manner of dismissal or from discrimination are more common, employers should resist this exclusion or at least limit it to matters not arising from any claim brought or threatened by the Executive at the date of the Agreement or not known about at the time of the agreement.

Clause 5.4: Only include if the business has been transferred within three months of dismissal and/or the dismissal was part of a large-scale redundancy exercise. These claims cannot be settled by a compromise agreement but the acknowledgement may have some evidential value.

Clause 6.3: If the Contract of Employment does not contain a definition of confidential information, include a definition, eg that contained in the Precedent Service Contract. Note that to include such a definition may be treated as introducing a restrictive covenant into the Agreement, which could have tax consequences – see comment in clause 13.

Clause 6.4: Only include this if the Executive is a shareholder.

Clause 7.1: Executives and their advisors will generally resist this clause since it leaves the executive vulnerable to future claims from the employer, defeating the object of achieving finality of all legal matters between the parties. From the employer's point of view, however, if it they later discover that there were grounds on which employment could have been terminated without notice and without compensation, then they have no remedy against the employee unless these clauses are included.

Clauses 7.2: This clause is generally resisted by departing Executives and their legal advisors. The advantages of this clause from the point of view of the employer is that it should flush out whether or not the Executive has other employment to go to. If he or she has, then the employer will know that any claim for notice pay and unfair dismissal is likely to be of little value (depending on the employee's earnings in the new job). The disadvantage for employees is that it may inhibit them from starting to look for other employment, in case they receive a job offer before this Compromise Agreement is finalised. Whether this clause is included is a matter for negotiation. A compromise may be reached whereby the Executive warrants only that he has not received a written offer of employment.

Clause 7.3: This is particularly useful as a significant deterrent on former employees from breaching restrictive covenants at least during the period that this agreement is being negotiated.

Clause 7.4: This gives the preceding sub-clauses teeth, creating a debt from the employee to the employer which can relatively easily be enforced. Again this clause is likely to be resisted by departing Executives and their advisors but and whether it can be included is a matter for negotiation.

Clause 9: Employers often seek to include a clause prohibiting derogatory comments from the departing executive. The executive or advisor then responds by asking for a similar obligation on the employer. Since employers comprise any number of employees, no employer could guarantee that no employee or other person representing the company will make a derogatory comment, so the obligation on the employer will have to be limited to directors or other narrowly defined classes of individuals.

Clauses 10 and 11: Parties to compromise agreements often seek to agree the wording of any reference to be provided to future employers and of any announcement made to staff. This gives the departing executive reassurance that his or her job prospects are not going to be damaged by adverse comments from the Company.

Clause 12: It is a requirement of the legislation that compromise agreements should state that the relevant requirements of the legislation are complied with. This means that the relevant provisions of all the applicable legislation must be referred to within the Compromise Agreement.

Clause 13: Set out any further restrictive covenants intended to be imposed by this Agreement. Some consideration should be attributed to any further restrictions, otherwise Her Majesty's Revenue and Customs will make its own assessment and attribute part or all of the consideration under this Agreement to the restrictive covenant, rendering it taxable under the Income Tax (Earnings and Pensions) Act 2003.

Clause 14: Where the employer is a company within a group of companies, this enables other companies in the group to gain the benefit and if necessary enforce through the courts any restrictive covenants or rules on confidentiality imposed by this agreement.

Clause 15: Payment should be tax free under a tax concession (A81) granted by the Inland Revenue (now her Majesty's Revenue and Customs) so long as the payee (who will normally be the relevant legal advisor) is a solicitor, payment is made directly to the solicitor under a term of an agreement such as this one and the advice relates only to the termination of employment (so advice on shares may be excluded).

Schedule 1: In order for a compromise agreement to be valid, the employee must have received advice from a qualified lawyer or certain other categories of advisor, including a barrister and a trade union representative who has been certified by the union as competent to provide advice. In most cases, the advisor is a solicitor. If it turns out that, despite what the employee has told you, that employee did not in fact get advice from a solicitor, then the agreement is invalid and the employee can still sue you for unfair dismissal or any of the other claims the agreement sought to settle. The employee would have to be fairly underhand to do this and an employment tribunal learning that an employee had done this would probably have little sympathy with that employee. However, not all tribunal members think in the way that the writer does, so the risk of an employee doing this can be reduced by:

– offering to pay or contribute to the employee's legal fees (clause 15);

– making it a condition of the agreement that the employee has sought legal advice on the agreement (clause 5.5); and

– requiring the advisor to sign a letter on headed note-paper confirming that he or she has advised the employee on the terms of the compromise agreement.

This may seem like overkill to deal with a situation which is highly unlikely to arise, but the requirement for an advisor to sign a certificate such as this has become standard procedure and will not come as any surprise to advisors of departing executives.

Schedule 4: Employers often ask employees to provide a suggested draft reference and then seek to agree the wording. Because of litigation arising from the giving of references, some employers are now extremely cautious about what is said in references, limiting them to purely factual information which could not possibly be disputed – such as positions held and periods of employment. The risk for the employer is that if the reference is too glowing, a future employer could sue on the basis that they were misled into employing someone unsuitable; and if it is not glowing enough, the employee could sue for defamation or negligent misstatement. Both types of claims have been made successfully in the past. If the reference is agreed, then the employee him or herself cannot complain if they later decide they do not like the reference or believe the reference caused them not to get a particular job. Keeping references purely factual, not expressing any subjective judgements at all whether directly or by implication, should avoid the risk of litigation. So phrases like 'highly competent', 'well-respected', 'excellent leadership qualities' should be avoided.

E4 COMPROMISE AGREEMENT (BASIC)

E4.1 USE

For an explanation of the use of Compromise agreements, see the notes to the Compromise Agreement for Executives precedent.

This precedent is designed for straightforward agreements where an employee's employment is terminated and the employer and employee have agreed a termination package. This agreement may then be used to record what has been agreed and to ensure that all possible disputes relating to the employment and its termination are resolved once and for all.

E4.2 Precedent

Compromise agreement

By this Agreement dated the [ ] day of [ ] 200, [insert name] ("the Employer") of [insert address] and [insert name] ("the Employee") of [insert address] agree as follows:

1. The Employee's employment with the Employer [will terminate/terminated] on [*date*] (the Termination Date) and the Employee will be/was paid his/her salary and has received all other benefits including accrued holiday pay [of [ ] days [less any further days of holiday taken during the period between the date of this Agreement and the Termination Date] for the period up to and including the Termination Date subject to appropriate deductions for tax and national insurance contributions.

2. The Employer will within [14] days of the Termination Date or (if later) within [14] days of the date of this Agreement pay the Employee the sum of £[ ] as compensation for [loss of office and] loss of employment to be paid without deduction of tax but any tax due in respect of any benefits received by the Employee under this Agreement shall be the Employee's liability and the Employee indemnifies the Employer in respect of any income tax, interest and penalties which the Employer pays on the Employee's behalf.

    Payment of these sums is in full and final settlement of the claims and complaints listed in clause 3 hereof.

3. The claims and complaints referred to in clause (2) hereof are:

    - any complaint of or claim for compensation for unfair dismissal;

    - any claim for a redundancy payment;

- any claim for arrears of wages, salary or bonus (other than as provided for in this Agreement) and any complaint that an unlawful deduction has been made from his/her wages contrary to the Employment Rights Act 1996;

- any other claim or complaint under the Employment Rights Act 1996 in relation to his/her employment with the Employer and/or the termination thereof;

- any claim or complaint under the Trade Union and Labour Relations (Consolidation) Act 1992;

- any complaint of or claim for compensation for wrongful dismissal, breach of contract (including a complaint that less notice has been given than that required by the Employee's contract) or for pay in lieu of notice;

- any complaint that he/she has been unlawfully discriminated against, harassed or victimised under the Sex Discrimination Act 1975, the Race Relations Act 1976, the Employment Equality (Sexual Orientation) Regulations 2003, the Employment Equality (Religion or Belief) Regulations 2003, the Employment Equality (Age) Regulations 2006 or the Disability Discrimination Act 1995;

- any complaint that the Employer has contravened the Working Time Regulations 1998 or the Working Time Directive, including any complaint that the Employer has failed to provide adequate weekly and daily rests or adequate rest breaks or has failed to permit or to pay for paid holiday entitlement;

- any claim for equal pay under the Equal Pay Act 1970;

- any claim under section 3 of the Protection from Harassment Act 1997;

- any claim under the National Minimum Wage Act 1998 or regulations made thereunder;

- [the complaint number [ ] which the Employee has presented to an Employment Tribunal and all other claims arising from or based on the facts and matters raised in that complaint.]

4. In addition, the Employee accepts the payments under this Agreement in full and final settlement of all and any other claims [he/she] may have against the Employer arising out of [his/her] employment with the Employer or the termination thereof with the exception of rights under any pension scheme accrued as at the date of termination of the Employee's employment [and with the

exception of any personal injury claim the basis of which is not known to the Employee at the date of this Agreement. The Employee warrants that he/she does not know of any grounds on which he/she may be entitled to seek compensation for any personal injury.]

5. The Employee agrees that [he/she] will not bring or pursue any claim or complaint of a type referred to in clause 3 hereof and if [he/she] has already brought such a claim [he/she] shall immediately withdraw it [and in particular shall write to the Employment Tribunal immediately on completion of this Agreement withdrawing complaint number [ ]]. [He/She] further agrees that if [he/she] breaches this clause, the payment referred to in clause 2 shall be immediately repayable to the Employer.

6. The Employee confirms and acknowledges [his/her] obligation not to divulge to any person or use for [his/her] own benefit information belonging to the Employer, including but not limited to information about the financial affairs and business affairs of the Employer and confirms and acknowledges that this obligation continues after the termination of his/her employment.

7. The Employer and Employee agree to keep the terms of this Agreement confidential and not to disclose its terms other than as may be required by law, and to their professional advisers. The Employee further agrees that if he/she breaches this clause 7 the Payment referred to in clause 2 shall be immediately repayable to the Employer.

8. The Employee agrees that [he/she] will not make or publish or cause to be published any malicious, unjustified or unsubstantiated statement or communication which might disparage the Employer. [The Employer shall procure that its directors shall not make any disparaging or derogatory statements about the Employee.]

9. The Employee will ensure that on or before the Termination Date [he/she] will return all the Employer's property which is in [his/her] possession, including but not limited to, documents, papers, records, files, computer disks, materials, and any copies or extracts of them; company credit card, lap-top computer, fax machine, keys, security pass [ ].

10. The Employee will not make, publish or issue or cause to be made, published or issued any disparaging or derogatory statements concerning the Employer or any company in the group of companies to which the Employer belongs, or any employee or officer of any such company]. [The Employer shall procure that its directors shall not make any disparaging or derogatory statements about the Employee.]

11. The Employer shall make the announcement set out in Schedule 2 to this Agreement to its staff.

12. The Employer shall provide the Employee with a reference in the form of Schedule 3 to this Agreement and shall not in response to any question from a prospective employer make any statement inconsistent with such reference.

13. The Employee confirms that [he/she] has received advice from a relevant independent adviser [ ] of [ ] Solicitors) about the terms and effect of this Agreement and in particular its effect on the Employee's ability to pursue any of the aforementioned claims before an Employment Tribunal, and [ ] confirms by signing a certificate in the form attached at Schedule 1 that [he/she] is a relevant independent adviser within the meaning of the Employment Rights Act 1996, the Trade Union and Labour Relations (Consolidation) Act 1992 the Sex Discrimination Act 1975, the Race Relations Act 1976, the Employment Equality (Sexual Orientation) Regulations 2003, the Employment Equality (Religion or Belief) Regulations 2003, the Employment Equality (Age) Regulations 2006, the Disability Discrimination Act 1995, the Equal Pay Act 1970, the Working Time Regulations, the National Minimum Wage Act 1998 ("the Legislation").

14. The conditions regulating compromise agreements under the Legislation are satisfied.

15. The Employer agrees to pay the Employee's reasonable legal fees for obtaining advice in connection with this Agreement up to a maximum of £[ ] [including/excluding] VAT on receipt of a copy invoice addressed to the Employee but marked payable by the Employer.

16. References to any statute and to any section of any statute shall be taken and understood to be references to any re-enactment or substantial re-enactment of such statute or section, whether such re-enactment be by way of consolidating legislation or otherwise.

SIGNED by the Employee

[NAME]

SIGNED by

Mr (the independent adviser)

SIGNED for and on behalf

of the Employer

Schedule 1

To be completed on the Advisor's headed notepaper

INDEPENDENT ADVISOR

I confirm that I am a relevant independent adviser for the purposes of the legislation referred to in clause 13 of the Compromise Agreement between [*Employer*] and [*Employee*] ('the Employee') and that I have advised the Employee on that Compromise Agreement and its effect on the Employee's right to bring a claim in an Employment Tribunal. I confirm that at the time the advice was given, there was in force a policy of insurance or there was an indemnity provided for members of a professional body covering any claim that might be brought by the Employee in respect of such advice.

Name .... Signature

Date ....

Schedule 2

Announcement to staff

It is with regret we have to announce that [ ] [has decided to resign from the Company] [is leaving the Company by mutual agreement] [will be leaving the Company by reason of redundancy] to pursue other interests. We would like to record our thanks to [ ] for [his/her] major contribution to the Company over the years and I am sure you will all join me in wishing [him/her] every success in the future.

Schedule 3

Reference

E4.3 DRAFTING POINTS

Clause 1: To ensure there is no disagreement about how much holiday pay is owing, it may be advisable to state how many days' holiday pay will be paid. If this agreement is finalised before the employment is terminated, you will have to include the section in square brackets to ensure that the employee does not take further holiday and then claim full holiday pay under the agreement.

The same could be said of any other contractual sums about which there could be disagreement, for example, any bonuses they may have become or will become due.

Clause 2: Only include reference to office-holder if the individual receives separate remuneration for holding that office.

Clause 3: Following a 2005 case care needs to be taken to ensure that all potential claims have been specifically identified and set out in the clause. This list includes just about every possible claim that could be brought. Claims that are obviously irrelevant could safely be deleted. Some employers and their advisors still leave in every claim. Otherwise, if the employer only includes claims they think the employee could bring, the employer could be putting ideas into the employee's head. Certain claims cannot be settled by compromise agreement – for example complaints of failure to inform and consult under the Transfer of Undertakings (Protection of Employment) Regulations 2006 (SI 2006/246) and complaints of failure to consult in respect of collective redundancies. If you want to settle such claims, you could use this agreement but recognise that it will not be enforceable or you could let the claim be brought and then ask the tribunal to record the agreement as a tribunal order.

The final bullet point should only be included if the employee has actually brought a complaint before an employment tribunal.

Clause 4: Many compromise agreements exclude personal injury claims from the settlement. Care needs to be taken with this. Employment tribunal claims for discrimination often contain claims for compensation for personal injury, so a blanket exclusion of all personal injury claims may still leave the employer vulnerable to tribunal claims. Employers should either refuse to exclude personal injury claims altogether; or (as here), limit the exclusion to claims of which the employee is unaware at the date of the agreement.

Clause 6: This clause is not essential but it is often regarded as useful to remind the employee of his or her obligations in respect of confidential information.

Clause 7: Again, this clause is not essential but it is often in the interests of both parties that the terms of the settlement are kept confidential.

Clause 9: Add anything else the employee may have which will need to be returned.

Clause 10: Employers often seek to include a clause prohibiting derogatory comments from the departing employee. The employee or advisor then responds by asking for a similar obligation on the employer. Since employers comprise any number of employees, no employer could guarantee that no employee or other person representing the company will make a derogatory comment, so the obligation on the employer will have to be limited to directors or other narrowly defined classes of individuals.

Clause 12: Parties to compromise agreements often seek to agree the wording of any reference to be provided to future employers and of any announcement made to staff. This gives the departing employee reassurance that his or her job prospects are not going to be damaged by adverse comments from the employer.

Clauses 13 and 14: It is a requirement of the legislation that compromise agreements should state that the relevant requirements of the legislation are complied with. This means that the relevant provisions of all the applicable legislation must be referred to within the Compromise Agreement.

Clause 15: Payment should be tax free under a tax concession (A81) granted by the Inland Revenue (now her Majesty's Revenue and Customs) so long as the payee (who will normally be the relevant legal advisor) is a solicitor, payment is made directly to the solicitor under a term of an agreement such as this one and the advice relates only to the termination of employment.

Schedule 1: In order for a compromise agreement to be valid, the employee must have received advice from a qualified lawyer or certain other categories of advisor, including a barrister and a trade union representative who has been certified by the union as competent to provide advice. In most cases, the advisor is a solicitor. If it turns out that, despite what the employee has told you, that employee did not in fact get advice from a solicitor, then the agreement is invalid and the employee can still sue you for unfair dismissal or any of the other claims the agreement sought to settle. The employee would have to be fairly underhand to do this and an employment tribunal learning that an employee had done this would probably have little sympathy with that employee. However, not all tribunal members think in the way that the writer does, so the risk of an employee doing this can be reduced by:

– offering to pay or contribute to the employee's legal fees (clause 15);

– making it a condition of the agreement that the employee has sought legal advice on the agreement (clause 5.5); and

– requiring the advisor to sign a letter on headed note-paper confirming that he or she has advised the employee on the terms of the compromise agreement.

Schedule 4: Employers are often wary about giving references because of the potential for litigation. If the reference is too glowing, a future employer could sue if the employee turns out to be less competent that they have been led to believe; and if it is not glowing enough, the employee could sue for defamation (although to succeed the employee would have to establish malice because references attract what is called 'qualified privilege') or negligent misstatement. Any reference given should be factual, setting out dates of employment, positions held and a brief description of what the employee did. Subjective phrases such as 'highly competent' and 'excellent team leader' should be avoided unless you are sure you could justify them if challenged.

E5 COMPROMISE AGREEMENT (SPECIFIC CLAIM)

E5.1 USE

This precedent compromise agreement may be used to compromise a specific claim before an employment tribunal. While settling the specific claim, most employers take the opportunity to settle all other possible claims by the employee. For more information about compromise agreements see the note to the precedent compromise agreement for executives.

E5.2   Precedent

Compromise agreement

By this Agreement dated the day of 20[ ] , [ ] (the Respondent) and [ ] (the Claimant) agree as follows:-

1. Without any admission of liability, the Respondent will pay the Claimant the sum of £[ ] in full and final settlement of all claims and complaints arising from the Claimant's employment with the Respondent or its termination, including but not limited to the Claimant's complaints raised by the Claimant in his/her application to the Employment Tribunal number [ ] and all other claims based on the same facts and matters as are raised by the Claimant in that claim.

2. The [first £30,000 of the] said sum of £ [ ] shall be paid without deduction of tax [but any tax due in respect of any benefits received by the Claimant under this Agreement shall be the Claimant's liability and the Claimant indemnifies the Respondent in respect of any tax which the Respondent pays on the Claimant's behalf.]

3. The Claimant agrees that [he/she] will immediately withdraw the complaint referred to in clause 1 hereof and will not bring or pursue any claim or complaint of a type referred to in clause 1 or based on the same facts as those set out the that complaint.

4. The Claimant confirms that [he/she] has received advice from a relevant independent adviser ([*name of advisor*] of [*advisor's firm*]) about the terms and effect of this Agreement and in particular its effect on the Claimant's ability to pursue any of the aforementioned claims before an Employment Tribunal, and [*name of advisor*] confirms and the Employee shall procure that the advisor signs a certificate on the advisor's headed note-paper in the form of Schedule 1 that [he/she] is a relevant independent adviser within the meaning of the Employment Rights Act 1996, the Trade Union and Labour Relations (Consolidation) Act 1992, the Sex

Discrimination Act 1975, the Race Relations Act 1976, the Employment Equality (Sexual Orientation) Regulations 2003, the Employment Equality (Religion or Belief) Regulations 2003, the Employment Equality (Age) Regulations 2006, the Disability Discrimination Act 1995, the Equal Pay Act 1970, the Working Time Regulations, the National Minimum Wage Act 1998 ("the Legislation").

5. The conditions regulating compromise agreements under the Legislation are satisfied.

6. References to any statute and to any section of any statute, shall be taken and understood to be references to any re-enactment or substantial re-enactment of such statute or section, whether such re-enactment be by way of consolidating legislation or otherwise.

SIGNED by the Claimant

SIGNED by Mr (the independent adviser)

SIGNED for and on behalf

of the Respondent.

Schedule 1

To be completed on the Advisor's headed notepaper

INDEPENDENT ADVISOR

I confirm that I am a relevant independent adviser for the purposes of the legislation referred to in clause 4 of the Compromise Agreement between [*Employer*] and [*Employee*] ('the Employee') and that I have advised the Employee on that Compromise Agreement and its effect on the Employee's right to bring a claim in an Employment Tribunal. I confirm that at the time the advice was given, there was in force a policy of insurance or there was an indemnity provided for members of a professional body covering any claim that might be brought by the Employee in respect of such advice.

Name .... Signature

                                                    Date ....

E5.3 DRAFTING POINTS

Clause 2: If the payment is more than £30,000, then the excess over £30,000 will be taxable. Any part of the payment which is taxable anyway (for example, if the agreement settles a claim for unlawful deductions from wages), that part will be taxable and will not count towards the tax-free £30,000.

Schedule 1: In order for a compromise agreement to be valid, the employee must have received advice from a qualified lawyer or certain other categories of advisor, including a barrister and a trade union representative who has been certified by the union as competent to provide advice. In most cases, the advisor is a solicitor. If it turns out that, despite what the employee has told you, that employee did not in fact get advice from a solicitor, then the agreement is invalid and the employee can still sue you for unfair dismissal or any of the other claims the agreement sought to settle. The employee would have to be fairly underhand to do this and an employment tribunal learning that an employee had done this would probably have little sympathy with that employee. However, not all tribunal members think in the way that the writer does, so the risk of an employee doing this can be reduced by:

- offering to pay or contribute to the employee's legal fees (see clause 15 of the basic compromise agreement);

- making it a condition of the agreement that the employee has sought legal advice on the agreement (clause 4); and

- requiring the advisor to sign a letter on headed note-paper confirming that he or she has advised the employee on the terms of the compromise agreement.

Other clauses: Other clauses may be included, depending on what can be negotiated. See the precedent basic compromise agreement.

E6 RELOCATION

E6.1 USE

This may be used to agree a relocation package either to new employees who are having to relocate in order to take up employment and in relation to existing employees who are required to relocate.

E6.2 Precedent

Relocation agreement

If you are required to move your place of work to a place that is further away from your home and is more than [ ] miles from your home, then you may be entitled to financial assistance with relocation. You may also be entitled to financial assistance if you are starting your employment with us and we have agreed as a condition of your employment to pay your relocation expenses.

We will pay up to £[ ] to assist you with relocation. This will only be paid once we have received invoices or other proof of payment. The expenses will be limited to the following:

– solicitors fees

– estate agents fees

– removal expenses.

We will also pay any rent and your expenses in travelling to work for a period of [ ] months and subject to an overall maximum of £[ ] while you look for somewhere permanent to live.

These figures may be reviewed from time to time, so you should check with [the Human resources Department] what the current figures are.

Because this represents a considerable investment for us, we do require reimbursement of these expenses or a proportion of them if you either do not take up this employment or if you leave within [ ] months of the final payment of expenses. The repayment will be determined by the following formula:

$$\frac{(\text{Total expenses paid}) \times (24 - \text{months of employment})}{24}$$

So, for example, if you left our employment after 16 months, you would repay one third of the expenses.

If you leave after two years of employment, there would be no repayment.

This requirement to repay will not apply if the reason for the termination of you employment is redundancy.

Any repayment required may be deducted from any wages or salary owing to you.

Signed on behalf of the employer:

Signed by the employee:

E6.3 DRAFTING POINTS

If you require repayment of relocation expenses where an employee, having received financial assistance, leaves employment after a short period, then the employee must have agreed to this in writing. The same applies if the repayment is deducted from salary.

It may be regarded as unfair to expect an employee to repay if the reason for the termination of their employment is outside their control – for example, because of redundancy.

It may also be unfair to expect someone to repay if they have worked for a significant period but less than two years. You will have received some benefit from the investment and therefore it is usual to reduce the repayment required by a proportion reflecting the length that they have worked (as is achieved by the formula set out in the precedent).

Certain tax exemptions may be available for relocation expenses. For advice on what exemptions may be available, you should consult your local tax office or a tax advisor.

E7　LOANS

E7.1　USE

This may be used to agree a loan to employees and to make provision for repayment of that loan. A written agreement is necessary because employers are not allowed to receive any payment from an employee or make any deduction from wages unless the employee has consented in writing or the employee has been notified that the employer's right to receive such repayment or make such deduction has been notified in writing.

E7.2　　　　　　　　　Precedent

Loan agreement

By this agreement dated [date] between:

[*name*] of [*address*] ('the Employee') and

[name] of [*address*] ('the Employer')

the Employer and the Employee agree as follows:

1. The Employer shall lend the Employee £[ ] ('the loan') on or before [*date*]. [Interest shall be applied at the rate of [ ] per cent for month on the balance outstanding.]

2. The Employee shall repay the loan by [ ] equal monthly instalments, the first such instalment being made on or before [*date*] and further payments shall be made [monthly/three-monthly] after that, each payment being made on or before the last day of the month in which it is due to be paid.

3. The Employee shall repay the whole of any outstanding part of the loan in any of the following circumstances:

    a. He/she defaults by not repaying any instalment by the required date

    b. His/her employment is terminated for any reason.

4. Any instalments owing under this agreement may be deducted from the employee's wages/salary.

Signed on behalf of the Employer

Signed by the Employee

F

STANDARD FORMS AND LETTERS

F1 ACCESS TO MEDICAL REPORTS – INFORMATION SHEET

F1.1 USE

Any employer who wishes to obtain a medical report on an employee needs to get the employee's consent in writing. The employee must be notified of his or her rights under the Access to Medical Reports Act 1988. The easiest way to do this is with an information sheet such as this, to be enclosed with the letter the employee requesting the employee's consent.

Employers may wish to obtain a medical report in cases of long-term or persistent absence.

F1.2   Precedent

Your rights under the Access to Medical Reports Act 1988

Please read the attached notes. If you are happy to consent to your GP, consultant or other health professional preparing and sending a report on your health, please sign and return the letter accompanying this form.

1. You do not have to consent to your GP, consultant or other health professional providing a medical report if you do not want to. However, if you do consent, we will be able to make a better-informed decision about how (if at all) we could facilitate your return to work, how to cope with your absence and your prospects of returning to work in the foreseeable future.

2. If you want, you can insist that you see a copy of the report before it is passed to us. Once you have seen the report you can, if you want, refuse your consent to our seeing it or ask that amendments be made before we see it.

3. You can ask your doctor for a copy of the report at any time, for a period of 6 months from the date it is supplied to us.

4. There are some circumstances in which, even if you ask for a copy

of the report, the doctor is entitled to refuse to let you see it. For example, the doctor need not show you the report if he thinks it might jeopardise your health.

F2 ACCESS TO MEDICAL REPORTS – LETTER SEEKING CONSENT

F2.1 USE

Please see the notes to the precedent Information Sheet.

F2.2 Precedent

Letter requesting consent to a medical report

Dear ....

I am sorry to hear that you are still unwell. [*or any other similarly sympathetic statement*]

In the meantime, I have to ensure the continued operation and success of the business. I propose to ask your Doctor for a report so that I can plan how to cope with your absence. [At the moment we are attempting to cope with your absence by [using agency staff and] spreading your workload amongst other employees but this is not proving satisfactory because [agency staff lack sufficient expertise and experience and] [it is putting unacceptable pressure on your colleagues. One of the options we may have to consider, therefore, is to appoint somebody on a permanent basis to replace you, which may mean that your employment would have to be terminated. We would only do this if no other options are reasonably practicable. If this were to happen, we would review sympathetically any future application from you for a job.]

This report will be used to help us to explore with you ways in which we might be able to facilitate your return to work, what steps we should take to cover your absence and whether and how we can continue to cope with your absence.

Would you please sign one copy of this letter where indicated below and return it to me, to mark your consent to my applying for a report.

I should inform you that you have the following rights under the Access to Medical Reports Act 1988:

1. You do not have to consent to this request if you do not want to. I would urge you to give your consent, however, for the reasons given above.

2. If you want, you can insist that you see a copy of the Doctor's report before it is passed to us. Once you have seen the report you can, if you want, refuse your consent to our seeing it or ask that amendments be made before we see it.

3. You can ask your doctor for a copy of the report at any time, for a period of 6 months from the date it is supplied to us.

4. There are some circumstances in which, even if you ask for a copy of the report, the doctor is entitled to refuse to let you see it. For example, the doctor need not show you the report if he thinks it might jeopardise your health.

The attached information sheet sets out your rights under the Act and should be retained by you.

If there is anything in this letter you do not understand or if you wish to discuss the matter further before giving your consent please do not hesitate to contact the undersigned.

I do hope you are feeling better and will be able to return to us soon [*or something else that sounds appropriately sympathetic*].

Yours sincerely,

I consent to your applying to my Doctor for a medical report.

....

My doctor/specialist (delete as appropriate) is:

Name:

Address:

I do(not) wish to have access to the report before it is supplied to you.

F2.3 DRAFTING POINTS

Only include the section in square brackets in the second paragraph if the point has been reached where you consider that termination of employment is a likely outcome.

F3 ACCESS TO MEDICAL REPORTS – LETTER TO DOCTOR

F3.1 USE

This letter should be used once you have obtained the employee's consent to applying for a medical report.

F3.2   Precedent

Letter to doctor

Dear Dr ....

I understand that you are [ ]'s Doctor. With his/her consent, I am writing to you for a medical report on. The purpose of this report is to enable me to decide what action to take in relation to [ ]'s future employment with the Company and whether there are any steps we can take to facilitate [ ]'s return to work. In particular, could you please answer the following:

(a)   Is [ ] likely to be fit for work within the next month?

(b)   If not, is he/she likely to be fit for work within the next two months?

(c)   If not, is he/she likely to be fit for work within the next three months?

(d)   Are there any types of work which you believe he/she would be fit for now or in the near future?

(e)   If so, how soon do you think he/she will be fit for that work?

(f)   Might he/she be able to return to work on reduced hours? If so, how many hours per week do you think he/she would be capable of work and how soon do you think he/she would be able to return on that basis?

(g)   Is there anything else you think we might be able to do to enable him/her to return any earlier than indicated in your answers to (a), (b) and (c) above?

[For your information, his/her current job is that of [ ]. This involves: *(Brief description of the job).*]

or

[Please see the attached job description, which sets out [ ]'s main duties.

I enclose a copy of a letter signed by [ ] [from which you will see that he/she has said that he/she would like to see the report before you supply it to me. Under Section 4(2) of the Access to Medical Reports Act 1988, you should not supply me with the report unless [ ] has seen it and has consented to its being supplied, or a period of 21 days has elapsed without hearing from [ ]. [ ] is entitled to ask you to amend the report. If you disagree with any amendments [ ] wants you to make, the report should be supplied without the amendments but with a statement of [ ]'s views.]*

We thank you for your assistance.

Yours etc.

*Delete if the employee had indicated he does not want to see the report beforehand.

F3.3 DRAFTING POINTS

The questions set out here are questions that might typically be asked, but in each case, these questions should be reviewed to check that they are appropriate and whether there are any other questions that should be asked.

The doctor will probably need to know a bit about the job. The easiest way to do this is often simply to provide a copy of the job description. However, job descriptions often get out of date or do not truly reflect the work of the employee. In that case, it would be better to summarise in the letter to the doctor what the employee's duties are.

F4 ACCESS TO MEDICAL REPORTS – LETTER WHERE ACCESS REQUESTED

F4.1 USE

This letter should be used if the employee has previously indicated that he or she wishes to see the report before consenting to supplying it to you.

F4.2　　　　　　　　Precedent

Letter where employee has requested access to report before its supply to you

Dear [   ]

I have today applied to your Doctor for medical report. You have indicated that you wish to have access to that report before it is supplied to me. Your Doctor cannot therefore supply me with the report unless he has allowed you access to it and you have consented to it being supplied to me, or unless 21 days elapse without the Doctor hearing from you.

Before giving your consent to the supply of the report, you are entitled to ask your Doctor to amend any part of the report which you think may be incorrect or misleading. Your Doctor may then either agree to amend the report, or simply attach to the report a statement of your views. Any request for the report to be amended should be made in writing.

Yours sincerely,

F5 CAPABILITY – INVITATION TO FORMAL MEETING

F5.1 USE

Before any dismissal or other disciplinary action, it is a statutory requirement (for dismissals/disciplinary action starting before 6 April 2009) and good practice (after that date) that the employee be invited to a meeting and informed of the reasons why you are contemplating dismissal or other disciplinary action. Disciplinary action for these purposes does not include warnings, but because a warning could, if insufficient improvement is achieved, lead to dismissal, it is advisable to follow the statutory procedure even in the case of warnings, to ensure that any subsequent dismissal is not held to be unfair on the grounds of an earlier unfair warning.

This precedent letter can be used to invite employees to the formal meeting. It should set out the complaints and evidence in sufficient detail for the employee to be able to prepare his or her defence.

F5.2 Precedent

Invitation to formal meeting

Dear [   ]

As we have discussed, the Company has a number of concerns about your performance. These are as follows: [*Set out details together with any documentary evidence – for example, output sheets showing poor level of output; documents showing mistakes that have been made; written complaints about the quality of work*].

Despite our discussions and [*set out steps that have been taken to improve performance, including training etc*], your performance is still not regarded as satisfactory. I would like to discuss this with you on [date] at [time] in [location]. [The outcome of this could be a written or final warning.] [In view of previous warnings you have received, the outcome could be a further warning or dismissal.]

You have the right to be accompanied to this meeting either by a colleague employed by this company or a representative of a trade union.

Yours sincerely,

F5.3 DRAFTING POINTS

Generally, it would not be regarded as fair to dismiss for incompetence without any prior warnings. If this is the first formal meeting to do with the employee's performance, the likely outcome is a warning (assuming the allegations are found to be proved). If there have been earlier warnings, however, then you should refer to this fact and explain that, because of these earlier warnings, a possible outcome could be the employee's dismissal.

F6 CAPABILITY – NO FURTHER ACTION

F6.1 USE

This form may be used where, following a meeting under the disciplinary or capability procedure, it is not proposed to take any further action.

F6.2 Precedent

No further action

Dear [   ]

Following out meeting on [*date*], I confirm that the Company does not propose to take any further action at this time. However, it is important that you continue to maintain a high standard of performance.

Yours sincerely

F7 CAPABILITY – WARNING FOR UNDER-PERFORMANCE

F7.1 USE

This precedent may be used for warnings for under-performance. Warnings for under-performance should generally offer more by way of guidance and support than warnings for misconduct.

F7.2 Precedent

Warning for under-performance

Dear [   ]

[Final] [Written] [Written notification of oral] warning

This is to confirm the outcome of the hearing under the Company's capability procedure held on [   ]. [I enclose for your information a note of the hearing.]

I have carefully considered all the evidence and the points you made at the hearing.

[S*et out some of the points made by the employee and your response to them.*]

I have concluded that the complaints of [*set out the complaints*] are made out and that some sort of action is appropriate. This letter, therefore, is a [final][written][written confirmation of an oral] warning. [I have taken account of the fact that you have already received [an oral] [a written] [a final written] warning.]

This warning will remain on your record for [   ] months. If there is no or insufficient improvement within the next [   ] months, then the next stage of the procedure will be invoked. [Since this is a final written warning, any further action could include dismissal.]

Specifically, the improvements we are looking for are: [*set out here reasonable and achievable targets for improvement with a reasonable timescale.*]

We have agreed the following actions which should help you to achieve the required standards: [*set out here any actions you may have agreed. These may include training, mentoring, regular review meetings.*]

You have a right of appeal against this warning. If you wish to appeal, please submit a written notice of appeal to [   ] within [   ] working days of the date of this letter. Please also set out the reasons why you disagree with the warning.

[*You may want to add something encouraging here like 'I very much hope that this warning and the support we have offered will achieve the improvements we are seeking and enable us to return to our previous good working relationship.*]

Yours sincerely

F7.3 DRAFTING POINTS

If you do not have a capability procedure, then you may use the Company's disciplinary procedure and the references in this letter to 'capability procedure' should be replaced by references to the 'disciplinary procedure'.

It is useful to prepare a note of the hearing and to send the employee a copy. This reduces the likelihood of the employee, at a later date (for example at an appeal or in an employment tribunal) claiming to have made a point which they did not make or disputing any evidence that may have been submitted to the hearing.

It is useful to set out some of the points the employee made at the hearing and your response to them. This will show that you have considered what the employee had to say and lessen the risk that an employment tribunal may conclude that the procedure you followed was just 'going through the motions'.

The capability procedure may determine how long the warning is to last for. If it does not, then you can choose an appropriate period. ACAS suggests six months for ordinary warnings and 12 months for a final warning.

The capability procedure will probably set out the period within which an appeal should be lodged. If it does not, then 5 working days should normally be sufficient. Under the statutory procedure, however, there is no set time limit and an appeal must be lodged within a 'reasonable' period. Therefore, if an employee submits a notice of appeal outside the usual time limits, you should consider whether it was submitted within a reasonable time. This may involve making enquiries about why the appeal was submitted so late. In some cases, employment tribunals have held that appeals well outside the time limit laid down in the Company's procedure were nevertheless submitted within a reasonable period. If you have reminded an employee of the period for appealing under your own procedures, it is more likely that an employment tribunal will treat a late appeal as outside a reasonable period.

F8 CAPABILITY – DISMISSAL LETTER

F8.1　USE

This precedent may be used for dismissals for under-performance. Generally, it will not be regarded as fair to dismiss for under-performance without prior warnings having been given. This precedent, therefore, assumes that previous warnings have been given.

F8.2　Precedent

Dismissal notice

Dear [   ]

Notice of dismissal

This is to confirm the outcome of the hearing under the Company's capability procedure held on [   ]. [I enclose for your information a note of the hearing.]

I have carefully considered all the evidence and the points you made at the hearing.

[*Set out some of the points made by the employee and your response to them.*]

I have concluded that the complaints of under-performance are made out. In particular [*set out a summary of the complaints and why you consider the evidence demonstrates under-performance sufficient to justify dismissal.*] In view of your previous warnings on [set out dates] I have concluded that your employment should be terminated. This letter is therefore notice of termination of employment [to take effect on [*date*]] [with immediate effect but with a payment in lieu of notice of £[   ]].

[You will not be required to work your notice.]

You have a right of appeal against. If you wish to appeal, please submit a written notice of appeal to [   ] within [   ] working days of the date of this letter. Please also set out the reasons why you disagree with the warning.

[*You may want to add something sympathetic here like:* 'I am sorry your employment with us has terminated in this way but I wish you every success in the future'.]

Yours sincerely

F8.3 DRAFTING POINTS

If you do not have a capability procedure, then you may use the Company's disciplinary procedure and the references in this letter to 'capability procedure' should be replaced by references to the 'disciplinary procedure'.

You may not wish the employee to work their notice, in which case this should be stated. The employee could either:

- be put on 'garden leave' for the period of notice (but if you do not have a right in your contract to place someone on garden leave, this may amount to a breach of contract, invalidating certain clauses in the contract of employment such as restrictive covenants); or

- be given a payment in lieu of notice. Again, if you do not have a right under the contract to dismiss with a payment in lieu of notice, there is a risk that this will be regarded as a breach of contract invalidating restrictive covenants.

It is useful to prepare a note of the hearing and to send the employee a copy. This reduces the likelihood of the employee, at a later date (for example at an appeal or in an employment tribunal) claiming to have made a point which they did not make or disputing any evidence that may have been submitted to the hearing.

It is useful to set out some of the points the employee made at the hearing and your response to them. For example, if the employee has blamed other people for not offering sufficient support or training, then explain why you think they did receive the support and training they needed and why you do not think that further support training would achieve anything. Generally, if some training has been provided and warnings have been given but there is still no or insufficient improvement, then that is sufficient to show that further support, training and warnings would not achieve anything. This will show that you have considered what the employee had to say and lessen the risk that an employment tribunal may conclude that the procedure you followed was just 'going through the motions'.

The letter should set out in broad terms why you have decided to dismiss.

The capability procedure will probably set out the period within which an appeal should be lodged. If it does not, then 5 working days should normally be sufficient. Under the statutory procedure, however, there is no set time limit and an appeal must be lodged within a 'reasonable' period. Therefore, if an employee submits a notice of appeal outside the usual time limits, you should consider whether it was submitted within a reasonable time. This may involve making enquiries about why the appeal was submitted so late. In some cases, employment tribunals have held that appeals well outside the time limit laid down in the disciplinary procedure were nevertheless submitted within a reasonable period. If you have reminded an employee of the period for appealing under your own procedures, it is more likely that an employment tribunal will treat a late appeal as outside a reasonable period.

F9 CAPABILITY – NOTICE OF APPEAL

F9.1 USE

This precedent may be used to acknowledge receipt of a notice of appeal against any action taken under the capability procedure and to notify the time, date and place of the appeal hearing.

F9.2 **Precedent**

Acknowledgement of notice of appeal

Dear

I have received your letter of [*date*] appealing against [*the decision appealed against*].

Please attend an appeal hearing at [*time and date*] at which [ ] will hear your appeal. The notes of the original hearing and any documents or other evidence given at that hearing will be made available to [ ]. If there is any other evidence you wish to rely on, please send it to [ ] at least 24 hours before the hearing.

You have the right to be accompanied by a work colleague or representative of a trade union.

If you have any queries about this letter or the process to be following, please contact [the Human Resources Department].

Yours sincerely

F10 COLLECTIVE CONSULTATION – REDUNDANCY INFORMATION LETTER

F10.1 USE

Legislation requires employers to consult with trade union or employee representatives when proposing 20 or more redundancies in a three-month period at one establishment and stipulates that there must be at least 30 days between the start of consultation and the date of the first redundancy or redundancies and at least 90 days where there are more than 100 proposed redundancies.

Some employers may consult employee representatives or trade union representatives over all redundancies irrespective of the number. They may be required to do this under a collective agreement with a recognised trade union.

Employers who do not recognise a trade union may need to arrange for the election of employee representatives – see Division D4 of *Jordans Employment Law Service* and the relevant precedent forms and precedent information sheets. It is up to the employer to arrange the ballot.

If required to consult, employers should write to the representatives of the recognised trade union or, if no union is recognised, to employee representatives explaining the proposals and in particular giving the following information:

– the reasons for the proposals;

– the numbers and descriptions of employees whom it is proposed to make redundant;

– the proposed method of selecting those who are to be made redundant;

– the total number of employees of that description;

– the proposed method of selecting those who are to be made redundant;

– the proposed method of carrying out the redundancies;

– how redundancy payments are to be calculated. The legislation determines the minimum redundancy payments that must be made but some employers may consider enhancing those payments, depending on the circumstances.

In consultation with the employee representatives and/or trade union representatives, the employer should then try to agree on all of the above points. If it becomes apparent that agreement cannot be reached on any particular point or points, then ultimately it is up to the employer to decide, taking account of any representations made by the representatives.

This precedent may be used to start the consultation process and provide the required information.

F10.2   **Precedent**

Collective consultation letter

[TO BE TYPED ON HEADED NOTEPAPER]

[For representatives of a recognised trade union, this letter should be hand delivered to them or posted to the union's head or main office, or such other address as may be requested by the union.]

[For elected employee representatives, this letter should be hand-delivered to the individual or posted to an address notified by them.]

[Date]

Dear [   ]

Proposed redundancies

We are supplying the following information to you as [trade union representatives/elected employee representatives] to enable us to consult with you as fully as possible regarding the possible collective redundancies.

We are considering this proposal because [*reasons*].

We are proposing that [*number/positions*] in [*department or some other way of describing the category of employees from which redundancies would be selected*] would be redundant.

The number of employees in [these departments] [in each of these categories] is: [*number of employees in each category*].

It is proposed that no dismissals would take effect before [*proposed date of first dismissal taking effect – if 20 or more employees are to be made redundant this must comply with the minimum consultation period of 30 or 90 days depending on the number to be made redundant*].

It is proposed that:

- the method of selection for redundant employees will be [*details*].

- all employees who are made redundant would receive statutory

F10 Collective Consultation – Redundancy Information Letter

redundancy pay calculated by reference to age and length of service in accordance with the relevant statutory provisions [enhanced by not applying the statutory cap on a week's pay and then multiplied by [ ]].

- [In the first instance, we are considering asking for volunteers for redundancy.]

- We propose that those made redundant [would receive a payment in lieu of notice] [should work throughout the notice period.]

- employees would be provided as early as practicable with an indication of the date upon which any proposed redundancy would be likely to take effect.

We enclose our Form HR1 which we have supplied to the Redundancy Payments Office.

We would like to discuss with you these proposals and in particular any means by which the need for redundancies might be avoided or the numbers of redundancies might be reduced, or any means by which the consequences of the proposed redundancies might be mitigated.

Yours sincerely

F10.3 DRAFTING POINTS

This sets out the information required to be given to representatives. Employers are also required to complete form HR1 and send it to the Redundancy Payments Office with a copy to the representatives.

You do not have to ask for volunteers for redundancy. The advantage of doing so is that you may reduce the number of compulsory redundancies, making the process more palatable, and it would be extremely difficult for a person who has volunteered for redundancy to argue that their redundancy was unfair. The disadvantage is that it may lead to an unbalanced workforce and you risk losing employees you would rather retain. In the notice asking for volunteers, you can state that you reserve the right not to accept an application for voluntary redundancy (see precedent request for volunteers).

F11 COLLECTIVE CONSULTATION – REQUESTS FOR NOMINATIONS (TUPE)

F11.1 USE

This may be used for inviting nominations for employee representatives for the purposes of consultation over business transfers.

F11.2 Precedent

Request for nominations (transfer)

[TO BE TYPED ON COMPANY HEADED PAPER]

[Date]

Dear [   ]

We are proposing to [sell/ contract out/ transfer] our [identify the part of the business that is being transferred] to [transferee].

This may affect your employment with the company. We would like to keep everyone informed and if appropriate to consult as fully as possible on any measures we may have to take in connection with the transfer, which could affect your employment. To achieve this, we would like to give you an opportunity to elect employee representatives. We will keep the elected representatives informed about the transfer including its implications for the employment of individuals including yourself and if any measures are proposed we will consult with those representatives.

We are therefore inviting employees to put themselves forward as candidates to be elected as employee representatives.

Initially we are seeking nominations for candidates to stand in the election. I enclose an information sheet explaining the election of employee representatives including the number of representatives that will be elected and the procedure that will be adopted during the election process.

If you have any queries in the meantime please feel free to speak to [   ].

Yours sincerely

F12 COLLECTIVE CONSULTATION – REQUESTS FOR NOMINATIONS (REDUNDANCY)

F12.1　USE

This should be used for inviting nominations for employee representatives for the purposes of consultation over collective redundancies.

F12.2　Precedent

Request for nominations

[TO BE TYPED ON COMPANY HEADED PAPER]

[Date]

Dear [　　　]

We are sorry to inform you that we are considering making a number of redundancies in the business. We will be providing more background information in due course but in general terms; redundancies are under consideration because [*details*]. [Your own position may be affected by these proposals.]

Before any decisions are made in this regard we wish to give you an opportunity to express your views. As part of that process we are giving you an opportunity to elect employee representatives whom we will consult on all aspects of the proposals including whether there is any way of avoiding redundancies, reducing the numbers affected or lessening the impact.

For the purposes of this consultation [*number*] elected employee representatives are required. We are therefore inviting employees to put themselves forward as candidates to be elected as employee representatives.

Initially we are seeking nominations for candidates to stand in the election. I enclose for your information details concerning the election of employee representatives including the number of representatives that will be elected and the procedure that will be adopted during the election process.

If you have any queries in the meantime please feel free to speak to [　].

Yours sincerely

F13 COLLECTIVE CONSULTATION – REQUEST FOR VOLUNTEERS

F13.1 USE

This precedent may be used to ask for volunteers for redundancy.

F13.2 Precedent

Request for volunteers

TO BE POSTED ON A NOTICE BOARD, THE INTRANET OR CIRCULATED TO ALL EMPLOYEES

[Date]

Dear [   ]

Request for volunteers for redundancy

[As you will know from recent discussions and announcements] we are considering making a number of redundancies because [*reasons*].

We are proposing that [*number/positions*] in [*department or some other way of describing the category of employees from which redundancies would be selected*] would be redundant.

We are now looking for volunteers for redundancy. If you would be interested, please contact [the Human Resources Department] for a confidential discussion about what this would mean for you and what your entitlement would be. Any requests for information about voluntary redundancy would be strictly confidential and will not be revealed to those who make the decision on who should be made redundant.

It is proposed that volunteers for redundancy would receive statutory redundancy pay calculated by reference to age and length of service in accordance with the relevant statutory provisions [enhanced by not applying the statutory cap on a week's pay and then multiplied by [ ]], together with a payment in lieu of notice [and a one-off ex gratia payment of [ ]]. We cannot guarantee that these payments would be available to anyone made compulsorily redundant.

We reserve the right not to accept an application for voluntary redundancy.

Yours sincerely

F13.3 DRAFTING POINTS

Many employers enhance the statutory redundancy payment, particularly for volunteers. The ways in which redundancy payments can be enhanced are now more restricted than previously because of the age discrimination legislation. The regulations on age discrimination recognised that most redundancy pay schemes (including the statutory one) to some extent discriminate on grounds of age. Rather than scrapping the redundancy pay scheme and starting again, an exemption was included within the regulations that exempts redundancy payments from age discrimination so long as the only departures from the statutory formula are the removal of the cap on a week's pay and multiplying the overall result by a factor. Many enhanced redundancy pay schemes do not quite work like this. The age discrimination legislation therefore limits the enhanced redundancy payments that are permissible. The formula set out here reflects most enhanced redundancy schemes. Another permissible option is to add a lump some which is the same for everyone to all redundancy payments. That could not possibly be discriminatory because all employees would be treated equally.

How you decide to enhance the redundancy payment may depend on which employees you want to encourage to volunteer. Lump sum payments may be more attractive to shorter serving employees because their redundancy payments alone could be significantly less than longer serving employees. Removing the statutory cap will be more attractive to the highly paid employees.

F14 COLLECTIVE CONSULTATION – TUPE INFORMATION LETTER

F14.1 USE

Transferors and transferees of a business are required by the Transfer of Undertakings (Protection of Employment) Regulations 2006 ('TUPE') to provide representatives of employees who may be affected by the transfer (that is employee representatives or representatives of a recognised trade union) with certain specified information in writing; and, if they propose measures in connection with the transfer. This applies most often to the transferor, since the transferor's employees are inevitably going to be affected by the transfer. The transferee may be required to inform and consult as well, however, if any of its employees are likely to be affected – for example, if the transferee plans to make redundancies after the two workforces (ie its own and the acquired workforce) have been combined. This precedent is drafted as if it is the transferor who is informing/consulting and should be adapted for use by the transferee.

F14.2 Precedent

Collective consultation letter

[TO BE TYPED ON COMPANY HEADED NOTEPAPER]

[For trade union representatives, this letter should be hand delivered to them or posted to the union's head or main office or such other address as may be requested by the union.]

[For elected employee representatives, this letter should be hand-delivered to them or posted to an address notified by the employee.]

[Date]

Dear [   ]

Business transfer

We supplying the following information to you as [trade union representatives/elected employee representatives] to enable us to consult with you on behalf of our employees as fully as possible regarding the transfer.

The transfer is to take place on or about [*date*]. The reason for the transfer is [*reason*].

The implications of this will be:

F14 Collective Consultation – TUPE Information Letter

- [that from the date of the transfer, everyone in the business transferred will be employed by [ ]] OR

- [that from the date of the transfer, those employees who work predominantly within the business to be transferred will be employed by [*transferee*]] OR

- [no employees are likely to transfer with the business to [*transferee*] because [*transferee*] already has sufficient staff to run the business and because there is nobody who works wholly or predominantly in the part of the business transferred. [This will mean a significant reduction in the amount of work available and there are likely, therefore, to be redundancies.]]

- [*any other implications, eg relocation*]

We have been told by [*the transferee*] that it envisages the following measures:

[*set out here the measures you have been told by the transferee that it envisage. These may include redundancy, relocation (which will probably constitute redundancy because the transferee will cease carrying on business at the place you carried on business), possibly changes to pensions schemes*]

[For the reasons explained above, it is envisaged that some redundancies may be necessary. The proposal is that [*insert number/positions*] would be redundant.

The number of employees affected would be: [*number of employees in each category*]].

[It is proposed that no redundancies would take effect before [insert proposed date of first dismissal taking effect – if 20 or more employees are to be made redundant, this must comply with the minimum consultation period of 30 or 90 days depending on the number to be made redundant].

[It is proposed that: set *out here the required information about redundancies, ie*

- the numbers and descriptions of employees whom it is proposed to make redundant

- the proposed method of selecting those who are to be made redundant

- the proposed method of carrying out the redundancies

- how redundancy payments are to be calculated

- The proposed time-scale]

We would like to discuss with you the transfer, its implications and the measures envisaged. We propose the first meeting should take pace at [*time and place*].

Yours sincerely

[ ]

For and on behalf of the Employer

F14.3 DRAFTING POINTS

Transferee's measures: The transferee is required to inform the transferor of what measures it envisages it will take in respect of affected employees. This is commonly done is what is often referred to as a measures letter. Typically, it may include any proposals for redundancies, or for reviewing the combined business before making any decisions. There is still considerable uncertainly about what constitutes a 'measure'. For example, pension rights do not transfer under TUPE. Does a proposal by the transferee to create a pension scheme for the acquired workforce amount to a measure which should be notified to the transferee? There is no clear answer to this yet and it is recommended that, until the law on this is clarified, the introduction of a new pension scheme should be treated as a measure.

Redundancies: If the transferee proposes 20 or more redundancies, then in addition to consulting under TUPE, consultation is required in respect of those redundancies and certain specified information must be provided at the start of the consultation process (see Precedent information letter for collective redundancies at **[F10.2]**). There must be at least 30 days between the start of consultation and the date of the first redundancy. If the transferee is hoping to make the redundancies at the point of transfer or shortly after, then consultation will have to start before the transfer, even though the redundancies will take place after the transfer. It is dangerous for the redundancies to take place before the transfer because the transferor may not have a valid reason for the redundancies. It has been held that the transferor may not rely on the transferee's reason for dismissal nor can they rely on the fact that the only way to sell the business would be to make the redundancies. There would be serious risk, therefore, of an unfair dismissal if redundancies are made before the transfer.

However, this means that consultation on the redundancies may have to start well before the transfer. This letter could be used to supply both the information required under TUPE and the information required for the redundancy consultation.

F15 DISCIPLINARY PROCEDURE – INVITATION TO INVESTIGATION MEETING

F15.1 USE

Disciplinary action including dismissal should generally only be taken after a reasonable investigation. In most cases, the investigation will include an interview with the person against whom allegations have been made. This precedent should be sent to the employee to invite him or her to an investigation meeting and to give the employee sufficient information for him or her to be able to prepare for it.

F15.2 Precedent

Invitation to investigation meeting

Dear [   ]

As we have discussed, the Company has the following concerns. [**Set out here what the concerns are explaining:**

- **what it is alleged the employee has or has not done which they should have done or not done;**

- **the date or dates of the events in question;**

- **the source of the information unless that source wishes to remain anonymous;**

- **any instructions, contractual provisions or work rules from which the employee should have known that such behaviour was unacceptable;**

- **any relevant parts of the disciplinary rules, in particular whether the conduct complained of could amount to gross misconduct.]**

We are currently investigating these matters. To help us with this investigation, could you please attend a meeting with [   ], who is carrying out the investigation.

[During the investigation and pending any disciplinary hearing, you are suspended on full pay and should not attend for work until further notified. During the period of your suspension, you should not contact any customer, client or supplier of the Company or any other employees.]

If there is any further information you need in order to prepare for the meeting, please let me know.

[You have the right to be accompanied to this meeting either by a colleague employed by this company or a representative of a trade union.]

Yours sincerely,

F15.3 DRAFTING POINTS

Take care to avoid any suggestion that the Company has already reached a conclusion on whether the employee committed the act complained of and, if so, whether any disciplinary action is appropriate. The misconduct alleged, therefore, should he expressed in neutral terms and it should be made clear that these are allegations only, not firm conclusions. For example, the section setting out the allegations should generally start with words such as:

'It has been alleged that' or 'One of your colleague has reported that ...'

Strictly, employees do not have the right to be accompanied at an investigation meeting. However, many disciplinary procedures do give employees that right. The final paragraph need only therefore be included if the disciplinary procedure gives a right to be accompanied at the meeting.

Generally the person conducting the investigation should not be the person who will conduct the disciplinary hearing. For those employers who do not have sufficient resources available to achieve this, it may be unavoidable that the investigator also conducts the hearing, in which case it may be unreasonable not to allow the employee to be accompanied at the investigation meeting.

You may wish to suspend the employee during the investigation and pending the disciplinary hearing. You can either notify the employee at the same time as inviting the employee to the investigation meeting or in a separate letter. Generally, suspension is only appropriate where gross misconduct is alleged and there is a risk either of further misconduct or of interference with the investigation if the employee is not suspended.

F16 DISCIPLINARY – SUSPENSION LETTER

F16.1 USE

This letter should be used to notify an employee that he or she is suspended during a disciplinary investigation. Generally, suspension is only appropriate where gross misconduct is alleged and there is a risk either of further misconduct or of interference with the investigation if the employee is not suspended.

F16.2 Precedent

Letter notifying suspension

Dear [   ],

Certain allegations have been made against you which are sufficiently serious for us to have to investigate them under the Company's disciplinary procedure. During this investigation, you will be suspended from your duties.

We will notify you in due course of the details of the allegations.

In the meantime, please do not attend for work or contact clients, customers, suppliers or other employees until further notification.

F17 DISCIPLINARY – INVITATION TO FORMAL MEETING

F17.1 USE

Once the investigation is completed, and assuming the investigation shows there is a case to answer, the employee should be invited to a disciplinary meeting and given sufficient information about the allegations and the evidence backing them up to be able to prepare his or her defence.

F17.2 Precedent

Invitation to formal meeting

Dear [   ]

As we have discussed, the Company has the following concerns. [**Set out here what the concerns are explaining:**

- what it is alleged the employee has or has not done which they should have done or not done;

- the date or dates of the events in question;

- the source of the information unless that source wishes to remain anonymous;

- any instructions, contractual provisions or work rules from which the employee should have known that such behaviour was unacceptable;

- any relevant parts of the disciplinary rules, in particular whether the conduct complained of could amount to gross misconduct.]

Please find enclosed [*list relevant documents, witness statement or notes of interviews and other evidence which will be used to back up the allegations*] and a copy of the Company's disciplinary procedure.

In order for the Company to decide what action, if any, to take, I would like to discuss this with you on [date] at [time] in [location]. The outcome of this meeting could be a written, a final warning or dismissal or the Company may decide that no disciplinary action is appropriate.

[You currently have a [written warning][final written warning] which may be taken into account in deciding what action, if any, to take.]

If there is any further information you need in order to prepare for the meeting, please let me know.

You have the right to be accompanied to this meeting either by a colleague employed by this company or a representative of a trade union.

Yours sincerely,

F17.3 DRAFTING POINTS

Take care to avoid any suggestion that the Company has already reached a conclusion on whether the employee committed the act complained of and, if so, whether any disciplinary action is appropriate. The misconduct alleged, therefore, should he expressed in neutral terms and it should be made clear that these are allegations only, not firm conclusions. For example, the section setting out the allegations should generally start with words such as:

'It has been alleged that' or 'One of your colleague has reported that …'

The employee must be given sufficient information about the allegations and the evidence backing them up to be able to prepare his or her defence. Generally, the easiest way to achieve this is to summarise the allegations in the letter and to enclose all relevant documentation. Occasionally, some witnesses wish to remain anonymous. If that is the case, that should be stated in the letter. As much information as possible should still be provided, if necessary by redacting the witness statements or notes of interview meetings so that the identity of the informant cannot be determined; or if that is not possible, a summary of what the anonymous informants are saying should be provided together with an explanation that the informants wish to remain anonymous. It is helpful to include a statement within the witness statements or interview notes that the informant wishes to remain anonymous.

F18 DISCIPLINARY – WARNING

F18.1 USE

This precedent may be used for warnings for misconduct. Warnings for under-performance should generally offer more by way of guidance and support – see the separate precedent warning.

F18.2 Precedent

Warning for misconduct

Dear [   ]

[Final] [Written] [Written notification of oral] warning

This is to confirm the outcome of the disciplinary hearing held on [ ]. [I enclose for your information a note of the disciplinary hearing.]

I have carefully considered all the evidence and the points you made at the hearing.

[S*et out some of the points made by the employee and your response to them.*]

I have concluded that the complaints of [*set out the complaints*] are made out and that some sort of disciplinary action is appropriate. This letter, therefore, is a [final][written] [written confirmation of an oral] warning. [I have taken account of the fact that you have already received [an oral] [a written] [a final written] warning.]

This warning will remain on your disciplinary record for [ ] months. If there is no improvement or if there is any further misconduct, then the next stage of the disciplinary procedure will be invoked. [Since this is a final written warning, any further misconduct could lead to dismissal.]

You have a right of appeal against this warning. If you wish to appeal, please submit a written notice of appeal to [ ] within [ ] working days of the date of this letter. Please also set out the reasons why you disagree with the warning.

[*You may want to add something encouraging here like 'I very much hope that this is the end of the matter (subject to any appeal you may wish to make) and that we can return to our previous good working relationship.*]

Yours sincerely

F18.3 DRAFTING POINTS

It is useful to prepare a note of the disciplinary hearing and to send the employee a copy. This reduces the likelihood of the employee, at a later date (for example at an appeal or in an employment tribunal) claiming to have made a point which they did not make or disputing any evidence that may have been submitted to the hearing.

It is useful to set out some of the points the employee made at the disciplinary hearing and your response to them. This will show that you have considered what the employee had to say and lessen the risk that an employment tribunal may conclude that the disciplinary procedure was just 'going through the motions'.

The disciplinary procedure may determine how long the warning is to last for. If it does not, then you can choose an appropriate period. ACAS suggests six months for ordinary warnings and 12 months for a final warning.

The disciplinary procedure will probably set out the period within which an appeal should be lodged. If it does not, then 5 working days should normally be sufficient. Under the statutory dismissal and grievance procedures, however, there is no set time limit and an appeal must be lodged within a 'reasonable' period. Therefore, if an employee submits a notice of appeal outside the usual time limits, you should consider whether it was submitted within a reasonable time. This may involve making enquiries about why the appeal was submitted so late. In some cases, employment tribunals have held that appeals well outside the time limit laid down in the disciplinary procedure were nevertheless submitted within a reasonable period. If you have reminded an employee of the period for appealing under your own procedures, it is more likely that an employment tribunal will treat a late appeal as outside a reasonable period. The statutory dismissal and grievance procedures are to be repealed for dismissals and grievances relating to incidents on or after 1 April 2009, so then it is more likely that employment tribunals will accept that employers will not need to deal with appeals or (in the case of warnings, grievances) submitted late.

F19 DISCIPLINARY – DISMISSAL LETTER

F19.1 USE

This precedent may be used for dismissals for misconduct.

F19.2   Precedent

Dismissal notice

Dear [   ]

Notice of [summary] dismissal

This is to confirm the outcome of the disciplinary hearing held on [   ]. [I enclose for your information a note of the disciplinary hearing.]

I have carefully considered all the evidence and the points you made at the hearing.

[S*et out some of the points made by the employee and your response to them.*]

I have concluded that the complaints of [*set out the complaints*] are made out and that some sort of disciplinary action is appropriate. In view of [the seriousness of the matter] [and taking account of your earlier warnings on [*dates*]] I have concluded that your employment should be terminated. This letter is therefore notice of termination of employment [with immediate effect] [to take effect on [*date*]] [with immediate effect but with a payment in lieu of notice of £[   ]].

[You will not be required to work your notice.]

You have a right of appeal against. If you wish to appeal, please submit a written notice of appeal to [   ] within [   ] working days of the date of this letter. Please also set out the reasons why you disagree with the warning.

[*You may want to add something sympathetic here like: 'I am sorry your employment with us has terminated in this way but I wish you every success in the future'.*]

Yours sincerely

F19.3 DRAFTING POINTS

Generally, summary dismissal should only be reserved for the most serious cases – those that are listed in your disciplinary procedure as amounting to gross misconduct. If the dismissal is not summary, then you should give the employee notice of dismissal. You may not wish the employee to work their notice, in which case this should be stated. The employee could either:

- be put on 'garden leave' for the period of notice (but if you do not have a right in your contract to place someone on garden leave, this may amount to a breach of contract, invalidating certain clauses in the contract of employment such as restrictive covenants); or

- be given a payment in lieu of notice. Again, if you do not have a right under the contract to dismiss with a payment in lieu of notice, there is a risk that this will be regarded as a breach of contract invalidating restrictive covenants.

It is useful to prepare a note of the disciplinary hearing and to send the employee a copy. This reduces the likelihood of the employee, at a later date (for example at an appeal or in an employment tribunal) claiming to have made a point which they did not make or disputing any evidence that may have been submitted to the hearing.

It is useful to set out some of the points the employee made at the disciplinary hearing and your response to them. This will show that you have considered what the employee had to say and lessen the risk that an employment tribunal may conclude that the disciplinary procedure was just 'going through the motions'.

The letter should set out in broad terms why you have decided to dismiss.

The disciplinary procedure will probably set out the period within which an appeal should be lodged. If it does not, then 5 working days should normally be sufficient. Under the statutory procedure (to be repealed from April 2009 in respect of dismissals where the process has started after that date), however, there is no set time limit and an appeal must be lodged within a 'reasonable' period. Therefore, if an employee submits a notice of appeal outside the usual time limits, you should consider whether it was submitted within a reasonable time. This may involve making enquiries about why the appeal was submitted so late. In some cases, employment tribunals have held that appeals well outside the time limit laid down in the disciplinary procedure were nevertheless submitted within a reasonable period. If you have reminded an employee of the period for appealing under your own procedures, it is more likely that an employment tribunal will treat a late appeal as outside a reasonable period.

F20 DISCIPLINARY – NO FURTHER ACTION

F20.1 USE

This form may be used where, following a meeting under the disciplinary procedure, it is not proposed to take any further action.

F20.2 Precedent

No further action

Dear [   ]

Following out meeting on [*date*], I confirm that the Company does not propose to take any further action at this time.

[*Add something encouraging and appreciative like:* I would like to thank you for the professional way in which you have conducted yourself throughout the disciplinary process, which I appreciate must have been a difficult time for you.]

Yours sincerely

F21 EMPLOYEE REPRESENTATIVES – CANDIDATE NOMINATION FORM

F21.1 USE

There are various situations where an employer may wish to appoint employee representatives. The main ones are:

– where the employer is required to consult employee representatives over proposed redundancies (see Division D4 of *Jordans Employment Law Service*);

– where the employer is required to consult over the transfer of a business (see Division D5 of *Jordans Employment Law Service*);

– where the employer wishes to enter a workforce agreement. There are certain matters which can only be achieved by a workforce or collective agreement – for example amendments to the Working Time Regulations 1998 (SI 1998/1833) (see Division C3 of *Jordans Employment Law Service*) or a procedure for dealing with requests for parental leave which differs from that laid down in the regulations (see Division C2 of *Jordans Employment Law Service*).

It is generally only necessary to appoint employee representatives where there is no recognised trade union. If there is a recognised trade union, then representatives of that union will be the employee representatives.

Employee representatives must be elected in a ballot which so far as is reasonably practicable should be secret. It is up to the employer to arrange the ballot. This form is the first step in that process.

As will be seen, it can be extremely simple.

F21.2 Precedent

Employee representative candidate nomination form

I wish to stand as a candidate as an employee representative

Name ....

Signed ....

Dated ....

F22 EMPLOYEE REPRESENTATIVES – INFORMATION SHEET (TUPE)

F22.1 USE

This can be used as an information sheet to explain to employees the process for nominating and then electing employee representatives for the purpose of consultation where a business is being transferred within the meaning of TUPE 2006.

F22.2 Precedent

Employee representatives for TUPE – election process

In order to consult with staff collectively about the transfer, its timing and implications, we wish to make arrangements for the election of employee representatives. We propose to have up to a total of [*number*] elect representatives from the following [*groups/departments*].

[*group/department*] [*number of representatives required*]

All employees in the above affected groups/departments are eligible to stand for election to represent their group/department.

The role of the employee representative is a very important one and will have the full support of the management team. Employee representatives' existing workload will be adjusted as necessary to make allowance for their new responsibilities. [Employee representatives will receive appropriate training.]

This document gives you information on:

- The role of the employee representative
- How to be nominated or to nominate someone else
- Time-scales for the election
- Eligibility to vote
- Voting procedures
- Elections rules

The role of the employee representative

Employee representatives are elected in order to consult with all staff regarding the transfer and its implications. In particular, consultation will cover the measures, including possible redundancies, we envisage we will take in connection with the transfer. Matters that will need to be discussed will be the proposed timing of any redundancies, the proposed selection process and the implications for the staff affected. It is envisaged that anyone elected will remain an employee representative for a period of [ ] weeks from the date of the announcement of the outcome of the ballot; that period is expected to cover the period of consultation and a short period after that.

[Arrangements will be made for the elected employee representatives to be briefed [and trained] to carry out the role].

Any employee, of any grade, within their affected [group/department] may be elected to be an employee representative.

[There are a number of key skills and attributes that we believe are important and will help representatives deliver in this role.

- **communication skills** – effective co-ordination of employees' feedback and concerns and putting forward constructive ideas and suggestions to the management team.

- **business understanding** – thorough understanding and appreciation of business issues and needs.

- **energy** – high levels of energy and commitment throughout the consultation process.

- **supportive** – providing support to those they are representing through listening to concerns and issues and responding to colleagues' requests in the most appropriate way.]

How to be nominated

You may put yourself forward as a candidate for the role of employee representative by competing the "Employee Representative Candidate Nomination Form" or you may nominate someone else who you think would be appropriate.

- **Time-scales for the elections**

    [   ] Nomination of employee representative begins
    [   ] Closing date/time for nominations
    [   ] Voting papers sent out and voting commences
    [   ] Closing date/time for voting
    [   ] Ballot Count
    [   ] Announce results of election

- **Eligibility to vote**

  All employees within each of the affected [group/department] are eligible to vote for candidates nominated from their [group/department].

- **Voting Procedures**

  - You may vote for up to [*number*] candidates. Your vote will not be counted if you vote for more than [*number*] candidates but you can vote for fewer candidates.

  - To vote you should mark the voting form with an "X" in the box adjacent to the name(s) of the candidate(s) for whom you wish to vote. Your vote may not be counted if you make additional marks on the form.

  - The [*number*] candidates with the greatest number of votes cast in their favour will be elected as the Employee Representatives. In the event that two or more candidates have each received the same number of votes, then all such tied candidates shall be elected as Employee Representatives.

  - You should return your completed voting form by placing it in the box provided in [*location*] by [*time and date*].

  - If you make a mistake when completing the form, you should hand the spoilt form to [ ] and ask for a replacement.

  - So far as possible, the ballot should be secret and no undue pressure should be put on anyone to vote in a particular way or not to vote. If you feel that the arrangements to ensure secrecy and the absence of undue pressure are not working, then please notify [the Human Resources Department].

  - If you have any questions you should contact [ ].

F23 EMPLOYEE REPRESENTATIVES – INFORMATION SHEET (REDUNDANCY)

F23.1 USE

This can be used as an information sheet to explain to employees the process for nominating and then electing employee representatives for the purpose of consultation where 20 or more redundancies are proposed.

F23.2 Precedent

Employee representatives for redundancy consultation – election process

In order to consult with staff collectively about the proposed redundancies, their timing and implications, how many redundancies we envisage, the proposed method of selection, we wish to make arrangements for the election of employee representatives. We propose to have up to a total of [*number*] elect representatives from the following [*groups/ departments*].

[*group/department*] [*number of representatives required*]

All employees in the above affected groups/departments are eligible to stand for election to represent their group/department.

The role of the employee representative is a very important one and will have the full support of the management team. Employee representatives' existing workload will be adjusted as necessary to make allowance for their new responsibilities. [Employee representatives will receive appropriate training.]

This document gives you information on:

- The role of the employee representative

- How to be nominated or to nominate someone else

- Time-scales for the election

- Eligibility to vote

- Voting procedures

- Elections rules

The role of the employee representative

Employee representatives are elected in order to consult with all staff regarding the proposed redundancies. The representatives will be provided with information about the proposals. They will discuss this information with all affected employees, either in a group or individually – that is up to them to decide. They will be the key channel of communication between us and the workforce and we want this consultation process to ensure that we implement these redundancies in a way that will help us to reach the fairest decision and provide as much assistance as we can to anyone who is made redundant. To do this, we do need a good process of communication between management and the workforce. The employee representatives will play a key role in this.

It is envisaged that anyone elected will remain an employee representative for a period of [ ] weeks from the date of the announcement of the outcome of the ballot; that period is expected to cover the period of consultation and a short period after that.

[Arrangements will be made for the elected employee representatives to be briefed [and trained] to carry out the role].

Any employee, of any grade, within their affected [group/department] may be elected to be an employee representative.

[There are a number of key skills and attributes that we believe are important and will help representatives deliver in this role.

- **communication skills** – effective co-ordination of employees' feedback and concerns and putting forward constructive ideas and suggestions to the management team.

- **business understanding** – thorough understanding and appreciation of business issues and needs.

- **energy** – high levels of energy and commitment throughout the consultation process.

- **supportive** – providing support to those they are representing through listening to concerns and issues and responding to colleagues' requests in the most appropriate way.]

How to be nominated

You may put yourself forward as a candidate for the role of employee representative by competing the "Employee Representative Candidate Nomination Form" or you may nominate someone else who you think would be appropriate.

- **Time-scales for the elections**

    | [   ] | Nomination of employee representative begins |
    | [   ] | Closing date/time for nominations |
    | [   ] | Voting papers sent out and voting commences |
    | [   ] | Closing date/time for voting |

- [   ] Ballot Count
- [   ] Announce results of election

- **Eligibility to vote**

  All employees within each of the affected [group/department] are eligible to vote for candidates nominated from their [group/department].

- **Voting Procedures**

  - You may vote for up to [*number*] candidates. Your vote will not be counted if you vote for more than [*number*] candidates but you can vote for fewer candidates.

  - To vote you should mark the voting form with an "X" in the box adjacent to the name(s) of the candidate(s) for whom you wish to vote. Your vote may not be counted if you make additional marks on the form.

  - The [*number*] candidates with the greatest number of votes cast in their favour will be elected as the Employee Representatives. In the event that two or more candidates have each received the same number of votes, then all such tied candidates shall be elected as Employee Representatives.

  - You should return your completed voting form by placing it in the box provided in [*location*] by [*time and date*].

  - If you make a mistake when completing the form, you should hand the spoilt form to [ ] and ask for a replacement.

  - So far as possible, the ballot should be secret and no undue pressure should be put on anyone to vote in a particular way or not to vote. If you feel that the arrangements to ensure secrecy and the absence of undue pressure are not working, then please notify [the Human Resources Department].

  - If you have any questions you should contact [ ].

F24 EMPLOYEE REPRESENTATIVES – BALLOT FORM

F24.1 USE

Employers must make appropriate arrangements for the election of employee representatives in certain situations. See notes to the Candidate nomination form.

F24.2 Precedent

Ballot form

ELECTION of EMPLOYEE REPRESENTATIVES

Candidate	Mark up to [ ] candidates with "X"
(Name)	

Before completing this voting form please read the following instructions:

1. You may vote for up to [*number*] candidates. However, you may vote for less than [*number*] candidates if you wish. Your vote will not be counted if you vote for more than [*number*] candidates.

2. To vote you should mark the voting form with an "X" in the box adjacent to the name(s) of the candidate(s) for whom you wish to vote. Your vote may not be counted if you make additional marks on the form.

3. The [*number*] candidates with the greatest number of votes cast in their favour will be elected as the Employee Representatives. In the event that two or more candidates have each received the same number of votes, then all such tied candidates shall be elected as Employee Representatives.

4. You should return your completed voting form by placing it in the box provided in [*location*] by [*time*] on [*date*].

5. If you make a mistake when completing the form, you should hand the spoilt form to [ ] and ask for a replacement.

6. If you have any questions you should contact [ ].

F25 FLEXIBLE WORKING – APPLICATION

F25.1 USE

Employees should be encouraged to use this form when applying for flexible working under the statutory procedure, although any written application setting out the required information will be sufficient to instigate the statutory procedure.

This form could be included within the Handbook and/or copies made available from the Human Resources Department. The advantage of having a standard form is that you can ensure that employees include in their application for flexible working all the information you will need to deal with the application.

F25.2 Precedent

Application for contract variation

> You do not have to use this form – any application in writing which sets out the information below will be sufficient. However, you are encouraged to use this form as it will ensure that you give us all the information we will need in order to deal with your application.
>
> **NAME:**
>
> **POSITION:**
>
> **DEPARTMENT:**
>
> **DATE:**
>
> **This is an application for flexible working under the Employment Rights Act 1996.**
>
> **I would like to request the following changes to my terms of employment:** [*The change must relate to hours, time or place of work*]
>
> **I would like this change to start on** [*DATE*]
>
> **I expect this change to have the following advantages for the Employer:** [*set out advantages*]
>
> **I expect this change may raise the following issues:** [*set out any potential problems you foresee*]
>
> **These issues could be dealt with as follows:** [*set out how you think those potential problems could be avoided, overcome or their impact lessened*]

These changes are to enable me to care for:

- **A child under the age of six of whom I am or my partner is parent, foster parent, adopter or guardian** ☐

- **A disabled child under the age of six of whom I am or my partner is parent, foster parent, adopter or guardian** ☐

- **An adult over the age of 18 of whom I am the spouse, partner or civil partner, parent, child, sibling, aunt, uncle or grandparent, including step, in-law and adoptive relationships or who lives at the same address as me** ☐

- **Please specify relationship:** [*explain relationship*] ☐

F26 FLEXIBLE WORKING – AGREEMENT TO REQUEST

F26.1 USE

This form should be used by the employer when agreeing to a request for flexible working.

F26.2 Precedent

Agreement to a flexible working request

Date:

Dear [   ]

That you for your request for a contract variation to enable you to work flexibly. We are pleased to say we can agree to your request [subject to the following modifications: *set out any modifications to the request.*]

Your terms of employment are therefore amended as follows:

[*Set out the changes to the terms and conditions of employment as a result of the change. These changes will typically include:*

– *changes to hours of work;*

– *changes to place of work;*

– *changes to wages/salary as a result of working different hours;*

– *changes to holiday pay and entitlement as a result of any changes in working hours.*]

All other terms of employment will remain unchanged.

If you have any queries about the effect of these changes, please contact [the Human Resources Department].

Yours sincerely

F27 FLEXIBLE WORKING – INVITATION TO DISCUSS REQUEST

F27.1 USE

This form should be used by the employer when not immediately agreeing to a request for flexible working. Where the employer does not agree to the request, a meeting must be held with the employee to discuss the request. This must be arranged within 28 days of receiving the request. The employee has the right to be accompanied by a work colleague or trade union representative.

F27.2 Precedent

Agreement to a flexible working request

> **Date:**
>
> Dear [   ]
>
> That you for your request for a contract variation to enable you to work flexibly. We would like to discuss this request with you. Could you please, therefore, attend a meeting at [*time, date and location*]
>
> You have the right to be accompanied by a work colleague or representative of a trade union.
>
> If you have any queries or if this time is inconvenient for you or the person you wish to accompany you, please contact [the Human Resources Department] to arrange an alternative time.
>
> Yours sincerely

F28 FLEXIBLE WORKING – REFUSAL OF REQUEST

F28.1 USE

This form should be used by the employer when refusing a request for flexible working following the required meeting to discuss the request. The notification must be in writing and must inform the employee of the right of appeal. The legislation only allows refusals on certain grounds and the applicable ground or grounds must be stated in this notification.

F28.2   Precedent

Agreement to a flexible working request

Date:

Dear [   ]

That you for attending the meeting on [ ] to discuss your request for flexible working.

Unfortunately, having considered the points you have made, we have concluded that we cannot agree to your request on the grounds of [*select one of the following:*

a.   *The burden of additional costs;*

b.   *There is a detrimental effect on the ability to meet customer demands;*

c.   *Inability to reorganise work of existing staff;*

d.   *Inability to recruit additional staff;*

e.   *Detrimental impact on quality;*

f.   *Detrimental effect on performance;*

g.   *Insufficiency of work during the periods the employee proposes to work; or*

h.   *Planned structural changes.*]

[*It may be helpful to add comments here about any points the employee may have made in the meeting and your answer to them. This will help the employee to understand more about your reasons for the refusal and show that you have thought carefully about the points the employee has made. This may also make it easier to justify a refusal if that refusal is challenged on the ground that it amounts to indirect discrimination – for example on grounds of sex or age.]*

You have the right to appeal against this decision. If you wish to appeal, please notify [the Human Resources Department/ the Chief executive/ the Managing Director] within [ ] working days.

If you have any queries about this, please contact [the Human Resources Department].

Yours sincerely

F29 FLEXIBLE WORKING – AGREEING REQUEST SUBJECT TO MODIFICATIONS

F29.1 USE

This form should be used by the employer when refusing a request for flexible working following the required meeting to discuss the request, but offering some different arrangement. This would technically be treated as a refusal, so a right of appeal must be offered and the refusal has to be on one of the specified grounds.

If an employer considers they have to refuse a request for flexible working, it is still worth considering whether some compromise could be offered. This may lead to a solution which is acceptable to both sides and will also make it easier to justify a refusal if the refusal is challenged.

F29.2　　　　　　　　　Precedent

Agreement to a flexible working request

Date:

Dear [   ]

That you for attending the meeting on [   ] to discuss your request for flexible working.

Unfortunately, having considered the points you have made, we have concluded that we cannot agree to your request on the grounds of [*select one of the following:*

a.   *The burden of additional costs;*

b.   *There is a detrimental effect on the ability to meet customer demands;*

c.   *Inability to reorganise work of existing staff;*

d.   *Inability to recruit additional staff;*

e.   *Detrimental impact on quality;*

f.   *Detrimental effect on performance;*

g.   *Insufficiency of work during the periods the employee proposes to work;* or

h.   *Planned structural changes.*]

F29 Flexible Working – Agreeing Request Subject to Modifications

[*It may be helpful to add comments here about any points the employee may have made in the meeting and your answer to them. This will help the employee to understand more about your reasons for the refusal and show that you have thought carefully about the points the employee has made. This may also make it easier to justify a refusal if that refusal is challenged on the ground that it amounts to indirect discrimination – for example on grounds of sex or age.*]

However, we can offer you the following, which we hope will go some way towards achieving the flexibility you are looking for.

[*Set out the proposed variation*]

You have the right to appeal against this decision. If you wish to appeal, please notify [the Human resources Department/ the Chief executive/ the Managing Director] within [ ] working days.

If you have any queries about this, please contact [the Human Resources Department].

Yours sincerely

F30 FLEXIBLE WORKING – APPEAL

F30.1 USE

This form should be used by the employee when appealing against a refusal of a request for flexible working or an agreement but only on terms different from those applied for. The statutory requirements for a notice of appeal are that it should be in writing, dated and should set out the grounds of appeal.

This form could be included within the Handbook and/or copies made available from the Human Resources Department. The advantage of having a standard form is that you can ensure that employees include in their notice of appeal all the information you will need to deal with the appeal.

F30.2 Precedent

Agreement to a flexible working request

> *You do not have to use this form – any application in writing which sets out the information below will be sufficient. However, you are encouraged to use this form as it will ensure that you give us all the information we will need in order to deal with your application.*

Date:

Dear [   ]

I wish to appeal against your decision to:

[refuse my application for a variation to my terms of employment for flexible working]

or

[agree my application for a variation to my terms of employment for flexible working but only on terms which I do not wish to accept.]

The grounds for my appeal are: [*set out grounds of appeal.*]

Yours sincerely

F31 GRIEVANCES – LETTER TO COMPLAINANT

F31.1 USE

This may be used to inform the person raising the grievance of the steps you are proposing to take to investigate the complaint. Not all grievances require investigation. In many cases, it is enough simply to arrange a meeting with the person raising the grievance. Sometimes, however, it will be necessary to investigate the matter, particularly where the grievance concerns the behaviour of another employee or other employees.

F31.2 Precedent

Letter to complainant

Dear [   ]

Thank you for drawing our attention to the matters you have raised. We take all grievances seriously and will now investigate your complaints thoroughly. I have arranged for [ ] to carry out the investigation. He/she will contact you to arrange a meeting to obtain details of the complaint. Please refer to the grievance procedure for the process.

Please do not discuss the content of your complaint with colleagues unless it is essential for you to do so so that you can provide the investigator with information relevant to the investigation.

[Because of the nature of the complaints, we consider it is appropriate to separate you from [ ]. The working arrangements to achieve this will be as follows. [*Set out arrangements*]]

[Because of the seriousness of the complaint, we are proposing to suspend [ ] on full pay for the duration of the investigation.]

If you have any queries about the process, please discuss these with [the Human resources Department].

Yours sincerely

F31.3 DRAFTING POINTS

In cases where the grievance is about the behaviour of a particular employee or particular employees, it may not always be practicable to separate the complaint from the person or persons complained about. If it is not practicable, you should consider what other steps may be necessary. For example, if it is inevitable that they will have to continue working together during the investigation, you could ask both of them not to comment on the investigation or complaint in any way.

You should only consider suspending the person or persons complained about in serious cases.

F32 GRIEVANCES – INSTRUCTIONS TO INVESTIGATOR

F32.1 USE

Not all grievances require investigation. It is often enough simply to invite the person complaining to a grievance hearing to listen to their grievance. An investigation may be necessary, however, where complaint is made about the behaviour of another employee or other employees, particularly where the facts are likely to be disputed.

Grievances often lead to claims in an employment tribunal. The employer may then be required to justify the outcome of the grievance. Without a thorough investigation, backed up by evidence from witnesses and documents, the employer may have to go through the whole process again, obtaining witness statements from those complained about and from any witnesses. It is important, therefore, that the investigator prepares statements or notes of interviews of summaries of what witnesses are saying that can be used, if necessary, in an employment tribunal.

If the investigator is an employee, then the employer has a reasonable degree of control over how the investigation is carried out. It is still useful for that employee to know what is expected of them. Occasionally, employers may wish to use an external investigator. A poor investigation then leaves the employer in a difficult position when trying to defend its decision on how to deal with the complaint.

Issuing the investigator with a copy of these instructions should help to ensure that the investigation is carried out in a way that would enable you to justify the decision and defend any employment tribunal claim.

F32.2 Precedent

Instructions to investigator

Thank you for agreeing to investigate the grievance raised by [ ]. Please find attached a copy of the grievance.

I should be grateful if you would investigate this grievance thoroughly and impartially. Ultimately, it is up to us to decide what action, if any, to take following your investigation. It is important, therefore, that we understand any conclusions that you have reached and that we understand why you have reached those conclusions.

While it is up to you to decide how the grievance should be investigated, we suggest the following steps:

Interviews: In most cases it will be necessary to interview:

- the complainant;

- those complained about; and

- any witnesses to any of the matters complained of.

Statements/interview notes/summaries: In order for us to understand the facts behind the grievance, it is helpful for us to have statements or interview notes or, if you prefer, as summary of the evidence given by each of the witnesses. These should be signed by the witness, to avoid any possibility of a witness later denying having said something you have recorded them as saying.

Those who wish to remain anonymous: Occasionally, witnesses prefer to remain anonymous. If that happens, then it is still useful to have signed statements, interview notes or summaries, but the versions provided to the complainant may be redacted to remove any information which could identify the witness. That would include removing the signature. Such statements, interview notes or summaries should contain a statement that the witness wishes to remain anonymous. You could explain this to the witness and reassure them that their statements will only be disclosed to the complainant in a form that the witness has approved and which will not reveal the identity of the informant.

[You may wish also to prepare a report setting out your overall conclusions, with comments about the credibility of witnesses, so that we can make an informed judgment. It is useful for us to know, for example, whether a witness gave inconsistent evidence or appeared unsure of what he or she was saying, or anything else which in your view might affect the credibility of a particular witness.]

Thank you once again for agreeing to carry out this investigation. If you would like to discuss the process or if you need any further information or access to any records or other documents, please contact [the Human Resources Department].

F32.3 DRAFTING POINTS

You should check your grievance procedure to ensure these instructions comply with it. For example, if the procedure requires the investigator to produce a report rather than merely gather the evidence, then that should be made clear. The above draft (the bracketed section) leaves this optional. What most employers actually need from an investigator is not the investigator's overall conclusions but a full understanding of the facts, which can be achieved by supplying only the statements, interview notes or summaries and any relevant documentation.

F33 GRIEVANCES – INVITATION TO HEARING

F33.1 USE

The statutory grievance procedure requires employers to invite the complainant to a hearing to determine what action, if any, to take following the investigation. From 6 April 2009 (when the statutory procedures are repealed), it will still be good practice to ensure that meetings are held in respect of all grievances.

F33.2 Precedent

Letter inviting to grievance hearing

Dear [   ]

[I confirm that the investigation into your grievance is now complete. Please find enclosed [*statements/notes of interviews with relevant witnesses/ a summary of what the witnesses have said*] [and a report prepared by the investigator].]

We would now like to discuss with you [the outcome of the investigation] [your grievance] and whether any action should be taken as a result. Would you please, therefore, attend a meeting at [*time and place*]. This will be conducted by [ ].

You may, if you wish, be accompanied by a work colleague or representative of a trade union.

If the time of this meeting is inconvenient for you or the person accompanying you, could you please contact [the Human resources Department] to arrange an alternative time.

If you have any queries about this letter or the process, please contact [the Human Resources Department].

Yours sincerely

F33.3 DRAFTING POINTS

Only include the first paragraph if there has been an investigation.

The investigator will normally have interviewed the complainant, the employee or employees complained about and any witnesses to any of the matters complained of. The investigator should have taken statements from those individuals or at least have prepared interview notes or a summary of what the individuals are saying. Ideally, the investigator should have got the witnesses to sign the statements, interview notes or summaries. This avoids any arguments about whether the witnesses really did say what the investigator says they did.

Occasionally, witnesses prefer to remain anonymous. If that happens, then it is still useful to have signed statements, interview notes or summaries, but the versions provided to the complainant may be redacted to remove any information which could identify the witness. That would include removing the signature. Such statements, interview notes or summaries should contain a statement that the witness wishes to remain anonymous.

You should check your grievance procedure to ensure this letter complies with it. For example, if the grievance procedure allows employees to be accompanied or represented by a friend or professional advisor, then the letter should mention that.

F34 GRIEVANCES – NOTICE OF OUTCOME

F34.1 USE

This may be used to notify the complainant of the outcome of the grievance procedure.

F34.2 Precedent

Letter notifying of outcome

Dear [   ]

Thank you for attending the meeting on [*date*]. I have now reviewed all the evidence and the points you have made and have reached the following conclusions.

[*Set out the conclusions – in particular, whether you have concluded that the matters complained of happened in the way the complainant has alleged and whether you consider the grievance should therefore be upheld.*]

You have said that the outcomes you are looking for are:

[*list the outcomes sought – for example:*

– *an apology*

– *disciplinary action or dismissal of anyone complained about*

– *financial compensation.*]

I have concluded that the following action should be taken:

[*List the action you consider should be taken. This does not necessarily have to be any of the actions sought by the complainant.*]

OR

I have concluded therefore that no further action should be taken in respect of your grievance.

[*You should now return to the previous working arrangements – i e* [*set out the previous working arrangements.*]

If you disagree with this decision, you have a right of appeal. If you wish to appeal, please submit your appeal in writing to [the Human Resources Department] within [ ] working days.

I should like to thank you for drawing these points to our attention. I appreciate this has been a difficult time for you.

Yours sincerely

F34.3 DRAFTING POINTS

The conclusions should be set out in broad terms and you should ensure that you are able to justify them from the evidence arising from the investigation.

If the complaint is found to be valid, then some sort of action should be taken, whether the complainant has asked for it or not.

If temporary arrangements have been made for the duration of the investigation, you should consider whether those arrangements should be made permanent, or whether the working arrangements should revert to what they were previously. You may, for example, have arranged for the complainant and the person or persons complained about to be split up so that contact between them could be minimised. If you decide they should go back to working together, you might wish to consider any steps you can take to build bridges between them – for example, a reconciliation meeting and regular reviews of the working relationship.

Your grievance procedure may lay down the time limit within which to appeal. If it does not, then you should specify a reasonable period – generally either 5 or 10 working days. Under the statutory grievance procedure, employees have a right of appeal within a 'reasonable period'. What is reasonable will depend on the circumstance, but one of those circumstances is the period for appealing stated in the letter or the grievance procedure. However, a later notice of appeal should not necessarily be rejected because there may be some good reason why the appeal was submitted late, in which case you may fall foul of the statutory grievance procedure by not allowing the appeal.

F35 HARASSMENT – LETTER INFORMING ALLEGED HARASSER

F35.1 USE

This may be used to inform the alleged harasser of any allegation of harassment.

F35.2   Precedent

Letter informing alleged harasser

Dear [   ]

This is to inform you that an allegation of harassment has been made against you. [Please refer to the Harassment Policy for the procedure for investigating such complaints.] This complaint will now be investigated by [ ] who will contact you to hear your side of the story in due course. Before that happens, we will provide you with full details of what is alleged.

Please do not discuss the investigation with any of your colleagues except where necessary to enable you to provide the investigator with information relevant to the investigation, as the contents of the investigation should remain confidential.

[In the meantime, we would like to ensure that you do not work in the same area as the complainant. Please therefore [*set out the arrangements to ensure the complainant and the alleged harasser to not work together.*]

[Because of the seriousness of the allegations, you will be suspended on full pay while the investigation proceeds.]

If you have any queries about the process, please discuss these with [the Human resources Department].

Yours sincerely

F35.3 DRAFTING POINTS

If there is a harassment policy, you should draw the employee's attention to it.

It is difficult to stop employees talking about a harassment complaint, but you should try to do so, otherwise there is a risk of employees colluding.

If practicable, you should try to separate the complainant and the alleged harasser. This may not always be practicable. For example, if it is inevitable that they will have to continue working together during the investigation, you could ask both of them not to comment on the investigation or complaint in any way, indicating that any breach of this instruction should be reported immediately and is likely to lead to disciplinary action.

In serous cases, you should consider suspending the alleged culprit for the duration of the investigation.

F36 HARASSMENT – LETTER TO COMPLAINANT

F36.1 USE

This may be used to inform the person complaining of harassment of the steps you are proposing to take to investigate the complaint.

F36.2 Precedent

Letter to complainant

Dear [   ]

Thank you for drawing our attention to the matters you have raised. We take all complaints of harassment seriously and will now investigate your complaints thoroughly. I have arranged for [ ] to carry out the investigation. He/she will contact you to arrange a meeting to obtain details of the complaint. Please refer to the harassment procedure for the process.

Please do not discuss the content of your complaint with colleagues unless it is essential for you to do so so that you can provide the investigator with information relevant to the investigation.

[Because of the nature of the complaints, we consider it is appropriate to separate you from [ ]. The working arrangements to achieve this will be as follows. [*Set out arrangements*].]

[Because of the seriousness of the complaint, we are proposing to suspend [ ] on full pay for the duration of the investigation.]

If you have any queries about the process, please discuss these with [the Human Resources Department].

Yours sincerely

F36.3 DRAFTING POINTS

It may not always be practicable to separate the complaint from the alleged harasser. If it is not practicable, you should consider what other steps may be necessary. For example, if it is inevitable that they will have to continue working together during the investigation, you could ask both of them not to comment on the investigation or complaint in any way, indicating that any breach of this instruction should be immediately reported and is likely to result in disciplinary action.

You should only consider suspending the alleged harasser in serious cases.

F37 HARASSMENT – INVITATION TO HEARING

F37.1 USE

The statutory grievance procedures (for grievances arising before 6 April 2009) and good practice (after that date), and probably also any harassment procedure you may have, require employers to invite the complainant to a hearing to determine what action, if any, to take following the investigation.

F37.2 Precedent

Letter inviting to harassment hearing

Dear [   ]

I confirm that the investigation into your complaint of harassment is now complete. Please find enclosed [*statements/notes of interviews with relevant witnesses/ a summary of what the witnesses have said*] [and a report prepared by the investigator].

We would now like to discuss with you the outcome of the investigation and whether any action should be taken as a result. Would you please, therefore, attend a meeting at [*time and place*]. This will be conducted by [ ].

You may, if you wish, be accompanied by a work colleague or representative of a trade union.

If the time of this meeting is inconvenient for you or the person accompanying you, could you please contact [the Human resources Department] to arrange an alternative time.

If you have any queries about this letter or the process, please contact [the Human Resources Department].

Yours sincerely

F37.3 DRAFTING POINTS

The investigator will normally have interviewed the complainant, the employee or employees complained about and any witnesses to any of the matters complained of. The investigator should have taken statements from those individuals or at least have prepared interview notes or a summary of what the individuals are saying. Ideally, the investigator should have got the witnesses to sign the statements, interview notes or summaries. This avoids any arguments about whether the witnesses really did say what the investigator says they did.

Occasionally, witnesses prefer to remain anonymous. If that happens, then it is still useful to have signed statements, interview notes or summaries, but the versions provided to the complainant may be redacted to remove any information which could identify the witness. That would include removing the signature. Such statements, interview notes or summaries should contain a statement that the witness wishes to remain anonymous.

You should check your harassment procedure or, if you do not have a harassment procedure, your grievance procedure, to ensure this letter complies with it. For example, if the harassment or grievance procedure allows employees to be accompanied or represented by a friend or professional advisor, then the letter should mention that.

F38 HARASSMENT – INSTRUCTIONS TO INVESTIGATOR

F38.1 USE

Complaints of harassment often lead to claims in an employment tribunal. The employer may then be required to justify the outcome of the harassment complaint. Without a thorough investigation, backed up by evidence from witnesses and documents, the employer may have to go through the whole process again, obtaining witness statements from the alleged harasser and from ay witnesses. It is important, therefore, that the investigator prepares statements or notes of interviews of summaries of what witnesses are saying that can be used, if necessary, in an employment tribunal.

If the investigator is an employee, then the employer has a reasonable degree of control over how the investigation is carried out. It is still useful for that employee to know what is expected of them. Occasionally, employers may wish to use an external investigator. A poor investigation then leaves the employer in a difficult position when trying to defend its decision on how to deal with the complaint.

Issuing the investigator with a copy of these instructions should help to ensure that the investigation is carried out in a way that would enable you to justify the decision and defend any employment tribunal claim.

F38.2 Precedent

Instructions to investigator

> Thank you for agreeing to investigate the complaint of harassment brought by [ ]. Please find attached a copy of the complaint.
>
> I should be grateful if you would investigate this complaint thoroughly and impartially. Ultimately, it is up to us to decide what action, if any, to take following your investigation. It is important, therefore, that we understand any conclusions that you have reached and that we understand why you have reached those conclusions.
>
> While it is up to you to decide how the complaint should be investigated, we suggest the following steps:
>
> *Interviews:* In most cases it will be necessary to interview:
>
> – the complainant;
>
> – the alleged harasser; and
>
> – any witnesses to any of the matters complained of.

Statements/interview notes/summaries: In order for us to understand the facts behind the complaint, it is helpful for us to have statements or interview notes or, if you prefer, as summary of the evidence given by each of the witnesses. These should be signed by the witness, to avoid any possibility of a witness later denying having said something you have recorded them as saying.

Those who wish to remain anonymous: Occasionally, witnesses prefer to remain anonymous. If that happens, then it is still useful to have signed statements, interview notes or summaries, but the versions provided to the complainant may be redacted to remove any information which could identify the witness. That would include removing the signature. Such statements, interview notes or summaries should contain a statement that the witness wishes to remain anonymous. You could explain this to the witness and reassure them that their statements will only be disclosed to the complainant in a form that the witness has approved and which will not reveal the identity of the informant.

[You may wish also to prepare a report setting out your overall conclusions, with comments about the credibility of witnesses, so that we can make an informed judgment. It is useful for us to know, for example, whether a witness gave inconsistent evidence or appeared unsure of what he or she was saying, or anything else which in your view might affect the credibility of a particular witness.]

Thank you once again for agreeing to carry out this investigation. If you would like to discuss the process or if you need any further information or access to any records or other documents, please contact [the Human Resources Department].

F38.3   DRAFTING POINTS

You should check your harassment procedure to ensure these instructions comply with it. For example, if the procedure requires the investigator to produce a report rather than merely gather the evidence, then that should be made clear. The above draft (the bracketed section) leaves this optional. What most employers actually need from an investigator is not the investigator's overall conclusions but a full understanding of the facts, which can be achieved by supplying only the statements, interview notes or summaries and any relevant documentation.

F39 HARASSMENT – NOTICE OF OUTCOME

F39.1 USE

This may be used to notify the complainant of the outcome of the harassment procedure.

F39.2 Precedent

Letter notifying of outcome

Dear [   ]

Thank you for attending the meeting on [*date*]. I have now reviewed all the evidence and the points you have made and have reached the following conclusions.

[*Set out the conclusions – in particular, whether you have concluded that the matters complained of happened in the way the complainant has alleged and whether you consider those matters amount to harassment.*]

You have said that the outcomes you are looking for are:

[*list the outcomes sought – for example:*

– an apology

– disciplinary action or dismissal of the person or persons complained about

– financial compensation.*]

I have concluded that the following action should be taken:

[*List the action you consider should be taken. This does not necessarily have to be any of the actions sought by the complainant. For example, if the complainant has not asked for disciplinary action against the alleged harasser but you consider the complaint is valid, you should take disciplinary action anyway.*]

OR

I have concluded therefore that no further action should be taken in respect of your complaint.

[*You should now return to the previous working arrangements – ie [set out the previous working arrangements.*]

If you disagree with this decision, you have a right of appeal. If you wish to appeal, please submit your appeal in writing to [the Human Resources Department] within [ ] working days.

I should like to thank you for drawing these points to our attention. I appreciate this has been a difficult time for you.

Yours sincerely

F39.3 DRAFTING POINTS

The conclusions should be set out in broad terms and you should ensure that you are able to justify them from the evidence arising from the investigation.

If the complaint is found to be valid, then some sort of action should be taken, whether the complainant has asked for it or not.

If temporary arrangements have been made for the duration of the investigation, you should consider whether those arrangements should be made permanent, or whether the working arrangements should revert to what they were previously. You may, for example, have arranged for the complainant and the alleged harasser to be split up so that contact between them could be minimised. If you decide they should go back to working together, you might wish to consider any steps you can take to build bridges between them – for example, a reconciliation meeting and regular reviews of the working relationship.

Your harassment procedure may lay down the time limit within which to appeal. If it does not, then you should specify a reasonable period – generally either 5 or 10 working days. Under the statutory grievance procedure (applicable for grievances where the matter complained of occurred or started on or before 5 April 2009), employees have a right of appeal within a 'reasonable period'. What is reasonable will depend on the circumstance, but one of those circumstances is the period for appealing stated in the letter or the harassment procedure. However, a later notice of appeal should not necessarily be rejected because there may be some good reason why the appeal was submitted late, in which case you may fall foul of the statutory grievance procedure by not allowing the appeal.

F40 REDUNDANCY – INVITATION TO MEETING

F40.1 USE

Redundancies may be unfair if:

– there was no genuine case for redundancy in the first place;

– the employer has not consulted over the redundancy;

– the selection process was unfair;

– the employer has not given proper consideration to alternative employment.

The consultation required here is consultation with individuals affected. This should be in addition to the collective consultation that is required where 20 or more redundancies are made.

This letter gives employees the required information to attend the initial meeting to discuss the redundancy.

F40.2 Precedent

Warning of redundancy

[ON COMPANY HEADED NOTEPAPER]

Dear [   ]

We are sorry to inform you that we are currently considering proposals that could result in redundancies.

[We have already consulted with [*the recognised trade union*][*employee representatives*] and in consultation with them have agreed the following: [*set out any matters that have been agreed*]]. [We have not managed to agree on all matters and but have taken into consideration all the points made during this consultation process.]

[In addition to the matters agreed with the representatives,] we are proposing [*set out other matters that you are proposing, such as selection criteria, whether redundancy payments are to be enhanced, timing etc if not agreed with the representatives.*]

We wish to inform you of this possibility in good time to give you the maximum opportunity to think of ways that could avoid the redundancies or, if that is not possible, to ensure that redundancies are with minimum disruption giving those affected by the redundancies the best possible chance of finding other employment as soon as possible.

The reasons for these proposals are [*insert brief reasons*].

These proposals, if implemented, may result in [*number*] redundancies at [*location*] in the following [*departments*].

It is possible, therefore, that you could be one of those who could be made redundant.

[We are proposing to select on the basis on [*set out the selection criteria*]. [Your scores under the relevant headings are:

[*set out scores*].

The attached table shows the scores of others in the department. This table does not indicate the names of the individuals affected for reasons of confidentiality.

On the basis of these scores, there is a risk that you could be selected for redundancy.]

No decisions have been made at this stage, however, and no decisions will be made until we have had the opportunity to consult with you and others affected.

I have arranged for a first consultative meeting with you to take place at [*time and place*]. We would welcome your views on the proposal and in particular would welcome your views on how the need for [redundancies/the redundancy] might be avoided and/or about any suitable alternative positions for which you might be considered.

[We would also welcome your comments on the proposed selection criteria and how they apply to you. If you disagree with any of your scores, or if you have any further information which you think could affect your score, then you should tell us why. If you need any further information to understand why you have been scored in the way that you have, please let [ ] know.]

If you wish, you may be accompanied at the meeting by a work colleague or representative of a trade union.

I you should have any comments or queries, or would like clarification on any of these points in the meantime, please feel free to contact me.

Yours sincerely

F40.3 DRAFTING POINTS

If you have already consulted with representatives of a recognised trade union or with employee representatives, then the points which have been agreed should be set out in this letter. If you have been unable to agree points such as selection criteria, enhancements to redundancy payment or anything else, then you will have to decide those points yourself, taking into account any points made in the course of collective consultation. Those points too should be explained in this letter.

If you have not consulted collectively, then you should simply state what your proposals are.

For dismissals in respect of which the invitation to the first meeting occurs on or before 5 April 2009, the statutory dismissal procedure applies. Even for dismissals after that date, it is recommended that this procedure is followed. Otherwise, the redundancy is likely to be an unfair dismissal under general principles. It is a requirement of the statutory dismissal procedure (which applies just as much to redundancies as to any other type of dismissal) that you invite the employee(s) to a meeting to discuss the proposals before any final decision is made; and that, before the meeting, you give the employee(s) sufficient in formation to understand why you are making the redundancies and why you are selecting them for redundancy. Where redundancy selection is on the basis of a matrix with various headings, you should explain the employee's individual score and give other scores without mentioning the names of others.

It is important to emphasise to the employee that no final decision has been made and no decision will be made before consultation is complete. You should ensure that nothing is said, whether in this letter or elsewhere, to suggest that you have made up your mind that the employee is to be made redundant.

F41 REDUNDANCY – INVITATION TO SECOND MEETING

F41.1 USE

It is useful to send the employee notes of the first consultation meeting, to avoid possible future disputes about what was said. This letter can be used to accompany those notes. It may also be useful to hold a second consultation meeting, particularly in the case of long-standing employees, to ensure that they have had every possible opportunity to make any points they wish to. This may not be necessary if there has already been collective consultation, since they will already have had an opportunity to make points via their representatives.

F41.2 Precedent

Letter accompanying notes of consultation meeting/ invitation to second meeting

[TO BE TYPED ON COMPANY HEADED NOTEPAPER]

[Name and address]

[Date]

Dear [   ]

I refer to our consultative meeting today and confirm that we are considering a proposal to make redundancies because [*set out brief reasons*]. [I enclose notes of our meeting].

[*Insert details of what was discussed at the first meeting. Confirm answers to any queries raised by the employee at that meeting*].

[No decisions have been made with regard to this proposal, however, and no decisions will be taken until we have had the opportunity to consult with you [and all others affected] personally. We particularly wish to hear any views which you may have on how the need for redundancy might be avoided, or whether any suitable alternative positions for which you might wish to be considered, as well as any comments you may have about the proposed method of selection.]

[I confirm that a list of vacancies will be [circulated to all those affected] [published on the notice board] [published on the intranet]. If there are any vacancies you would be interested in, please let [the Human resources Department] know and they will discuss the vacancy with you.]

[We have arranged a further meeting at [*time and place*] so that you have a opportunity to let us have any further considered views. [I confirm that in order to allow you the opportunity to reflect on these proposals, you may take paid leave until our further meeting (please note that this will not be deducted from any holiday entitlement).] If you wish, you maybe accompanied at this meeting by a colleague or representative of a trade union.]

Please do not hesitate to contact me by telephone or in writing, however, if you wish to put forward any views or raise any questions in the meantime.

Yours sincerely

F41.3 DRAFTING POINTS

If you have decided to hold a second consultation meeting, include the third and fifth paragraphs.

If there are vacancies in other parts of the business or, in the case of a group of companies, in other parts of the group, make suitable arrangements to notify those at risk of redundancy of those vacancies. It is recommended that you provide a list of all vacancies, whether you regard them as suitable or not. This will avoid any possible arguments in the future about whether you should have notified a particular vacancy.

F42 REDUNDANCY – NOTIFICATION OF REDUNDANCY

F42.1 USE

Once consultation over the redundancies is completed and you have decided whom to make redundant, this precedent can be used to notify the affected employees.

F42.2 Precedent

Notification of redundancy

[ON COMPANY HEADED NOTEPAPER]

Dear

Following our recent discussions I now regret to inform you that we have decided to make you redundant with effect from [*date*]. You will be paid in the normal way up to that date. [or you will receive a payment in lieu of notice in respect of the remainder of your notice period].

[We considered the points you raised at our meeting on [*date*] [*set out the points and your answers.*]

You will be entitled to a redundancy payment of £[ ] [and a payment in lieu of notice of £[ ]]. You will also be entitled to accrued holiday pay up to the date of termination. These payments are calculated as follows: [*set out calculation*].

I am very sorry that this action has had to be taken. However, I wish you every success for the future. If we can be of assistance, for example in provision of a reference or in any other way in helping you obtain new employment, please let me know and I will be only too pleased to help.

[During the notice period, you are entitled to reasonable paid time off to look for other employment. If you wish to do so, please notify [the Human resources Department].]

[We will continue to notify you of any vacancies that arise during the notice period [by circulating a vacancy list] [by posting all vacancies on the notice board] [via the intranet]. If you are interested in any vacancies please contact [the Human Resources Department] who will discuss the vacancy with you.]

If you wish to appeal against this decision, please notify [the Human Resources Department] in writing within [ ] days of the date of this letter setting out why you disagree with the decision. An appeal hearing will then be arranged.

Yours sincerely

F42.3 DRAFTING POINTS

It is useful to set out any points that the employee made in the course of consultation and give your response. This shows that you have thought about what the employee said and you were not just 'going through the motions'.

You may either terminate employment immediately with a payment in lieu of notice (which may be taxable if there is a term in the contract of employment requiring a payment in lieu of notice or if such a term can be implied through custom and practice); or you may terminate with notice.

It is a statutory requirement that the calculation of the redundancy payment is explained.

If you terminate with notice and require the employee to work that notice, then the employee has a right to reasonable paid time off to look for other employment. The fifth paragraph should then be included. Similarly, you should continue to notify any vacancies that arise during the notice period. Failure to do so could render the redundancy unfair.

Any letter terminating employment should inform the employee of the right of appeal. If you have a dismissal procedure, that will lay down the time limit within which to appeal. If you do not, then you should specify a reasonable period – generally either 5 or 10 working days. Under the statutory dismissal procedure (applying to dismissals where the process has started before 6 April 2009), employees have a right of appeal within a 'reasonable period'. What is reasonable will depend on the circumstance, but one of those circumstances is the period for appealing stated in the redundancy letter or the dismissal procedure. However, a later notice of appeal should not necessarily be rejected because there may be some good reason why the appeal was submitted late, in which case you may fall foul of the statutory dismissal procedure by not allowing the appeal.

F43 REDUNDANCY – CONFIRMATION OF REDUNDANCY AFTER APPEAL

F43.1 USE

This precedent may be used to notify an employee that the decision to make the employee redundant has been upheld following an appeal.

F43.2 Precedent

Confirmation of redundancy following appeal

[ON COMPANY HEADED NOTEPAPER]

Dear

Following our recent discussions I regret to inform you that I have decided to uphold the decision to make you redundant with effect from [*date*].

[I considered the points you raised at our meeting on [*date*] [*set out the points and your answers.*]

I regret that this action has had to be taken and wish you every success for the future. If we can be of assistance in helping you obtain new employment, please let me know and I will be only too pleased to help.

Yours sincerely

F43.3 DRAFTING POINTS

You do note have to include the section in square brackets, but it is useful if the employee challenges the fairness of the redundancy in proving that the appeal process was genuine and that you did think about the points raised.

F44 REDUNDANCY – LETTER OVERTURNING REDUNDANCY

F44.1 USE

This precedent may be used to notify an employee that the decision to make the employee redundant has been overturned on appeal.

F44.2 Precedent

Overturning redundancy following appeal

[ON COMPANY HEADED NOTEPAPER]

Dear

Following our recent discussions this is to inform you that I have decided to uphold your appeal and overturn the decision to make you redundant.

This means that you are reinstated and your employment will continue as if you had been employed continuously since the termination of your employment. You will be paid full back pay for this period and your period of continuous employment will not be treated as broken.

I suggest you return to work on [date]. If for any reason this is inconvenient for you, please discuss your return date with [the Human resources Department].

[This means that you will have to repay the redundancy payment and payment in lieu of notice you have received.]

Briefly, the reasons for my conclusions are [set out reasons].

Yours sincerely

F44.3 DRAFTING POINTS

You should consider whether there are any other consequences of overturning the redundancy decision. For example, if the employee would have benefited from a pay rise during the period, that pay rise should be granted and an appropriate adjustment to remuneration should be made.

If the employee has already received the redundancy payment and a payment in lieu of notice, then that should be repaid. Strictly, payments can only be received from employees, and deductions can only be made from pay, if the employee has consented in writing or the employee has been informed in writing that such payment can be received or deducted from wages. The precedent redundancy policy includes such a term. If you do not have a provision this effect in the redundancy procedure, then it would be worth obtaining the employee's agreement to your receiving the payment or making the deduction before the decision is notified.

F45 RETIREMENT – RETIREMENT NOTIFICATION

F45.1 USE

See notes on the retirement policy for a summary of the rules on age discrimination and unfair dismissal as they affect retirement.

Retirement must be notified by the employer between 6 and 12 months before the retirement date and the retirement notification should explain to the employee the right to request working beyond retirement age.

F45.2 Precedent

Sample notification of retirement

[Date]

Dear

Notification of retirement

The Company's current retirement age is 65. I understand you will reach your 65th birthday on [date]. Your last day of employment, therefore, will be [date].

I would like to thank you for your work for the Company during your employment. We shall be sorry to see you go but wish you a happy retirement.

If you would like us to consider continuing your employment beyond retirement age, please complete and return the attached form as soon as possible, but in any event at least 3 months before your retirement date.

Yours sincerely

F46 RETIREMENT – REQUEST TO CONTINUE WORKING

F46.1 USE

Providing a form for employees to use when requesting continued working beyond retirement age ensures that the employee gives you all the information you will need to deal with the request. Employees do not have to use this form but if you make it easily available to them, then they are likely to use it.

F46.2 Precedent

Sample request to continue working

Name:

Please consider this request to continue working beyond retirement age. I would like to continue in:

- ☐ My current role
- ☐ Another role (please specify)

On

- ☐ My current terms of employment
- ☐ The following terms of employment (please specify

I would like my employment to continue:

- ☐ Indefinitely (ie, until either you or I give notice to terminate it)
- ☐ Until   (specify date)
- ☐ For   months (specify period)

Once you have submitted a request, it will either be agreed to or we will hold a meeting with you to discuss the request.

If you wish, you may set out here any points you would like us to consider in support of your request:

This request is made pursuant to paragraph 5 of Schedule 6 to the Employment Equality (Age Discrimination) Regulations 2006.

Signed ....

F47 RETIREMENT – INVITATION TO MEETING

F47.1 USE

See notes on the retirement policy for a summary of the rules on age discrimination and unfair dismissal as they affect retirement.

If you do not immediately agree the request for continued working beyond retirement age, then a meeting must be held to discuss the request.

F47.2 Precedent

Invitation to meeting

[Date]

Dear

Invitation to meeting

Thank you for request to continue working beyond retirement age.

Could you please attend a meeting on [day] at [time] in [location]? All reasonable steps must be taken to attend this meeting, but if you are unable to attend the meeting, please let me know as soon as possible.

You have a right to be accompanied by a colleague employed by us.

Yours sincerely

F48 RETIREMENT – NOTIFICATION OF DECISION

F48.1 USE

The decision following a meeting to discuss a request to continue working beyond retirement age must be notified in writing, setting out the reasons for refusing a request or, if the request is granted but not on the terms sought by the employee, the reasons must be stated and an explanation of the new terms that are to apply must be given.

F48.2 Precedent

Sample letter notifying decision

[Date]

Dear

Thank you for attending the meeting on [date] to discuss your request to continue working beyond retirement.

> We have decided to refuse your request because
>
> [*specify reasons. It is useful here to set out some of the points the employee has made in the course of the meeting – see drafting notes.*].
>
> Accordingly, subject to your right of appeal, you will retire on [ ].
>
> If you wish to appeal against this decision, please write to [ ] within [ ] working days setting out why you disagree with the decision.

> We have decided to agree to your request on the following terms:
>
> Your employment will continue [indefinitely]/[until   ]
>
> Your terms of employment will [remain unchanged]/[be amended as follows
> [*set out the changes*]
> The reasons why we have not agreed to exactly what you have asked for are: [*set out the reasons. It is useful here to set out some of the points the employee has made in the course of the meeting – see drafting notes.*].
>
> If there is anything in this decision you are not happy with, you have a right of appeal. If you wish to appeal, please write to [   ] within [   ]   working days setting out why you disagree with this decision.

Yours sincerely

F48.3 DRAFTING POINTS

The reasons for a refusal should be set out in broad terms. One or two sentences should be sufficient. It may be helpful, to include here any points the employee has made in the course of the meeting and your response to them. This will help to prove, if it is necessary to do so, that you did give proper consideration to the request and that the procedure was more, therefore, than just going through the motions. If the procedure is followed, then the employee cannot bring an employment tribunal complaint of age discrimination or unfair dismissal, but could possibly bring claims for other forms of discrimination if, for example, you generally do allow employees to continue working beyond retirement age should they so wish but have refused one particular request because the employee is disabled and may not therefore be as productive as other able-bodied employees.

F49 RETIREMENT – APPEAL LETTER

F49.1 USE

You do not have to provide a precedent letter for employees to appeal against a refusal of a request, but employees must be informed of their right to appeal. This letter may help employees to prepare their appeal notice properly.

F49.2　　　　　　　　Precedent

Appeal letter

Dear

I would like to appeal against

[the decision to refuse my request to continue working beyond my proposed retirement date]

[the terms of employment on which you are prepared to allow me to continue working beyond my proposed retirement date.]

My reasons for disagreeing with the decision are:

Yours sincerely

G

CONTENTIOUS PRECEDENTS

G1 CLAIM FOR WRONGFUL DISMISSAL IN HIGH COURT

G1.1 USE

'Wrongful dismissal' is the term usually used to describe a dismissal which breaches the contract of employment – for example, because the employer has not given the employee the notice it is required to give under the contract of employment.

This is a precedent for a claim for wrongful dismissal in the High Court. Claims for breach of a contract of employment can be commenced in the High Court, a county court or an employment tribunal. Claims in employment tribunals for breach of contract are subject to a jurisdictional limit which is currently £25,000. If such a claim is brought and ruled upon by the Employment Tribunal it will not be possible to claim any outstanding balance beyond the relevant jurisdictional limit in either the High Court or a county court. It follows that the jurisdictional issue must be carefully considered before proceedings are commenced.

An employment related claim could also be commenced in the Chancery Division although proceeding in the QBD is more common. If the claim can in truth be described as a commercial action it could also be commenced in the Commercial Court although this is rare.

The normal rules for commencing proceedings in the High Court or a county court are governed by the Civil Procedure Rules 1998 (SI 1998/3132) and these will need to be complied with.

It is important to include the relevant terms as to notice which it is claimed are breached as well as the remuneration which it is alleged has been lost. Although the burden of proof in relation to mitigation rests on the Defendants, the Civil Procedure Rules 1998 (SI 1998/3132) require the Claimant to plead any matters relevant to the mitigation of loss in the Particulars of Claim. It is normal for these details to be updated in the course of proceedings by way of a further updated Schedule of Loss.

For an explanation of the law relating to wrongful dismissal, see Division D2 of *Jordans Employment Law Service*.

G1.2 **Precedent**

Claim for wrongful dismissal

IN THE HIGH COURT OF JUSTICE
QUEEN'S BENCH DIVISION
B E T W E E N:

[AB]

Claimant

and

[BC]

Defendant

PARTICULARS OF CLAIM

1. The Claimant was employed by the Defendant as a [job title] pursuant to the terms of a written contract of employment dated [insert date]. A copy of the contract of employment is attached to this statement of case.

2. The following were express terms of the contract of employment:

    (a) by clause [x] of his contract of employment the Claimant was entitled to [y] months' notice of the termination of his employment;

    (b) [set out the other key terms of the contract of employment which are relied upon in the claim such as remuneration, bonuses, pension etc.]

3. The Claimant served the Defendant faithfully and lawfully pursuant to the terms of his contract of employment.

4. By means of a letter dated [date] the Defendant [gave [z] weeks' notice of the termination of the Claimant's contract of employment] [terminated the Claimant's contract of employment without giving any advance notice]. A copy of this letter is attached to this statement of case.

5. The termination of the Claimant's contract of employment by the Defendant was in breach of the express term referred to at paragraph 2(a) above and was wrongful.

6. By reason of the facts and matters set out above the Claimant has sustained loss and damage.

PARTICULARS

[Set out here the losses sustained by the Claimant by reason of his wrongful dismissal]

7. The Claimant has taken steps to mitigate his losses. Without prejudice to the contention that the burden of proof is on the Defendant to establish any failure to mitigate the Claimant shall rely upon the attached Schedule of Mitigation.

8. Further the Claimant claims interest on the sums found to be due to him at such rate and for such periods as the Court deems fit pursuant to Section 35A of the Supreme Court Act 1981.

AND the Claimant claims:

(1) DAMAGES to be assessed; and

(2) INTEREST to be assessed pursuant to Section 35A of the Supreme Court Act 1981.

Dated

Statement of truth etc.

G1.3 DRAFTING POINTS

Paragraph 3: Copies of all key documents referred to in the Particulars of Claim should be attached to the document.

Paragraph 7: Although the legal burden of proof remains on the Defendant to establish any failure to mitigate on behalf of the Claimant the Civil Procedure Rules 1998 (SI 1998/3132) provide that a Claimant should set out in its claim the details of any steps taken in relation to mitigation. This might include, for example, steps taken to find other employment; earnings from other employment; lists of job advertisements responded to; details of recruitment agencies registered with.

Paragraph 8: If the claim is for a specific sum, the interest needs to be calculated in the claim. However this precedent relates to a claim for damages rather than a specific sum.

Statement of truth: The Particulars of Claim must be accompanied by the relevant statement of truth: see Civil Procedure Rules 1998 (SI 1998/3132).

G2 DEFENCE TO CLAIM FOR WRONGFUL DISMISSAL

G2.1 USE

'Wrongful dismissal' is the term usually used to describe a dismissal which is in breach of contract, for example because the employer has not given the required period of notice. Possible defences might be:

– the notice period asserted by the Claimant is not correct and the Defendant in fact gave the correct period of notice – see *Jordans Employment Law Service*, at D2[4]–[5];

– the Defendant was entitled to dismiss without notice because the Claimant had fundamentally breached the contract of employment – see J *Jordans Employment Law Service*, at D2[12]–[14].

This precedent is the Defence to the claim for wrongful dismissal as set out at **[G1.2]**. It provides an example of how to challenge the terms as pleaded in the Particulars of Claim and also puts into dispute the issue of mitigation and loss.

G2.2 Precedent

Defence to claim for wrongful dismissal

IN THE HIGH COURT OF JUSTICE

QUEEN'S BENCH DIVISION

B E T W E E N:

[AB]

Claimant

and

[BC]

Defendant

DEFENCE

1. Other than as set out at paragraph 2 below paragraphs 1 to 3 of the Particulars of Claim are admitted.

2. [It is denied that the Claimant was entitled to [ ] months' notice of the termination of his employment as alleged at paragraph 2(a) of the Particulars of Claim. The relevant provision regarding the Claimant's notice was set out in the letter of offer of employment from the Defendant to the Claimant dated [insert date]. That letter made it clear that the normal contractual provision regarding

notice would not apply for the first [ ] months of the Claimant's employment. During this initial [ ]-month period the relevant period of notice would be [ ] weeks. A copy of the relevant letter is attached to this statement of case.]

[AND/OR]

[By reason of the Claimant's conduct, the Defendant was entitled to and did terminate the Claimant's contract of employment without notice. The conduct was as follows: [*set out the conduct alleged to have entitled the employer to dismiss summarily*].]

3. [Save that it is admitted that the Claimant was given [ ] weeks' notice of the termination of his contract] paragraphs 4 and 5 of the Particulars of Claim are denied. By reason of the matters set out at paragraph 2 above the Claimant's employment was lawfully terminated.

4. It is denied that the Claimant has suffered the loss and damage pleaded at paragraph 6 of the Particulars of Claim or any loss and damage.

5. Paragraph 7 of the Particulars of Claim is denied. The Claimant is a well qualified [insert] and the job market for such positions is currently buoyant. Furthermore the Defendant is aware that the Claimant elected to take a [ ] month holiday after the termination of his employment and in the circumstances he has failed to mitigate his loss.

6. The claim to interest is not admitted.

Dated.

Statement of truth.

G2.3 DRAFTING POINTS

Paragraph 2: Set out here the reasons why the notice period claim by the Claimant is disputed. The text here is an example of the sorts of points that might be made.

For an explanation of the sort of conduct that might constitute a fundamental breach of contract entitling the employer to dismiss without notice, see *Jordans Employment Law Service*, at D2[10]–[15].

G3 HIGH COURT CLAIM FOR BONUS

G3.1 USE

This precedent is for a contractual claim for bonus in the High Court. It is necessary for such a claim to include details of the relevant contractual entitlement as well as the way in which this entitlement is alleged to have been breached. The relevant rules of the Civil Procedure Rules 1998 (SI 1998/3132) need to be complied with.

Some bonuses are stated to be discretionary, but that does not necessarily mean that there can be no contractual claim if a bonus is not paid. Courts and tribunals have sometimes held that bonus schemes which are stated to be discretionary and non-contractual are nevertheless subject to implied terms. For example, there is likely to be an implied term that the discretion will be exercised rationally and in accordance with any stated objectives of the bonus scheme (eg to reward exceptional performance, or encourage loyalty). It is important to include relevant particulars of how it is alleged that the relevant discretion has not been exercised lawfully.

For relevant details on jurisdiction please refer to the details as set out for Precedent Claim for Wrongful Dismissal (at [G1.2]).

G3.2 Precedent

High Court claim for bonus

IN THE HIGH COURT OF JUSTICE
QUEEN'S BENCH DIVISION
B E T W E E N:

[AB]

Claimant

and

[BC]

Defendant

PARTICULARS OF CLAIM

1. At all material times the Claimant was employed by the Defendant as [state position] pursuant to the terms of a written contract of employment dated [insert date] supplemented by [list any other documents which set out details and rules of the bonus scheme]. Copies of the relevant contract of employment and other relevant contractual documents are attached to this statement of case.

2. The following were express terms of the Claimant's contract of employment:

(a) the Claimant was entitled to participate in the Defendant's annual bonus scheme [set out further details as relevant];

(b) accordingly, the Claimant was entitled to an annual bonus calculated as follows [set out how bonuses are calculated] which amounted in the case of the Claimant for the period [identify period] to [insert relevant figure];

(c) [set out any other relevant terms].

3. The following were implied terms of the Claimant's contract of employment:

(a) that the Defendant would not without justification act in a manner which was calculated or likely to destroy the relationship of trust and confidence between it and the Claimant; and

(b) that the Defendant would exercise its discretion under the bonus scheme referred to at paragraph 2(a) above rationally and in good faith and in accordance with the stated objectives of the scheme.

4. The Claimant served the Defendant faithfully and lawfully pursuant to the terms of his contract of employment.

5. On or about [date] the Defendant informed the Claimant that [his annual bonus would be [insert the relevant sum]] [he would not be awarded annual bonus for the year [ ]].

6. In [arriving at the figure set out at paragraph 5 above] [declining to award an annual bonus] the Defendant acted unlawfully and in breach of the express term set out at paragraph 2(a) above and/or the implied terms set out at paragraph 3 above.

PARTICULARS

[Set out here the allegations as to why the bonus figure arrived at or the decision not to award a bonus was unlawful. For example:

The Claimant's reached a higher level of performance than in the previous year, in particular by winning more work for the Defendant and generating a higher level of fees than in the previous year. His bonus for the year [ ] had been £[ ] and his bonus for the year [ ] should, had the Defendant acted in accordance with the implied terms set out in paragraph 3 above, have been at least £[ ]. In fact the bonus awarded was £[ ].]

7. By reason of the matters aforesaid the Claimant has sustained loss and damage.

PARTICULARS

[Set out here the level of bonus that it is contended the Claimant should have been awarded and all relevant facts and matters relied upon. For example:

The Claimant should have been awarded a bonus of £[ ] for the reasons set out in paragraph 6 above but was in fact awarded a bonus of £[ ]. The Claimant submitted a grievance complaining about the level of the bonus. The grievance was heard by Mr [ ] of the Defendant. The Defendant failed to provide any rational explanation of why the bonus was so low but did comment that it had not helped that the Claimant's brother, who was married to the daughter of the Defendant's Managing Director, was seeking a divorce. The defendant in allowing that fact to influence the level of the Claimant's bonus took account of a matter which, according to the stated objectives of the bonus scheme should have been irrelevant.]

8. Further the Claimant claims interest pursuant to Section 35A of the Supreme Court Act 1981.

AND the Claimant claims:

(1) DAMAGES;

(2) INTEREST pursuant to Section 35A of the Supreme Court Act 1981.

Dated etc.

Statement of truth.

G4 DEFENCE TO CLAIM FOR DISCRETIONARY BONUS

G4.1 USE

This precedent is the Defence to the claim for the failure to pay a contractual bonus as set out at **[G3.2]**. It provides an example of how to challenge the allegation that a bonus was not awarded in good faith.

G4.2 Precedent

Defence to claim for discretionary bonus

IN THE HIGH COURT OF JUSTICE
QUEEN'S BENCH DIVISION
B E T W E E N:

[AB]

Claimant

and

[BC]

Defendant

DEFENCE

1. Paragraphs 1 to 4 of the Particulars of Claim are admitted save that it is denied that the Claimant was entitled to the bonus asserted in paragraph 2(b) of the Particulars of Claim.

2. Paragraph 5 of the Particulars of Claim is admitted. It is further contended that the Claimant was provided with a written explanation for the calculation of his bonus figure. A copy of this document is attached to this statement of case.

3. Paragraph 6 of the Particulars of Claim is denied. The decision to award the Claimant a bonus of [insert] was a reasonable decision taken in good faith and based upon all the relevant material. [Set out further particulars here as necessary.] It is admitted that the Claimant won more work for the Defendant during the relevant period than during the equivalent period in the previous year but the Defendant was entitled to and did take account of other material factors including the facts that in winning that work he had considerable assistance from [ ], that all other employees in the Claimant's position had won more work during the relevant period than during the previous year and that the Claimant had made significant errors during the year which had jeopardised the relationship with an important customer of the Defendant.

4. It is denied that the Claimant has sustained the loss and damage as alleged at paragraph 7 of the Particulars of Claim or any loss and damage.

5. Without prejudice to the generality of the foregoing it is denied that the Claimant could conceivably have been awarded the level of bonus contended by him at paragraph 7 of the Particulars of Claim. [Set out here any further detail as relevant, for example, denying any assertions made that the Defendant took account of irrelevant matters or failed to take account of relevant matters].

6. The entitlement to interest is not admitted.

Dated.

Statement of truth.

G5 CLAIM FOR UNPAID BONUS AND REPUDIATORY BREACH

G5.1 USE

This is a precedent for a claim in the High Court relating to a failure to pay a guaranteed annual bonus where that failure is alleged was a repudiatory breach of contract entitling the employee to resign. This precedent is also based upon a breach of the implied term of trust and confidence.

A claim for a bonus may either be brought in the Civil Courts (High Court of county court) or in an employment tribunal. Claims in an employment tribunal may be brought using one of two jurisdictions available to employment tribunals:

1. A claim for unlawful deductions from wages. Payment of a bonus at a level which is less than the correct amount of the bonus counts as a deduction. Deductions are unlawful unless authorised by legislation or by contract. Such claims must be brought within three months of the deduction complained of or, in the case of a series of deductions, within three months from the last of the series. This time limit is extended by three months if the Claimant has brought a written grievance (this provision is expected to be repealed in April 2009). For more information about complaints of unlawful deductions from wages, see *Jordans Employment Law Service*, at C1[57]–[105].

2. The bonus could be claimed as a remedy for breach of contract where the bonus is required by a term of the contract of employment. Breach of contract claims can be brought, in limited circumstances, in an employment tribunal. First, the claim must arise or be outstanding on termination of employment. Where a bonus or other sums are claimed in conjunction with an unfair dismissal claim, then this condition is likely to be satisfied. Secondly, the maximum amount an employment tribunal can award for a breach of contract claim is £25,000 (see *Jordans Employment Law Service*, at D2[24]). If the bonus claim is any more than this, the Claimant will have to proceed in the county court of High Court.

Complaints by an employee that an employer has breached the contract of employment and forced the employee to resign are known as 'constructive dismissal' claims. Complaints of constructive dismissal are normally brought in an employment tribunal (see *Jordans Employment Law Service*, at D1[26] and D3[5]). A constructive dismissal may be an unfair dismissal or may amount to discrimination. However, remedies for such claims may not be available in all cases (for example, because the employee does not have sufficient service) or may not provide adequate compensation because of the limits on compensation for unfair dismissal. In those cases, it may be possible to sue for the breach of contract in the High Court or a county court. The losses arising from the forced resignation, including loss of earnings as a result of the resignation, may be recovered.

As it is a claim in the High Court the Civil Procedure Rules 1998 (SI 1998/3132) must be followed.

For relevant details on jurisdiction please refer to the details as set out for Precedent Claim for Wrongful dismissal (at [G1.2]).

G5.2 **Precedent**

Claim in High Court for bonus and constructive dismissal

IN THE HIGH COURT OF JUSTICE
QUEEN'S BENCH DIVISION
B E T W E E N:

[AB]

Claimant

and

[AB]

Defendant

PARTICULARS OF CLAIM

1. The Claimant was employed by the Defendant as a [job title] pursuant to the terms of a written contract of employment dated [insert date] supplemented by [list any other documents which set out details and rules of the bonus scheme]. Copies of the relevant contract of employment and other relevant contractual documents are attached to this statement of case.

2. The following were express terms of the Claimant's contract of employment:

    (a) the Claimant was entitled to participate in the Defendant's annual bonus scheme [set out further details as relevant];

    (b) accordingly, the Claimant was entitled to an annual bonus calculated as follows [set out how bonuses are calculated] which amounted in the case of the Claimant for the period [identify period] to [insert relevant figure];

    (c) [insert other terms as necessary].

3. The following were implied terms of the contract of employment:

G5 Claim for Unpaid Bonus and Repudiatory Breach

    (a)   the Defendant would not without justification act in a manner which was calculated or likely to undermine the relationship of trust and confidence between the Claimant and the Defendant;

    (b)   that the Defendant would exercise its discretion under the bonus scheme referred to at paragraph 2(a) above rationally and in good faith and in accordance with the stated objectives of the scheme;

    (c)   the Defendant would deal with any grievance raised by the Claimant promptly and in good faith.

4. On or about [date] the Claimant was informed that he would not be paid an annual bonus [of [insert figure] but would instead receive the lower figure of [insert figure]].

5. On or about [date] the Claimant raised a grievance with his line manager regarding the failure to pay him his full annual bonus in accordance with the express and implied terms set out at paragraph 2 and 3 above.

6. [Set out any further relevant facts, for exmple:] On or about [date] the Claimant was informed by his line manager that he could "take it or leave it" and that he would not be paid any higher level of bonus. The Claimant was also told that the matter was closed and that there would be no further discussion on the issue.

7. By reason of the matters aforesaid the Defendant was in breach and/or in anticipatory breach of the express term set out at paragraph 2(a) above and/or the implied terms set out at paragraph 3 above. These breaches, whether taken individually or cumulatively, amounted to the repudiation of the Claimant's contract of employment by the Defendant.

8. By reason of the matters set out at paragraph 7 above the Claimant resigned from his employment with the Defendant with immediate effect by means of a letter dated [insert date] and accepted the Defendant's repudiation of his contract of employment.

9. By reason of the matters set out above the Claimant has suffered loss and damage.

PARTICULARS

    (a)   the Claimant is entitled to the sum of [insert sum] by way of his annual bonus under paragraph 2(a) above;

    (b)   the Claimant is also entitled to his lost remuneration and the value of all other benefits to which he would have been entitled during the notice period under his contract of employment had the Claimant not resigned as a result of the Defendant's repudiation of the contract of employment. This amounts to [insert figure].

10. Further the Claimant claims interest pursuant to Section 35A of the Supreme Court Act 1981 at the rate of [insert]. In relation to the sum of [insert] claimed under paragraph 9(a) above this amounts to [insert] as at the date of issue and continuing at the rate of [insert] per day. In relation to the damages claimed under paragraph 9(b) above the sum remains to be assessed.

AND the Claimant claims:

(1) the sum of [insert] under paragraph 9(a) above and interest thereon amounting to [insert details];

(2) damages under paragraph 9(b) above to be assessed; and

(3) interest pursuant to Section 35A of the Supreme Court Act 1981.

Dated etc.

Statement of truth.

G5.3 DRAFTING POINTS

Paragraphs 2 and 3: Set out here all the terms of employment, express or implied, which it is alleged the Defendant (the employer) has breached. Paragraph 2(a) in this precedent sets out the implied term most often relied on, but there are other implied terms, such as the duty not to do anything to undermine a particular benefit which would otherwise be available to the employee. For example, if there is an enhanced redundancy scheme there may be an implied term not to deliberately avoid the redundancy scheme by concocting some false reason for dismissal; or if there is a permanent health insurance scheme which provides benefits to those who are off sick for six months or more, there may be an implied term not to defeat the purpose of such a scheme by dismissing shortly before the end of the sixth month of absence. For more information on implied terms generally, see *Jordans Employment Law Service*, at B2[209]–[381].

Paragraph 5: At least for the moment, employees are required to submit a grievance before pursuing certain types of claim in an employment tribunal. That requirement is to be repealed with effect from April 2009. It is, therefore, standard practice to include within employment tribunal claims a statement of when the grievance was submitted. There is not strictly any need to do this in High Court proceedings. It does at least show, however, that the Claimant has tried to resolve the dispute using the employer's internal grievance procedures.

Paragraph 6: For the same reason, it is useful to include reference to any conversations the Claimant may have had with the employer to demonstrate that the Defendant (the Employer) that the bonus would not be paid.

Paragraph 7: the requirements for a constructive dismissal, for the purposes of unfair dismissal law, are:

- that the employer has fundamentally breached the contract of employment;

- that as a result the employee has resigned;

- the Claimant has not delayed too long between the breach and the resignation (see *Jordans Employment Law Service*, at D3[5]).

A series of incidents may cumulatively amount to a breach. It is generally sensible, where the Claimant is relying on a series of incidents, to assert that each incident by itself amounts to a breach sufficient to entitle the Claimant to resign without notice. If a court or tribunal concludes that one or more of the incidents in the series are not as asserted by the Claimant, then the Claimant can still rely on the other incidents pleaded.

Paragraph 9: Generally, because employers are always entitled under the contract of employment to terminate the employment by giving the notice specified in the contract, the most that can be claimed as damages for breach of contract is the value of remuneration and other benefits that would have been earned during the notice period. As the law currently stands, no further damages can be claimed by reason of the manner of the dismissal. For more information on compensation that may be claimed for a wrongful dismissal, see *Jordans Employment Law Service*, at D2[32]–[55].

G6 DEFENCE TO HIGH COURT CLAIM FOR A BONUS AND CONSTRUCTIVE DISMISSAL

G6.1 USE

This precedent is the Defence to the claim for a failure to pay a bonus which is alleged to be a repudiatory breach entitling the employee to resign as set out at [G5.2]. It includes an allegation of waiver and/or variation of the contract – ie that the reason the bonus was not paid was that the Claimant had agreed to a variation in his or her contract entitling the Defendant not to pay or had accepted that the Defendant need not pay the bonus.

Defences to a claim for a bonus may include:

– that the bonus was entirely discretionary and there was no entitlement to it under the contract;

– that even if the bonus was contractual, the criteria for earning the bonus were not met;

– even if the bonus was contractual and the criteria met, the Claimant may have calculated the amount of the bonus incorrectly;

– even if none of the above apply, the Claimant has agreed to the non-payment of the bonus or to payment of a lesser amount.

Criteria for earning the bonus are often related to the performance of the individual or of the business or both, and may include conditions such as that the employee must still be in employment at the date of payment; or that employees under notice of termination of employment are excluded.

G6.2 **Precedent**

Defence to claim for bonus and constructive dismissal

IN THE HIGH COURT OF JUSTICE
QUEEN'S BENCH DIVISION
B E T W E E N:

[A.B.]

Claimant

and

[A.B.]

Defendant

DEFENCE

1. Paragraphs 1 [to][and] 3 of the Particulars of Claim are admitted.

2. [Paragraph 2 of the Particulars of Claim is denied. There was no term of the Claimant's contract of employment, whether express or implied, entitling the Claimant to a bonus.]

2. Paragraph 4 of the Particulars of Claim is admitted. It is further contended that the Claimant was provided with a written explanation as to [why no bonus was due][the calculation of the bonus]. This was because:

   [the bonus is discretionary and no employee has a contractual right to a bonus]

   [of the financial situation of the Defendant of which the Claimant was aware]

   [the criteria for qualifying for a bonus set out in the terms of the bonus scheme had not been met]

   [it is a condition of qualifying for the bonus that, as at the date on which bonuses are due to be paid, the employee is still in the employment of the Defendant and no notice of termination of employment has been served either by the Claimant or the Defendant]

   [of the facts and matters asserted at paragraphs 4 and 6 below.]

   A copy of the relevant document is attached to this statement of case.

3. Paragraph 5 of the Particulars of Claim is admitted.

4. Paragraph 6 of the Particulars of Claim is denied. The Claimant

was given a full opportunity to raise his grievance and his grievance was discussed directly with him during meetings on [insert dates]. The Claimant was informed of [the reasons why no bonus had been paid][how the bonus had been calculated]. The Claimant stated that he understood the position [and that he was prepared to accept the lower figure [on the understanding that he would be viewed favourably for a bonus in the future if the financial position of the Defendant improved.]]

5. In the circumstances it is denied that the Defendant has acted unlawfully as alleged or at all and paragraph 7 of the Particulars of Claim is denied.

6. Further and in the alternative if, which is denied, the Defendant had acted unlawfully as alleged then the Claimant either waived any such breach or consented to a variation of his contractual terms by reason of the facts and matters set out at paragraph 4 above.

7. It is admitted that the Claimant resigned from his employment with the Defendant by means of a letter dated [date] as alleged at paragraph 8 of the Particulars of Claim. It is denied that the Claimant was entitled to resign by reason of any alleged repudiation of contract (which is in any event denied) on behalf of the Defendant.

8. It is denied that the Claimant has suffered the loss and damage as alleged at paragraph 9 of the Particulars of Claim or at all.

9. No admissions are made to the claim for interest.

Dated.

Statement of truth.

G6.3 DRAFTING POINTS

Paragraph 4: There is no need strictly to explain how any grievance was dealt with. However, setting this information out in the defence draws attention to the Respondents attempts at resolving the matter.

If the Claimant, by his or her actions, may be said to have agreed to the non-payment or reduction in the bonus, then the facts upon which that assertion is based should be set out here.

Paragraph 6: This should be included where it is alleged that the Claimant, by words or actions, has agreed to the non-payment or reduction in the bonus.

Paragraph 7: A resignation can be treated as a dismissal for the purposes of unfair dismissal and redundancy payments if the resignation was in response to a fundamental breach of contract by the employer. The fact that a person may be treated as dismissed for unfair dismissal purposes in such circumstances does not mean that they can be treated as dismissed for all other purposes. An employee who believes he or she has been constructively dismissed cannot therefore sue on that basis for wrongful dismissal. But they could sue for breach of contract (the breach being the fundamental reach relied on) and argue that the loss of earnings as a result of the resignation was a loss for which they should be compensated.

For an explanation of the circumstances in which an employee may resign and be treated as dismissed, see *Jordans Employment Law Service*, at D3[5].

G7 UNFAIR DISMISSAL CLAIM

G7.1 USE

This precedent illustrates a standard claim for unfair dismissal. The claim must be commenced in the Employment Tribunal and the Employment Tribunal Rules will apply (see *Jordans Employment Law Service*, at H1[10]–[26]).

As with all complaints to an employment tribunal, the form ET1 must be used. A Claim submitted on any other form, even if it contains all the required information, will not be accepted. This Form is available from the Employment Tribunals' website. Claims can be completed and submitted online. The Form asks for standard information such as the identity of the employer, the Claimant's address and contact details and information about earnings. Box 5.1 on the Form ET1 asks the Claimant to set out the grounds for saying the dismissal was unfair. That box can be filled in with the precedent set out below.

A dismissal may be unfair because a tribunal concludes there are insufficient grounds for dismissing. For example, in cases of dismissal for misconduct, a tribunal may conclude that the misconduct was not serious enough to justify dismissal, or that the misconduct has not been sufficiently proved.

A dismissal may also be procedurally unfair if the employer has not followed a fair procedure before dismissing; or it may be automatically unfair if the employer has not followed the statutory dismissal procedure (the statutory dismissal procedure is to be repealed in April 2009). Generally, it is better for Claimants not to rely solely on procedural unfairness, because the tribunal may hold that, even though unfair, the employee would still have been dismissed even if a fair procedure had been followed. The tribunal may then award either no compensation or only limited compensation.

This precedent sets out grounds for both substantive and procedural unfairness.

G7.2   **Precedent**

Unfair dismissal claim (to be completed on Form ET1)

IN THE EMPLOYMENT TRIBUNALS   CASE NO: .../2009
[LOCATION]
B E T W E E N:

[AB]
Claimant

– and –

[CD]
Respondent

PARTICULARS OF CLAIM

The parties

1. The Claimant was employed by the Respondent as a [position] from 1st October 2005 until he was dismissed with effect from 15th May 2007.

2. At all material times, the Respondent has been a company in the business of building widgets and is based in [address].

The claims

3. The Claimant brings the following claims against the Respondent:

   (1) Unfair Dismissal, contrary to sections 94 and 98 Employment Rights Act 1996 ("ERA 1996"); and

   (2) Automatically Unfair Dismissal, contrary to sections 94 and 98A ERA 1996.

Jurisdiction

4. The Claimant's claims relate to dismissal only and, therefore, no grievance issues arise in this case.

Background

5. The Claimant has been a Shop Floor Manager for many years. On or about 10th May 2007, the Claimant was walking past Widget Machine 1 when he saw an altercation between Mr Ian Brown and Mr David Johnson, both Machine Workers.

6. The Claimant interrupted this altercation and a scuffle occurred.

The Claimant told both men to behave themselves and he then went on with his normal duties and thought nothing further of it.

7. To the Claimant's surprise, later that day, Mr Kevin Williams (the Claimant's Line Manager) called the Claimant to his office and informed the Claimant that he was being suspended for fighting. The Claimant explained what had happened, but Mr Williams would not listen to the Claimant's version of events and the Claimant was sent home immediately.

8. On 11th May 2007, the Claimant received a letter explaining that he was suspended pending an investigation into alleged gross misconduct, namely fighting.

9. On 13th May 2007, the Claimant received a letter calling him to a disciplinary hearing. The hearing took place on 15th May 2007. At that hearing the Claimant was summarily dismissed for fighting. The Claimant received a letter on 17th May 2007, confirming that he was dismissed with effect from 15th May 2007. The Claimant was not given a right of appeal.

The claimant's claims

UNFAIR DISMISSAL: SUBSTANTIVE UNFAIRNESS

10. It is the Claimant's case that his dismissal was substantively unfair.

11. The Claimant was dismissed for alleged gross misconduct, namely fighting. The Claimant denies that he was fighting on 10th May 2007. In fact, as set out above, the Claimant was (in his managerial role) breaking up an altercation between Mr Brown and Mr Johnson. The Claimant did not strike either Mr Brown or Mr Johnson. The Claimant was very surprised to face any disciplinary action whatsoever in respect of the events of 10th May 2007 and it is averred that his dismissal for alleged fighting is entirely unfair.

12. Further and in any event, the Claimant avers that his dismissal for this one-off incident on 10th May 2007 was wholly unfair and disproportionate for the following reasons:

    (1) firstly, the Claimant's version of the events of 10th May 2007 is the true and correct version, not the Respondent's. The Claimant's conduct throughout the incident on 10th May 2007 was reasonable and professional and cannot be classified as misconduct, let alone gross misconduct;

    (2) secondly, even if the Respondent's version of events of the incident on 10th May 2007 were correct, this would not reasonably justify dismissing the Claimant. This was, on both parties' cases, a one-off incident. The Claimant was a

good employee, good at his job, had a clean disciplinary record, was in a managerial position and had great expertise in his area;

  (3) In the circumstances, it was not fair to dismiss the Claimant, even if the Respondent's version of events of the 1st September 2006 was correct.

13. In the circumstances, it is denied that the Respondent had the required, reasonable belief that the Claimant had (allegedly) committed an act of (gross) misconduct. It is, further, denied that dismissal was within the band of reasonable responses.

14. The Claimant claims that his dismissal was substantively unfair, contrary to sections 94 and 98 ERA 1996.

UNFAIR DISMISSAL: PROCEDURAL UNFAIRNESS

15. It is the Claimant's case that his dismissal was procedurally unfair, for the following reasons:

  (1) It was unfair to call the Claimant to a Disciplinary Hearing without holding an Investigatory Hearing first;

  (2) It was unfair (and in breach of natural justice) that Mr Williams heard the Claimant's Disciplinary Hearing and also suspended him;

  (3) The content of the disciplinary hearing letter dated 13th May 2007 was unfair in that it did not allege that any of the Respondent's disciplinary rules had been breached by the Claimant (and, if the Claimant had breached such a rule, which rule he had allegedly breached);

  (4) It was unfair that the Claimant was never given the opportunity to question any witnesses and, in particular, the crucial other employees involved in the incident on 10th May 2007 – ie Mr Brown and Mr Johnson;

  (5) It was unfair that the Claimant was not given a right of appeal.

16. In the circumstances, the Claimant claims that his dismissal was procedurally unfair, contrary to sections 94 and 98 ERA 1996.

17. In the circumstances, the Claimant claims that his dismissal was both procedurally and substantively unfair.

AUTOMATICALLY UNFAIR DISMISSAL

18. The Claimant avers that he was not given the right to an appeal after his dismissal.

19. In the circumstances, the Respondent acted in breach of section 98A ERA 1996. In particular, the Respondent failed to follow step 2(4) of Chapter 1 of the (standard) dismissal procedure set out in Part 1 of Schedule 2 to the Employment Act 2002 – ie the Respondent failed to notify the Claimant of the right to appeal the decision to dismiss him.

20. In the circumstances, the Claimant's dismissal was automatically unfair.

Conclusion

21. The Claimant accordingly brings the following claims against the Respondent:

   (i) Unfair Dismissal;

   (ii) Automatically Unfair Dismissal;

   (iii) Damages;

   (iv) Further and other relief.

G7.3 DRAFTING POINTS

Paragraphs 5 to 9: These paragraphs set out the facts behind the dismissal from the Claimant's point of view. Paragraph 9 also asserts that one of the steps in the statutory dismissal procedure (namely providing a right of appeal) was not followed by the Respondent. An employer is required to inform the employee of the right of appeal. Failure to do so renders the dismissal automatically unfair. It probably also makes the dismissal procedurally unfair irrespective of the statutory dismissal procedure.

Paragraphs 11 to 14: These paragraphs explain the arguments why the dismissal was substantively unfair. In this example, it is denied that there was any misconduct, let alone gross misconduct. What matters in an unfair dismissal claim, however, is whether the employer had reasonable grounds for believing that the employee had committed gross misconduct – not whether the employee had actually committed gross misconduct. The test for fairness in misconduct cases is whether the employers had a reasonable and genuine belief in the misconduct, based on reasonable grounds and following a reasonable investigation; and whether dismissal was within the range of reasonable responses to that misconduct. Here, the Claimant alleges that there were no reasonable grounds for the

Respondent's belief; and that, in view of the Claimant's employment record, dismissal would have been an unreasonable response. For a fuller explanation of when a dismissal may be unfair, and for the factors which may make other types of dismissal (eg dismissals for redundancy, ill health or capability) unfair, see Division D3 of *Jordans Employment Law Service*.

Paragraphs 15 to 17: These paragraphs set out reasons why the dismissal was also procedurally unfair. For more details, see *Jordans Employment Law Service*, at D3[29]–[53].

Paragraphs 18 to 20: These paragraphs set out why the dismissal was automatically unfair because the Respondent had not followed the statutory dismissal procedure. The statutory dismissal procedure is to be repealed in April 2009, but factors such as those mentioned here, even after April 2009, are still likely to make the dismissal unfair on general principles.

G8 RESPONSE TO UNFAIR DISMISSAL CLAIM

G8.1 USE

This precedent is a defence to an unfair dismissal claim (see precedent at [G7.2]).

As with all responses to complaints to an employment tribunal, the form ET3 must be used. A response submitted on any other form, even if it contains all the required information, will not be accepted. This Form is available from the Employment Tribunals' website. Responses can be completed and submitted online. The Form asks for standard information such as the identity of the employer, the number of employees and contact details and information about earnings. One of the boxes asks the Respondent to set out the grounds on which the claim is to be resisted. This precedent sets out a suggested response to be included in that box.

In this precedent, the Claimant has argued that the dismissal was both substantively and procedurally unfair, and that the statutory dismissal procedure was not followed (because the Claimant was not informed of his right to appeal). These terms are explained in the notes to the precedent Claim form (at [G7.2]). The respondent must, therefore, explain why it was thought that dismissal was within the range of reasonable responses for a reasonable employer; and set out the procedure followed, arguing that it was fair. Alternatively, if the dismissal was unfair for procedural reasons only, this precedent argues that dismissal was nevertheless an appropriate response so that, if the Claimant had not been unfairly dismissed, he would inevitably have been fairly dismissed; and/or the Claimant had contributed wholly or mainly to his dismissal. Either way, this precedent argues, the Claimant should not be entitled to any compensation or compensation should be substantially reduced.

For an explanation of the law of unfair dismissal, see Division D3 of *Jordans Employment Law Service*.

The Employment Tribunal Rules apply.

G8.2   **Precedent**

Response to unfair dismissal claim (to be completed on Form ET3)

IN THE EMPLOYMENT TRIBUNALS   CASE NO: .../2009
[LOCATION]
B E T W E E N:

                               [AB]
                                                   Claimant
                              – and –
                                [CD]
                                                   Respondent

GROUNDS OF RESISTANCE

The parties

1. It is admitted that at all material times the Claimant was employed by the Respondent as a [position]. It is admitted that he was so employed from 1st October 2005 until he was dismissed for gross misconduct (namely fighting), with effect from 15th May 2007.

2. It is admitted that at all material times the Respondent has been a company in the business of building widgets.

Summary of the respondent's case

3. The Claimant brings claims for (1) unfair dismissal and (2) automatic unfair dismissal.

4. The Respondent's summarised case is as follows:

    (1) It was the Claimant who was the aggressor on 10th May 2007;

    (2) Mr Brown and Mr Johnson were having a playful discussion that day when the Claimant (who is known to dislike the other two men) came over and physically attacked them both;

    (3) Mr Brown and Mr Johnson both complained to Mr Williams (the Claimant's Line Manager) about this;

    (4) An independent witness, Mrs Robinson confirmed Mr Brown's and Mr Johnson's version of events;

    (5) In any event, during the disciplinary hearing held on 15th May 2007, the Claimant admitted to hitting both Mr Brown and Mr Johnson;

(6) In the circumstances, it was both procedurally and substantively fair to dismiss the Claimant for the gross misconduct offence of fighting, particularly when he admitted as much;

(7) It is admitted that the Claimant was not informed of the right of appeal. However, it is averred that (particularly in light of the Claimant's admission during the disciplinary hearing) no appeal was necessary or appropriate in this case. The Claimant was in any case aware of his right of appeal, having been sent a copy of the Respondent's disciplinary procedure;

(8) In the circumstances, it is denied that the Respondent is liable to the Claimant as alleged or at all.

Background

5. It is admitted that the Claimant has been a [position] for many years. It is denied that, on or about 10th May 2007, the Claimant was walking past Widget Machine 1 when he saw an altercation between Mr Brown and Mr Johnson.

6. As set out above, Mr Brown and Mr Johnson were involved in nothing more than a playful discussion. The Claimant interrupted this discussion and without any provocation or reason for doing so, attacked both Mr Brown and Mr Johnson. He punched both of them and shouted at them. The attack was entirely unprovoked, although it is well known at the Respondent that the Claimant does not like Mr Brown or Mr Johnson. Mrs Robinson witnessed the entire incident and supported Mr Brown's and Mr Johnson's version of events entirely.

7. Later that day, the Claimant's Line Manager, Mr Williams, called the Claimant to his office and informed the Claimant that he was being suspended for fighting. It is admitted that, in accordance with standard company procedure, the Claimant was sent home immediately.

8. The Claimant was sent a letter explaining that he was suspended pending an investigation into alleged gross misconduct, namely fighting.

9. The Claimant was sent a letter calling him to a disciplinary hearing and the hearing took place on 15th May 2007. At that hearing the Claimant was summarily dismissed for fighting. The Claimant was sent a letter confirming that he was dismissed with effect from 15th May 2007. It is admitted that the Claimant was not informed of his right of appeal.

Alleged unfair dismissal

10. The Claimant's dismissal was both procedurally and substantively entirely fair.

11. The Claimant was dismissed for alleged gross misconduct, namely fighting. Both Mr Brown and Mr Johnson complained to Mr Williams on 10th May 2007 that they had been physically attacked by the Claimant. Mrs Robinson, an entirely independent witness (who works in a different area and just happened to be passing), gave a statement that supported Mr Brown's and Mr Johnson's version of events. Mr Brown, Mr Johnson and Mrs Robinson all gave consistent evidence about the Claimant's behaviour on 10th May 2007 during the disciplinary investigation. During the disciplinary hearing, the Claimant admitted to striking both Mr Brown and Mr Johnson.

12. It was entirely fair to dismiss the Claimant for this one-off incident on 10th May 2007. The Claimant's dismissal was in no way unfair or disproportionate:

    (1) The Claimant's version of the events of 10th May 2007 is not the true and correct version. The Claimant's conduct throughout the incident on 10th May 2007 was not reasonable or professional and certainly amounted to gross misconduct. In any event, the correct test is whether or not the reasonable employer could reasonably believe (after a reasonable investigation) that the Claimant committed this act of gross misconduct. In light of the above, the Respondent avers that this was the case;

    (2) Despite the fact that the Claimant was a good employee, good at his job, was in a managerial position and had great expertise in his area, the Respondent's policy on fighting is strict. The Claimant admitted hitting Mr Brown and Mr Johnson and Mrs Robinson stated that the Claimant was the aggressor. The Respondent will not tolerate this kind of behaviour and it was entirely fair to dismiss the Claimant in these circumstances.

13. In the circumstances, it is averred that the Respondent had the required, reasonable belief that the Claimant had committed an act of gross misconduct. It is, further, averred that dismissal was within the band of reasonable responses.

14. In the circumstances, the Claimant's dismissal was substantively fair.

Unfair dismissal: procedural unfairness

15. The Claimant's dismissal was procedurally fair:

(1) It was fair to call the Claimant to a disciplinary hearing without holding an investigatory hearing first. The Respondent's standard policy does not require an investigatory hearing first. The Respondent had all the information needed to hold the disciplinary hearing without any further investigation.

(2) It was entirely fair for Mr Williams to hear the Claimant's disciplinary hearing even though he had also suspended him. Mr Williams was the Claimant's line manager and he had been in no way prejudiced or biased by any prior knowledge of the incident before hearing the disciplinary hearing.

(3) The content of the disciplinary hearing letter dated 13th May 2007 was fair. It set out what the Claimant had done wrong. It was obvious that this was an allegation of fighting and gross misconduct.

(4) It was fair that the Claimant was not given the opportunity to question any witnesses. This is the Respondent's standard procedure. In any event, the question is the Respondent's belief, not the Claimant's.

(5) In view of Mr Brown's, Mr Johnson's and Mrs Robinson's evidence and the Claimant's above admission, it is averred that it was not unfair that the Claimant was not given a right of appeal.

16. In the circumstances, the Claimant's dismissal was procedurally entirely fair.

17. If, which is denied, the Claimant was unfairly dismissed, as alleged or at all, it is averred that the Claimant would have been dismissed in any event for gross misconduct.

18. If, which is denied, the Claimant was unfairly dismissed, as alleged or at all, it is averred that the Claimant contributed 100% or substantially to his dismissal.

Alleged automatic unfair dismissal

19. It is admitted that the Claimant was not informed of his right to an appeal after his dismissal.

20. However, it is averred that (particularly in light of the Claimant's admission during the disciplinary hearing) no appeal was necessary or appropriate in this case. In any case, the Claimant was aware of his right under the disciplinary procedure to an appeal, having been sent a copy of the disciplinary procedure.

21. If, which is denied, the Claimant was automatically unfairly dismissed, as alleged or at all, it is averred that the Claimant would have been dismissed in any event for gross misconduct.

22. If, which is denied, the Claimant was automatically unfairly dismissed, as alleged or at all, it is averred that the Claimant contributed 100% to his alleged dismissal.

Alleged losses

23. The Claimant is put to strict proof of all his alleged losses. Further and in any event, it is not admitted that the Claimant has taken reasonable steps to mitigate his losses.

Conclusion

24. Save where specifically denied, not admitted or admitted, each and every allegation made against the Respondent is denied as though the same were individually set out herein and traversed. In the circumstances and for the reasons set out above, the Claimant is not entitled to the relief claimed against the Respondent or to any other relief, and it is denied that the Respondent is in any way liable to the Claimant.

G8.3 DRAFTING POINTS

Paragraphs 1 and 24: It is not strictly necessary in employment tribunal proceedings to indicate which points in the Claim the Respondent admits and which he denies. However, the risk of not specifically denying points that the Respondent disagrees with is that any failure to deny a particular point may be taken as evidence that the Respondent accepts that it is true.

Paragraph 4: This sets out a summary of the Respondent's case. One weakness in the respondent's case is that the Claimant was not informed of his right to appeal. That is a breach of the statutory dismissal procedure and so (at least until Aril 2009) renders the dismissal automatically unfair. The Respondent can still argue that that defect in procedure made no difference, so that, even if the dismissal was unfair, no compensation should be awarded. Paragraph 4(7) sets out the facts upon which this argument could be based.

Paragraphs 5 to 14: These paragraphs set out the facts on which the Respondent relies to establish that the dismissal was within the range of reasonable responses. Fighting is generally so obviously a serious matter that there is no need here to set out why the Claimant's conduct was regarded as so serious. In less clear cases, the Response should explain why the conduct was regarded as so serious. For example, if the conduct falls within a category which is defined in the disciplinary rules as gross misconduct, then that fact should be stated in the Response form. Here, in paragraph 12(1), the Respondent relies not only on the fighting but the fact that the Claimant was not truthful in his explanation of what happened.

Paragraph 15: This paragraph deals with the Claimant's assertion that an unfair procedure was followed. For details of what constitutes a fair dismissal procedure, see *Jordans Employment Law Service*, at D3[32]. Generally, a dismissal for misconduct will be fair if the employer had a reasonable and genuine belief in the misconduct following a reasonable investigation; and dismissal was within the range of reasonable responses to that misconduct.

Paragraph 15(1): Here, there was very little in the way of an investigation, but it is argued that there was no need for an investigation as the facts were so clear.

Paragraph 15(2): Generally, the person who takes the decision to dismiss should not have had any previous involvement in the matter, either as the investigating officer or as a witness. Here, the Claimant had argued that the dismissing officer (Mr Williams) had had previous involvement and so should not have conducted the dismissal hearing. The Respondent's answer to that is that Mr Williams' previous involvement was not such as to make him prejudiced or biased.

Paragraph 15(4): There is no absolute rule that witnesses must be made available at the disciplinary/dismissal hearing. What matters is whether the Claimant was given a fair opportunity to challenge the allegations of misconduct. It might have been better to have witnesses present in this case, because there is such a difference between what the Claimant asserts happened and what the other witnesses say. Someone is obviously lying and the dismissing officer had to decide who was telling the truth. The Claimant will argue that, even though there is no absolute rule that witnesses should be made available, in this case the only way that Mr Williams could fairly make an assessment of who was telling the truth was to have the witnesses present at the hearing. The tribunal may accept that, given the weight of the evidence against the Claimant, and the fact that he had admitted striking another employee, there was no need for the presence of witnesses.

Paragraph 17: This is the argument that the Claimant would have been dismissed in any event, whether or not a fair procedure had been followed. If the tribunal accepts this, then no compensation, or only limited compensation, will be awarded.

Paragraph 18: In addition to the argument that the Claimant would have been dismissed in any event, the Respondent may argue that the Claimant was wholly or substantially to blame for his dismissal. The advantages of arguing this in addition to the argument in paragraph 17 are first, that it gives the Respondent two arguments for reducing compensation and so increases the chances of a tribunal awarding no or little compensation; and secondly, if the tribunal accepts for example, that there would have been a 50% chance that the Claimant would have been dismissed anyway and that the Claimant contributed 50% to his dismissal, then compensation should be reduced twice by 50% – ie reduced to 25%.

Paragraphs 19 to 22: These paragraphs attempt to argue that the failure to inform the Claimant of his right to appeal did not make the dismissal automatically unfair. Under the current rules (to be repealed in April 2009), however, a failure to complete the statutory dismissal procedure makes the dismissal automatically unfair. A tribunal is likely to conclude that the statutory procedure has not been completed because of the Respondent's failure to comply with the procedure. The Respondent can still argue, however, that no compensation should be awarded.

Paragraph 23: For an explanation of how compensation for unfair dismissal is determined, see *Jordans Employment Law Service*, at H2[29]–[52].

G9 CLAIM FOR UNFAIR DISMISSAL ON THE GROUNDS OF UNION MEMBERSHIP AND/OR ACTIVITIES AND/OR NON-MEMBERSHIP ETC

G9.1 USE

This precedent sets out how to make a claim in relation to the statutory protection from dismissal for a reason relating to union membership, non-membership or activities contained in the Trade Union and Labour Relations (Consolidation) Act 1992. Such claims may only be made to an employment tribunal. For details of the protection from dismissal on these grounds, see *Jordans Employment Law Service*, at F6[9].

The usual time limit for presenting a complaint applies – that is three months from the date of dismissal. That time limit may be extended if:

– it was not reasonably practicable to bring the complaint within that time limit and the Claimant then presented the claim within a reasonable period; or

– at the time of the expiry of the three-month time limit, the Claimant reasonably believed that the dismissal procedure was still continuing. This may be the case if, for example, the Claimant has appealed against the dismissal and the appeal hearing has not yet been held.

If the Claimant can establish that the reason for the dismissal was:

– that the Claimant was a member or official of a trade union;

– the Claimant was not a member of a trade union;

– the Claimant took part in the activities of a trade union at an appropriate time – that is either outside working hours or during working hours at a time when the Respondent gave its consent to taking part in union activities;

– the Claimant made use of services provided by a trade union;

– the Claimant did not accept an inducement from the employer not to belong to a trade union or not to take part in the activities of the trade union or not to use the services of a trade union

then the dismissal is automatically unfair.

G9 Claim for Unfair Dismissal – Union Membership/Non-membership

Where pressure to dismiss was exerted by a trade union, that trade union may be joined as a party to the proceedings (see *Jordans Employment Law Service*, at F6[15]). This may be on the application of the Claimant or of the Respondent.

The Claimant may apply for 'interim relief- ie an order that the contract of employment should be treated as continuing until the matter is determined by an employment tribunal. The tribunal must consider any such application and will order interim relief if it considers that the Claimant is more likely than not to succeed (se *Jordans Employment Law Service*, at F6[24]–[27]).

As with all complaints to an employment tribunal, the form ET1 must be used. A Claim submitted on any other form, even if it contains all the required information, will not be accepted. This Form is available from the Employment Tribunals' website. Claims can be completed and submitted online. The Form asks for standard information such as the identity of the employer, the Claimant's address and contact details and information about earnings. One of the boxes on the Form ET1 asks the Claimant to set out the grounds of complaint. That box can be filled in with the precedent set out below.

The Employment Tribunal Rules apply.

G9.2　　　　　　　　Precedent

Complaint of unfair dismissal relating to trade union membership (to be completed on Form ET1)

    IN THE EMPLOYMENT TRIBUNALS　　　　CASE NO: …/2009
    [LOCATION]
    B E T W E E N:

                          [AB]

                                              Claimant

                 – and –

                         [BC]

                                              Respondent

    DETAILS OF CLAIM:
    Claim for unfair dismissal on grounds related to
    union membership, activities, or non-membership

        1.   The Claimant's complaint is that his employer (the Respondent) has unfairly dismissed him on grounds related to his [union membership] [and/*or* union activities] [and/or making use of the services of a trade union] [and/or refusing to accept an inducement not to belong to a trade union] [*or* non-membership] contrary to

section 152 of the Trade Union and Labour Relations (Consolidation) Act 1992 ('TULR(C)A 1992').

2. The grounds of the claim are as follows (set out details as in the following example):

    (1) [The Claimant is a member of] [*or* The Claimant proposed to become a member of] the Workers' Preferred Union (WPU), an independent trade union not recognised by the Respondent for bargaining purposes. [*Or* The Claimant is not a member of any trade union].

    (2) On [date] the Claimant was dismissed by the Respondent without notice or pay in lieu of notice.

    (3) The reason or principal reason for the Claimant's dismissal was that:

    (a) *(union membership):* [The Claimant was a member of] [*or* The Claimant proposed to become a member of] the WPU; *or*

    (b) *(union activities):* on [date] the Claimant had taken part [*or* proposed to take part] in the activities of the trade union [outside his working hours] [*or* within his working hours at which, in accordance with arrangements agreed with or consent given by the Respondent, it was permissible for him to take part in the activities of the trade union]. The activities in which the Claimant [took part] [proposed to take part] were [specify – for example] to prepare for a meeting of trade union members and to enlist the support of other members for a resolution he proposed to put to the meeting;

    (c) *(union services):* The Claimant had made use [*or* proposed to make use] of trade union services [outside his working hours] [*or* within his working hours at which, in accordance with arrangements agreed with or consent given by the Respondent, it was permissible for him to make use of trade union services];

    (i) *(example):* The WPU raised a matter on behalf of the Claimant as one of its members.

    (d) *(refusal to accept inducement):* The Claimant had failed to accept an offer made to him by the Respondent for the sole or main purpose of inducing him

G9 Claim for Unfair Dismissal – Union Membership/Non-membership

           (i)   [not to be or seek to become a member of the WPU]

           (ii)   [*or* not to take part in the activities of the WPU [outside his working hours] [*or* within his working hours at which, in accordance with arrangements agreed with or consent given by the Respondent, it was permissible for him to take part in the activities of the trade union];

           (iii) [*or* not to make use of trade union services [outside his working hours] [*or* within his working hours at which, in accordance with arrangements agreed with or consent given by the Respondent, it was permissible for him to make use of trade union services]];

           (iv) [*or* to be or become a member [of any trade union] [*or* of a particular trade union, namely the Employer's Favourite Union ('EFU')]].

  (e)   *(union non-membership):* [The Claimant was not a member of any trade union [*or* of the Employers' Favourite Union (EFU)]] [*or* The Claimant had refused [*or* proposed to refuse] to become [*or* remain]] a member of the Employers' Favourite Union (EFU), which the Respondent required him to join;

           (i)   *(example: payment in lieu of union membership):* [The Claimant refused to make a payment in lieu of membership of the EFU trade union] [*or* The Claimant objected to the Respondent deducting from his wages a payment in lieu of his membership of the EFU trade union].

(4)   The dismissal was therefore automatically unfair under s 152 of the Trade union and Labour Relations (Consolidation) Act 1992.

(5)   Alternatively, the dismissal was unfair because the Respondent had no valid or supportable reason under s 98 of the Employment Rights Act 1996.

(6)   The Respondent failed to act reasonably in dismissing the Claimant in that [*set out reasons why the Respondent failed to act reasonably – for example*] it failed to follow any fair procedure before dismissing, it failed to inform the

Claimant of the true reason for dismissal and failed to give the Claimant an adequate opportunity to challenge the dismissal.

(7) In the circumstances, the Claimant's dismissal was unfair.

(8) [The Respondent was induced to dismiss the Claimant on the ground that the Claimant [was not a member of any trade union] [*or* had refused to join the EFU trade union] by the exercise of pressure by the EFU trade union [*or other third party*] on the Respondent, by calling [*or* organising] [*or* procuring] [*or* financing] a strike [*or* other industrial action], [*or* by threatening to do so] if the Claimant did not join that union. The Claimant therefore requests that the EFU be joined as a party to the proceedings under section 160 of TULR(C)A 1992.]

3. Accordingly, the Claimant seeks:

(1) [interim relief of reinstatement or re-engagement under section 161 of TULR(C)A 1992 pending the determination of his unfair dismissal complaint [and the Claimant encloses a certificate signed by AB, an authorised official of the WPU trade union (as required by section 161(5) of that Act) stating (a) that at the date of his dismissal the Claimant [was *or* proposed to become] a member of that union, and (b) that there appear to be reasonable grounds for supposing that the [principal] reason for his dismissal was that the Claimant [was *or* proposed to become] a member of that union [*or* that the Claimant had taken part in the activities of that union at an appropriate time];

(2) a declaration that the Respondent unfairly dismissed him on grounds related to his [union membership] [and/*or* union activities][and/*or* making use of union services][and/*or* failing to accept the employer's inducement] [*or* non-membership] contrary to section 152 of TULR(C)A 1992;

(3) alternatively, a declaration that the dismissal was unfair under s 98 of the Employment Rights Act 1996;

(4) a minimum basic award under section 156 of TULR(C)A 1992;

(5) a compensatory award.

(Signature)

Dated .... 20...

G9.3 DRAFTING NOTES

Paragraphs 2(5 and 2(6)): If the Claimant does not persuade the tribunal that the reason for dismissal was to do with trade union membership, non-membership, activities etc, then the claim will fail. The Claimant may wish to argue that, even if he/she fails to persuade the tribunal that that was the reason, the dismissal was nevertheless unfair because the Respondent had no valid reason for dismissing. Generally, a dismissal is only fair if the employer can establish one of the reasons for dismissal set out in s 98 of the Employment Rights Act 1996; and the tribunal is then satisfied that the employer acted reasonably in treating that reason as a reason for dismissal. It is up to the Respondent to prove the reason for dismissal; but in determining whether dismissal was reasonable, the 'burden of proof' is neutral – ie it is not up to the Respondent to prove the dismissal was reasonable or the Claimant to prove it was unreasonable. The tribunal must decide that on the basis of all the evidence before it.

There are some circumstances where a Claimant can only succeed by proving an inadmissible reason for dismissal such as trade union membership. For example, normally employees need to have worked continuously for their employer for a period of at least 12 months before they are entitled to present a claim to an employment tribunal. That rule does not apply, however, where the reason for dismissal is an inadmissible one. In such cases there is no point in including these two paragraphs.

Paragraph 2(8): This paragraph should be included if the Claimant wishes to extend the claim to the trade union, if the Claimant believes that the employer's actions were induced by the trade union.

Paragraph 3(1): See notes under 'Use' above for an explanation of why this paragraph should normally be included in complaints of unfair dismissal on grounds of union membership etc.

G10 RESPONSE TO CLAIM FOR UNFAIR DISMISSAL ON THE GROUNDS OF UNION MEMBERSHIP AND/OR ACTIVITIES OR NON-MEMBERSHIP ETC

G10.1 USE

This precedent sets out the Grounds of Resistance to the claims made in the precedent claim for unfair dismissal on grounds of trade union membership etc. It must be included on form ET3 and the Employment Tribunal Rules apply.

For an explanation of the various claims to which this is a response, see notes to the precedent claim.

As with all responses to complaints to an employment tribunal, the form ET3 must be used. A response submitted on any other form, even if it contains all the required information, will not be accepted. This Form is available from the Employment Tribunals' website. Responses can be completed and submitted online. The Form asks for standard information such as the identity of the employer, the number of employees and contact details and information about earnings. One of the boxes asks the Respondent to set out the grounds on which the claim is to be resisted. This precedent sets out a suggested response to be included in that box.

The precedent includes the defence that the action taken against the Claimant was induced by the pressure exercised on the Respondent by the relevant trade union. Using this defence automatically makes the trade union a party to the proceedings.

For an explanation of the rules making dismissals for trade union-related reasons unfair, see *Jordans Employment Law Service*, at F6[9]–[27].

G10.2 Precedent

Response to claim for unfair dismissal on grounds of union members and/or activities or non-membership etc [to be completed on Form ET3]

IN THE EMPLOYMENT TRIBUNALS   CASE NO: .../2009
[LOCATION]

B E T W E E N:

[AB]

Claimant

– and –

[BC]

Respondent

GROUNDS OF RESISTANCE:
Claim for unfair dismissal on grounds related to union membership, activities, or non-membership

1. It is denied that the Claimant was dismissed for the reason(s) alleged in the Details of Claim.

2. It is averred that the reason or principal reason for the Claimant's dismissal related to his [capability] [or conduct] [or is retirement] [or is that he was redundant] [or is that he could not continue to work in the position which he held without contravention of a duty or restriction imposed by or under an enactment] [or some other substantial reason of a kind such as to justify the dismissal of an employee holding the position which he held [in each case give details – for example]

    (1) On [date] the Claimant refused to carry out a reasonable instruction from his manager to [set out the instruction] and then became abusive and threatening towards the manager.

    (2) The Claimant was invited to a disciplinary hearing to answer the allegation. The Claimant provided no reasonable excuse or explanation for his actions. Accordingly, the Claimant was summarily dismissed.

    (3) The Claimant appealed but the decision to dismiss was upheld.

    (4) The Respondent acted reasonably in deciding to treat the Claimants conduct as sufficient to warrant dismissal.

    (5) Accordingly, the dismissal was fair.

[Or

3. It is admitted that the Claimant was dismissed for the reason(s) stated in his Details of Claim.

4. The Respondent was induced to dismiss the Claimant by pressure exercised on the Respondent by the EFU trade union, by it calling [or organising] [or procuring] [or financing] a strike [or other industrial action], [or by threatening to do so] *(set out details of inducement)*.

5. The Respondent therefore applies for the EFU union to be joined as a party to the proceedings, and that any award of compensation to the Claimant be paid wholly by that union.]

(Signature)

Dated .... 20...

G10.3 DRAFTING POINTS

Paragraph 2: If the Respondent does not set out and establish what it claims to be the true reason for the dismissal, then the tribunal may accept that the reason asserted by the Claimant was correct – there having been no other reason asserted. The Respondent should also include here enough information to demonstrate that the dismissal was fair for the reason it has asserted. For a fuller example of a defence to a claim for unfair dismissal, see Precedent at **[G8.2]**.

Paragraphs 3 to 5: These paragraphs should be included if the Respondent admits that the reason for dismissal did have something to do with the fact that the Claimant was not a member of any trade union or was not a member of a particular trade union. It would be theoretically possible to include this as an alternative defence – ie that there was some reason for dismissal other than non-membership of a trade union but that, if the tribunal concludes that that was the reason, then the dismissal was induced by pressure from the trade union. In most cases, however, asserting that dismissal was induced by a trade union would amount to an admission that the reason had something to do with trade union membership or non-membership.

G11 CLAIM FOR UNLAWFUL DEDUCTIONS FROM WAGES IN EMPLOYMENT TRIBUNAL

G11.1 USE

This is a precedent for a claim for unlawful deductions from wages under the Employment Rights Act 1996. The claim can only be commenced in the Employment Tribunal. It must therefore be commenced on Form ET1. This precedent sets out the grounds for the claim which should be inserted in answer to question 8 on the form ET1. The claim must comply with the Employment Tribunal Rules – see Division H1, Section 2 of *Jordans Employment Law Service*. In particular, claims must be brought within three months of the deduction or, where a grievance has been brought, within six months of the deduction (this extension to six months is expected to be repealed in April 2009). In the case of a series of deductions, the claim must be brought within three months (or six months where a grievance has been brought) of the last deduction in the series.

Such a claim may also be brought in the High Court or a county court on the basis that the employer has breached the contract of employment by not paying the correct amount of wages. Claims in the High Court or county court are subject to a six-year limitation period.

G11.2 Precedent

Claim for unlawful deductions from wages [to be completed on Form ET1]

IN THE EMPLOYMENT TRIBUNALS   CASE NO: …/2009
[LOCATION]
B E T W E E N:

[AB]

Claimant

– and –

[BC]

Respondent

DETAILS OF CLAIM:
Claim for unauthorised deductions from wages

1. The Claimant's complaint is that his employer (the Respondent) has made a deduction from his wages in contravention of section 13 of the Employment Rights Act 1996.

2. The grounds of the claim are as follows (set out details as in the following example):

(1) The Claimant commenced employment with the Respondent as a Sales Assistant on [date]. He is still so employed. His gross wages are £[ ] per month.

(2) On receiving his payslip for the month ending [date], the Claimant discovered that the Respondent had made deductions from his wages in the sum of £[ ].

(3) The Claimant sent a written statement of grievance to the Respondent on [date] complaining about the deduction.

(4) The Respondent has to date given no or no adequate explanation for making such deductions.

(5) These deductions were unauthorised as the Claimant had not previously signified in writing his agreement or consent to any such deductions being made nor is the deduction required or authorised to be made by any statutory provision or relevant term of his contract.

3. Accordingly, the Claimant seeks:

(1) a declaration that the Respondent has made a deduction from his wages in contravention of section 13 of the Employment Rights Act 1996;

(2) an order that the Respondent do pay to the Claimant the amount of any deduction made in contravention of section 13.

(*Signature*)

Dated .... 20....

G11.3 DRAFTING POINTS

Paragraph 2(3): As with most other types of tribunal claims not concerning dismissal, the Claimant must, before commencing tribunal proceedings, have brought a grievance in respect of the subject matter of the claim and must have waited at least 28 days before submitting the claim to the tribunal. The rules about grievances are to be repealed in April 2009. For an explanation of these rules, see *Jordans Employment Law Service*, at C6[41].

Question 3 on the form ET1 requires the Claimant to state, by ticking the relevant boxes, whether a grievance was brought and if so when. There is strictly no need to explain how and when the grievance was brought. The advantage of mentioning the grievance here, however, is that the grounds for the claim then set out a more complete picture of what happened and it gives the Claimant an opportunity assert to the tribunal at an early stage that the grievance was not dealt with properly by the Respondent.

G12 RESPONSE TO CLAIM FOR UNLAWFUL DEDUCTION FROM WAGES IN EMPLOYMENT TRIBUNAL

G12.1 USE

This is a precedent for Grounds of Resistance to a claim for unlawful deductions as set out in the precedent at **[G11.2]**. It must be inserted into Form ET3. This form is available from the Employment Tribunals' website. Responses on any other form will not be accepted. The Form asks for various pieces of information, such as the identity of the employer and whether the Respondent agrees with the information about wages etc included on the Claim Form. The grounds on which the claim is resisted must be included in Box 5.2 of the Response Form.

The Employment Tribunal Rules must be complied with.

This Precedent alleges that the deductions in question were not unlawful and were permitted by the contract of employment.

For an explanation of the rules about deductions from wages and other possible defences, see *Jordans Employment Law Service*, at C1[57]–[106]. Possible defences to the claim may be:

– that no deduction was made and the Claimant was in fact paid the correct amount that he or she was entitled to under the contract;

– that the contract or legislation permitted the deduction;

– that the deduction was permitted by the terms of some other agreement;

– that the Claimant was taking industrial action during the period in respect of which the deduction was made.

G12.2 **Precedent**

Response to claim for unlawful deduction from wages in employment tribunal (to be completed on Form ET3)

IN THE EMPLOYMENT TRIBUNALS   CASE NO: …/2009
[LOCATION]
B E T W E E N:

    [AB]
                   Claimant

   – and –

    [AB]
                   Respondent

GROUNDS OF RESISTANCE:
Claim for unauthorised deductions from wages

1. The Respondent admits that on [date] it deducted the sum of [£.....] from the Claimant's wages.

2. The deduction was lawful in that:

    (1)   [it was required or authorised to be made by virtue of a written term of the Claimant's contract of employment, a copy of which the Respondent gave to the Claimant on [date], which occasion was prior to the Respondent making the deduction in question]; or

    (2)   [it was made in accordance with an [express *or* implied] term of the Claimant's contract of employment, the existence and effect of which the Respondent notified to the Claimant in writing on [date], which occasion was prior to the Respondent making the deduction in question]; or

    (3)   [It was required or authorised to be made by virtue of a statutory provision, namely [ ]].

    (4)   [before the deduction was made, by an agreement on [date] the Claimant had signified in writing his agreement or consent to the making of the deduction]; or

    (5)   [add any other relevant matters – for example that the Claimant was taking industrial action during the period in respect of which he or she claims a deduction was made (which is one of the defences to such a claim). The Claimant was not therefore entitled to the amount claimed and the Respondent was entitled by reason of the

industrial action to deduct from the amount normally payable for such period the sum of £[ ].

3. The Respondent wrote to the Claimant on [date] setting out its response to his grievance in the terms set out above.

4. In the circumstances, it is denied that the Respondent has made any unlawful deduction from the Claimant's wages as alleged or at all.

(*Signature*)

Dated .... 20....

G12.3 DRAFTING POINTS

Paragraph 1: If the Respondent believes that the correct amount was in fact paid, then this paragraph should deny that any deduction was made and assert that the Claimant was paid the correct amount, determined in accordance with the contract of employment or an agreed variation of the contract of employment.

Paragraph 2: Generally, defences to claims for unlawful deductions from wages are those set out here. If none of these apply, then specialist advice should be obtained to check that there are no other defences. If there is no defence to the claim, it is better to repay the deduction and if the Claimant owes the Defendant the amount deducted, the Respondent should sue for it in the High Court of county court. Otherwise, any tribunal ruling that an unlawful deduction was made will prevent the Respondent from recovering the sums owed by the Claimant.

G13 EMPLOYMENT TRIBUNAL CLAIM FOR UNLAWFUL DEDUCTION FROM BONUS

G13.1 USE

Claims for a bonus can be pursued in a number of ways:

- as claims to enforce a contract or for compensation for a breach of contract, which may be made in the High Court or a county court, or in an employment tribunal on termination of employment (see precedents at [G5.2] and [G20.2]);

- complaints of unlawful deductions from wages.

Any failure by an employer to pay the full amount of earnings due to an employee is a deduction from wages. Employers may only make deductions if certain conditions are satisfied. Broadly, the deduction must be authorised by statute, or the contract of employment or by some other contract. Complete non-payment amounts to a deduction. For more information on this, see *Jordans Employment Law Service*, at C1[57]–[90].

As with other employment tribunal complaints, the complaint must be set out on form ET1, available from the employment tribunal's website. A complaint submitted on any other form, even if it contains all the required information, will not be accepted. The Form asks for various pieces of information. Box 5(1) asks for information about complaints relating to dismissal. (including constructive dismissal). Where the claim for a bonus is combined with an unfair dismissal complaint, Box 5(1) should therefore be completed in relation to the dismissal (see precedent unfair dismissal claim at [G7.2]); Box 8 is the box to complete for complaints of unlawful deductions from wages. The precedent set out below may be used to complete Box 8.

G13.2 Precedent

Employment tribunal claim for unlawful deduction from bonus

Grounds of complaint

1. The Claimant is employed by the Respondent as a sales director pursuant to a written contract of employment dated [ ].

2. Clause 10 of the Claimant's contract of employment is as follows:

    10. *The employee is entitled to an annual bonus calculated at the rate of 10% of all sales attributed to the efforts of the employee during the financial year. The payment shall be made within 28 days of the end of the financial year.*

3. During the [ ] financial year the value of sales to the Claimant's clients amounted to £[ ]. In the circumstances the Claimant was entitled to an annual bonus of £[ ]. This bonus became due and payable on [ ].

4. The Respondent failed to pay the £[ ]. Instead the Claimant was informed by letter dated [ ] that due to the financial position of the Respondent the Claimant would only receive a bonus of £[ ] for the [ ] financial year. This payment was made on [ ].

5. In the circumstances the sum of £[ ] remains due and owing to the Claimant from the Respondent.

6. The Claimant contends that the failure of the Respondent to pay the sum of £[ ] amounts to a deduction from his wages for the purposes of section 13 of the Employment Rights Act 1996. Accordingly the Claimant seeks a declaration that he has suffered an unlawful deduction from his wages pursuant to section 13 of the 1996 Act and payment of the said sum of £[ ] pursuant to section 24(a) of the 1996 Act.

G13.3 DRAFTING POINTS

Paragraph 2: Set out here the contractual terms relied on. This precedent assumes that there is an express contractual term providing a right to a bonus. Many contracts of employment provide that bonuses are discretionary and non-contractual. In such cases, the Claimant may have to rely on implied terms – for example, that the amount of the bonus should not be decided capriciously or irrationally. Often, statements by the employer about the purpose of the bonus can be used to support an implied term. For example, a statement that bonuses are to reward good performance may be used to argue that other factors, such as the financial state of the company, should be irrelevant. All facts, including the precise implied term relied on and any statements made by the Respondent to support the right to a bonus should be set out here.

Paragraph 3: Here, the Claimant should set out all the factors which he or she contends should have been used to determine the amount of the bonus. For example, if the purpose of the bonus is stated to be to reward good performance or good sales results, details of the performance and/or the sales results should be set out here.

Paragraph 4: Here the Claimant should set out what he or she contends the bonus should have been and what was in fact paid, asserting that the difference amounts to an unlawful deduction from wages (as is asserted in paragraph 6).

G14 RESPONSE TO EMPLOYMENT TRIBUNAL CLAIM FOR UNLAWFUL DEDUCTION FROM BONUS

G14.1 USE

This is a precedent response to an employment tribunal complaint that an unlawful deduction has been made from a bonus. It must be inserted into Form ET3. This form is available from the Employment Tribunals' website. Responses on any other form will not be accepted. The Form asks for various pieces of information, such as the identity of the employer and whether the Respondent agrees with the information about wages etc included on the Claim Form. The grounds on which the claim is resisted must be included in Box 5.2 of the Response Form.

The Employment Tribunal Rules must be complied with.

Possible defences to a complaint of unlawful deductions from wages (in this case, for a bonus) include:

– That there was no contractual right to the bonus in the first place (although sometimes a mere expectation is sufficient to form the basis of a claim), so the employer was entitled to decide whether to pay the bonus and the amount;

– that the bonus payment made was in fact correctly calculated;

– that the contract of employment or legislation permitted the deduction;

– that the deduction was permitted by statute or by the terms of some other agreement which the employee has signed to indicate consent;

– that the Claimant was taking industrial action during the period in respect of which the deduction was made.

For an explanation of the rules about deductions from wages and other possible defences, see *Jordans Employment Law Service*, at C1[57]–[106].

G14.2   **Precedent**

Response to employment tribunal claim for unlawful deduction from bonus

IN THE EMPLOYMENT TRIBUNALS   CASE NO: …/2009
[LOCATION]

B E T W E E N:

[AB]

Claimant

– and –

[BC]

Respondent

GROUNDS OF RESISTANCE

1. The Claimant was employed by the Respondent as a sales director pursuant to a written contract of employment dated [ ]. Clause 10 of that contract of employment was as stated by the Claimant at paragraph 2 of his Grounds of Complaint.

2. By letter dated [ ], the Respondent informed all of its sales staff, including the Claimant, that due to adverse trading conditions a decision had to be made as to whether or not to make redundancies amongst the sales staff. The Respondent indicated its preference for the sales staff to agree to a reduction in their annual bonus payments in order to avoid the need for redundancies. The sales staff unanimously agreed to a reduction in bonuses at a meeting on [ ]. The Claimant was present at that meeting and voted in favour of the plan to avoid redundancies. At that meeting it was agreed by all sales staff, including the Claimant, that the level of bonus payable for the [ ] financial year would be in the discretion of the Respondent.

3. Paragraph 3 of the Grounds of Complaint is admitted to the extent of the sales figures there referred to. By reason of paragraph 2 above it is denied that the relevant sum claimed was due and owing to the Claimant as alleged or at all.

4. Paragraph 4 of the Grounds of Complaint is admitted. The letter referred to by the Claimant set out in detail the Respondent's approach to the bonus award for the [ ] financial year. In particular it provided a full breakdown of the sums saved and the corresponding way in which those sums ensured that no redundancies would be made amongst the sales staff.

5. In the circumstances the Respondent contends that:

    (a) the Claimant has been paid his full contractual entitlement to bonus; and

(b) there is no sum due and owing to the Claimant as alleged or at all.

6. It follows that paragraphs 5 and 6 of the Grounds of Complaint are denied.

G14.3 DRAFTING POINTS

Paragraph 1: If the Respondent believes that the correct amount was in fact paid, then this paragraph should deny that any deduction was made and assert that the Claimant was paid the correct amount, determined in accordance with the contract of employment or an agreed variation of the contract of employment.

Where the Respondent believes that the bonus was discretionary and non-contractual, this paragraph should set out any provision in the contract of other document (eg a letter of appointment or other correspondence) which establishes that and should then assert that the amount of the bonus was properly determined by the Respondent in exercise of its discretion. Note, however, that paying less than the amount which was in the reasonable contemplation of the parties, whether or not that amount was contractual, has been held to be a 'deduction' (see *Jordans Employment Law Service*, at C1[59].

Paragraph 2: Generally, defences to claims for unlawful deductions from wages are those set out under 'Use' above. If none of these apply, then specialist advice should be obtained to check that there are no other defences.

Here, the defence is that the proper amount was paid in the first place because the amount of the bonus had been changed by agreement with the workforce, so there was no deduction. The Respondent might be able to add as a further defence that the Claimant had agreed to the deduction; that would only be necessary as an alternative line of defence in case the tribunal thinks that the agreement referred to here did amount to an agreement to make a deduction (rather than an agreement to alter the amount of the bonus). But for such an agreement to be relied on, then the employee must have signed to indicate his or her consent.

If there is no defence to the claim, it is better to repay the deduction and if the Claimant owes the Defendant the amount deducted, the Respondent should sue for it in the High Court of county court. Otherwise, any tribunal ruling that an unlawful deduction was made will prevent the Respondent from recovering the sums owed by the Claimant.

G15 EMPLOYMENT TRIBUNAL CLAIM FOR UNLAWFUL DEDUCTIONS FROM HOLIDAY PAY

G15.1 USE

Most employment contracts give employees a right to paid holiday. Employees are also entitled to paid holiday under the Working Time Regulations 1998 (SI 1998/1833). A complaint of failure to pay the holiday pay owing under a contract of employment may be brought in an employment tribunal under the 'unlawful deductions from wages' provisions of the Employment Rights Act 1996 (*Jordans Employment Law Service*, at C1[60]).

Under the current rules about statutory grievances, employees must, before bringing a tribunal complaint, have submitted to the employer a written grievance. They must then wait 28 days before putting in the tribunal complaint. Provided they have done this, the time limit for bringing a complaint is six months from the date of the unlawful deduction or, in the case of a series of deductions, from the last such deduction. This requirement is to be repealed from April 2009.

As with other employment tribunal complaints, the complaint must be set out on form ET1, available from the employment tribunal's website. A complaint submitted on any other form, even if it contains all the required information, will not be accepted. The Form asks for various pieces of information. Box 8 is the box to complete for complaints of failure to pay holiday pay. The precedent set out below may be used to complete Box 8.

G15.2 Precedent

Employment tribunal claim for unlawful deductions from holiday pay

IN THE EMPLOYMENT TRIBUNALS   CASE NO: …/2009
[LOCATION]

B E T W E E N:

[AB]

Claimant

– and –

[CD]

Respondent

PARTICULARS OF CLAIM

The parties

1. The Claimant has been employed by the Respondent as a Shop Floor Manager from 1st October 2005 to date.

2. At all material times, the Respondent has been a company in the business of building widgets and is based in King's Cross, London.

The Claim

3. The Claimant brings a claim against the Respondent for unauthorised deductions from wages, pursuant to sections 13 and 23 Employment Rights Act 1996 ("ERA 1996").

Jurisdiction

4. The Claimant submitted a relevant, written grievance on 7th October 2008 and, therefore, the Tribunal has jurisdiction to hear the Claimant's claim (which was presented on or about 5th December 2008).

The contract

5. By a written Contract of Employment signed and dated on or about 1st October 2005, it was expressly provided (amongst other things) that the Claimant is entitled to four weeks' annual leave. The Claimant is entitled to be paid at the rate of a week's pay for each of those weeks. The Claimant is paid £1,000 gross per week.

6. It was also an express term of the Contract of Employment that the Claimant is to be paid on the last day of every month. The Claimant's leave year commences on 1st January.

Unauthorised deduction

7. The Claimant took two weeks' annual leave in September 2008. However, the Claimant was only paid two weeks' wages on 30th September 2008. In the circumstances, wrongfully and in breach of section 13 ERA 1996, the Respondent made an unauthorised deduction from the Claimant's wages paid to him on 30th September 2008.

8. The Claimant raised this immediately with his Line Manager, Mr Brown. Mr Brown refused to discuss the matter. Therefore, the Claimant wrote a formal grievance letter and handed it to Mr Brown on 7th October 2008. However, despite many requests, the Respondent has failed to pay to the Claimant the outstanding sum of two weeks' pay owed to him.

Conclusion

9. In the circumstances, the Claimant presented this claim on or about 5th December 2008.

10. The Claimant accordingly brings a claim against the Respondent for unauthorised deductions from wages, pursuant to sections 13 and 23 ERA 1996, in the sum of £2,000 (ie two weeks' pay) and the Claimant seeks:

    (1) a declaration that the said deduction was unauthorised; and

    (2) an Order for payment of the amount of the deduction, namely an Order that the Respondent does pay to the Claimant the sum of £2,000.

G15.3 DRAFTING POINTS

Paragraph 4: Claimants may not bring a complaint in an employment tribunal under any of the provisions listed in Schedule 4 to the Employment Act 2002 (which includes complaints of unlawful deductions from wages) unless they have first brought a grievance and then waited at least 28 days. This requirement is to be repealed for deductions made on or after 1 April 2009.

G16 RESPONSE TO EMPLOYMENT TRIBUNAL COMPLAINT OF UNAUTHORISED DEDUCTION FROM HOLIDAY PAY

G16.1 USE

For an explanation of the various ways in which an employee may enforce a contractual right to holiday pay, see notes to precedent claim at **[G15.2]**. This is a precedent response to a claim that an unauthorised deduction has been made from holiday pay.

As with other responses to employment tribunal complaints, the response must be set out on form ET3, available from the employment tribunal's website. A response submitted on any other form, even if it contains all the required information, will not be accepted. The Form asks for various pieces of information. The precedent set out below may be used to complete Box 5.2.

G16.2 Precedent

Response to employment tribunal complaint of unauthorised deduction from holiday pay

IN THE EMPLOYMENT TRIBUNALS	CASE NO: .../2009
[LOCATION]	

B E T W E E N:

[AB]

Claimant

– and –

[CD]

Respondent

GROUNDS OF RESISTANCE

The parties

1. It is admitted that the Claimant has at all material times been employed by the Respondent as a Shop Floor Manager. It is admitted that he has been so employed since 1st October 2005 to date.

2. It is admitted that at all material times the Respondent has been a company in the business of building widgets and is based in King's Cross, London.

The claim and jurisdiction

3. The Claimant's claim for unauthorised deductions from wages is denied in its entirety for the reasons set out more fully below.

4. It is admitted that the Claimant submitted a relevant, written grievance on 7th October 2008 and it is admitted that the Tribunal has jurisdiction to hear the Claimant's claim. However, it is averred that the Claimant refused to attend the grievance meeting arranged.

The contract

5. It is admitted that the Claimant's Contract of Employment expressly provides that the Claimant is entitled (1) to four weeks' annual leave, (2) to be paid at the rate of a week's pay for each of those weeks, (3) to be paid £1,000 gross per week and (4) to be paid on the last day of every month. It is also admitted that the Claimant's leave year commences on 1st January.

6. It is averred that the Claimant's contract also expressly provides that deductions can be made from the Claimant's wages if agreed in writing and in advance by the Claimant.

Alleged unauthorised deduction

7. On or about 5th August 2008, the Claimant asked his Line Manager, Mr Brown if he could be paid two weeks of his September 2008 wages early because he wanted extra spending money for his holiday in September 2008.

8. Mr Brown said that this could be agreed, but only if the Claimant agreed in writing to being paid the extra two weeks' wages in his August 2008 wages and two weeks' less pay in his September 2008 wages. The Claimant agreed to this and a written agreement was signed by the Claimant to this effect on or about 5th August 2008.

9. The Claimant was duly paid the extra two weeks' wages on 31st August 2008 and two weeks' less pay on 30th September 2008. In the circumstances, it is denied that the Respondent wrongfully and/or in breach of section 13 ERA 1996 made an unauthorised deduction from the Claimant's wages on 30th September 2008.

10. It is admitted that (as agreed) the Respondent paid the Claimant two weeks' less pay on 30th September 2008. It is admitted that the Claimant raised this with Mr Brown. However, Mr Brown replied to the Claimant that he had signed a written agreement as above that explained why he was to be paid two weeks' less pay on 30th September 2008. It is admitted that, at the time, Mr Brown refused to discuss the matter further.

11. It is admitted that the Claimant handed a grievance letter to Mr Brown on 7th October 2008. However, as set out above, the Claimant refused to attend the grievance meeting arranged.

12. It is admitted that the Respondent has refused to pay to the Claimant the allegedly outstanding sum of two weeks' pay allegedly owed to him. The Respondent has refused to do so and has not "failed" to do so, as alleged. The reason for the refusal is that, as set out above, the Claimant agreed in writing to be paid two weeks' less pay on 30th September 2008 because he (asked to be and) was paid two weeks' extra pay on 31st August 2008.

Conclusion

13. In the circumstances, the Claimant's claim is denied in its entirety.

14. If, which is denied, the Claimant's claim succeeds in whole or in part, the Claimant's claim should be reduced by 10% to 50% (in accordance with section 31 Employment Act 2002) because he refused to attend the grievance meeting arranged.

15. Save where specifically denied, not admitted or admitted, each and every allegation made against the Respondent is denied as though the same were individually set out herein and traversed. In the circumstances and for the reasons set out above, the Claimant is not entitled to the relief claimed against the Respondent or to any other relief, and it is denied that the Respondent is in any way liable to the Claimant.

G16.3   DRAFTING POINTS

Paragraph 4: For complaints (other than those relating to dismissal) made in respect of matters arising before April 2009, the statutory grievance procedures apply. No complaint may be presented to an employment tribunal unless the Claimant has first submitted a grievance to the employer. This paragraph simply acknowledges that a grievance has been submitted and that, therefore, the tribunal has jurisdiction to hear the claim. This will be unnecessary for complaints relating to matters arising on or after 1 April 2009. Here, the Respondent relies on the fact that the Claimant failed to attend the grievance hearing, which would reduce the amount of any award the tribunal makes.

Paragraphs 7 to 10: Here set out the grounds on which the claim is resisted. In this precedent, the grounds are that the Claimant had in fact agreed to the deduction. Other possible defences may include:

– that the Claimant has simply miscalculated his or her holiday pay;

– that the holiday was not authorised and so, under the Respondents rules about paid holiday, the Claimant did not qualify for payment in the first place.

For an explanation of the right to holiday pay, see *Jordans Employment Law Service*, at C7[1]–[15]; and for possible defences to complaints of unauthorised deductions from wages, see *Jordans Employment Law Service*, at C1[71]–[90].

Paragraph 14: If the Claimant has not complied with the grievance procedure with the result that the procedure was not completed, then the tribunal may make a reduction in the compensation award of up to 50%. For an explanation of the statutory grievance procedure, see *Jordans Employment Law Service*, at C6[32]–[43].

G17 EMPLOYMENT TRIBUNAL CLAIM FOR HOLIDAY PAY UNDER WORKING TIME REGULATIONS

G17.1 USE

Most employment contracts give employees a right to paid holiday. Employees are also entitled to paid holiday under the Working Time Regulations 1998 (SI 1998/1833). For holiday years commencing on or after 1 April 2009, the annual entitlement (including bank holidays) under the regulations is 5.6 weeks (28 days for those who work a five day week). See *Jordans Employment Law Service*, at C7[7]–[15].

Employees may complain to an employment tribunal if they have not been allowed to take their entitlement to paid holiday under the regulations. The complaint must be made within three months of the date of the failure to pay. Such complaints may not be made under the 'unlawful deductions from wages' provisions of the ERA1996, where the time limits for bringing claims would be more generous to employees – see *Jordans Employment Law Service*, at C7[12].

As with other employment tribunal complaints, the complaint must be set out on form ET1, available from the employment tribunal's website. A complaint submitted on any other form, even if it contains all the required information, will not be accepted. The Form asks for various pieces of information. Box 8 is the box to complete for complaints of failure to pay holiday pay. The precedent set out below may be used to complete Box 8.

G17.2   **Precedent**

Employment tribunal claim for holiday pay under working time regulations

IN THE EMPLOYMENT TRIBUNALS   CASE NO: …/2009
[LOCATION]
B E T W E E N:

[AB]

Claimant

– and –

[CD]

Respondent

GROUNDS OF RESISTANCE

The parties

1. The Claimant has been employed by the Respondent as a Shop Floor Manager from 1st October 2005 to date.

2. At all material times, the Respondent has been a company in the business of building widgets and is based in King's Cross, London.

The Claim

3. The Claimant brings a claim against the Respondent for a failure to pay holiday pay, pursuant to Regulations 16(1) and 30 Working Time Regulations 1998 ("WTR 1998") (1998/1833).

The contract

4. By a written Contract of Employment signed and dated on or about 1st October 2005, it was expressly provided (amongst other things) that the Claimant is entitled to four weeks' annual leave in addition to bank and statutory holidays. The Claimant is entitled to be paid at the rate of a week's pay for each of those weeks. The Claimant's leave year commences on 1st January. The Claimant is paid £1,000 gross per week.

Failure to pay holiday pay

5. The Claimant took two weeks' annual leave in September 2008. However, the Claimant was only paid two weeks' wages for September 2008. In the circumstances, wrongfully and in breach of Regulation 16(1) WTR 1998, the Respondent has failed to pay the Claimant's holiday pay owed to him.

Conclusion

6. In failing to pay the Claimant for the said weeks, the Respondent was in breach of Regulation 16(1) WTR 1998. The Claimant is accordingly entitled to recover the sum of £2,000 and the Claimant seeks an Order that that the Respondent pay to the Claimant the sum of £2,000.

G18 RESPONSE TO EMPLOYMENT TRIBUNAL CLAIM FOR HOLIDAY PAY UNDER WORKING TIME REGULATIONS

G18.1 USE

This precedent is a response to a claim for holiday pay made under the Working Time Regulations 1998 (1998/1833).

As with other responses to employment tribunal complaints, the response must be set out on form ET3, available from the employment tribunal's website. A response submitted on any other form, even if it contains all the required information, will not be accepted. The Form asks for various pieces of information. The precedent set out below may be used to complete Box 5.2.

G18.2 Precedent

Response to ET claim for holiday pay under working time regulations

IN THE EMPLOYMENT TRIBUNALS CASE NO: .../2009
[LOCATION]

B E T W E E N:

[AB]

Claimant

– and –

[CD]

Respondent

GROUNDS OF RESISTANCE

The parties

1. It is admitted that the Claimant has at all material times been employed by the Respondent as a Shop Floor Manager. It is admitted that he has been so employed since 1 October 2005 to date.

2. It is admitted that at all material times the Respondent has been a company in the business of building widgets and is based in King's Cross, London.

The claim

3. The Claimant's claim for alleged failure to pay holiday pay is denied in its entirety for the reasons set out below.

The contract

4. It is admitted that the Claimant's Contract of Employment expressly provides that the Claimant is entitled (1) to four weeks' annual leave in addition to statutory and public holidays, (2) to be paid at the rate of a week's pay for each of those weeks and (3) to be paid £1,000 gross per week. It is also admitted that the Claimant's leave year commences on 1st January.

Alleged failure to pay holiday pay

5. The Claimant took annual leave for two weeks in February 2008 and for a further two weeks in July 2008. The Claimant was paid in respect of all four weeks' annual leave.

6. It is admitted that the Claimant took two weeks' further annual leave in September 2008. It is admitted that the Respondent did not pay the Claimant in respect of the two weeks' leave that he took in September 2008. The reason that it did not do so was that the Claimant had exhausted his annual leave entitlement by that date, having taken four weeks' leave on the dates referred to above. The Claimant was informed in September 2008 that if he took two weeks' leave in September 2008, it would be treated as unpaid leave.

7. In the circumstances, it is denied that the Respondent wrongfully and/or in breach of Regulation 16(1) of the Working Time Regulations 1998 (SI 1998/1833) failed to pay the Claimant's holiday pay (allegedly) owed to him.

Conclusion

8. In the circumstances, the Claimant's claim is denied in its entirety.

9. Save where specifically denied, not admitted or admitted, each and every allegation made against the Respondent is denied as though the same were individually set out herein and traversed. In the circumstances and for the reasons set out above, the Claimant is not entitled to the relief claimed against the Respondent or to any other relief, and it is denied that the Respondent is in any way liable to the Claimant.

G18.3   DRAFTING POINTS

Paragraphs 5 and 6: Here set out the grounds for resisting the complaint. In this precedent, the Claimant is simply mistaken about the amount of holiday he has taken. Other possible defences might include:

– that the employee was not authorised to take the holiday;

- that the employee was in fact paid holiday pay. If the dispute is about the amount of holiday pay, then the reasons why the Respondent considers the amount paid was correct should be set out here.

G19 CLAIM FOR REDUNDANCY PAYMENT

G19.1 USE

This Claim may be used where an employee has been made redundant and either has not received a redundancy payment or does not believe that the payment has been made correctly.

A complaint must be submitted to the employer, generally within six months of the redundancy taking effect. So long as the Claimant has done this, the complaint to the tribunal may be brought at any time within 6 years.

As with all employment tribunal complaints, the complaint must be submitted on form ET1. A Claim submitted on any other form, even if it contains all the required information, will not be accepted. This Form is available from the Employment Tribunals' website. Claims can be completed and submitted online. The Form asks for standard information such as the identity of the employer, the Claimant's address and contact details and information about earnings. Box 7 on the Form ET1 asks the Claimant to set out the reasons why the Claimant believes he or she is entitled to a redundancy payment. That box can be filled in with the precedent set out below.

The rules on entitlement to redundancy payments and how they are calculated are explain in Division D4 of *Jordans Employment Law Service*.

G19.2   **Precedent**

Claim for redundancy payment

IN THE EMPLOYMENT TRIBUNALS   CASE NO: …/2009
[LOCATION]

B E T W E E N:

[A DISGRUNTLED EMPLOYEE]

Claimant

– and –

[WIDGETS 'R' US PLC]

Respondent

PARTICULARS OF CLAIM

The parties

1. The Claimant was an employee employed by the Respondent as a Branch Manager at its branch in Cardiff from 1 April 1997 to 31 March 2009.

2. At all material times, the Respondent was a company in the business of manufacturing and retailing widgets and with a head office based in Silicon Valley, Swansea.

The claim

3. The Claimant brings a claim against the Respondent under section 163 of the Employment Rights Act ('ERA') 1996 for a redundancy payment.

The redundancy dismissal

4. On (date) the Claimant was informed by the Respondents that, as part of a business reorganisation, it was closing down the retail side of its business and that the Claimant job as a Branch Manager would no longer exist.

5. The Respondent offered alternative employment to the Claimant as an Office Manager based in its Head Office at a lower rate of pay. When the Claimant refused to accept this offer as not being suitable alternative employment, the Respondent dismissed him and refused to pay him a redundancy payment.

6. In the circumstances, the Claimant was dismissed by reason of redundancy and is entitled to a redundancy payment in the sum of [£sum].

Conclusion

7. Accordingly, the Claimant seeks:

　　(1)　a declaration that the Respondent has failed to make a redundancy payment to him; and

　　(2)　an Order that the Respondent make a redundancy payment to the Claimant in the sum of [£sum].

G19.3　DRAFTING POINTS

Paragraph 4: Here, set out the circumstances which the Claimant says amount to a redundancy situation and the reasons why he or she claims that that was the reason for the dismissal.

Paragraph 5: Employers may have a defence to a claim for a redundancy payment if they offered suitable alternative employment and it was unreasonably refused (see *Jordans Employment Law Service*, at D4[71], [72]. In this precedent, the employee has anticipated this argument and provided a response to it.

Paragraph 6: If the employer has made a redundancy payment but the Claimant thinks it is not the right amount, the Claimant should set out how much the employer has paid and explain why it is considered that this is not the correct amount.

G20 EMPLOYMENT TRIBUNAL CLAIM FOR BONUS ON TERMINATION OF EMPLOYMENT

G20.1 USE

On termination of employment, employees may bring complaints in an employment tribunal for breach of contract so long as the claim is outstanding on or arises out of the termination of the employment (see *Jordans Employment Law Service*, at D2[61]). A claim may also be made for unlawful deduction from wages where the amount outstanding is for wages. A bonus counts as wages. This precedent is a claim for a bonus which makes use both of the right to complain of a breach of contract and the right to complain of unlawful deductions from wages.

As with all employment tribunal claims, the claim must be made on form ET1 – see the precedent claim for unlawful deductions at **[G11.2]**.

G20.2 Precedent

Employment tribunal claim for bonus on termination of employment

1. The Claimant was employed by the Respondent as a sales director pursuant to a written contract of employment dated [ ].

2. The following were express terms of the Claimant's contract of employment with the Respondent:

    1. *The employee is entitled to 3 months notice of the termination of his employment.*

    2. *The employee is entitled to an annual bonus payment calculated at the rate of 10% of the sales achieved by the employee during the financial year. This sum shall be payable within 28 days of the end of the relevant financial year.*

    3. *In the case of the termination of the employee's employment before the end of the financial year the employee shall be entitled to a bonus payment calculated on the basis of the sales achieved by the employee as at the date of termination. The bonus as calculated shall become due and owing on the termination of the Claimant's employment.*

3. On [ ] the Claimant was given 3 months notice of the termination of his employment. His employment with the respondent lawfully terminated on [ ].

4. From the beginning of the financial year up until the date of the

termination of his employment the Claimant achieved sales of £ [ ]. In the circumstances he was entitled to a bonus payment of £ [ ] which was due and payable on the termination of his employment.

5. The Respondent has failed to pay the relevant bonus to the Claimant. In the circumstances this amounts to a deduction for the purposes of section 13 of the Employment Rights Act 1996 and the Claimant seeks a declaration to this effect and payment of the relevant sum accordingly. In the alternative the failure to pay amounts to a breach of contract and the Claimant seeks payment of the sum of £[ ] under the Employment Tribunal's contractual jurisdiction.

G20.3 DRAFTING POINTS

See the drafting points for the precedent tribunal claim for unlawful deductions from a bonus.

G21 EMPLOYMENT TRIBUNAL CLAIM FOR MINIMUM WAGE

G21.1 USE

For details of the right to the national minimum wage, see *Jordans Employment Law Service*, at C1[1]–[50].

The contract of employment is treated as modified, so that any terms of employment which provide for payment at less than the national minimum wage are treated as amended to bring the wages up to the national minimum wage. This means that employees seeking to enforce their right to receive the minimum wage have a number of options:

– they could sue in the county court for their arrears of wages and for a declaration that they are entitled to the national minimum wage;

– they could sue in an employment tribunal under the 'unlawful deductions from wages' provisions (see *Jordans Employment Law Service*, at C1[57]–[105];

– they could notify the enforcement agency (Her Majesty's Revenue and Customs), which has powers to force employers to pay the national minimum wage.

This precedent is for a complaint in an employment tribunal.

As with other employment tribunal complaints, the complaint must be set out on form ET1, available from the employment tribunal's website. A complaint submitted on any other form, even if it contains all the required information, will not be accepted. The Form asks for various pieces of information. Box 8 is the box to complete for complaints of unlawful deductions from wages. The precedent set out below may be used to complete Box 8.

G21.2 Precedent

Employment tribunal claim for minimum wage

IN THE EMPLOYMENT TRIBUNALS CASE NO: . . . /2009
[LOCATION]

B E T W E E N:

[AB]

Claimant

– and –

[CD]

Respondent

PARTICULARS OF CLAIM

The parties

1. The Claimant has been employed by the Respondent as a Shop Floor Manager from 1st October 2005 to date.

2. At all material times, the Respondent has been a company in the business of building widgets and is based in King's Cross, London.

The claim

3. The Claimant brings a claim against the Respondent for a failure to pay minimum wage, contrary to Section 1 of the National Minimum Wage Act 1998 ("NMWA 1998").

The contract

4. By a written Contract of Employment signed and dated on or about 1 October 2005, it was provided (amongst other things) that the Claimant was to be paid at the rate of £202 for a 40-hour week. This was increased on 1st October every year.

Failure to pay minimum wage

5. On 1 October 2008, the Claimant's weekly pay was increased to £220 per week. As a result, the Claimant now receives £5.50 per hour for a 40-hour week, which is less than the national minimum wage (of £5.73 per hour).

Conclusion

6. In failing to pay the Claimant £5.73 per hour, the Respondent is in breach of Section 1 NMWA 1998. In failing to pay the Claimant the wages to which the Claimant is entitled, the Respondent has

made a series of unlawful deductions from wages in breach of s 13 Employment Rights Act 1996. The Claimant is accordingly entitled to recover the difference between what he has been paid and what he should have been paid in accordance with the national minimum wage.

7. The Claimant seeks:

   (1) a declaration under s 11 Employment Rights Act 1996 that his rate of pay is less than the national minimum wage;

   (2) an Order that the Respondent increases his rate of pay to £5.73 per hour; and

   (3) an Order for payment of the difference between what he has been paid and what he should have been paid, if he were paid in accordance with the national minimum wage.

G22 RESPONSE TO EMPLOYMENT TRIBUNAL CLAIM FOR MINIMUM WAGE

G22.1 USE

This precedent is for a complaint in an employment tribunal.

For details of the right to the national minimum wage, see *Jordans Employment Law Service*, at C1[1]–[50]. An explanation of the various ways in which the minimum wage may be enforced appears in the notes to the precedent claim at [G21.2].

As with other responses to tribunal claims, the response must be set out on form ET3, available from the employment tribunal's website. A response submitted on any other form, even if it contains all the required information, will not be accepted. The Form asks for various pieces of information. The precedent set out below may be used to complete Box 5.2.

G22.2 Precedent

Response to employment tribunal claim for minimum wage

IN THE EMPLOYMENT TRIBUNALS　　　　CASE NO: …/2009

[LOCATION]

B E T W E E N:

[AB]

Claimant

- and -

[CD]

Respondent

GROUNDS OF RESISTANCE

The parties

1. It is admitted that the Claimant has at all material times been employed by the Respondent as a Shop Floor Manager. It is admitted that he has been so employed since 1st October 2005 to date.

2. It is admitted that at all material times the Respondent has been a company in the business of building widgets and is based in King's Cross, London.

The claim

3. The Claimant's claim for alleged failure to pay minimum wage is denied in its entirety for the reasons set out more fully below.

The contract

4. It is admitted that the Claimant's Contract of Employment provided that the Claimant was to be paid at the rate of £202 for a 40-hour week. It is also admitted that this was increased on 1st October every year.

Alleged failure to pay minimum wage

5. It is admitted that on 1st October 2008, the Claimant's weekly pay was increased to £220 per week. It is averred that, at the same time, the number of hours worked by the Claimant was reduced (with the Claimant's signed, written consent) to 35 hours per week. As a result, the Claimant now receives £6.29 per hour for his 35-hour week, which is more than the national minimum wage of £5.73 per hour.

Conclusion

6. In the circumstances, the Claimant's claim is denied in its entirety.

7. Save where specifically denied, not admitted or admitted, each and every allegation made against the Respondent is denied as though the same were individually set out herein and traversed. In the circumstances and for the reasons set out above, the Claimant is not entitled to the relief claimed against the Respondent or to any other relief, and it is denied that the Respondent is in any way liable to the Claimant.

G22.3 DRAFTING POINTS

Paragraph 5: Here set out the reasons why the claim is disputed. The reasons may be straightforward, as here – ie that the Claimant has not taken account of a reduction in hours. Other possible defences may be that:

– the Claimant has received other benefits which should be taken into account in determine his or her pay. The extent to which other payments and benefits may be taken into account is limited – see *Jordans Employment Law Service*, at C1[17]–[21];

– the Claimant has not taken account of unpaid breaks, which would reduce the number of working hours.

G23 EMPLOYMENT TRIBUNAL COMPLAINT OF FAILURE TO INFORM/CONSULT OVER BUSINESS TRANSFER

G23.1 USE

This Precedent may be used for claims by recognised trade unions that an employer has not provided the required written information and has not consulted over transfers of business, as required by the Transfer of Undertakings (Protection of Employment) Regulations 2006 ('TUPE') (SI 2006/246). The remedy is a payment of up to 13 weeks' pay for those employees specified by the tribunal.

The rules requiring employers involved in a transfer of a business to provide certain specified written information and (in some cases) to consult with appropriate representatives are laid down by regulations 13 to 16 of TUPE. For details, see Division D5 of *Jordans Employment Law Service*.

Representatives of recognised trade unions or (if no union is recognised) elected employee representatives (ie representatives who have been elected for the purpose by the workforce) may complain to an employment tribunal that the employer has not provided the required information in writing or, where required to do so, has not consulted the representatives.

If there is no recognised trade union and employee representatives have not been appointed, then the complaint can be presented by any affected employee.

As with all employment tribunal complaints, the complaint must be submitted on form ET1. A Claim submitted on any other form, even if it contains all the required information, will not be accepted. This Form is available from the Employment Tribunals' website. Claims can be completed and submitted online. The Form asks for standard information such as the identity of the employer, the Claimant's address and contact details and information about earnings. Box 9.1 on the Form ET1 asks the Claimant to set out the grounds for the complaint. That box can be filled in with the precedent set out below.

G23.2   **Precedent**

Complaint of failure to inform/consult over business transfer

IN THE EMPLOYMENT TRIBUNALS   CASE NO: …/2009
[LOCATION]

B E T W E E N:

[A TRADE UNION]

Claimant

– and –

[WIDGETS 'R' US PLC]

Respondent

PARTICULARS OF CLAIM

The parties

1. The Claimant is an independent trade union recognised by the Respondent in respect of its retail staff for the purposes of Regulation 13(3)(a) of the Transfer of Undertakings (Protection of Employment) Regulations ('TUPE') 2006 (SI 2006/246).

2. At all material times, the Respondent has been a company in the business of manufacturing and retailing widgets, with head offices based in Silicon Valley, Wales.

The claim

3. The Claimant brings a claim against the Respondent under Regulation 15(1) for a declaration that the Respondent failed to inform and consult with it in accordance with TUPE and a compensatory award pursuant to Regulation 15(8).

The transfer

4. On 1 March 2009 the Respondent transferor transferred 10 of its retail branches to Oligarchy Ltd. A list of the affected branches is attached. The proposed exercise was a relevant transfer within the meaning of Regulation 3(1)(a) of TUPE.

5. In accordance with Regulation 13 the Respondent was obliged to supply prescribed information to the Claimant long enough before the transfer to enable the Respondent to consult with the Claimant in its capacity as an appropriate representative of the affected employees.

6. The Respondent failed to supply the requisite information in accordance with Regulation 13(2) with the result that no

consultation concerning the transfer could (or did) take place with the Claimant under Regulation 13(6).

Conclusion

7. Accordingly, the Claimant seeks:

   (1) a Declaration that the Respondent has failed to inform and/or consult the Claimant under Regulation 13 of TUPE; and

   (2) an Order that the Respondent pay appropriate compensation to such descriptions of affected employees as may be specified in the award.

G23.3 DRAFTING POINTS

Paragraph 1: Where the complaint is brought by elected employee representatives or, in the absence of such representatives, affected employees, this paragraph should simply identify who is bringing the claim. It should assert that the representatives are representatives of employees who have been affected by the transfer or (if there are no representatives) that those bringing the Claim are affected. In this Precedent, the affected employees are identified by the phrase 'retail staff'. It is obvious here, and so does not require any further explanation, that retail staff would be affected by the sale of the retail branches. Where it is not so obvious, the form should identify who the affected employees are and should explain that the representatives represent some or all of those affected employees.

For complaints brought by affected employees, this paragraph should explain that there is no recognised trade union and that the transferor has not organised the election of employee representatives.

Paragraph 4: Both the transferor and the transferee of a business are required to provide the written information and, in certain cases, consult representatives if any of their own employees will be affected. Employees of the transferor will almost always be affected, but there are circumstances where employees of the transferee will also be affected – for example, if the transferee proposes to merge its workforce with the acquired workforce and then make redundancies from the combined workforce. This precedent assumes that the complaint is against the transferor but could be adapted for complaints against the transferee.

Where the transferor is found liable, the transferee is jointly and severally liable. At some point, the transferee is likely to become a party to the proceedings. The Claimant can include the transferee as a Respondent in the Claim form, but there is no need to do so. The transferee can be joined in at a later date.

Paragraph 4: Sufficient information should be included here to identify the business which is alleged to have been transferred.

Paragraph 6: This should set out all the respects in which it is alleged that the transferor (or transferee) has failed to comply with its obligations under regulation 13 of the Transfer of Undertakings (Protection of Employment) Regulations 2006 (SI 2006/246). Details of all the requirements of regulation 13 appear at *Jordans Employment Law Service*, at D5[69]–[80].

G24 CLAIM FOR FAILURE TO CONSULT OVER COLLECTIVE REDUNDANCIES

G24.1 USE

This Precedent may be used for claims for a protective award for breach of the requirement to inform in writing and consult employee representatives over collective redundancies. The claim is normally made by a recognised trade union or by elected employee representatives but can (in the absence of any other representatives) be made by the employees whom it was proposed to make redundant.

The rules requiring employers to provide specified written information and to consult with appropriate representatives over collective redundancies are set out in sections 188 to 192. The rules apply when an employer proposes 20 or more redundancies within a 3-month period. At least 30 days must be allowed for consultation, or 90 days where 100 or more redundancies are proposed within a 90-day period. The remedy for failure to consult is a 'protective award' – ie an award that the employer must continue to pay the specified employees for a period of up to 90 days. For details, see Division D5 of *Jordans Employment Law Service*.

Representatives of recognised trade unions or (if no union is recognised) elected employee representatives (ie representatives who have been elected for the purpose by the workforce) may complain to an employment tribunal that the employer has not provided the required written information to and/or has not consulted the representatives as required by the legislation.

If there is no recognised trade union and employee representatives have not been appointed, then the complaint can be presented by any affected employee.

As with all employment tribunal complaints, the complaint must be submitted on form ET1. A Claim submitted on any other form, even if it contains all the required information, will not be accepted. This Form is available from the Employment Tribunals' website. Claims can be completed and submitted online. The Form asks for standard information such as the identity of the employer, the Claimant's address and contact details and information about earnings. Box 9.1 on the Form ET1 asks the Claimant to set out the grounds for the complaint. That box can be filled in with the precedent set out below.

G24.2   **Precedent**

Claim for failure to consult over collective redundancies

IN THE EMPLOYMENT TRIBUNALS   CASE NO: …/2009
[LOCATION]

B E T W E E N:

[A TRADE UNION]

Claimant

– and –

[WIDGETS 'R' US PLC]

Respondent

PARTICULARS OF CLAIM

The parties

1. The Claimant is an independent trade union recognised by the Respondent in respect of its retail staff employed at its branch in Cardiff.

2. At all material times, the Respondent was a company in the business of manufacturing and retailing widgets and with a head office based in Silicon Valley, Swansea.

The claim

3. The Claimant brings a claim against the Respondent under section 189(2) of the Trade Union and Labour Relations (Consolidation) Act ('TULRCA') 1992 for a declaration that the Respondent failed to consult with it in accordance with section 188 and for a protective award under sections 189(2) to (4).

The collective redundancies

4. On 1 March 2009 the Human Resources Director of the Respondent orally informed the General Secretary of the Claimant union that the Respondent proposed to dismiss by reason of redundancy 55 retail staff at its branch in Cardiff. The first of the proposed dismissals was due to take effect on 11 March 2009 which was 10 days later.

5. The first of the dismissals in fact took place on 5 March and the remainder on 7 March.

6. The Respondent failed to comply with the provisions of section 188 of TULRCA 1992 in that:

    a. the consultations did not take place in good time and did not, in any event, take place at least 30 days before the first of the proposed dismissals took effect, as required by section 188(2)(b);

        b.   the information given by the Respondent was not delivered in writing and was, in any event, deficient in that it did not disclose the reasons for the proposals, or the method of selection of those employees who were to be dismissed, or the proposed method of carrying out the dismissals;

        c.   the Respondent failed to consider the representations made by the representatives of the Claimant union on 3 March and/or failed to reply to those representations and/or failed to give their reasons for rejecting them.

Conclusion

7.   Accordingly, the Claimant union seeks:

        (1)   a declaration that the Respondent has failed to consult in accordance with the requirements of section 188 of the TULRCA 1992; and

        (2)   an Order that the Respondent pay a protective award pay in respect of the retail staff dismissed by the Respondent.

G24.3   DRAFTING POINTS

Paragraph 1: Where the complaint is brought by elected employee representatives or, in the absence of such representatives, affected employees, this paragraph should simply identify who is bringing the claim. It should assert that the representatives are representatives of those the employer has proposed to make redundant. In this Precedent, those employees are identified by the phrase 'retail staff'.

For complaints brought by affected employees, this paragraph should explain that there is no recognised trade union and that the employer has not organised the election of employee representatives.

Paragraph 6: This paragraph should set out all the respects in which it is alleged that the employer failed to comply with its obligations under section 188 of the Trade Union and Labour Relations (Consolidation) Act 1992. This precedent alleges breaches of all the main provisions of section 188.

G25 PARTICULARS OF COMPLAINT IN A WHISTLE-BLOWING (PUBLIC INTEREST DISCLOSURE) CLAIM

G25.1 USE

This is a precedent for a complaint of being subjected to a detriment and being constructively dismissed because of 'whistleblowing' (ie making a 'protected disclosure') under the Employment Rights Act 1996.

Employees are protected if they have made a disclosure to someone within the employer's organisation or to an appropriate outside organisation such as the Health and Safety Executive. The law and the terminology used are set out in Division E5 of *Jordans Employment Law Service*.

Such claims must be commenced in the Employment Tribunal and the Employment Tribunal Rules must be followed.

In view of the complexity of these claims it is common practice for the factual allegations to be relied upon to be set out in some detail. The claim must be set out on form ET1. For comment on how this form must be used, see the notes to the Precedent unfair dismissal claim at **[G11.2]**.

G25.2 Precedent

Particulars of Complaint in a whistle-blowing (public interest disclosure) claim (to be completed on Form ET1)

IN THE EMPLOYMENT TRIBUNALS　　　CASE NO: .../2009
[LOCATION]
B E T W E E N:

[AB]

Claimant

– and –

[BC]

Respondent

PARTICULARS OF COMPLAINT

Introduction

1. These Particulars of Complaint should be read in conjunction with the ET1 "Claim to an Employment Tribunal" completed by the Claimant. The purpose of the Particulars of Complaint is to provide the details required by sections 5.1 and 9.1 of the ET1.

Claimant's claims

2. The Claimant makes the following claims against the Respondent:

    (a) That she was constructively and unfairly dismissed by the Respondent by reason of the fact that she had made a protected disclosure (see sections 43KA(1)(C), 95(1)(c) and 103A of the Employment Rights Act 1996 (the "ERA, 1996")).

    (b) That she was subjected to "detriment/s" on the ground that she had made a protected disclosure (see sections 43KA(1)(b) and 47B of the ERA, 1996). Particulars of the same are provided in paragraphs 7, 9 to 11, 13 to 14, 16 to 17, 19 to 29 and 31 to 35 below.

Background

3. From [date] until she was constructively dismissed the Claimant served as a [complete]. By the date of her constructive dismissal the Claimant had reached the position of [complete].

4. For the purposes of sections 47B and 103A of the ERA, 1996, the Claimant is to be treated as an employee employed by the Respondent under a contract of employment.

5. In or around [date] the Claimant became concerned about the activities and conduct of her colleague(s) [X – identify those against whom the allegations are made.].

6. The Claimant orally reported her concerns to [identify whom the disclosure was made to – eg] her line managers. The Claimant's reports to her line managers amounted to "protected disclosures" as defined by sections 43A to 43C of the ERA 1996. The information provided by the Claimant regarding the activities and conduct of her colleague(s) amounted to allegations that "criminal offences [had] been committed" (section 43B(1)(a) of the ERA 1996) and/or that her colleagues were "failing ... to comply with a legal obligation to which [they were] subject" (section 43B(1)(b) of the ERA 1996). Further, the information provided by the Claimant about the activities and conduct of her colleague(s) fell within the Respondent's "Whistleblowing Guide".

7. Contrary to the provisions of the Respondent's "Whistleblowing Guide" the Claimant's line managers failed: (i) to acknowledge in writing the concerns raised by the Claimant; (ii) to investigate the same either locally or centrally; or (iii) to inform the Claimant of the outcome of any investigation. The Claimant's line managers failed to take the Claimant's concerns and complaint seriously and the Claimant was made to feel like a "trouble-maker" for having raised such concerns.

8. On [date] the Claimant completed a written report regarding the alleged activities of her colleague(s) which the Claimant believed amounted to [criminal offences/ breaches of legal obligations]. This report was also a "protected disclosure" as defined by sections 43A to 43C of the ERA 1996. Further, the information provided by the Claimant fell within the categories defined in the Respondent's "Whistleblowing Guide".

9. As a result of having raised the allegations against her colleague(s) the Claimant [list the actions of the employer which it is alleged amounted to subjecting her to a detriment – for example:] was removed from her existing role and was posted to a less prestigious role.

10. The said treatment was as a direct result of the fact that she had raised allegations against her colleague(s). Such actions:

    (a) Amounted to "detriments" for the purposes of section 47B of the ERA 1996;

    (b) Were contrary to the provisions of the Respondent's "Whistleblowing Guide".

11. Whilst the Claimant was working on her new role she was subjected to the following further detriments by her colleagues [list any further detriments – for example:

    (a) Her line manager made the comment, overheard by the Claimant: "... well, she should know better." This was a direct reference to the fact that she had made a protected disclosure, raising concerns about the conduct and activities of her colleague(s).

    (b) Normal co-operation and support was not extended to the Claimant by her colleagues and her superior officers.

    (c) The Claimant was ostracised by her colleagues. She was ignored. Colleagues who would normally sit with her in the canteen/bar area would deliberately sit elsewhere.

12. On [date] the Claimant submitted a detailed, written report outlining the alleged [criminal activities/ breaches of legal obligations] of her colleague(s). This written report was also a "protected disclosure" as defined by sections 43A to 43C of the ERA, 1996. Further, the information provided fell within the categories defined in the Respondent's "Whistleblowing Guide."

13. On [date] the Claimant made a request to her line manager for a return to her former role (ie her substantive role).

14. Later on [date] the Claimant's line manager informed her that her request to return to her substantive role had been refused. She was

handed a copy of an e-mail confirming this. The refusal to permit the Claimant to return to her substantive post amounted to a "detriment" for the purposes of section 47B of the ERA 1996.

15. On [date] the Claimant attended a meeting with her line managers. The Claimant was refused any information regarding the outcome of her complaint against her colleague(s). This was contrary to the provisions of the Respondent's Whistleblowing Policy and amounted to a "detriment" for the purposes of section 47B of the ERA 1996.

16. The Claimant was also informed that no "wrongdoings" had been found against her as a result of the investigation. This was the first time that the Claimant had been told that any allegations had been made against her that required investigation. The making of unwarranted allegations (by an unidentified person) and the failure to inform the Claimant that she was the subject-matter of investigation amounted to "detriments" for the purposes of section 47B of the ERA 1996.

17. [ ] gave no indication that any steps would be taken to protect the Claimant or to ensure that she was not subjected to adverse treatment by her colleagues and superiors on the grounds that she had made the protected disclosures, nor were any such steps taken. The comments made by [ ] and the failure to take steps to protect her from adverse treatment amounted to "detriments" for the purposes of section 47B of the ERA, 1996.

18. On [date] the Claimant was informed that her colleagues were "unhappy" that the Claimant was returning to her substantive role. [ ] indicated that the understanding of the Claimant's colleagues was that [X] had been moved even though he had not been interviewed about the allegations made by the Claimant and nothing had been proven against him. This amounted to a detriment for the purposes of section 47B of the ERA 1996.

19. The Respondent had failed to properly investigate the Claimant's complaint [in accordance with the provisions of the Whistleblowing Policy]. Further, the Respondent had taken no steps to communicate the outcome of any investigation that had been carried out to colleagues of the Claimant and [X]. The Respondent had thereby permitted inaccurate and damaging "rumours" to circulate and had failed to correct them. These failures amounted to "detriments" for the purposes of section 47B of the ERA 1996.

20. On [date] [ ] informed the Claimant that her colleagues had refused to work with the Claimant stating that they could not trust her. The Claimant was told that she would, therefore, not now be permitted to return to her substantive role and that she would be posted to [other position]. The refusal by the colleagues to work with the Claimant amounted to a "detriment" for the purposes of section 47B of the ERA 1996. The refusal to permit the Claimant

to return to her substantive role and her compulsory posting to [other position] amounted to "detriments" for the purposes of section 47B of the ERA 1996.

21. On [date] the Claimant was informed that a review of the decision had been carried out and that she would now be permitted to return to her substantive role. The Claimant's return was, however, to be subject to an "action plan" being implemented in respect of her. Such an action plan was not, and should not have been, required; the Claimant had done nothing wrong by raising the complaint in the proper manner. The imposition of an action plan amounted to a "detriment" for the purposes of section 47B of the ERA 1996.

22. The Respondent continued to refuse to provide the Claimant with any information regarding the outcome of the investigation of her complaint. Nor was the outcome made known to the Claimant's colleagues in order to dispel the inaccurate and damaging rumours that were circulating regarding the Claimant's complaint. This amounted to a further detriment for the purposes of s 47B of the ERA, 1996.

23. On [date] the Claimant submitted a formal, written request to the Managing Director for information about the investigation, the procedures followed and the outcome. The Claimant has not yet receive a response to this letter. It was simply ignored.

24. On [date] the Claimant was informed that [X] had been posted back to his old position. This was directly contrary to the assurance that the Claimant had been given that she would not be required to work at the same station as [X]. The posting of [X] to the same department as the Claimant amounted to a "detriment" for the purposes of section 47B of the ERA 1996.

25. In the period from [date] until her resignation on [date] the Claimant was shunned and ostracised by her colleagues whenever she came into contact with them. Further, the Respondent has failed and refused to address any of the Claimant's questions regarding the investigation of her complaint. An answer to her letter to the Managing Director dated [date] is still outstanding. Further, the Respondent has failed to take any steps to prevent the adverse treatment of the Claimant by her colleagues and by her superiors. The above-listed acts and omissions were continuing up to the date of the Claimant's resignation and amount to continuing "detriments" for the purposes of section 47B of the ERA 1996.

26. On [date] the Claimant received a letter from [the Respondent. The letter was in response to a request made by the Claimant pursuant to section 7 of the Data Protection Act 1998, and enclosed copies of documents held by the Respondent which related to the Claimant. The documents were heavily redacted. The disclosed

documents included the following (only examples are given at this stage and the Claimant will refer to the entirety of the disclosed documents at the hearing of this matter):

[set out relevant details here]

27. The comments made in the various documents referred to above were inaccurate, untrue and inconsistent with the Claimant's Personal Development Reviews. The Claimant had no opportunity to comment on or correct the inaccuracies or to challenge the false assertions made as to her mental health and stability. The comments were, obviously, made as a direct result of the Claimant's "protected disclosures" (ie the complaints that she had raised against [X]). The comments amounted to "detriments" for the purposes of section 47B of the ERA 1996.

28. The disclosed documents also included a heavily redacted copy of a document [set out details].

29. It is, therefore, acknowledged by the author of the investigation report that the investigation carried out into the Claimant's allegations was "limited." The Claimant was not interviewed as part of the investigation in order to clarify any alleged "misunderstandings" (although such "misunderstandings" are only suggested in respect of 2 of the many allegations made by the Claimant).

30. The documents disclosed on behalf of the Respondent on [date] were the final straw in destroying the relationship of trust and confidence between the Claimant and the Respondent. As a result, the Applicant resigned from her position as [complete] with immediate effect by a letter dated [date].

31. The Claimant's resignation amounted to a dismissal pursuant to section 95(1)(c) of the ERA 1996. The reason (or the principal reason) for the dismissal was that the Claimant had made a protected disclosure and, consequently, it was automatically unfair pursuant to the provisions of section 103A of the ERA 1996.

Dated etc.

G25.3 DRAFTING POINTS

Paragraph 2(a): This paragraph assumes that as a result of the treated complained of in this application, the Claimant resigned. If part of the treatment complained of was that the Claimant was actually dismissed, then this paragraph should simply assert that the Claimant was dismissed because she had made a protected disclosure.

Paragraph 2(b): The Claim should set out all the actions of the Respondent which the Claimant says were in response to her making the protected disclosure. This paragraph should list all the paragraphs in which those actions are described.

Paragraphs 6 and 7: If the Respondent has a policy on whistle-blowing, then the Claim should mention that and identify any breaches of that policy. This will make it more difficult for the Respondent to argue that it handled the complaints correctly.

The history of events should then be set out chronologically, identifying all the communications, whether oral or in writing, in which the allegations were made to the Respondent (for example, in this Precedent, these are paragraphs 8, 12, 23); and all the actions of the employer which the Claimant says were in response to her having made the protected disclosure (in this Precedent, paragraphs 9, 11, 14 to 28) and should assert that these amounted to detriments (paragraphs 10, 14 to 28).

Paragraph 26: For an explanation of the rights of employees under the Data Protection Act 1998 and in particular the subject access rights, se *Jordans Employment Law Service*, at C9[56]–[59]. Subject access requests under the Data Protection Act 1998 can be a useful method for Claimants to obtain information about what others may have said relating to the Claimant, to back up a claim.

Paragraph 30 and 31: Any constructive dismissal claim should set out the Respondent's actions which the Claimant says amounted to a breach of contract and the fact that the Claimant resigned as a result of those breaches. If the Respondent has breached one or more of the written terms of the contract of employment, this should be mentioned her. Often, Claimants can only allege breaches of implied terms. One of those implied terms most often relied on is the duty of an employer not, without reasonable cause, to do anything to destroy mutual trust and confidence.

G26 RESPONSE TO EQUAL PAY CLAIM

G26.1 USE

This precedent illustrates how to defend an equal pay claim under the Equal Pay Act 1970 and European Law. The proceedings must be commenced in the Employment Tribunal and the Employment Tribunal Rules, as modified for equal pay claims, apply. The grounds must be set out in form ET3.

It is normal in such cases for the facts relied upon to be set out in some detail. This is because the interim stages in such cases are often vital in identifying the precise issues in dispute and a fully pleaded Grounds of Resistance is relevant to this task.

G26.2 Precedent

Response to equal pay claim (to be completed on Form ET3)

IN THE EMPLOYMENT TRIBUNALS CASE NO: …/2009
[LOCATION]
B E T W E E N:

[AB]

Claimant

– and –

[AB]

Respondent

GROUNDS OF RESISTANCE

Claimant's claims

1. The Claimant has raised claims for equal pay against the Respondent pursuant to section 1(2) of the Equal Pay Act 1970, and/or Article 141 of the EU Treaty and/or the Equal Pay Directive 75/107.

2. The Respondent is not an emanation of the state. Consequently, the Claimant cannot, as a matter of law, pursue any claims against the Respondent pursuant to Article 141 of the EU Treaty and/or the Equal Pay Directive 75/107. Claims for equal pay can only be pursued by the Claimant under the Equal Pay Act.

3. It is the Respondent's understanding that the Claimant makes the following claims for equal pay:

    (a) That she is paid less than certain of her male colleagues in the Resources Department. It is the Respondent's understanding that the Claimant relies on the following comparators whom she alleges were employed on like work or work of equal value to her role as [set out relevant details]; and/or

    (b)   That she is paid less than [set out relevant details].

Respondent's response

EQUAL PAY CLAIM – COLLEAGUES IN THE RESOURCES DEPARTMENT

4.   In respect of the employment of the Claimant and of her colleagues in the Resources Department the Respondent admits and avers as follows:

    (a)   That with effect from [date] until the date of submission of her ET1 on [date], the Claimant was employed by the Respondent as a [complete].

    (b)   That [comparator 1] was employed by the Respondent as [complete] with effect from [date].

    (c)   That [comparator 2] was employed by the Respondent as [complete] with effect from [date].

    (d)   That [comparator1] and [comparator 2] had both transferred into the Respondent's Resources Department from posts which attracted a higher salary than that paid in respect of the posts to which they transferred. Comparator 1 had held the position of [complete], a managerial role within the [complete] Department. The role attracted a higher salary than that of the [complete]. [Comparator 2] had held the position of [complete] within the [complete] Department. The role attracted a higher salary than that of [complete]. The posts held by [Comparator 1] and [Comparator 2] became redundant. In accordance with the general policy of the Respondent they were both afforded salary protection such that their salary was not reduced following the transfer into the redeployed posts. Further details are provided below.

    (e)   That following the pay review implemented on [complete], the salaries of those working in the [complete] Department were as follows: [set out the details of the relevant salaries].

5.   It is admitted that the Claimant was employed on like work or work of equal value to [Comparator 1] and [Comparator 2].

6.   It is further admitted that the Claimant was paid a lower annual salary than [Comparator 1] and [Comparator 2]. The salary differential was attributable to the salary protection offered to

[Comparator 1] and [Comparator 2], in accordance with the Respondent's policy, following their transfers from higher paid posts.

7. Salary protection is paid by the Respondent to a total of 40 employees of whom 30 (75%) are female and 10 (25%) are male.

8. It is denied, if it is alleged, that the payment of salary protection directly or indirectly discriminates against women employed by the Respondent in general, or the Claimant in particular, on grounds of their/her sex.

9. In summary, the response of the Respondent to the Claimant's equal pay claim, based on a comparison with male colleagues working in the [complete], is as follows:

    (a) it is admitted that the Claimant is employed on like work or work of equal value to her male comparators, [Comparator 1] and [Comparator 2].

    (b) it is admitted that the Claimant is paid a lower annual salary than her male comparators.

    (c) the salary differential is attributable to salary protection offered to the comparators, in accordance with the Respondent's policy, following their transfer from higher paid positions.

    (d) the salary protection, and the consequent salary differential, constitute a "genuine material factor which is not the difference of sex" for the purposes of section 1(3) of the Equal Pay Act.

    (e) salary protection is offered by the Respondent to a total of 40 employees, 30 of which are female. It is denied, if it is alleged by the Claimant, that the operation of salary protection is directly or indirectly discriminatory on grounds of sex against women employed/engaged by the Respondent in general or against the Claimant in particular.

    (f) it is denied that the Claimant is entitled to a Declaration or damages pursuant to the Equal Pay Act.

EQUAL PAY CLAIM – [COMPLETE]

10. In respect of the position of [Comparator 3]:

    (a) the position was held at the relevant time by [Comparator 3].

(b) following the pay review implemented with effect from [complete] Comparator 3's position was graded at Grade RL and [Comparator 3] received the annual salary that was appropriate for a Grade RL post, namely [complete].

(c) the position of [complete] held by the Claimant was graded at Grade CC and attracted an annual salary of [complete].

11. It is denied that the position of [complete] held by the Claimant was work of equal value to the position of [complete] held by [Comparator 3]. In addition to the evidence that will be given on behalf of the Respondent regarding the fundamental differences between the roles of the Claimant and the role of [Comparator 3], the Respondent will, amongst other matters, rely on the following in support of this denial: [set out the relevant factors, for example:]

11.1 [Comparator 3] often had to work in difficult, unpleasant and dangerous working conditions whereas the Claimant worked for most of the time in an office;

11.2 [Comparator 3] was responsible for ensuring the safety of other employees and visitors whereas the Claimant had no such responsibility nor any comparable responsibility;

11.3 [Comparator 3]regularly had to deal with and resolve complex technical problems for which he had received special training whereas the Claimant had no such duty nor any comparable duty.

12. In the event, that the Tribunal determines, contrary to the Respondent's case, that the roles of [complete] and [complete] are work of equal value, the Respondent will rely on a Genuine Material Factor (GMF) defence pursuant to section 1(3) of the Equal Pay Act, namely, that a higher salary was necessary in order to recruit and retain a suitable candidate in the role of [complete].

13. The particulars of the GMF defence are as follows:

(a) that the Respondent had advertised for a period of 18 months to attempt to recruit a [complete]. No suitable candidates had applied before the application was received from [complete].

(b) that there is a known shortage of candidates qualified for the [complete] across the industry.

(c) that the [complete] employed by the Respondent's main competitor, [complete], are paid a higher salary than the [complete] employed by the Respondent.

(d) that it was necessary to offer a salary of [complete] to [complete] in order to secure his acceptance of the post.

14. It is denied that the Claimant is entitled to a Declaration or damages pursuant to the Equal Pay Act.

Dated etc.

G26.3 DRAFTING POINTS

Paragraph 2: Claimants may rely on Article 141 of the treaty of Rome. The Equal Pay Act 1970 should give workers all rights which they have under Article 141. Article 141 is binding on Member States. It can therefore only be relied on where the employer is the state or an 'emanation of the State'. So for private sector employers against whom a Claimant is seeking to rely on Article 141, the paragraph should be included. For more information about the impact of European law on equal pay, see *Jordans Employment Law Service*, at E1[2].

Paragraph 3: The first point a Claimant needs to establish is that she (or he) is employed on work which is comparable with that of her comparator. The Claimant's work and that of the comparator must be:

– like work (see *Jordans Employment Law Service*, at E1[27]);

– work rated as equivalent (see *Jordans Employment Law Service*, at E1[35]); or

– work of equal value (see *Jordans Employment Law Service*, at E1[43].

The first ground on which a Respondent may wish to challenge an equal pay claim, therefore, is that the work is not comparable in any of the above ways.

In this example, the Respondent accepts that the Claimant's work is comparable with that of two of the comparators named by the Claimant; but denies this in respect of the third comparator (paragraph 11).

Paragraph 4 to 6 and paragraph 12: If the Claimant can establish that her work is comparable to one or more of her chosen comparators, she is entitled to be paid the same as the comparators unless the employers can establish that there is a genuine material factor which is not itself discriminatory and which explains the difference in pay – see *Jordans Employment Law Service*, at E1[60] for examples of factors which may be regarded as genuine material factors. The genuine material factors relied on here are pay protection and market forces.

Paragraph 7 and 8: The Claimant may have anticipated in the Claim form that pay protection would be relied on by the Respondent and have alleged that the pay protection scheme is itself discriminatory. This example sets out the sort of facts a Respondent may rely on to establish that the scheme is not discriminatory.

G27 EMPLOYMENT TRIBUNAL'S DIRECTIONS IN EQUAL PAY FOR VALUE CASE

G27.1 USE

This precedent sets out a template for the type of directions which may be sought in an equal pay claim where the Claimant relies on a comparator whose work, the Claimant asserts, if of equal value to that of the Claimant. The proceedings must be brought in an employment tribunal and the Employment Tribunal Rules apply to such cases. This precedent illustrates the type of directions that will often be sought from the tribunal particularly in relation to matters such as the identification of comparators and other relevant matters. For the tribunal procedure in equal value claims and an explanation of the terminology used below, see *Jordans Employment Law Service*, at E1[43].

In this example, the Respondent is not only challenging whether the Claimant's work is of equal value to that of the comparator, but is also relying on the 'genuine material factor' defence (see *Jordans Employment Law Service*, at E1[60].

G27.2 Precedent

Employment tribunal's directions in equal pay for value case

IN THE EMPLOYMENT TRIBUNALS　　　　CASE NO: .../2009
[LOCATION]
B E T W E E N:

[AB]

Claimant

– and –

[BC]

Respondent

PROPOSED DIRECTIONS

Equal pay claim – genuine material factor defence

1. A hearing be listed with a time estimate of 3 days to determine the issue of whether the salary differential is genuinely due to a material factor which is not the difference in sex (section 1(3) of the Equal Pay Act 1970) (the "GMF Issue").

2. Disclosure by list limited to the GMF issue by 4-00 p.m. on _____.

3. Inspection by provision of copies on request by 4-00 p.m. on _____.

4. Preparation of Bundles for hearing:

   (a) The Claimant to prepare a draft Bundle Index and to serve the same on the Respondent on or before 4-00 p.m. on **[35 days before the hearing date]**.

   (b) The Respondent to provide comments on the draft Bundle Index on or before 4-00 p.m. on **[28 days before the hearing date]**.

   (c) The Claimant to prepare 5 copies of the Bundle (in addition to those prepared for its own use) serving 1 copy on the Respondent by 4-00 p.m. on **[21days before the hearing date]** and bringing 4 copies to the Tribunal on the first day of the hearing.

5. Simultaneous exchange of witness statements by 4-00 p.m. on **[14 days before the hearing date]**.

6. The parties to agree: (i) a Bundle of Authorities; and (ii) a Chronology of Relevant Events and to bring the same to the Tribunal on the first day of the hearing.

Equal pay claims

7. The Tribunal will list a Stage 1 Equal Value Hearing in accordance with the provisions of Rule 4(1) of the Employment Tribunals (Equal Value) Rules of Procedure 2004 (the "2004 Rules"), with a time estimate of ½ day, to determine whether the Claimant's claim that her work is of equal value to that of [Comparator] should be:

   (a) Struck out in accordance with the provisions of section 2A(2) of the Equal Pay Act 1970; or

   (b) Determined by a Tribunal; or

   (c) Referred to a member of the panel of independent experts to prepare a report with respect to that question

   and to give directions for the further conduct of this aspect of the claim in accordance with Rule 5 of the 2004 Rules.

8. The parties to disclose any documents relevant to the matters to be determined at the Stage 1 Equal Value hearing by 4-00 p.m. on _____.

9. The parties to agree a Bundle of documents to be used at the Stage 1 Equal Value hearing by 4-00p.m. on **[21 days before the hearing]**.

10. The parties to simultaneously exchange any witness statements relevant to the matters to be determined at the Stage 1 Equal Value hearing by 4-00 p.m. on **[14 days before the hearing]**.

Dated etc

> # G28 GROUNDS OF RESISTANCE TO DISCRIMINATION COMPLAINT IN EMPLOYMENT TRIBUNAL

G28.1 USE

This precedent sets out the grounds of resistance to a claim for unlawful discrimination on grounds of sex, race, religion, belief and sexual orientation. Complaints of disability discrimination require slightly different treatment because of differences in the definitions of discrimination. For an explanation of what constitutes unlawful discrimination, see Division E2 of *Jordans Employment Law Service*.

Such claims must be brought in the Employment Tribunal and the Employment Tribunal Rules will apply.

As with all complaints to an employment tribunal, the form ET3 must be used. A Response submitted on any other form, even if it contains all the required information, will not be accepted. This Form is available from the Employment Tribunals' website. Responses can be completed and submitted online. The Form asks for standard information such as the identity of the employer, and whether the Respondent agrees with the information about earnings, job title etc provided by the Claimant. One of the boxes on the Form ET3 asks the Respondent to set out the grounds of complaint. That box can be filled in with the precedent set out below.

In view of the burden of proof provisions (see *Jordans Employment Law Service*, at E2[280]–[287], it is normally desirable for the factual basis of the Response to be set out in some detail in order to try and prevent the burden of proof shifting to the Respondent. This means not only denying the events claimed by the Claimant but also setting out the Respondent's version of events and anything else which may be helpful to the Respondent – for example, other actions of those alleged to have discriminated which appear inconsistent with a discriminatory attitude; and the Claimant's reaction to events which he or she, in the Claim Form, claims to have caused offence and to have amounted to unlawful discrimination, including in particular any failure by the Claimant to complain at the time of the alleged incident. It is worth responding fully even to allegations that the Claimant has since withdrawn or accepted do not amount to discrimination, particularly if the Response sets out facts inconsistent with a discriminatory attitude.

This precedent also includes an example of how to plead the statutory defence, that even if the employee was discriminated against, the employer should not be liable because the discrimination was the act of an employee and the employer had taken all reasonably practicable steps to prevent such discrimination from occurring (see *Jordans Employment Law*

Service, at E2[191]). This is a difficult defence to run and should be set out in sufficient detail at an early stage of the proceedings.

G28.2   Precedent

Grounds of resistance to discrimination complaint in employment tribunal (to be inserted into Form ET3)

IN THE EMPLOYMENT TRIBUNALS   CASE NO: …/2009
LOCATION
B E T W E E N:

[AB]

Claimant

– and –

[BC]

Respondent

GROUNDS OF RESISTANCE

1. It is denied that the Claimant was discriminated against on grounds of [state the grounds alleged by the Claimant] whether as alleged or at all.

2. As to paragraph 2 [set out the Respondent's case in respect of each allegation made in the Claim, explaining whether the allegation is admitted or denied, and setting out any further points which the Respondent may wish to use in defending the Claim. As explained above, it is worth it only denying the Claimant's version of events but also setting out what the Respondent says actually happened. For example]:

    (a) It is denied that the Claimant was "subject to unwanted and distressing comments of a racial nature from the early stages of her employment." Save for comments alleged to have been made by [complete], the Claimant has failed to identify: (i) when the alleged comments were made; (ii) by whom; or (iii) what was said.

    (b) It is denied that [complete] made "comments to the Claimant which clearly indicated that she found it difficult to work with the Claimant because the Claimant is black." The Claimant has failed to identify: (i) what comments were made which gave that indication (whether clearly or otherwise); or (ii) when such comments were allegedly made.

    (c) It is denied that [complete] made the comment: "My daughter went out with a black man, I hated it." It is averred that [complete] did have a conversation with the

Claimant, outside of the workplace, in which she told the Claimant that her daughter had dated a Nigerian man and that she did not like him because he treated her daughter badly. The Claimant responded that Nigerian men were notorious for treating women badly. It is denied that the said discussion amounted to less favourable treatment of the Claimant on grounds of her race. It was a discussion in which the Claimant actively participated.

(d) It is denied that [complete] made the comment: "Don't you think black people, especially the old ones, look funny in black and white photographs." [complete] made no such comment.

Save as aforesaid, paragraph 2 is denied.

3. As to paragraph 3:

(a) It is denied that [complete] made the comment: "The NHS is in such a state because of all the bloody foreigners in the country."

(b) It is admitted that there was a discussion in the office at lunchtime regarding an article in the national press about medical treatment being sought under the NHS by asylum seekers and people from abroad. It was common practice for topical press articles to be discussed in this way. The discussion was not addressed to or at the Claimant. The Claimant raised this issue with [complete] who expressed the view that the discussion was not addressed at the Claimant and that it was one of many discussions that took place in the office about topical issues reported in the press. The Claimant seemed satisfied with the explanation and did not raise it further. The Claimant did not indicate that she wished the matter to be formally investigated or that any action should be taken against those involved in the discussion.

Save as aforesaid, paragraph 3 is denied.

4. As to paragraph 4:

(a) The Respondent is unable to respond to the allegation that there were a "number of incidents in the workplace" since the Claimant has not identified the alleged incidents.

(b) It is denied that the Claimant's colleagues "left her to struggle with a caller making racist comments." It is, unfortunately, not uncommon for members of the public to make aggressive and insulting comments when calling the Respondent's offices. As soon as [complete] realised the nature of the conversation he took the telephone from the

Claimant and handled the abusive caller. The Claimant made no complaint at the time with regard to the manner in which [complete], or any other employee of the Respondent, handled the matter.

5. As to paragraph 5:

   (a) The Respondent is unable to respond to the Claimant's allegation that there was a "very hostile attitude towards her" on her return from the rest room (which she used when she was pregnant) since she has not identified who was allegedly present.

   (b) The Respondent is unable to respond to the allegation of a "further series of incidents in the office" since the Claimant has not particularised the alleged incidents.

   (c) It is denied that the Claimant was shouted at and belittled by [complete]. It is further denied that the treatment of the Claimant was on grounds of [set out grounds alleged].

   (d) It is averred that the Claimant confided in [complete] that she was pregnant but stated that she did not wish the pregnancy to become common knowledge in the office. [Complete] respected her wish. The Claimant also confided in [complete]: (i) that she was suffering from morning sickness; (ii) that she was homesick; and (iii) that she was worried about the pregnancy. [Complete] recommended various remedies for the Claimant's morning sickness and loaned her travel sickness bands. She also escorted the Claimant to the shops in her lunch hour in order to recommend shops in which the Claimant could purchase maternity and baby clothes.

6. As to paragraph 6:

   (a) It is denied that the Claimant raised any allegations of discrimination with [complete] on her return to work. Save for the informal discussion outlined above, the Claimant did not raise any allegations of discrimination until she purported to submit a grievance pursuant to the statutory grievance procedures on [complete]. That was almost 6 months after the termination of her employment.

   (b) It is denied that the Claimant raised, or attempted to raise, allegations of discrimination at the meeting at which she was dismissed. The Claimant simply suggested that [complete] had been "rude to [her]." The meeting was to review the Claimant's 6-month probationary period and to consider whether her employment was to be terminated. Those issues were, correctly, the issues focused upon at the meeting.

(c) It is denied that the Claimant's dismissal was an act of discrimination or victimisation. It is further denied that the Claimant's dismissal was on grounds of her pregnancy. The Claimant had been warned at the review meeting that her continued probationary employment was at risk if her performance did not improve. Her performance had not improved when the 6-month review was conducted. Consequently, the decision was taken to terminate the Claimant's probationary employment.

7. As to paragraph 7, the Claimant has now clarified that she does not make any allegations of discrimination, victimisation or less favourable treatment arising out of the telephone call from [complete]. [Complete] enquired about the health of the Claimant and her baby and requested that the Claimant bring the baby into the office and send e-mail pictures of the baby to her. She also arranged for a note of congratulations to be sent to the Claimant.

8. Paragraphs 8 to 10 are denied. It is denied that the Claimant was discriminated against or treated less favourably on grounds of race, sex or pregnancy, whether as alleged or at all. It is further denied that the Claimant was victimised.

9. In the event that the Tribunal finds, contrary to the Respondent's case, that the Claimant was discriminated against or treated less favourably by [complete] or any other employee or agent of the Respondent, the Respondent "took such steps as were reasonably practicable to prevent those employees from doing that act or from doing in the course of [their] employment acts of that description" (see section 41(3) of the Sex Discrimination Act 1975; section 32(3) of the Race Relations Act 1976; regulation 22(1) of the Employment Equality (Religion and Belief) Regulations 2003 (SI 2003/1660); and regulation 22(1) of the Employment Equality (Sexual Orientation) Regulations 2003 (SI 2003/1661)).

10. The Respondent will rely on the following facts and matters in support of its statutory defence [set out here all the actions the Respondent has taken to try to prevent discrimination from occurring, for example:]

   (a) The Respondent has implemented and publicised a Confidential Reporting Policy under which employees can confidentially raise allegations of discrimination.

   (b) The Respondent has implemented and publicised a Racial Incident Reporting Policy allowing for the reporting and monitoring of any incident reported as racially motivated.

   (c) The Respondent has implemented and publicised a written Comprehensive Equality Policy.

(d) The Respondent has implemented and publicised a written Dignity at Work Policy.

(e) The Respondent's has a Committee formally tasked with the monitoring and co-ordination of the Respondent's equalities policies.

(f) There are regular discussions about equal opportunities issues at Staff Meetings.

(g) Grievances raised by employees that include allegations of discrimination are extensively investigated by the Respondent. The Respondent will refer to and rely on the investigation conducted as a result of an allegation raised by [complete].

(h) All permanent employees of the Respondent, including [complete] are required to, and have, attended appropriate training courses on equal opportunities and the Respondent's Equality Policy. The relevant details are as follows: [Complete, setting out in particular the training received by those who are alleged to have discriminated].

Dated etc

G28.3 DRAFTING POINTS

Paragraphs 2(a), (b) and (d): These are straightforward denials. If the Claimant has not made clear exactly what the allegation is, then a simple denial may be all the Respondent can say.

Paragraphs 3(c), 4(b): This is a denial coupled with a statement by the Respondent of what actually happened. Where possible, Respondents should state their version of events rather than simply deny the Claimant's. It looks more convincing and should help to avoid the burden of proof shifting to the Respondent.

Paragraph 5(d): Where the Respondent agrees with facts stated in the Claim form, admit them as is done in this paragraph and add any further points relevant to those facts which help to demonstrate that the Respondent did not discriminate.

Paragraph 6(a): Point out any other facts that may cast doubt on the Claimant's complaints, for example, the fact that no complaint was made at the time.

Paragraph 9: The defence that the employer took all reasonably practicable steps to prevent discrimination occurring can be used even if it is established that the Claimant was discriminated against. The effect could be, if the defence succeeds, that the Claimant proceeds with his or her claim against the individual alleged to have discriminated but not against the employer respondent. Using this defence could therefore put pressure on the individual accused of discriminating – which can be an effective way of discouraging employees from discriminating. They will know that, if they are found to have discriminated unlawfully, they could have to face the claim and any compensation due without assistance from their employer.

G29 REQUEST FOR FURTHER INFORMATION ABOUT RESPONSE

G29.1 USE

Either on the application of a party or of its own motion, a tribunal may order a party to provide additional information about any assertions made in the Claim form or the Response. The purpose should be to enable one party to know the case it will have to meet in the tribunal. It can also be used to establish facts prior to the hearing and prior to witness statements being exchanged, so that evidence on those facts will not need to be given at the hearing itself.

Here, for example, the Claimant is applying for further information about two matters. First, he wants to know the basis of the allegation that the Claimant was 'known to dislike the other two men. The Claimant may dispute that, but in order to prepare for how to deal with that contention at the hearing, it will be useful for the Claimant to know what the Respondent bases that assertion on. For example, the Respondent may be intending to call evidence of incidents in the past when the Claimant has shown a dislike for the two men. The Claimant will want to know what those incidents are, so that he can include an explanation of those incidents in his witness statement or so that he can identify other witnesses who may be able to cast some doubt on whether that contention is true.

The second piece of information requested is confirmation of two points which might cast doubt on the Respondent's assertion that Mrs Robinson was an 'independent witness'. If the Respondent denies that Mrs Robinson is Mr Johnson's long-term partner, then the Claimant will know that he will have to bring evidence to prove it. If the Respondent admits this, then no evidence will be required on this point because it will already have been established prior to the hearing.

Requests for information should not be used simply to find out what the various witnesses are going to say. There must be a good reason why providing the information in advance is necessary to enable the party applying for the information to have it in advance – for example, so that it knows what evidence it will need to bring or to avoid unnecessary costs being incurred, or to avoid the risk that the hearing may need to be adjourned.

The Claimant may initially just send the Respondent a list of questions. If the Respondent does not respond, then the Claimant should write to the tribunal explaining why it is necessary to ensure that justice is done, that unnecessary legal costs are not incurred, that the hearing is not unnecessarily lengthened and/or that the risk of an adjournment of the hearing while further evidence is gathered is avoided. The tribunal may then order the other party to provide the information. Failure then to provide the information may lead to the claim or the response being struck out – although normally this is only done after an 'unless' order, ie an order that unless the information is provided by a certain date, the claim or response will be struck out.

This example seeks further information about the Response. A Respondent may equally wish to obtain further information about the Claim, and can apply in a similar way.

For more information about applications for additional information, see *Jordans Employment Law Service*, at H1[38].

G29.2   Precedent

Request for further information about Response

         IN THE EMPLOYMENT TRIBUNALS   CASE NO:…/2009
         [LOCATION]
         B E T W E E N:

                               [AB]

                                                        Claimant

                             – and –

                               [CD]

                                                    Respondent

REQUEST FOR FURTHER PARTICULARS OF THE GROUNDS OF RESISTANCE

Please answer the following written questions. Please provide your answers in writing to … of … on or before … 2007. You can do this by post to …, by e-mail to … or by fax to …

Under paragraph 4(2)

        OF: "…the Claimant (who is known to dislike the other two men)…"

        REQUEST:

        1.   Please identify who allegedly has this alleged knowledge.

        2.   Please identify any evidence to support this allegation.

Under paragraph 11

        OF: "Mrs Robinson, an entirely independent witness (who works in a different area and just happened to be passing)…"

REQUEST:

3. Please confirm that Mrs Robinson is the long-term partner of Mr Johnson.

4. Please confirm that Mrs Robinson has previously faced disciplinary warnings for spending time away from her workstation with Mr Johnson and Mr Brown.

5. Please confirm that, in the circumstances, Mrs Robinson was not an "independent" witness at all.

Please could you provide your responses to the above questions as soon as possible and, in any event, by no later than [date], failing which we shall apply to the tribunal for an appropriate order.

We look forward to hearing from you.

G29.3 DRAFTING POINTS

It is helpful, as is done here, to quote exactly the wording of the Claim or Response form and then to set out the further information required. This then makes it easier for the tribunal to see why the information is needed, should an order from the tribunal be sought. This is not absolutely necessary, however, and a simple list of questions set out in letter form is also perfectly acceptable.

The party seeking the information should set out the date by which it is required. Generally, the other party should be given at least seven days to assemble the information. The request should be made long enough before the hearing to allow time for an application to be made to the tribunal if this proves necessary.

G30 RESPONSE TO REQUEST FOR FURTHER INFORMATION

G30.1 USE

A party faced with a request for further information should first decide whether the party applying for the information is entitled to have it in advance of witness statements being exchanged. If the request is just a request for the contents of the Respondent's witness statements, then the information could be refused. If the parties cannot agree whether the information should be provided in advance, then an application can be made to the tribunal for a decision on that point.

Full details do not need to be provided. All that is necessary is sufficient information for the party applying for the information to know what the other party's case is. Here, the response simply states that relevant evidence will be provided in the usual way – ie by exchange of witness statements at the time directed by the tribunal.

G30.2 Precedent

Response to request for further information

IN THE EMPLOYMENT TRIBUNALS   CASE NO: .../2009
[LOCATION]
B E T W E E N:

[AB]

Claimant

– and –

[CD]

Respondent

RESPONSE TO REQUEST FOR FURTHER PARTICULARS OF THE GROUNDS OF RESISTANCE

Please find below our response to your written questions. Please confirm receipt.

Under paragraph 4(2)

OF: "...the Claimant (who is known to dislike the other two men)..."

REQUEST:

1.   Please identify who allegedly has this alleged knowledge.

2. Please identify any evidence to support this allegation.

RESPONSE:

1. The said knowledge was had by all relevant staff who worked in the same area as the Claimant. It was common knowledge and commonly the topic of staffroom discussions.

2. Relevant witness statements will be provided at the appropriate stage of this litigation.

Under paragraph 11

OF: "Mrs Robinson, an entirely independent witness (who works in a different area and just happened to be passing)…"

REQUEST:

3. Please confirm that Mrs Robinson is the long-term partner of Mr Johnson.

4. Please confirm that Mrs Robinson has previously faced disciplinary warnings for spending time away from her workstation with Mr Johnson and Mr Brown.

5. Please confirm that, in the circumstances, Mrs Robinson was not an "independent" witness at all.

RESPONSE:

3. This is confirmed.

4. This is confirmed.

5. This is denied. Mrs Robinson will give her relevant witness evidence at the relevant stage of this litigation. For sake of clarification, however, Mrs Robinson provided an independent statement on 10th May 2007 to Mr Williams that confirmed Mr Johnson's and Mr Brown's version of events.

G30.3 DRAFTING POINTS

For the sake of clarity, it is useful to set out precisely what the question being answered is and then to provide the answer.

Requests for further information are often just requests for the contents of witness statements. Where, as here, the Respondent considers that that is the purpose of the request, then the Respondent can simply indicate that the relevant evidence will be given on exchange of witness statements.

G31 NOTICE OF APPEAL TO THE EMPLOYMENT APPEAL TRIBUNAL

G31.1 USE

This precedent sets out the form of an appeal to the Employment Appeal Tribunal (EAT). This must comply with the Employment Appeal Tribunal Rules and the relevant practice direction – see *Jordans Employment Law Service*, at H2[71] onwards. The documents to accompany the Notice of Appeal include the judgement or order appealed from, the reasons, the Claim and the Response. The Practice direction should be checked carefully before sending the appeal. If the correct documents have not been included, the appeal may not be accepted. The EAT may contact the appellant to point out what further needs to be lodged, but if they cannot do that if the appeal is lodged just before the deadline for appealing.

The deadline is strict – generally 42 days from the date the reasons for the decision were sent to the parties. The notice of appeal must be received by the EAT before 4pm on the deadline date. Documents received after 4pm are deemed to have been received on the next working day.

An appeal to the EAT is nearly always restricted to an appeal on points of law. The EAT will not interfere with a tribunal's conclusions on the facts – even if the appellant knows that the tribunal has got all the facts wrong, has believed the witnesses the appellant believes were lying etc. Notices of Appeal need to set out an explanation of the errors of law relied upon – for example, that the tribunal applied the wrong test, or took into account an irrelevant factor, or failed to take into account a relevant factor. If the appellant's disagreement with a tribunal's decision cannot be expressed in this sort of way, then it is probably not worth appealing, however outrageous the tribunal's decision. It is possible to appeal on the ground that the tribunal's decision was 'perverse', but successful appeals on this ground are rare.

The EAT performs a robust sifting process to try and weed out any claims which in reality do not involve any points of law. It is important, therefore, to identify clearly where the tribunal went wrong and to express this in a way that suggests an error of law. If you do not, then the appeal may fall at the 'sift' stage, by when it may be too late to put in a revised Notice of Appeal.

For an explanation of the appeal process, see *Jordans Employment Law Service*, at H2[71]–[76].

G31.2 **Precedent**

Notice of Appeal to the Employment Appeal Tribunal

[*Precedent for an appeal to the Employment Appeal Tribunal from a decision of the Employment Tribunal striking out the Appellant's claim of unfair dismissal*].

IN THE EMPLOYMENT APPEAL TRIBUNAL   EAT/...

B E T W E E N:

[AB]

Appellant

- and -

[BC]

Respondent

NOTICE OF APPEAL FROM DECISION OF THE EMPLOYMENT TRIBUNAL

To: The Registrar
       Employment Appeal Tribunal
       58 Victoria Embankment
       London EC4Y 0DS

1. The Appellant is [AB] of [address].

2. Any communication relating to this appeal may be sent to the Appellant's solicitors at the following address:

   [Complete Address]

   Tel: [complete]

   Fax: [complete]

   Any communications should be marked for the attention of **[Solicitors Name]** and should bear the reference: **[Reference]**.

3. The Appellant appeals from the decision of the Employment Tribunal [chaired by **[Judge]**, sitting alone] at a [Pre-Hearing Review [*or* hearing] conducted on **[Date]**.

4. The Judgment and Written Reasons were sent to the parties on **[Date]**. [*Set out summary of judgment, for example:*] The Tribunal determined that the Appellant's complaints of unfair and wrongful dismissal should be struck out on the grounds that they had no reasonable prospects of success. The basis of the decision was the Tribunal's conclusion that the Appellant had not been dismissed since he had subsequently been offered re-instatement (albeit that

the offer was later withdrawn and the dismissal re-confirmed). In the absence of a dismissal the Appellant could not claim unfair or wrongful dismissal.

5. The party to the proceedings before the Employment Tribunal, other than the Appellant was the Respondent, [bc] of **[Address]**. Any communication relating to this appeal should be sent to the Respondent's representatives, **[Name and Address of Solicitors]**, marked for the attention of **[Name]** and bearing the reference: **[Complete]**. The telephone number is: **[Complete]**.

6. Copies of the following documents are attached to this Notice:

    (a) The Judgment and Written Reasons for the Tribunal's decision, dated **[Complete]**.

    (b) The Claim Form (ET1) submitted by the Appellant, dated **[Complete]**.

    (c) The Respondent's Response (ET3), dated **[Complete]**.

    (d) Copies of all relevant correspondence between the Respondent and the Appellant as referred to in the Summary Chronology of Events (see below).

7. The Appellant has not made an application to the Tribunal for a Review of any Judgment or decision.

Summary chronology of events

8. The Chronology of Events relevant to the issue of [*set out relevant issue, for example:*] whether the Appellant was dismissed by the Respondent was as follows:

    [Here set out succinct summary of the case]

Grounds of appeal

9. The grounds upon which this appeal is brought are as follows:

    [*Here set out the relevant grounds of appeal, for example:*]

10. The Tribunal erred in law in striking out the Appellant's claims in circumstances in which there were clear issues of fact and/or law to be determined as to whether:

    (a) The offer of reinstatement made by the Respondent was a genuine offer;

    (b) the offer of reinstatement made by the Respondent was unreasonable given that it imposed a deadline for return on a date when as the Respondent was aware that the Appellant was working abroad and would be unable to return. The deadline imposed by the Respondent was [date]. The Appellant was due to return to the United Kingdom on [date]. No explanation was given by the Respondent as to why the deadline could not be extended to after that date;

(c) it was practicable for the Appellant to return by the deadline unilaterally imposed by the Respondent. The Tribunal had heard no evidence in this regard.

(d) it was reasonable for the Appellant to refuse the offer of reinstatement given the manner in which he had been treated by the Respondent (being unfairly dismissed) and the imposition of an unreasonable deadline for return (at a time when the Respondent was aware that the Appellant was working abroad and not due to return until mid-March 2007); and/or

(e) The offer of reinstatement rendered the dismissal inoperable in law.

The Tribunal failed to properly apply the decision in **North Glamorgan NHS Trust v Ezsias [2007] IRLR 603** that: "it would only be in an exceptional case that an application … will be struck out as having no reasonable prospect of success when the central facts are in dispute." In this case, the central fact of whether the offer of re-instatement was genuine and reasonable was firmly in dispute.

11. The Tribunal erred in law in failing to conclude that the Appellant was dismissed with effect from [date] such that he had the right to make claims for unfair and wrongful dismissal. The merits of such claims should have been determined at a full Tribunal hearing.

12. The Tribunal erred in law in failing to understand that the case of **Roberts v West Coast Trains Limited [2004] IRLR 788,** which determined that there was no dismissal in circumstances "where a contractual disciplinary procedure permits the employers, on appeal, to impose a sanction of demotion in place of an earlier decision to dismiss." There was no such contractual disciplinary procedure in this case. The Tribunal failed to address the issue of the status of the disciplinary procedure at all. It simply found that the "contract was revived as a result of the letter dated [ ]." Such finding was unexplained and amounted to an error of law.

13. The Tribunal erred in law in failing to recognise that it would be contrary to public policy for an employer to be able to unfairly dismiss an employee but to avoid liability in respect thereof by offering re-instatement on terms with which the employee was unable to comply (for example, a date by which the employee must

return to work). The Tribunal was not in a position to make findings of fact as to the Appellant's ability to comply with the unreasonable deadline imposed by the Respondent since it had heard no evidence.

14. The Tribunal erred in law in failing to consider the impact of, and make findings as to the legal effect of, the withdrawal of the offer of reinstatement on [date] and the Respondent's express confirmation that the "dismissal stands as confirmed in writing on [date]." Even if, which is denied, the effect in law of the offer of reinstatement was to revive the contract, the withdrawal of that offer of reinstatement constituted dismissal. The Tribunal were aware that the offer of reinstatement had been withdrawn but failed to address and make findings as to the consequences of that withdrawal.

15. It is averred that the effect of the withdrawal must be that the Appellant was dismissed either:

    (a) with effect from the date the Appellant was dismissed initially as the Respondent suggested in its letter; or

    (b) with effect from the date the offer of reinstatement was withdrawn.

In either event the Appellant was dismissed and had the right to make claims for unfair and wrongful dismissal.

Order sought

16. The Order sought by the Appellant is that the decision to strike out his claims be overturned and that his claims be ordered to proceed to a full merits hearing.

Dated etc.

G31.3 DRAFTING POINTS

Paragraphs 10–15: In this example, the employment tribunal had struck out a claim at a pre-hearing review on the grounds that in the tribunal's view the claim had no reasonable prospects of success. For more details of the circumstances in which a tribunal may strike out a claim on these grounds, see *Jordans Employment Law Service*, at H1[35]. Generally, when trying to identify errors of law, one should set out the rule or rules that the tribunal should have applied and then explain the respects in which the tribunal failed to follow that rule. Then one should consider what factors may be relevant, and should therefore be taken into account, when applying that rule. If the tribunal failed to take a relevant matter into account or was influenced by some matter which should, if it had applied the rule correctly, had no bearing on the application of the rule, then that too might indicate an error of law.

In this example, the tribunal could only have reached the conclusion that there were no reasonable prospects of success if, whatever evidence is provided at a full hearing, there would still be no reasonable chance of the claim succeeding. Reliance by the tribunal on conclusions of fact which should not have been determined until evidence was heard at a full hearing would amount to an error of law – hence the points made in paragraph 10 above that there were questions of fact which needed to be determined at a full hearing.

This example lists numerous other errors of law – so many it is hoped that no tribunal could ever come to such an incompetent decision!

In paragraph 12, the point is made that the tribunal applied a rule about disciplinary demotions permitted by the contract of employment to a situation where the employer simply offered reinstatement following a dismissal. The tribunal applied the rule to the wrong circumstances.

Paragraph 13 points out the ludicrous consequences of applying the rule in the way the tribunal applied in this case.

Paragraph 14 makes the point that the tribunal failed to take account of relevant matters – here the withdrawal of the offer of reinstatement and the Respondent's assertion that the original dismissal still stood.

INDEX

References are to paragraph numbers.

Absence *see* Sickness; Time off work
Access to Medical Reports Act 1988
  employees right under   F1.1, F1.2, F2.2
Accident *see also* Health and Safety
Accident reporting
  policy   D15.1, D15.2
  staff handbook   D1.1
Adopted child
  arrival of, time off for *see* Adoption leave
  parental leave   D23.2
Adoption leave
  additional rights from employer   D26.3
  commencement   D26.2
  eligibility   D26.2
  entitlement   D26.2
  'keep in touch days'   D26.2
  notice of intention to take   D26.2
  pay (contractual)   D26.3
  pay, statutory   D26.1, D26.2
    rate   D26.2
    period of   D26.2
  policy   D26.2, D26.3
  return to work right   D26.2
    early return, notification   D26.2
  statutory right   D26.1, D26.2
Age *see also* Retirement
  discrimination
    claims   G28.1
    grounds for resistance   G28.1
    harassment on grounds of   D12.1
    behaviour constituting   D12.2
AIDS policy
  staff handbook   D1.1
Alcohol and drugs
  abuse
    staff handbook   D1.1
  driving under the influence of   D21.2
Applicant (job) *see also* Application form; Recruitment
  checks on   A1.1
    criminal convictions   A1.1, A1.3
  discrimination protection *see* Recruitment

Applicant (job) —*continued*
  entitlement to work in UK   A1.1
  foreign worker *see* Foreign worker
  monitoring   A1.2, A1.3
  qualifications   A1.1, A1.3
    foreign   A1.3
  successful candidate
    offer letter   A2.1, A2.2, A2.3
    precedent   A2.2
  work with children   A1.1, A1.3
    Criminal Records Bureau checks   A1.1, A1.3
Application form
  accompanying documentation   A1.2
  content   A1.1, A1.2
  criminal conviction details   A1.1, A1.3
  incorrect information provided by applicant   A1.1
  monitoring   A1.2, A1.3
  precedent   A1.2
  warranty   A1.2
Appraisal
  policy   D18.1, D18.2
  staff handbook   D1.1
Bereavement
  policy
    staff handbook   D1.1
Betting worker
  Sunday working
    opting-out notice   B6.1, B6.2
    statutory rights   B6.1, B6.2
Bonus
  claim, High Court in   G3.2
    defences for employer   G4.1, G4.2
  contractual claim for   G3.1
  deductions from pay
    employment tribunal, complaint to   G13.1, G13.2, G13.3
    response   G14.1, G14.2, G14.3
  discretionary   B2.3, G3.1
  employment tribunal claim   G20.1, G20.2

Bonus—*continued*
guaranteed
    High Court claim   G5.2, G5.3
        defences for employer   G6.1,
                      G6.2, G6.3
        repudiatory breach   G5.1
        jurisdiction of claims   G5.1
    termination, claim on   G20.1, G20.2
    wrongful dismissal damages
        calculation   G3.1

Breach of contract *see* **Contract (employment)**

Bullying
    behaviour constituting   D12.2

Capability (employee)
    disability discrimination and   D5.1
    dismissal
        right to appeal   D5.2, D5.3
    invitation to formal meeting   F5.1,
                      F5.2, F5.3
        statutory requirement   F5.1, F5.2
    monitoring   D5.2
    opportunity to improve   D5.1
    policy   D5.2, D5.3
    poor performance
        causes   D5.2, D5.3
        evidence   D5.2
    procedure   D5.1, D5.2, D5.3, F5.1,
                      F5.2, F5.3
        dismissal
            appeal right   F9.1
            acknowledgement of
                notice   F9.2
            notice of   F8.1, F8.2, F8.3
        formal   D5.2
        informal   D5.2
        no further action   F6.1
            notice of   F6.2
        short   D6.1, D6.2
        warning, under-performance
            for   F7.1, F7.2, F7.3
            time limit   F7.3
    standards expected   D5.2
    termination   D5.2
    unfair dismissal and   D5.1

Casual workers
    terms of employment for   B4.1, B4.2

Collective agreement   B2.2
    employee representative
        nomination form   F21.1
    lay-off   C3.1, C3.3
    parental leave   D23.1
        incorporation into
            contract   D23.3
    redundancy
        duty to consult   F10.1
        short-time   C3.1, C3.3

Commission for Equality and Human Rights
    Codes of Practice   D22.1

Company car
    accidents and breakdown   D21.2
    allowances   D21.2
    entitlement, criteria   D21.2
    fines
        employee responsibility   D21.2
    health and safety issues   D21.2
    insurance   D21.2
    leasing schemes   D21.2
    maintenance, expenses
        employer responsibility   D21.2
    policy   D21.2
    return on termination of
        employment   D21.2
    smoking in   D21.2
    tax implications   D21.2
    use of   B1.2, D21.1

Company interests
    protection of
        clause in contract   B1.2

Compromise agreement
    basic   E4.1, E4.2, E4.3
    executives   E3.1, E3.2, E3.3
        conditions   E3.2, E3.3
        confidentiality   E3.2, E3.3
        purpose   E3.1
        'relevent independent
            advisor'   E3.2
        restrictive covenants   E3.2, E3.3
    specific claim   E5.1, E5.2, E5.3

Computer
    access   C1.1, C1.2, C1.3
    copyright   D3.2
    use by employee   C1.1, C1.2, C1.3, D3.2, D3.3

Conduct (employee's)
    general rules   D2.1, D2.2
    gross misconduct   D2.2

Constructive dismissal
    disciplinary procedure, failure to
        follow   D7.3
    High Court action   G5.2, G5.3
        defences for employer   G6.1, G6.2, G6.3
    lay-off/short-time   C3.1
    repudiatory breach of
        contract   G5.1

Consultant
    agreement for
        duration   B3.2
        purpose   B3.1
        termination   B3.2, B3.3
    confidentiality   B3.2, B3.3
    duties   B3.2, B3.3
    employee, treated as   B3.1
    fees and expenses   B3.2, B3.3
    indemnity   B3.2, B3.3
    self-employed status   B3.1, B3.3
    services   B3.2, B3.3
    tax status   B3.1

Index

Consultation *see also* Redundancy;
    Transfer of Undertaking
  lay-off   C3.1, C3.3
  redundancy   D9.1, D9.2, D9.3,
                                  F10.1, F10.2, F10.3
  redundancy, with employee
    representatives *see*
    Employee representative;
    Redundancy
  short-time   C3.1, C3.3
  'smoke-free' policy   D28.1, D28.2
    enforcement   D28.2
Continuous employment
  break in   B2.3
  period of   B2.3
Contract (employment)   B1.1, B1.2,
                                       B1.3
  car, use of   B1.2
  company interest, protection
    of   B1.2
  confidential information   B1.2
  content   B1.2, B1.3
    place of work specified in   B1.2
  data protection   B1.2
  draft   A2.1, A2.3
  duties of employment   B1.2
  expenses   B1.2
  garden leave
    meaning   B1.3
  holiday entitlement   B1.2
  information technology, rules
    for   D3.1
  insurance benefits   B1.2
  inventions   B1.2
  lay-off *see* Lay-off
  media communications   C4.1, C4.2
  offer and acceptance   B1.1
  offer letter as   A2.1, A2.3
  precedent   B1.2, B1.3
  remuneration   B1.2
  repudiatory breach of   G2.1
  restraint of trade clause   B1.2
  sickness   B1.2
  signature, effect of   A2.1
  signing
    effect of   B1.1
    failure to   B1.1
    statutory requirement   B1.1
  termination clause   B1.2
  terms   A2.1
    discrepancy with offer
      letter   A2.3
    employee's objection to   A2.1
  terms of employment   B1.1
  third party interests   B1.2
Criminal conviction *see* Criminal
  record
Criminal record
  Criminal Records Bureau   A1.1,
                                         A1.3
  spent convictions   A1.1

Data protection
  personal data   B1.2, B2.2
Demotion
  circumstances where allowed   D7.1
Dimissal
  misconduct for
    appeal right   F19.3
    notice of   F19.1, F19.2, F19.3
Director
  contract, terms *see* Service
    agreement
Disability
  harassment
    behaviour constituting   D12.2
  harassment on grounds of
    behaviour constituting   D12.1
Disability discrimination
  less favourable treatment   D22.2
Disability Rights Commission
  Codes of Practice   D22.1
Disciplinary procedures *see also*
    Grievance procedure   D7.1,
                                   D7.2, D7.3,
  appeals   D7.2
  capability   D5.1
    invitation to formal meeting   F5.1,
                                         F5.2
    statutory requirement   F5.1,
                                         F5.2
    no further action   F6.1
    notice of   F6.2
  demotion   D7.1
  exemptions   D7.1
  gross misconduct   D7.2, D7.3
    categories   D7.3
    grounds   D7.1
    notification   D7.2, D7.3
  hearing   D7.2, D7.3, F17.1, F17.3
    invitation to   F17.2
    re-arranging time   D7.3
  investigation   D7.3
    prior to   F15.1, F15.2, F15.3
    suspension during   D7.2
  misconduct
    dismissal
      appeal right   F19.3
      notice   F19.3
    dismissal, notice   F19.1, F19.2
    warning for   F18.1, F18.2, F18.3
    no further action
      notification of   F20.1, F20.2
    outcome   D7.2
    persistent absenteeism   D29.2, D29.3
  policy
    staff handbook   D1.1
    statutory   D7.1
  suspension   D7.1
    during investigation   F16.1, F16.2
Disclosure
  media communications and   C4.1,
                                       C4.2

Discrimination
  direct
    meaning   D22.2
  indirect
    meaning   D22.2
Dismissal
  appeal from decision   D8.2
  compliance with procedure   D7.1
  grounds   D7.1, D8.1
    capability   D5.1, F5.1
      right to appeal   D5.2, D5.3
    notification   D8.2
  hearing   D8.2
    re-arranging time for   D8.2
  investigation   D8.2
  persistent absenteeism   D29.2
  procedure   D8.1, D8.2
  right to be accompanied   D8.2
  statutory   D8.1
  unfair dismissal
    failure to follow statutory
      procedure   D8.1
Doctor
  letter to obtain medical
    reports   F3.1, F3.2, F3.3

E-mail, use of   D3.2, D3.3
  policy
    staff handbook   D1.1
    unauthorised use   D3.2
Employee
  notification of information   D4.1,
                                          D4.2
  personal property of
    protection policy   D14.1, D14.2,
                                        D14.3
  purchase of goods   C2.1, C2.2, C2.3
  representative *see* Employee
    representative
  self-employed person
    compared   B3.1
Employee representative
  election
    ballot form   F24.1, F24.2
    nominations   F11.1, F11.2, F12.1,
                                      F12.2
    form   F21.1, F21.2
    process   F22.1, F22.2
    voting procedure   F22.2
    invitation to be nominated   F11.1,
                    F11.2, F12.1, F12.2
  redundancies
    consultation   F10.1, F10.2, F10.3
    election
      process   F23.1, F23.2
      role of   F23.2
    role of   F22.2
    when needed   F21.1
Employer
  goods of
    right to search employee   C2.2
    staff purchase   C2.1, C2.2, C2.3

Employment appeal tribunal
  notice of appeal to   G31.1, G31.2,
                                       G31.3
  grounds for   G31.2, G31.3
  points of law   G31.1
  time limits   G31.1
  procedure   G31.1, G31.2, G31.3
Employment tribunal
  proceedings
    bonus, termination on   G20.1,
                                       G20.2
    collective redundancies
      claim, failure to consult,
        for   G24.1, G24.2, G24.3
    discrimination cases   G28.1,
                                 G28.2, G28.3
      grounds of resistance   G28.1,
                                 G28.2, G28.3
    equal pay claim   G26.1, G26.2,
                                       G26.3
      directions   G27.1, G27.2
      response to   G26.1, G26.2,
                                     G26.3
    ET1 form   G7.1, G7.2, G9.1,
                        G9.2, G11.2, G11.3
    ET3 form   G8.1, G8.2, G8.3,
                  G10.1, G10.2, G10.3
    holiday pay, claim under
      Working Time
      Regulations   G17.1, G17.2,
                  G18.1, G18.2, G18.3
    national minimum wage, claim
      for   G21.1, G21.2, G22.1,
                      G22.2, G22.3
    redundancy payment
      claim   G19.1, G19.2, G19.3
    request for further
      information   G29.1, G29.2,
                                  G29.3
      response to   G30.1, G30.2,
                                  G30.3
    TUPE, complaint
      regarding   G23.1, G23.2,
                                 G23.3
    unlawful deductions
      bonus, from   G13.1, G13.2,
          G13.3, G14.1, G14.2, G14.3
      holiday pay, from   G15.1,
          G15.2, G15.3, G16.1, G16.2,
                                 G16.3
      wages, from   G11.1, G11.2,
          G11.3, G12.1, G12.2, G12.3
    whistleblowing   G25.1, G25.2,
                                 G25.3
Equal opportunities
  Codes of Practice   D22.2
  legal duty to promote   D22.1
  policy   D22.1, D22.2, D22.3
    disciplinary procedures   D22.2,
                                     D22.3
    grievances   D22.2
    harassment   D22.2

Index

Equal opportunities—*continued*
  policy—*continued*
    monitoring and review   D22.2, D22.3
    need for   D22.1
    objectives   D22.1
    people with disabilities   D22.2
      less favourable treatment   D22.2
    promotion and training   D22.2, D22.3
    recruitment and selection   D22.2, D22.3
    right to hold personal data   B1.2, B2.2
    victimisation   D22.2
  relevant legislation   D22.2, D22.3
Equal Opportunities Commission
  Codes of Practice   D22.1
Equal opportunities policy
  monitoring   A1.2
Equal pay
  claim for
    employment tribunal's directions   G27.1, G27.2
    response to   G26.1, G26.2, G26.3
Executive
  contract, terms *see* Service agreement

Flexible working
  additional rights from employer   D27.3
  agreement of request   F26.1
    modifications, subject to   F29.1, F29.2
    notice of   F26.2
  appeal right   D27.2, F30.1, F30.2
  company's decision on   D27.2
  applications for   D27.1, D27.2
    form of   F25.1, F25.2
  care for child as purpose of   D27.1
  carers   D27.1
  eligibility   D27.2
  grounds for refusal   D27.2
  procedure   D27.1, D27.2
    duration of   D27.2
    employer's consideration of request   D27.2
    meeting to discuss   F27.1, F27.2
    refusal of request   F28.1
      form of notice   F28.2
    request in writing   D27.2
    trial period   D27.2
  qualifying conditions   D27.2
  refusal of request
    appeal right   F30.1, F30.2
    right to request   D27.1, D27.2
Foreign worker
  recruitment of
    equivalent qualifications   A1.3

Foreign worker—*continued*
  recruitment of—*continued*
    permission to work in UK   A1.2, A2.3
    documentation required   A1.2, A2.3

Garden leave
  restrictive covenant/restraint of trade   B1.3
Gender re-assignment
  harassment on grounds of   D12.1
  behaviour constituting   D12.2
Grievance procedure *see also*
  Disciplinary procedures
  accompanying at meeting/hearing   D10.2
  appeals   D10.2
  contractual obligation
    incorporation into contract   D10.1
  employment tribunal claim   D10.1, D10.2
  formal stage   D10.2, D10.3
  good practice guidelines   D10.1
  hearing
    invitation to complainant   F33.1, F33.2, F33.3
  informal stage   D10.2, D10.3
    problems for employer   D10.3
  investigation
    instructions to investigator   F32.1, F32.2, F32.3
    notification to complainant   F31.1, F31.2, F31.3
  meeting   D10.2
    re-arrangement   D10.2
  outcome, notice of   D10.2, F34.1, F34.2, F34.3
  purpose and scope   D10.1
  short version   D11.1, D11.2, D11.3
  statutory   D10.3
    harassment complaint   D12.1, D12.2
    requirements   D10.3
  termination   D10.2

Handbook *see* Staff handbook
Harassment
  alleged harasser
    notification of complaint   F35.1, F35.2, F35.3
  behaviour constituting   D12.2, D12.3
  complaints procedure
    formal   D12.2, D12.3
    informal   D12.2, D12.3
  criminal offence as   D12.1
  definition   D12.2
  hearing   F37.1, F37.3
    letter inviting   F37.2

Harassment—*continued*
   investigation   D12.2
      instructions to investigator   F38.1,
                                    F38.2, F38.3
   notification to
      complainant   F36.1, F36.2,
                                          F36.3
   outcome   F39.1, F39.3
      notification of   F39.2
   policy   D12.1, D12.2, D12.3
   statutory grievance
      procedure   D12.1
Health and safety
   accidents, reporting of   D15.1,
                                          D15.2
   company car, use of   D21.2
   dangerous machinery   D15.2, D15.3
Holiday *see also* Sunday working;
   Time off work
   entitlement
      contract in   B1.2
      part-time workers   B2.3
   pay on termination
      accrued pay   B2.3
Holiday pay
   claim for
      Working Time Regulations,
         under   G17.1, G17.2
         response to   G18.1, G18.2,
                                          G18.3
      contractual entitlement   G15.1,
                                          G15.3
      unlawful deductions
         claim for   G15.1, G15.2, G15.3
         response to   G16.1, G16.2,
                                          G16.3

Immigration
   employment
      work permit requiring   A1.1,
                                        A1.2, A1.3
Information
   employees, notification of   D4.1,
                                          D4.2
Insurance
   benefits   B1.2
Internet, use of   D3.2, D3.3
   unauthorised use   D3.2

Lay-off
   consultation   C3.1, C3.3
   definition   C3.1
   dismissal   C3.1
   pay   C3.1
   policy   C3.1, C3.2
      impact   C3.3
   redundancy
      entitlement to   C3.1
      pay   C3.1
Loan
   agreement   E7.1, E7.2

Maternity
   ante natal care, time off for   D24.2
   contractual rights/obligations   D24.2
   leave   D24.1
      additional   D24.2
      commencement   D24.2
      consecutive periods of   D24.2
      contractual rights during   D24.2
      length of   D24.2
      ordinary   D24.2
      policy   D24.2, D24.3
   notification by employee   D24.2
   pay (contractual)   D24.2, D24.3
   pay (SMP) *see* Statutory
      maternity pay
   return to work   D24.2
   rights
      policy
         staff handbook   D1.1
Media
   communication with, policy   C4.1,
                                           C4.2
Medical report
   access to   F1.1, F1.2, F2.1, F2.2,
                F3.1, F3.2, F3.3, F4.1, F4.2
   consent of employee   F1.1, F1.2,
                                           F2.1
      letter requesting   F2.2
   doctor
      letter to   F3.1, F3.2, F3.3
   employee, by, prior to
      supply   F4.1, F4.2
   long-term or persistent
      absence   D29.2, F1.1, F1.2
   notification of rights   F1.1, F1.2,
                                           F2.2
Misconduct
   dismissal
      appeal right   F19.3
      notice   F19.1, F19.2, F19.3
   written warning for   F18.1, F18.2,
                                           F18.3
Monitoring
   applicant (job)   A1.2, A1.3
   discrimination protection   A1.3

National minimum wage *see* **Wages**

Offer letter *see* Offer of
   employment
Offer of employment
   offer letter   A2.1, A2.2, A2.3
      acceptance   A2.1
      constituting contract of
         employment   A2.1
      content   A2.1, A2.2, A2.3
         precedent   A2.2
   documentation of entitlement
      to work   A2.3
      precedent   A2.2

Parental leave
birth/adoption of child,
    connected with *see*
    Adoption leave; Maternity;
    Paternity leave
child born after 15 December
    1999, in respect of   D23.2
disabled child, parents of   D23.2
eligibility   D23.2
entitlement to   D23.2
    proof of   D23.2
interaction with paternity
    leave   D23.2
notification requirements   D23.2
parental responsibility
    meaning   D23.2
policy   D23.1, D23.2
    staff handbook   D1.1
postponing   D23.2
right to   D23.1
rights during   D23.2
when taken   D23.2

Paternity leave
additional rights from
    employer   D25.3
contractual right co-existing   D23.3
eligibility   D25.2
entitlement   D23.2
interaction with parental
    leave   D23.2
notice of   D25.2
pay
    statutory   D25.1, D25.2
    rate   D25.2
pay (contractual)   D25.3
period of   D25.2
policy   D25.1, D25.2, D25.3
    staff handbook   D1.1
return to work right   D25.2
statutory right   D25.1, D25.2

Pay
bonuses
    wrongful dismissal
        damages   G3.1
entitlement
    contract in   B1.2

Personal property
employees of
    protection policy   D14.1, D14.2, D14.3

Press
communication with *see* Media

Public interest disclosure *see* Whistleblowing

Recruitment
discrimination protection   A1.1, A1.3
offer letter   A2.1, A2.2, A2.3
    precedent   A2.2

Redundancy
appeal
    confirmation following   F43.1, F43.2
    decision overturned   F44.1, F44.2, F44.3
appeal from decision   D9.2, D9.3
collective   F10.1, F10.2, F10.3
    failure to consult trade
        unions/representatives
        complaint   G24.1, G24.2, G24.3
consultation   D9.1, D9.2, D9.3, F10.1, F10.2, F10.3
    collective   D9.2, D9.3
employee representative
    election process   F23.1, F23.2
    invitation to be nominated   F12.1, F12.2
    nomination form   F21.1
    role of   F23.2
investigation prior to   D9.2
lay-off
    meaning   C3.1
    redundancy payment claim   C3.1, C3.3
meetings   D9.2, D9.3
    right to be accompanied   D9.2
    no statutory requirement   D9.1
notice (of dismissal)   D9.2, D9.3
notification   F40.2, F40.3, F42.1, F42.2, F42.3
    second meeting to   F41.1, F41.2, F41.3
payment   D9.2, F13.3, G19.1
    age limit removed   F13.3
    calculation   G19.1
    claim   G19.2, G19.3
    enforcement in tribunal   G19.1, G19.2, G19.3
    enhanced   D9.3, F13.3
    lump sum   F13.3
    notice of claim   G19.1
    right to   G19.1
    statutory   F13.3
    time limit   G19.1
period of notice   D9.2
procedure   D9.1, D9.2, D9.3
    meeting, invitation to   F40.1, F40.2, F40.3
    second meeting, invitation
        to   F41.1, F41.2, F41.3
selection for   D9.2, D9.3
    absence/sickness   D9.2
    disciplinary record   D9.2
    length of service   D9.2
    performance   D9.2
short-time
    meaning   C3.1
    redundancy payment claim   C3.1, C3.3
vacancies, notification of   D9.2, D9.3

Redundancy—*continued*
  voluntary   F10.3
  requests for   F13.1, F13.2, F13.3
Religion or belief
  discrimination
    claims   G28.1
    grounds for resistance   G28.1
    harassment on grounds of   D12.1
    behaviour constituting   D12.2
Relocation
  agreement   E6.1, E6.2, E6.3
Remuneration *see* Pay; Wages
Repudiatory breach of contract
  constructive dismissal   G5.1
  guarateed bonus, failure to
    pay   G5.1
  wrongful dismissal   G2.1
Restraint of trade
  enforceability of restraint
    clause   B1.3
  garden leave clause   B1.3
  terms of, contract in   B1.2
Retirement
  age discrimination,
    avoidance   D16.1
  appeal right   F49.1, F49.2
  decision
    notification   F48.1, F48.2, F48.3
  employees' rights   D16.1
  meeting   F47.1, F47.2
  'normal retirement age'   D16.2, D16.3
  notification   F45.1, F45.2
  policy   D16.1, D16.2, D16.3
  staff handbook   D1.1
  procedure   D16.1, D16.2, D16.3
  request to continue working   D16.3
    employer's decision   D16.2
    form of   F46.1, F46.2
    refusal, appeal right   D16.2
  unfair dismissal   D16.1
  working after retirement age   D16.2, D16.3

Service agreement
  contract of employment as   B1.1
  director/executive   B1.2
    car, use of   B1.2
    company interest, protection
      of   B1.2
    confidential information   B1.2
    content   B1.2
      place of work specified
        in   B1.2
    duties of employment   B1.2
    expenses   B1.2
    holiday entitlement   B1.2
    insurance benefits   B1.2
    inventions   B1.2
    precedent   B1.2
    remuneration   B1.2
    restraint of trade clause   B1.2

Service agreement—*continued*
  director/executive—*continued*
    termination clause   B1.2
    third party interests   B1.2
  information technology, rules
    for   D3.1
  media communications   C4.1, C4.2
Sex and race
  discrimination
    claims   G28.1
    grounds for resistance   G28.1
    recruitment   A1.1
    harassment on grounds of   D12.1
    behaviour constituting   D12.2
Sexual orientation
  discrimination
    claims   G28.1
    grounds for resistance   G28.1
    harassment on grounds of   D12.1
    behaviour constituting   D12.2
Shop worker
  Sunday working
    policy   B5.2
    statutory rights   B5.1, B5.2
Short-time *see also* Lay-off
  consultation   C3.1, C3.3
  definition   C3.1
  dismissal   C3.1
  pay   C3.1
  policy   C3.1, C3.2
    impact   C3.3
  redundancy
    entitlement to   C3.1
    pay   C3.1
Sickness *see also* Medical report
  long-term   D29.1
    disability   D29.3
    employee's duties   D29.2
    termination on grounds of   D29.1, D29.3
  payment   D29.1, D29.2, D29.3
  persistent absenteeism   D29.1
    acceptable levels   D29.2
    disciplinary procedure   D29.2, D29.3
  policy   D29.1, D29.2, D29.3
    absence reporting   D29.1
    staff handbook in   D29.1
    provision in contract   B1.2
Smoking policy
  company car in   D21.2
  consultation   D28.1
  'smoke-free' policy   D28.1, D28.2
    assistance for smokers   D28.1, D28.2
  staff handbook   D1.1
  statutory requirements   D28.1, D28.2
Staff handbook
  accident reporting   D1.1, D15.1
  AIDS policy   D1.1
  alcohol and drug abuse   D1.1
  appraisals   D1.1

Index

Staff handbook—*continued*
bereavement	D1.1
changes to	D1.1
computer, use of	C1.1, C1.2, C1.3
contents	B2.2, D1.1, D1.2
e-mail, use of	D1.1
forms	D1.1, D1.2
grievance procedure	B2.1, D10.1
incorporation of contractual terms	D1.1
lay-off, impact of	C3.3
maternity rights	D1.1
parental leave	D1.1
protection of personal property	D14.1
retirement policy	D1.1
rules	D1.1, D1.2
behaviour	D1.1
sick pay	B2.3
short-time, impact of	C3.3
sickness policy	D29.1
smoking policy	D1.1
summary of benefits	D1.1

Staff purchase
authorisation	C2.3
deduction from wages	C2.2
unauthorised deductions	C2.3
defective goods	C2.2
discount	C2.2
policy	C2.1, C2.2, C2.3
procedure	C2.2

Statement of terms
agreement to	B2.1
changes to	B2.1
notification	B2.1
collective agreement	B2.2
conditions of employment	B2.2
confidentiality	B2.2
content	B2.1, B2.2
data protection	B2.2
duties	B2.2
employer's interests protection of	B2.2
grievance procedure	B2.1, B2.2
holiday entitlement	B2.2
public holidays	B2.2
hours of work	B2.2
information technology, rules for	D3.1
pension details	B2.1, B2.2
place of work specified in	B2.2
precedent	B2.2
restrictive covenants	B2.1
sick pay	B2.1, B2.2
termination clause	B2.2

Statutory maternity pay D24.1
eligibility	D24.2
'keep in touch days'	D24.2
period of	D24.2
policy	D24.2, D24.3

Statutory rights
adoption leave	D26.1, D26.2
maternity leave	D24.1, D24.2, D24.3

Statutory rights—*continued*
parental leave	D23.1
paternity leave	D25.1, D25.2
time off work	D20.3

Sunday working
betting workers	B6.1, B6.2
opting-out notice	B5.1, B5.2
shop workers, by	B5.1
statutory rights	B5.2

Suspension
circumstances where allowed	D7.1
letter notifying	F16.1, F16.2

Termination
capability, lack of	D5.2
clause in contract	B1.2
consultancy agreement	B3.2, B3.3
grievance brought after	D10.2
grounds for	B1.2
long-term sickness for	D29.1, D29.3
return of company car	D21.2

Third party
employee injured by reimbursement of employer	B1.2, B1.3

Time off work
ante natal care for	D24.2
entitlement	D20.1, D20.2, D20.3
jury service	D20.2
parental leave *see* Parental leave	
policy	D20.1, D20.2, D20.3
public duties	
pay	D20.1, D20.2, D20.3
'reasonable time'	D20.1, D20.2
statutory right	D20.3
reserve or auxiliary forces, participation	D20.2
training for	E2.1, E2.2

Trade union
consultation with	F10.1, F10.2
redundancy	D9.1, D9.2, D9.3
dismissal for membership/activities	G9.1, G10.1, G10.2, G10.3
automatically unfair	G9.1
claim for	G9.1, G9.3
ET1 form	G9.1, G9.2
particulars of claim	G9.2
grounds of resistance	G10.1, G10.2, G10.3
ET3 form	G10.1, G10.2, G10.3
reason	G9.3
statutory protection	G9.1
time limit for complaint	G9.1
dismissal for non-membership	G9.1, G10.1, G10.2, G10.3
automatically unfair	G9.1
claim for	G9.1, G9.3
ET1 form	G9.1, G9.2
particulars of claim	G9.2
grounds of resistance	G10.1, G10.2, G10.3
ET3 form	G10.1, G10.2, G10.3

Trade union—*continued*
  dismissal for
    non-membership—*continued*
      reason   G9.3
      statutory protection   G9.1
      time limit for complaint   G9.1

Training
  agreement   E2.1, E2.2
    expenses   E2.2
    parties to   E2.2
    policy   D17.1, D17.2
  employee not staying in
    employment, agreement for
      refund of fees   E2.1, E2.2, E2.3
    course fees, payment of   E2.2
    proportion of   E2.2
    salary   E2.3
  policy
    staff handbook   D1.1

Transfer of undertaking
  continuity of employment   B2.3
  employee representative
    election process   F22.1, F22.2
      voting procedure   F22.2
    invitation to be nominated   F11.1, F11.2
    nomination form   F21.1
    role of   F22.2
  failure to consult trade
    unions/representatives
      complaint   G23.1, G23.2, G23.3
      remedies   G23.1
  information duty   F14.1, F14.2, F14.3
  redundancy   F14.3
  regulations for   F14.1, F14.2, F14.3
  transferee, duties   F14.3

Unfair dismissal
  capability   D5.1
  claim for
    commencement of
      proceedings   G7.1
    ET1 form   G7.1, G7.2, G7.3
    grounds for   G7.1, G7.2, G7.3
      procedural   G7.1, G7.2
      substantive   G7.1, G7.2
  compensation   D8.1
  employee's right to   D7.1
  failure to follow statutory
    procedure   D8.1
  insufficient grounds for
    dismissal   G7.1
  reasons (general)   G7.3
  response to claim   G8.1, G8.2, G8.3
    ET3 form   G8.1, G8.2, G8.3
    submission of   G8.1, G8.3
  statutory dismissal procedure   G7.1, G7.3

Wages
  claim for, employment
    tribunal   G21.1, G21.2
    response to   G22.1, G22.2, G22.3
  deductions from
    staff purchases   C2.2
    unauthorised deductions   C2.3
  deductions from pay
    employment tribunal,
      complaint to   G11.1, G11.2, G11.3
    ET1 form   G11.2, G11.3
    response to claim   G12.1, G12.2, G12.3
      ET3 form   G12.2
    time limit   G11.1, G11.2, G11.3
    High Court action   G11.1
  national minimum
    enforcement   G21.1, G21.2

Whistleblowing
  constructive dismissal claim   G25.1, G25.2, G25.3
  particulars   G25.1, G25.2, G25.3
  employer, disclosure to
    good faith requirement   D13.1
    policy   D13.1, D13.2, D13.3
    no legal requirement for   D13.1
    procedure   D13.2
    'protected disclosure'   D13.1
    protection of workers   D13.1
    statutory provisions   D13.1
    unfair dismissal protection   D13.1
  workers
    Crown employees   D13.3

Worker representative *see* **Employee representative**

Workforce agreement
  employee representative
    nomination form   F21.1
  parental leave   D23.1
    incorporation into
      contract   D23.3

Working time
  48-hour week
    agreement to opt-out   D19.2, E1.1, E1.2, E1.3
    termination by notice   E1.3
  opt-out
    records of working
      hours   D19.2
  daily rest period   D19.2
  holiday pay, claim for   G17.1, G17.2
    response to   G18.1, G18.2, G18.3
  holidays   D19.2
  hours of work   D19.2
  policy   D19.1, D19.2, E1.1, E1.2, E1.3
  procedure   D19.2
  rest breaks   D19.2
  weekly rest period   D19.2

Written particulars of employment
  agreement to   B2.1

Written particulars of employment—*continued*

changes to	B2.1
notification	B2.1
collective agreement	B2.2
conditions of employment	B2.2, B2.3
confidentiality	B2.2, B2.3
content	B2.1, B2.2
data protection	B2.2
discretionary benefits	B2.3
duties	B2.2
statutory requirements	B2.3
employer's interests	
protection of	B2.2
grievance procedure	B2.1, B2.2, B2.3
holiday entitlement	B2.2, B2.3
part-time workers	B2.3
public holidays	B2.2
hours of work	B2.2
pension details	B2.1, B2.2
stakeholder pensions	B2.3
place of work specified in	B2.2
precedent	B2.2, B2.3
restrictive covenants	B2.1

Written particulars of employment—*continued*

sick pay	B2.1, B2.2
discretionary	B2.3
termination clause	B2.2

Wrongful dismissal

damages	G1.3
defences for employer	G2.1, G2.3
form of	G2.2
employment tribunal, claim in	
limit on award	G1.1
subsequent High Court proceedings	G1.1
forum for claim	G1.1
employment tribunal	G1.1
High Court action	
claim for	G1.1, G1.2, G1.3
accompanying documents	G1.3
damages	G1.3
specific sum	G1.3
jurisdiction for claim	G1.1
notice period requirements	
common law	G2.1
disputed	G2.3
repudiatory breach	G2.1
unpaid bonus	G5.1